TH
SECRET O

THE
SECRET OFFENSIVE

Active Measures:
A Saga of Deception, Disinformation, Subversion,
Terrorism, Sabotage and Assassination

CHAPMAN PINCHER

SIDGWICK & JACKSON
LONDON

To the all too few who care enough to give tongue

First published in Great Britain in 1985
by Sidgwick and Jackson Limited

Copyright © 1985 by Chapman Pincher

ISBN: 0-283-99262-X

Typeset by Rapidset and Design Limited, London WC1
Printed in Great Britain by
The Garden City Press, Letchworth, Hertfordshire
for Sidgwick and Jackson Limited
1 Tavistock Chambers, Bloomsbury Way
London WC1A 2SG

Contents

	Introduction	1
1	Tailor-made for Moscow	7
2	The Lie Machinery	24
3	The *Der Spiegel* Affair	32
4	Mission Accomplished	46
5	Kremlin Conspiracy Exposed	56
6	The Great Missile Deception	68
7	The Long March through the Media	87
8	The Agencies as Agents	117
9	Seeing Red	131
10	The Disinformation Game	146
11	Agents of Influence	162
12	Active Measures and the Trade Unions	181
13	The Offensive Called 'Peace'	196
14	The Détente Deception	203
15	The Neutron Bomb Offensive	210
16	'Cruise' and the CND	218
17	'Star Wars'	231
18	The Sharp Edge of Active Measures	237
19	Counter-Offensive?	259

Biographical Notes 275
Notes and Sources 281
Selected Bibliography 306
Index 307

Introduction

'The extension of Communist control over vast areas and populations since the end of the Second World War has owed more to the propaganda and disinformation offensive of the Communist countries than to the power of their arms.'

Reed Irvine

Since the end of the Soviet Union's reluctant wartime alliance with the true democracies the peoples of the West have been repeatedly shocked when the excesses of the Politburo, the Communist Party's ruling faction in the Kremlin, have been exposed. They find it hard, in peacetime, to comprehend events like the deliberate shooting-down of a laden Korean airliner, the murder of a uniformed American officer on official duty, the assassination of political opponents, the enforced psychiatric treatment of dissidents, the training and arming of terrorists, the massive scale of Soviet espionage, the wholesale theft of technological secrets, the cheating on solemn arms agreements. In Western eyes such activities are permissible, if at all, only in war and therein lies the Politburo's reason for pursuing them – the Politburo considers that the Soviet State and all the Soviet people who are its servants *are* at war. The morality of the measures being used to win the war is, therefore, not an issue.

To the Western mind peace is the absence of war and a state of friendliness to other countries. To those few in the Kremlin, and to the millions never given any option but to agree with them, peace means what Lenin proclaimed – that there can be no peace until

1

there is Communist world control and the struggle for that control must be ceaseless. High-level Soviet defectors, like Arkady Shevchenko, who was personal assistant to Gromyko, the Soviet Foreign Minister, have confirmed that the Politburo's long-term purpose, the steady extension of Soviet hegemony world-wide, has not changed and is unlikely to do so.[1] The self-perpetuating minority clique which seized power illegally, and has held on to it by force and intimidation ever since, believes that it is surrounded by enemies – including millions of its own people – and that it must subdue them to survive. In pursuit of 'establishing the security of its own borders' it continues the Tsarist tradition of dominating or seizing more and more territory, Afghanistan being its current victim.

To Western politicians war is the continuation of politics by other means. To the Politburo, with its ideological compulsion to invert reality as free societies see it – which I call 'the upside-down ploy' – politics is the continuation of war by other means. These other means, now known in the Soviet jargon as 'active measures', form the major subject of this book. They comprise sophisticated techniques of deception, disinformation, forgery, blackmail, subversion, penetration and manipulation, the insidious use of agents of influence, the organization of mass demonstrations with the promotion of violence and other criminal acts and even military violations. The scale on which this underhand offensive is being relentlessly pursued in the Politburo's game-plan against countries of the free world, and especially against the US, Britain, West Germany, France and the Scandinavian states, is far greater and much more menacing than is generally appreciated, especially as so little is being done to combat it. As things are going, the West is on a hiding to nothing, and it is the purpose of this book to stimulate some defensive action by exposing the Kremlin's clandestine stratagems.

The Politburo is pouring ever more money and resources into active measures because they are achieving such positive results. This book will chronicle Moscow's major triumphs in the undeclared war – like the worldwide manipulation of the 'peace' movements to maintain Soviet military superiority; like the elimination of the stalwart anti-Communist, Franz Josef Strauss, from the West German leadership by the process of character assassination; like the current state of the British Labour Party which, whatever its motives, is committed to doing exactly what the Politburo wants in the field of defence, if and when it achieves power. It will document, with details, dates and names, how institutions and people at all levels have been seduced into serving as conscious agents of the Soviet active-measures machinery. It will also expose the extent to which institutions and individuals have been duped into being its unwitting agents – what are known in intelligence parlance as 'willies'.

The situation during the recent miners' strike showed, more vividly than a thousand books, how fragile our freedoms are and how easily the apparently sturdy oak of democracy could crash down to reveal itself as a husk, gnawed away by pro-Soviet termites concentrating on the heartwood of the trade unions, Parliament, the media, the education system and even the churches. The strike was a long-planned challenge to a democratically elected government and the government's survival was more close-run than it cares to admit. All that saved it was the fluke existence of massive coal stocks which gave the authorities time to organize alternative fuels for the power stations. Without them a quick surrender, as industry ground to a halt, might have seemed so inevitable that the left-wing leaders of the dockers, railmen, seamen and others could have induced their members to join what would have been, effectively, a general strike. If they had mounted violent mass pickets, as they would have been encouraged to do, law and order would almost certainly have surrendered to violence and intimidation. With the miners alone, the police were stretched almost to the limit, and mass picketing in the major industries, with extremist militants and perhaps many of the unemployed joining in for the kill, could not have been contained. Neither could the deliberate extension of the violence into the so-called deprived areas in the cities, which have seen riots before. With the use of troops as the only hope for containment, it is the opinion of high authorities close to the action that such a situation could have come near to civil war, though they would deny it publicly, preferring to perpetuate the dangerous belief that 'it could never happen here'.

Whether the miners' leaders called themselves pro-Soviet Communists or just behaved like them, their preference was for a pseudo-democracy – a government that can never be defeated in an election, like that of the Soviet Union. Those afflicted by the it-could-never-happen-here syndrome should recall that when successful Communist revolutions have been accomplished it has been by small minorities prepared to use force and deceit to install a small ruling clique and to maintain it. Pro-Soviet revolutionaries, and especially those with the intimidatory threat of Soviet military strength behind them, have only to win once.

The miners' strike also demonstrated two of the human factors which make Soviet active measures so successful when applied over many years: the gullibility of what Communists call 'the masses' and their readiness to shrug off excesses which may have shocked them deeply for a few days. Miners have, traditionally, been hard-headed men, not easily fooled, but many among them were prepared to swallow the patent lies and deceptions of their leaders when these were exposed again and again by events. Though each striker lost heavily and gained nothing, many seemed prepared to continue following their rabble-rousers and to hold them in esteem. Watching the behaviour of the miners, not least in the context of their violence to colleagues who disagreed with them, it became easier to understand how an intelligent people like the Germans submitted to the monstrous rantings of Hitler and fastened the chains of a murderous tyranny around themselves. Again, those who are confident that it could not happen here because the British are not so easily led should realize that Arthur Scargill, an Englishman from the heart of England, and Mick McGahey, a heartland Scot, each a product of a Communist upbringing, were able to organize a totally unnecessary and essentially political strike without a ballot and to rally enough support to keep it going long enough to inflict damage costing at least £4,000 million on the nation.[2]

The strike, with its saturation media coverage, ably exploited by Scargill and so often biased against the police, must have been closely monitored on behalf of the Politburo by harder and hardier men than Scargill, especially through television, and it must have given them heart to continue what they call 'the long march through the institutions of the West' – through the trade unions, the Labour Party, Parliament, the media, the educational system and the churches. The Soviet leaders are nothing if not patient, and the techniques of deception and intimidation have worked successfully against their own people and their satellite populations to keep them at the pinnacle of power for nearly seventy years. It does not seem to be sufficiently appreciated that the major liability of the Soviet 'dictatorship of the élite' from liberty's viewpoint – that it can never be ousted by popular vote – is a pillar of strength in the 'struggle' against other nations. The Soviet Government has total continuity of power, so its foreign policy, of which active measures are an integral part, can be held subservient to the long-term ideological intention, with the immediate interests of the Soviet people, such as its material welfare, remaining in the discard.[3]

The Politburo's standard reaction to exposures of its true nature and odious activities is a set-piece deception exercise in itself: charges of 'anti-Soviet lies' and 'reds-under-the-beds hysteria' being promoted on behalf of 'aggressive circles' against the 'peace-loving socialist democracies'. Any such defence against the statements made in this book will be systematically riddled in the following pages by the evidence of witnesses who worked in the Kremlin or its out-stations and off-shoots, like the KGB, and can say, without fear of effective denial, 'I was there!' It will be refuted with evidence provided from counter-intelligence agencies like MI5, GCHQ, the CIA and the FBI and the results of my own investigative experiences over forty years. The evidence will be documented in copious source notes.

In collecting my information I owe a particular debt to Sir James Goldsmith who, at my request, granted me access to the mass of documents acquired in the preparation for his defence of the libel action brought by the West German magazine, *Der Spiegel*, and which was never utilized because, at the magazine's instigation, the case was settled out of court with a legal statement vindicating Sir James, as detailed in Chapters 3, 4 and 5. My indebtedness to many others will be acknowledged in the source notes, but there are some who, for professional reasons, need to remain unnamed.

Friends complain that my books frighten them. The more research I do into Soviet behaviour the more it frightens me. Those of us who enjoy real freedom can never be too aware of the dreadful circumstances that those responsible for active measures, and those who knowingly assist them, would like to thrust upon us. The KGB defector, Stanislav Levchenko, on his return to his native Russia after service in Japan, described the whole Soviet Union as 'like a vast land of exiles ruled by wardens who ceaselessly conduct militant active measures against their wards'.[4] Everything was a lie.

Looking for hope, he saw 'in the tired, forlorn faces of the people only hopelessness'. While the rulers proclaimed 'unremitting progress', everybody with eyes could see accelerating deterioration. The system corrupted everybody and the 'dictatorship of the proletariat' was really a 'dictatorship of the élite', these being the fourteen men of the Politburo, their relations and the dependent bureaucracy – the so-called *nomenklatura* – who kept the leadership in control and themselves in privileged positions.

What should be cause for grave concern is the number of people in all countries of the West who are fully aware of the truth about conditions in the Soviet Union and the gross incompetence of the Communist system, yet are determined to impose that kind of society on their own kith and kin to satisfy their personal lust for power and their warped ideological yearnings. These Trojan horsemen are every bit as dangerous as full-blown traitors and spies in furthering the secret offensive designed to replace the free range of true democracy with the prison camp of Communism.

By his writings, his utterances and his actions Hitler made his intentions plain, yet governments and many people chose to ignore them. The intentions of the Politburo and its supporters are equally manifest and even more menacing.

Chapter 1

Tailor-made for Moscow

'It is useless for the sheep to pass resolutions in favour of veg-etarianism when the wolf remains of a different opinion.'
                                                              Dean Inge

The British Labour Party's defence policy for the next general election, which must be held in or before 1988, could hardly be more suited to the requirements of the Politburo. Indeed, as laid out in the latest official pronouncement on the subject it could scarcely do more to achieve the Politburo's prime foreign-policy targets had it been formulated by that ill-disposed clique itself. Table 1 lists what the Kremlin has striven for since 1945 and what the Labour Party is committed to delivering, as stated clearly and unequivocally in the *Statement on Defence and Security for Britain* issued by the Labour Party's National Executive Committee in advance of the 1984 Annual Conference.[1]

None of these moves, which spell not only the end of Britain as a military, air and naval power of consequence but the collapse of NATO and the withdrawal of American military support in Europe, requires any comparable action by the Soviet Union. They are all unilateral and depend for any reciprocal action on the goodwill of the Politburo, as Czechoslovakia and other countries of Eastern Europe were made to rely on Stalin's goodwill to promote free elections.

Apart from the rapid decommissioning of the Polaris submarines, which form the nation's deterrent to nuclear attack, and the immediate cancellation of the Trident programme, the successor to Polaris, no specific time-scale is given, but the tone of the document, and what has been said since by Labour spokesmen, indicate that all the measures would be implemented as quickly as possible and certainly within four years because of the danger that Labour might be elected for only one term. The Labour Party's aim is to make all the defence changes irreversible by future governments, so the nation's basic nuclear defence assets, like the Aldermaston research station and the plutonium production facilities, would be disbanded.

Table 1

What the Politburo wants	What the Labour Party promises to deliver
No battlefield nuclear weapons to be available to NATO.	All battlefield nuclear weapons to be taken away from the British Army and RAF units in Germany. To press for the withdrawal of all NATO battlefield nuclear weapons from Europe.
No neutron weapons to be available to NATO.	Refusal to permit neutron weapons to be deployed in Britain or with British forces in Europe. Opposition to the introduction of neutron weapons with any other NATO forces.
The scrapping of all NATO's cruise and Pershing 2 missiles.	The unconditional removal of all cruise missiles from Britain and the elimination of the cruise missile bases.
An end to the use of Britain as an advance base for American nuclear missiles.	The unconditional removal of all American nuclear weapons, including those on submarines, from British territory and territorial waters. This would entail the expulsion of the Americans from their base at Holy Loch.
No independent strategic nuclear weapons in British hands.	The Royal Navy's Polaris force to be decommissioned and the weapons to be scrapped. Trident, the replacement for Polaris, to be cancelled immediately.

What the Politburo wants	*What the Labour Party promises to deliver*
While NATO retains its nuclear weapons, a guarantee that it would never be first to use them.	Pressure on NATO to announce a 'No first use' of nuclear weapons.
An end to the use of Britain as a forward base for American conventional forces (a move which would spell the end of NATO).	American bases housing F111 aircraft to be removed. The presence of conventional American forces in Britain to be 'regularized' to ensure a physical British veto over the use of such facilities.
Europe free of all nuclear weapons, giving the USSR an inevitable preponderance in conventional might, especially in tanks and aircraft.	Britain to be defended by conventional forces only. Pressure on other NATO members to follow suit.
The elimination of NATO and the Warsaw Pact, requiring the permanent withdrawal of US forces from Europe, leaving Soviet forces poised for a quick return, if required.	Pressure for the 'phasing out' of NATO and the Warsaw Pact.
A 'freeze' on long-range nuclear weapons while the Soviet Union has superiority.	Pressure for a 'freeze' on the testing, production and deployment of all nuclear weapons.
A return to détente, which previously permitted the USSR to achieve nuclear superiority while still pursuing its global aims.	A firm commitment to détente.
A ban on the 'Star Wars' (Strategic Defence Initiative) defence system.	Opposition to 'Star Wars'.
Support for the Soviet Union's 'peace' campaign.	Full support for the Campaign for European Nuclear Disarmament.

The Labour Party is professing a wish to remain in NATO (the North Atlantic Treaty Organization) until some arrangement can be made for its demise along with that of the Warsaw Pact, when it will 'look for protection of our national interests through the United Nations', a notoriously ineffective organization packed with Soviet client states. There can be little doubt, however, that NATO would quickly cease to exist without any decline in the Warsaw Pact's strength, if the Labour Party achieved its main objectives. The emasculation of the British forces alone, which is what removal of their nuclear weapons would amount to, would be a savage blow to NATO, but the elimination of the American nuclear forces from Britain, which is central to Labour's agenda, would almost certainly be mortal.

NATO strategy depends on being able to stem a Soviet attack for a few days and then to defeat it with massive reinforcements flown from the US mainland via Britain, the 'unsinkable aircraft carrier', where many of the nuclear and conventional weapons for the American forces are stored. It is not logistically feasible for these weapons and stores to be based in the US and to be flown from there in an emergency. Britain is the only country through which the US could reinforce its NATO troops at the necessary speed, and, without the certainty that reinforcements could arrive in time, no American government would dare to leave its resident troops in Europe as hostages to fortune.

The Labour Party's alleged belief that the American forces would remain in Britain in a purely conventional role, having been deprived of their nuclear weapons, is totally unrealistic. Their planning and training are based on the concept of being able to use nuclear weapons if the Soviets use them first or look like succeeding with a massive armoured thrust. Their aircraft have a dual-purpose conventional/nuclear role and it is most unlikely that the US Forces chiefs and their government would even consider allowing them to remain as purely conventional machines. The British action would mean that the Americans would be unable to respond effectively with nuclear battlefield weapons, even if these were being widely used by Soviet forces in a major invasion of Europe, as Soviet military manuals indicate they would be.[2]

Neither the US Government nor the American people could be expected to continue to make financial sacrifices to help to defend a nation which had expelled them from their bases, in which huge sums have been invested since a former Labour government allowed American nuclear weapons to be stored in Britain in 1948.[3] Nor would they be likely to continue the special relationship between two English-speaking peoples which has been so carefully fostered for forty years.

As will be shown, the Politburo has been deploying every kind of active measure to loosen the alliance between Britain and the US and to prise American forces out of Europe. So it is hardly surprising that *Pravda* has strongly welcomed Labour's new defence policy as promising to remove what the Kremlin calls 'obstacles to progress'. There can be no reasonable doubt that these promises would be implemented in the event of Labour's election to power. The policies derive from the hard left but the leadership is totally committed to them publicly, missing no opportunity to promote them, and those moderates who privately oppose unilateral disarmament because they do not trust the Soviet Union have trimmed, irretrievably, to maintain Party unity and their own positions.[4]

Currently, Labour is taking the conveniently craven line that, having forced all American nuclear weapons back to the US mainland, where most of them would be useless at such range, Britain would still enjoy protection from the deterrent 'umbrella' of America's intercontinental missiles. But would the Politburo really believe that any American administration would be prepared to risk the destruction of its own cities to protect a nation which had, deliberately, done what the Soviets wanted? Would not any American administration feel it necessary to make clear to its own electorate that, so far as Britain was concerned, the umbrella had been folded?

An indication of what Washington's understandable reaction would be has recently been provided by its attitude to the New Zealand Government's decision to ban visits to its ports or territorial waters by any American ship which might be nuclear-powered or be carrying nuclear weapons. Washington immediately cut off the supply of sensitive intelligence to New Zealand, barred further training of New Zealand officers in the US and suspended New Zealand's favoured status for the purchase of defence equipment.[5] This was done not simply as a gesture but because the US feels that it can no longer trust such an unreliable ally. The British Labour Party is determined to ban all similar American ships from British waters and the consequence could be an end to the intelligence interchange between the US and Britain. While the US would lose the assistance it receives from Britain's radio-interception agency, GCHQ, Britain would suffer infinitely more. The British defence chiefs rely heavily on information supplied daily by Washington from American spy-satellites. As Britain has no independent facility for putting such satellites into orbit and could not afford the enormous cost of creat-

11

ing one, it would become virtually blind to what is going on behind the Iron Curtain – another big strategic plus for the Kremlin.[6]

Many inside the Labour Party are already pressing for withdrawal from NATO to a 'Fortress Britain', defended only by conventional weapons, and the current pro-NATO stance of the Party Conference may be no more than a temporary façade.[7] With or without Britain, there is no possibility that any group of European countries could form an effective counterforce to the Soviet Union. The Soviet Union has become a military super-power and only another super-power, the US, can stand in its way. The withdrawal of American forces would, inevitably, force West Germany, Norway, Denmark and possibly others to make separate treaty arrangements with the Soviet Union, which could then be guaranteed to deal with them piecemeal as it has dealt with Finland, bringing them into its 'sphere of influence'. Under continuing Labour government Britain would seem to be committed to becoming progressively neutral, like Sweden, and to suffering the same fate. While Sweden puts up a brave front on defence it has no real hope of preventing a Soviet take-over, should that ever suit the Kremlin's purpose, and has to countenance continual espionage intrusions and other insults with ineffective response, as described in Chapter 18.

Is it just coincidence that what Labour intends to do, action by action, would fulfil the Kremlin's catalogue of strategic and political requirements? This book will attempt to show that it is not coincidence and that what will constitute a major triumph for the Soviet Union, if Labour is elected, will be the result of deliberate active measures planned and put into effect by the Politburo over many years during its 'long march through the institutions of the West', the Labour Party and the associated trade unions being two of the targets on which it has concentrated most effort. How and why the Labour Party and the trade-union movement were successfully converted to Trojan horses in the Kremlin's bid to take the citadel of Western Europe can best be appreciated by a brief examination of East–West relations since Soviet and Allied troops linked arms in Germany in the spring of 1945.

When Stalin surveyed the geo-political scene on the surrender of the German forces, the future of Soviet Communism, battered though it was, must have seemed unbelievably auspicious. His leadership of the Bolshevik revolution, which had taken over the vast Russian Empire in 1917, had already increased its territory by seizing half of Poland, the three Baltic states, part of Finland and Transcaucasia. Under the incredibly favourable agreements he had reached with the Americans and British at Yalta and Potsdam he had a free hand to impose virtual enslavement over the rest of Poland, Czechoslovakia, Hungary, Romania, Bulgaria and that part of Eastern Germany occupied by the Red Army. The rest of Germany lay in ruins, physically, politically and morally. France had no effective military forces and it would take a generation for morale to be resuscitated after her dishonourable performance in the struggle against Hitler. While the British and American forces, yearning for peace and feeling homesick, wanted only to return to their families, the Red Army could be made to do whatever Stalin required, for, unlike his Western counterparts who were answerable to their electorates, there was no way, short of death, that he could lose his absolute power. What better opportunity was ever likely to be presented to convert the whole of Germany to a pro-Soviet Communist state, a project which had been the prime aim of Moscow's pre-war thrust to achieve international Communism in pursuit of Lenin's dictum, 'Whoever has Germany has Europe'? Western Germany was literally the ideologue's 'seed-bed' of capitalist ruins on which Soviet-style Communism could be erected.

Stalin's personal position was extraordinarily appropriate to his purpose. His 'Uncle Joe' image and the phenomenal way he had converted what had seemed like a quick defeat into total victory had made him a popular figure throughout the free world and, to the unsuspecting, one who could be trusted. He had asserted a moral ascendancy over the American leaders who held him in respect bordering on awe, and, after the way he had hoodwinked Roosevelt at Yalta, this master of the art of political deception must have believed in his ability to exploit the opportunity and that it was his ideological duty to do so. After the appalling behaviour of the German forces in the Soviet Union he could claim, with apparent justice and considerable sympathy, that any bid to Communize the rest of Germany through political pressure was no more than trying to ensure the security of his motherland's borders. All he had to do was to wait for the Allied forces, and the Americans in particular, to withdraw, and then intimidation by the presence of the Red Army alone might achieve his objectives. Within a year the Allied forces in

13

Europe which had totalled 5 million were reduced to less than 900,000 and most of them had been demobilized. The Soviet Union retained about 6 million in arms.[8] There had never been any intention for the Red Army to be withdrawn from the conquered territories. On the contrary, as the former German intelligence chief, Reinhard Gehlen, was to write in his memoirs, nostalgically perhaps but truthfully, 'While the Soviet Union restocked Hitler's depleted munitions dumps in Eastern Europe, the Western Allies destroyed the arms factories and industrial installations in their zones of Germany.'[9]

Stalin's opportunity was to slip away, however, as the Soviet attitude at various Allied conferences made his purposes too plain. As early as September 1945 the Canadian Prime Minister, Mackenzie King, recorded in his diary 'great alarm at the encroachment which Russia is making in various parts of the world' and noted that the Soviet Union was 'blocking whatever seemed to stand in Russia's way to increase her power and world control'.[10] An event then occurred which exacerbated the growing estrangement between East and West, soon to be called the Cold War, and which has been given insufficient attention by historians. A young Soviet officer called Igor Gouzenko defected from the Soviet Embassy in Ottawa with a bundle of secret documents and verbal information which proved that, while professing friendship, the Soviet leadership had been undermining its wartime allies with the possibility of a further hot war in mind. Soviet agents identified by Gouzenko, several of whom were later convicted, were being required, as a matter of urgency, to report on the rates of American and Canadian demobilization and to provide other information relevant only to contingency planning for a new outbreak of hostilities to be instigated by the Soviets. Gouzenko's documents proved that while the Canadian, American and British Governments, and their peoples, had been giving sacrificial assistance to the Russians during the war, the Politburo's professional agents, posing as diplomats, had been subverting scientists, politicians, civil servants and others to spy and serve as agents of influence against their own countries and in the Soviet interest. And, as Gouzenko stressed, what he could reveal was only a fragment of the total treachery.[11]

Mackenzie King's diaries record the horror which the discovery of this duplicity generated in the minds of Clement Attlee, the

British Prime Minister, and Harry Truman, the US President, as well as in his own. Stalin's supremely cynical behaviour in signing the pre-war pact with Communism's arch-enemy, Hitler, which facilitated the German invasion of Poland and the victories in Europe, had been forgotten or forgiven in the euphoria of Allied victory. Gouzenko's information faced the Western leaders with a historic truth so alien to their ethical standards that neither they nor their successors could fully appreciate its implication – that nothing the Soviets do or say can be safely taken at face value. There has been a deception component in every decision of consequence taken by the Politburo since Lenin decreed that the Soviet state must 'resort to all sorts of tricks, slyness, illegal methods and concealment of truth' – the devices now known as active measures. It is grotesque to imagine a British Cabinet, having decided an aspect of foreign policy, addressing itself to the questions, 'Will we be able to improve our position by cheating?', 'How can this be used for deception purposes to undermine our adversaries?' Yet this is routine procedure with the Politburo and always has been. As the next chapter will show, there is a particular individual listening to the Politburo's deliberations who is expected to put up ideas for the exploitation of new developments by active measures and has a huge department and unlimited resources for putting them into effect, once the Politburo has agreed to them.

Gouzenko's revelations also made it clear that the only factor which appeared to have delayed Stalin's plans for 'asserting the further power of the Soviets' was the American possession of the atomic bomb.[12] On that issue the Communist newspapers in the West, assisted covertly by pro-Soviet journalists in the 'liberal' media, were already pressing for the sharing of nuclear secrets with the Kremlin and the outlawing of atomic weapons which, to their apparent distress, were negating the massive Soviet superiority in conventional arms. They were to be helped over the ensuing years by powerful agents of influence, including several of the scientists who had been involved in the Anglo–American effort to produce the atomic bomb and others who had worked in the defence field. As Chapter 11 will describe in some detail, the use of such agents is a prime component of active measures.

The first clear sign of Western resolve to stem the Communist tide resulted from the Kremlin's crude pressure on Turkey and its support for a Greek Communist minority trying to seize control of their country. In the spring of 1947 Truman offered economic and military assistance to any nation resisting Communist aggression, direct or indirect, and this was followed, in July, by the American Programme for European Recovery, popularly called the Marshall Plan, which, on its acceptance by West Germany in particular, gave the Kremlin the disappointing news that the US intended to maintain a military presence in Western Europe, if only as an earnest of its determination to help defend it.[13] The Politburo reacted to the aid plan with expected bitterness and declined to take any part in it. Instead its propaganda machine and the Western media it could control or influence were turned on to discredit the recovery programme and make the false assertion that America's 'imperialist' purpose was to build up West Germany to take part in a war of revenge against the Soviet Union and the other 'peace-loving democracies' – a typical example of the upside-down ploy. The Kremlin's patient purpose was, and still remains, to induce the Western European governments and peoples to turn against the Americans and secure the removal of their forces, and then totally to decouple the US from Europe, and from Britain in particular. At the same time it has striven, with remarkable success, to counter the atomic obstruction to its long-term plans by achieving and maintaining nuclear superiority, a process in which active measures have been employed with brilliance, as described in Chapter 6.

British Communists had been told by Lenin that they should support the Labour Party, 'as the rope supports the hanged man', but they were unable to do so when the Labour Government under Attlee decided that Britain must play its part in deterring Soviet aggression by becoming an independent nuclear power.[14] It was also a Labour Government which decided that Britain should join NATO, the organization dedicated to the defence of Europe against aggression from the only possible source, the Soviet Union. On Soviet instructions the British Communists began to appear to forsake their dedication and joined the Labour Party to penetrate the trade unions which can influence Labour Party policies through members on the Party's National Executive Committee, their card votes at conferences and the large number of Labour MPs whom they sponsor.

This threat from Soviet-inspired Communist activities was per-

16

ceived so clearly by Attlee and his Foreign Secretary, Ernest Bevin, that they set up a special secret committee under General Sir Gerald Templer to assess its nature and extent. After taking evidence from many witnesses, including the heads of the secret services, the committee concluded that the Communists would continue to penetrate the Labour Party and the trade unions and that action needed to be taken against them. The other prime targets would be the media and the higher educational system.[15]

Labour's programme of nuclear bomb production was continued by Conservative governments with the support of the later leader of the Labour Party Hugh Gaitskell, who, with some difficulty and considerable political courage, fought off a sustained attempt to foist a policy of unilateral nuclear disarmament on the Party. While the pro-Soviet penetration of the Party had made insufficient ground at that stage, it had been more successful in the trade unions. In 1960 the Union of Shop, Distributive and Allied Workers (USDAW) voted in favour of unilateral disarmament and several other unions followed suit. This movement in the Kremlin's desired direction was assisted by the Campaign for Nuclear Disarmament (CND), as described in Chapter 16, and by pro-Soviet sections of the British media, both overt and covert.

The peculiar death of Gaitskell in 1963 removed a genuine social democrat so hated by the Politburo that Khrushchev is on record as saying that 'If Communism were to triumph, Gaitskell would be among the first to be shot outside the Houses of Parliament as a traitor to the working class', meaning that he had declined to do what the Politburo wanted. The possibility that his removal was the result of an extreme Soviet active measure, assassination, remains a serious consideration by the security authorities, as described in Chapter 18. Active measures were, unquestionably, involved in the defeat of the Conservative government in 1964 through the Kremlin's exploitation of the political aspects of the Profumo Affair, as I have argued at length elsewhere.[16]

The Labour Prime Minister, Harold Wilson, who had secured the Party leadership by 'talking left' and promising to get rid of the nuclear deterrent, then taking shape in the form of four Polaris submarines, must have disappointed the Kremlin severely. On taking office in 1964 he not only retained the Polaris fleet but improved it and, during his later premiership, spent £1,000 million to ensure

17

that the Polaris warheads could penetrate the Soviet defences.[17] He also continued Attlee's policy of welcoming American air-power to Britain. In 1976 his administration allowed the Americans to more than double the number of F111 warplanes in Britain and the nuclear weapons for them. Again, the purpose was to help to deter aggression by the Soviets, who were still seen by the Labour leaders as bent on the long-term objective of world-wide Communism subservient to Moscow. The number of pro-Soviet, unilateralist Labour Members of Parliament had steadily increased, some of them being paid Soviet-Bloc agents, but there were few among the Labour leadership at that stage who did not believe that it was essentially the nuclear deterrent which had maintained the peace in Europe. Further, most of them were convinced that the independence of the British deterrent increased the credibility of the total Western deterrent in the eyes of the Soviet leaders because of their uncertainty about what Britain might do with it in an emergency. The Politburo had witnessed Britain's lone, defiant stance against the Nazi might and its ultimate survival against all the odds.

With the trade unions increasingly under the control of Communist and former Communist leaders, often elected for life by blatantly undemocratic means and prepared to use their enormous card-votes to influence Labour Party policy in their desired direction, the Labour leadership was forced to make some major concessions to the far left. The most welcome of these to the Kremlin was the decision at the 1973 Labour Party Conference to abolish the proscribed list of Communist front organizations which members of the Labour Party had been forbidden to join under penalty of expulsion. These multifarious fronts, which will be discussed in some detail later, are essentially tools of the Politburo for promoting active measures against its adversaries, and a study of their use leaves little doubt that the undermining of the Labour Party by the pro-Soviet left was accelerated by the ending of their proscription.[18]

Resolutions for unilateral nuclear disarmament were passed at the Labour Party's annual conferences in 1972 and 1973 but had little impact on policy because that was decided by the leadership and elected Labour MPs in the House of Commons. Though the Kremlin pressed on with its active measures, making what use it could of the 'peace' movements, it could see little hope of prising the Americans out of Britain or breaking the log-jam of Western nuclear disar-

18

mament in the foreseeable future. The outlook from Moscow was to change dramatically, however, in 1980 with the surprise election of Michael Foot as Leader of the Labour Party and of the Opposition.

Foot, a backbench gad-fly in the mould of a nineteenth-century pamphleteer, had been a founder member of the Campaign for Nuclear Disarmament and had regularly appeared on its marches and at its meetings.[19] He represented the basic pacifism of the old Labour Party which has always been susceptible to active measures playing on the fear and horrors of war. When he had been in the Wilson government, Foot had not been consulted concerning nuclear decisions, though he did not resign in protest when he knew they had been taken. His election to the leadership, after the defeat of James Callaghan by Margaret Thatcher, was an indication of the extent to which the Labour Party as a whole, as well as the Labour MPs, had moved, inexorably, to the left, the left-wing take-over of the National Executive being due mainly to the trade unions. It was inevitable that, with Foot in command and the militants and trade unions behind him, the Party would move to an unequivocal unilateralist stance. In 1982 the Party adopted unilateral nuclear disarmament as its official policy for the next general election by the necessary two-thirds majority. This could only be seen by the Politburo and its foreign supporters as a triumph for active measures patiently applied at many points over many years and a clear indication to continue with them.

The election of Foot and the further swing to the left carried a further bonus: the new leadership was aggressively anti-American and not only on the issue of defence. This owed much to elements of the British media and particularly television which tends to seize on any topic that can be given an anti-American slant. It probably owed more to the infiltration of the Party by would-be revolutionaries posing as social democrats, a process which continues on such a scale that it now has a name – 'entryism'. One of the reasons why official membership of the Communist Party has decreased so much over recent years is that so many have left to infiltrate the Labour Party, which then tends to lose its disgusted moderates, thereby increasing the extreme left bias even more.[20] Many Labour Party members, and Scargill is an example, openly scorn the ballot box in favour of revolutionary processes. Communists are now able to speak openly of 'the battle for the Labour Movement' and the 'historical necessity' of ousting true social democrats. They boast about the extent to which Communist ideas have been adopted by Labour.[21]

Entryism is also being practised with success by the breakaway brands of Communists such as Trotskyites, Socialist Workers and other revolutionary militants. While such groups squabble with the pro-Soviet Communists and among themselves, they all share a common aim – the overthrow of democratically elected government – and they are united in their hatred of a free society in which they have no hope of power. While the breakaway extremists, who are very vocal and active in promoting strikes and picket-line violence, may seem to be currently more effective than standard Communists, they would be quickly eliminated in the event of a successful revolution. Unlike the pro-Soviet Communist Party which would have the intimidatory support of the Politburo and its Red Army, the fringe militants have no military backing.

Labour went into the 1983 General Election with the firm policy of unilaterally abandoning nuclear weapons and of prising the Americans out of their nuclear bases, thereby making Britain a 'nuclear-free zone'. There were high hopes that the disproportionate publicity given, over many months, to the 'peace' movements by the media would swing votes in Labour's favour, but, for the first time for many years, the Conservatives chose to make defence a major election issue, relying on the good sense of the electorate. Their confidence was not misplaced. Labour was disastrously defeated and, while the failure was due in some measure to Foot's inept leadership and total lack of charisma, there can be little doubt that the prospect of relying on the Politburo's goodwill frightened many voters.

In spite of that, Foot's more credible successor, Neil Kinnock, has not only taken up the unilateralist policy but expanded it along with an increasingly anti-American stance. When President Reagan was due to visit Britain in 1984 a large group of Labour MPs, including Kinnock, joined trade unionists, overt Communists and Trotskyist extremists in sponsoring advertisements urging people to picket the American Embassy on his arrival.[22]

The constitution of the Working Party that drew up the report, *Defence and Security for Britain*, on behalf of Labour's National Executive, which is summarized in Table 1, speaks for itself. Its chairman was Alex Kitson who, when representing the Labour Party at the 1977 celebrations of sixty years of Communism in Moscow, told Soviet radio audiences that Russia had achieved so much that Britain was still far from achieving. The Working Party included several Marxist MPs, like Jo Richardson and Eric Heffer, and university representatives associated with CND, such as Mary Kaldor, Bill Niven and Malcolm Chalmers, as well as far-left trade unionists. Their conclusions have been repeatedly endorsed by Kinnock. In 1984 he called for a 'nuclear freeze', which happened to be the Soviet line at that moment. In February 1985 the BBC reported that he had written to the New Zealand Premier to congratulate him for refusing to allow any American warships that might be carrying nuclear weapons to dock in New Zealand ports. A month later he visited NATO headquarters in Brussels and reiterated Labour's decision to remove American cruise missiles from Britain. No politician I have consulted believes that Kinnock could change his attitude, once in power, as Wilson did, because the leader is now much more firmly under the control of the Party machinery.

To bolster the unilateralist policy, Labour politicians, ably assisted by far-left writers, have been promoting the thesis that Britain has been taken over by American forces and converted into an advance base essentially in the US interest. The most impressive of these efforts is an astonishingly detailed book, *The Unsinkable Aircraft Carrier*, by the left-wing journalist Duncan Campbell who has also advised the Labour Party on intelligence matters.[23] The lists of air and storage bases, all for the purpose of supporting NATO, and of intelligence-gathering centres, most of which are shared with Britain, are calculated to influence the gullible, but what the book really does, for the discerning, is to underscore the immensity of the American investment in anti-Soviet defence in Britain and the inevitability of American dismay and resentment if the US is forced to abandon it. The investment has been made on long-term understandings with British governments, most of them Labour, and if these are renegued on by a future Labour administration the American commitment to NATO, and therefore NATO itself, are doomed without a shot being fired.

The current Labour argument is that unilateral disarmament and trust in the Soviets have never been tried and should be given a chance. They have been tried and the results demonstrate just how much faith can really be placed in Labour's belief that the Politburo would be likely to follow a lead. After the Second World War Britain's capability to make gas-warfare weapons was abandoned in conformity with the Geneva Convention. In 1969, following receipt of disinformation planted by Soviet active-measures agents, President Nixon announced the end of the production of chemical and biological weapons in the hope that the Soviet Union would reciprocate. As a result, NATO forces in Europe have no gas weapons and no training in their offensive use. The Politburo's response has been to stockpile more than 300,000 tons of poison gas for use against NATO forces, including those of Britain. Every Red Army infantry unit has a chemical section with troops specializing in the launching of rockets carrying warheads armed with poison gas, while the Red Air Force is equipped with poison bombs. The stockpiles include nerve gases but the bulk consists of cyanide because this quickly disperses once it has been dropped and affected areas could be entered by Soviet troops who carry antidotes, routinely. Soviet training manuals claim that the gas would kill 40 per cent of troops and civilians exposed to it. Intelligence reports, defector evidence and the regular mock use of gas weapons in military exercises show that the Politburo has every intention of using them from Day One in any large-scale conflict because, currently, there is no risk of retaliation.[24]

As with the Politburo's nuclear build-up, complaints about the Soviet production and storage of chemical weapons are never heard from the Labour left, which is vocal against the Americans.

While the electorate rejected unilateral disarmament in 1983 there is no certainty that it will do so again. At the time of writing, Labour is ahead in the opinion polls and, under the influence of the 'peace' propaganda, more and more people, especially young voters, seem to be swallowing Labour's simplistic line that making Britain non-nuclear would make them less likely to suffer the horrors of a nuclear attack. It is, of course, no coincidence that nuclear war is being projected as much more likely than ever before, though there is no evidence that it is. The World Peace Council and the Politburo's other fronts continue to stoke up this false fear and 'willies' could help to swing the next General Election in Labour's favour, especially as it is likely to be dominated by domestic issues such as unemployment and rating. Further, the British electorate has a habit of voting governments out, sometimes irrespective of what the opposing party has to offer.

Labour's West German counterpart, the Social Democratic Party (SPD), which has long been a prime target for Communist infiltration and manipulation, has also been pushed further to the left during its current period of opposition so that it too now advocates renunciation of nuclear deterrence, the creation of an atom-free zone in Europe, a halt to NATO's modernization and a cut in spending on conventional defence – all welcome to the Politburo.

It is, therefore, by no means unlikely that the irreversible measures listed in Table 1 could be implemented before the end of this decade with consequences that could be catastrophic for the British way of life, for Europe and for the West in general. In that event, the Soviet Union would achieve its main initial objectives without firing a shot and, in the Politburo, the credit would be given to its cherished invention which it calls, with some pride, *aktivnyye meropriyatiya*.

Chapter 2

The Lie Machinery

'To speak the truth is a petty bourgeois prejudice. To lie, on the other hand, is often justified by its ends.'

Lenin

Most countries conduct their foreign policy aims through diplomacy, economic means, such as trade and aid, intelligence operations and military means which, in extreme cases, involve armed conflict. In keeping with its pathological preoccupation with deception, the Politburo has added a further arm – active measures (*aktivnyye meropriyatiya*), a euphemistic term for its array of peacetime offensive actions against those considered to be its adversaries and against the US, Britain and West Germany in particular. Active measures have the prime purpose of sapping and destroying the Western will to resist the expansion of the Soviet Union's influence and territorial acquisition. They can be roughly equated with undeclared psychological warfare in cold war conditions and, while they include propaganda of the aggressive kind which has become generally acceptable through its constant use, they are essentially a much more deliberately offensive instrument requiring a high degree of planning and control.

Like all aspects of Soviet foreign and domestic policy, active measures are firmly controlled by the Communist Party through the Politburo, which has at its command three powerful and heavily endowed departments for the purpose. They are the International

Department, the International Information Department and the Committee for State Security, the KGB.[1]

The International Department, of which no counterpart exists in the West, was founded in 1957 as a lineal descendant of the Comintern, the worldwide subversive organization set up by Lenin to promote Soviet-style revolutions in as many countries as possible, with the clear understanding that any new Communist governments would be subservient to Moscow. Headed by a former executive of the Comintern, Boris Ponomarev, a very senior and prestigious figure, the International Department is responsible for suggesting active-measures operations to the Politburo and, when these are approved, it directs and orchestrates them. Ponomarev is a non-voting member of the Politburo: he needs no vote, for his function is to listen to the deliberations by the Party chiefs and then, or later, to suggest how their decisions might be exploited.[2]

With a staff of several hundred officers, some of whom are delegated to the embassies abroad, the International Department controls all the Communist front organizations operating in target countries under various guises, funds them when necessary and ensures that they follow Moscow's requirements. It liaises with foreign Communist Parties, ensuring that, so far as possible, they do its bidding, controls clandestine radio stations operating under deceptive names, plans disinformation operations, plants forgeries, recruits and operates agents of influence and is involved in the support of 'national liberation' movements and some kinds of international terrorism.

The activities of the International Department clearly overlap those of the Foreign Ministry and, as defectors and intelligence operations have revealed, it exerts considerable power over Soviet foreign policy, being responsible for approving Foreign Ministry appointments. The fact that Ponomarev, aged eighty at the time of writing, has controlled the International Department for thirty years and holds the rank of a Central Committee Secretary is some indication of the success of his activities in the Politburo's eyes. Described as short, unprepossessing, with a toothbrush moustache and bright round eyes giving him the look of a surprised terrier, he also resembles that creature in his tenacity.[3] The successor whom the new Politburo leader, Gorbachov, is likely to appoint can be expected to be as cunning and ruthless and perhaps even more energetic.

The second agency available for active-measures operations, the International Information Department, was established in March 1978 to intensify the propaganda offensive abroad and to control and counter the effects of foreign news which might be picked up by Soviet citizens listening to broadcasts. As many defectors have testified, it is fundamental to the survival of the Soviet hierarchy that the people they are supposed to serve should never be told the truth. The whole Soviet way of life is based on a gigantic deception, particularly about the true nature of capitalist countries, and maintaining this deception is a major function of the International Information Department which is currently headed by Leonid Zamyatin, a former chief of the TASS telegraph agency and now a full member of the Communist Party's Central Committee. The fact that he accompanied Gorbachov to London in December 1984 and laid the ritual wreath on the tomb of Karl Marx, in Highgate Cemetery, gives some indication of his standing.

The boundary between overt and covert active measures is often blurred, so both the International Department and the International Information Department are regularly involved in the same operation, as is the third and more sinister active-measures agency, the KGB – the power-house through which the Politburo exerts its control.

The Committee for State Security, the KGB, also referred to in the Soviet Union as 'The Troops of the Invisible Front', is so huge and so well entrenched in target countries for espionage and subversion purposes that it is, inevitably, concerned with active measures and especially those which might be included in the term 'dirty tricks'.[4] Its services are in such demand for surreptitious work that a large section of its First Directorate, called Service A, is devoted exclusively to active-measures operations and therefore functions as the executive arm of the International Department. Service A is heavily staffed with personable officers selected from the new generation of graduates trained under Yuri Andropov when he headed the KGB from 1967 to 1982. Usually fluent in at least two foreign languages, they are in sharp contrast to the baggy-trousered, trench-coated thug beloved of cartoonists. There are about 200 such men and women in Service A headquarters, with many more in the field posing as officials in embassies, consulates, trade missions, Soviet media and the various delegations to United Nations agencies. Many pose as journalists, one of the most senior of these, Major Stanislav Levchenko, having defected from his Service A post in Japan, since when he has described his tasks and those of others like him in such detail that I will comment on them at various separate points.[5] Suffice it to say, at this stage, that Service A KGB field officers recruit foreign journalists to plant pro-Soviet forgeries and other disinformation, acquire stationery letterheads and signatures for use by the forgery 'factory' in Moscow, and deliver money to Communist Parties, Communist fronts and Communist publications.

The KGB's increasing involvement in active measures derives from a major change in KGB policy taken in 1959 and steadily developed ever since. Before that the operations were run by a relatively small department, 'D', specializing mainly in the character assassination of foreigners on the Kremlin's list of people who were 'obstructing progress'. Department D was headed by Colonel (later General) Ivan Agayants, a tall, thin Armenian who was ingenious and effective.[6] In 1958, however, the KGB acquired a new chief, Aleksandr Shelepin, who had new ideas for the whole organization. Cultivated, intellectually able and impressive, Shelepin was nevertheless a dedicated revolutionary who had already been involved publicly in the assassination of two Ukrainian political exiles. After taking office he reported to the Politburo that, under his predecessor, the KGB had become a highly efficient espionage organization, successful at penetrating the secrets of Western governments, but had done little to help the strategic, political, economic and ideological struggle with the capitalist powers. He suggested that the KGB should concern itself more with creative political activity, under the firm direction of the Party leadership, and with a much more important role being given to disinformation aimed at distorting Western perceptions of the Soviet Union's real intentions. Shelepin was encouraged to develop this thesis and, in May 1959, a huge conference of some 2,000 KGB officers recalled from the various out-stations was held in Moscow and attended by Ministers.[7]

Shelepin told his officers of the new political tasks against the 'main enemies' which he listed as the US, Britain, France, West Germany and all other NATO countries and Japan. The security and intelligence services of the whole Soviet Bloc were to be mobilized to influence international relations in the directions required by the Politburo's new long-range policy to destabilize the main enemies and weaken the alliances between them.

In pursuit of these aims Department D recruited more staff, was renamed Department A in 1968 and, after further expansion, was upgraded to Service A in 1970. According to John Barron, the leading American authority on the KGB, Service A doubled its size in the ensuing decade and continues to expand as more tasks are given to it. Andropov was an active-measures enthusiast during his leadership of the KGB and his influence in that area continued when he became chief of the Politburo.

While the International Department itself is lavishly funded, according to various defectors, the total available for active-measures operations is vastly increased through Service A because of the virtually unlimited resources which the Politburo makes available to the KGB in the interests of its own survival. All told, according to the American intelligence analysts Richard Shultz and Roy Godson, between 10,000 and 15,000 people are employed full-time on Soviet active measures. Annual costs are likely to be in excess of £2,000 million.[8]

These figures and the resulting effort in active measures are effectively boosted by the heavy participation of the Soviet satellite intelligence agencies and 'information' departments. From the time of Lenin the KGB has preferred to use non-Soviet agents for operations which would be particularly embarrassing if exposed, and all the Soviet satellites are required to take on their share of unpleasant activities. First-hand evidence of this has been provided by several important defectors, such as Major Ladislav Bittman, who defected from the Czech intelligence service to the US after the brutal invasion of his country by Soviet forces in August 1968. He had spent two of his fourteen years' service as deputy-chief of the department responsible for active measures and professed himself to be particularly appalled at the extent to which the KGB used disinformation, forgeries, influence agents and other techniques against their Socialist opponents in Czechoslovakia. 'The Soviets do not hesitate to utilize active measures against their own friends and allies if they feel they are becoming too independent' he told a US Congressional Committee on Intelligence in February 1980.[9]

Bittman told his CIA debriefers that, in 1965 alone, the Czechs conducted more than 100 active-measures operations on behalf of the Soviet Union, half of them based on forgeries. He confirmed that the KGB kept very tight control on the satellite agencies through Service A officers assigned to them. This Czech involvement has been independently confirmed by the more senior defector, Major-General Jan Sejna, while others have disclosed that the East German intelligence service specializes in forgeries, having its own 'factory', the Bulgarian service concentrates on assassinations, while the Polish has specialized, successfully, in acquiring secret technology.

All the informants testify to the importance of feed-back to headquarters so that evaluations of results can be monitored and new instructions for furthering the measures issued to the field operators.[10] The latter track the progress of the operations and Service A prepares a secret daily bulletin on active-measures developments worldwide. This is passed to the International Department which, after further evaluation, informs the Politburo, enabling it to keep its fingers on the pulse of the secret offensive. There is the closest collaboration with the particularly secret section of the KGB's First Directorate concerned with the planting of 'moles' in the intelligence and security services of the target countries, because these are often the most trustworthy sources about the effects being exerted by active-measures operations. Implanted spies, as Kim Philby was in the British Secret Intelligence Service, Anthony Blunt was in MI5 and Donald Maclean was in the Foreign Office, have access to intelligence assessments of the greatest value in assessing the progress of active measures. For that reason, Shelepin stressed, at the start of the intensification of the active-measures offensive, the continuous penetration of foreign secret services was essential to success.[11]

While the International Department and Service A are geared to respond at short notice to a sudden opportunity, they prefer to plan their operations well in advance, with Politburo agreement, after deep thought has been given to all the political consequences. Because of the centralized system, which is not answerable in any way to the Soviet people, risks can be taken which would be politically dangerous in a free democracy and the danger of political embarrassment abroad is regarded as a justifiable risk, with some cover-plan always available to minimize it.

Active measures being planned against important targets are invariably complex and organized so that they can be applied at different points using several techniques designed to combine with maximum impact at the most suitable time. Meticulous attention is paid to this combining of various measures such as the planting of falsified reports in foreign media, the surfacing of a relevant forgery, perhaps in a different part of the world but intended to generate wide publicity, a whispering campaign by well-placed agents of influence, followed, maybe, by some significant act of violence.

In the ideal scenario, what is happening to the target, whether an individual or an institution, should appear to be due to events which are spontaneous and coincidental. There should be no awareness of the operation by the target, at least until maximum damage has been inflicted. Then, if Soviet active measures are suspected, it should be near-impossible to trace them back to Moscow. The planners, therefore, do all they can to conceal their activities in advance and during the operation. The field KGB officers will use paid agents, or other intermediaries to reduce the risk of exposure when, for example, planting a damaging report with a foreign newspaper or magazine. In the event that the Kremlin might be accused of involvement there is always a detailed cover-plan, usually some variant of the upside-down ploy, inverting the truth so that the blame can be laid on the US or another adversary.

In the most important operations active measures achieve their objectives through the cumulative effect of many separate episodes covering several years and, though there may be a sudden climax which appears to be spectacular, it is the planned result of a long campaign waged with ruthlessness, patience and ingenuity to make the terminal event possible. Such triumphs after so much effort and expense generate great rejoicing and mutual congratulation in the International Department and the KGB.

As several trustworthy defectors have testified, there has never been more back-slapping satisfaction than on the occasion of the first major victory in the active-measures offensive initiated by Ponomarev and Shelepin and in which the Politburo had been intimately involved at every stage because the target was a political figure of prime importance. The victory was the removal of the staunchly anti-Communist West German Defence Minister, Franz Josef Strauss, from the political scene. The terminal event in the

Kremlin's determined campaign to eliminate him is recorded in the post-war history of Western Europe as 'the *Der Spiegel* Affair'.

Chapter 3

The *Der Spiegel* Affair

'With West Germany in our hands we would control the whole of Western Europe and could liquidate NATO.'

Alexei Adjubei
Khrushchev's son-in-law; while Editor of Izvestia

As the Soviet active-measures exponents have toiled so patiently to mould the British Labour Party to their requirements and to get it into power, so they have worked on its West German counterpart, the Social Democratic Party (SPD) in pursuit of Lenin's dictum, – 'Whoever has Germany has Europe'. As an essential part of this process they have devoted immense effort to sapping the political strength and will of the SPD's main opponents, the Christian Democrats (CDU) and the Christian Social Union Party (CSU). Of these opponents one man in particular, Franz Josef Strauss of the Christian Social Union Party, was reviled by the Politburo as being such an uncompromising obstacle in the path of the onward march of its influence and ascendancy that he had to be removed. Details of how this requirement was passed to the active-measures experts for action and how they used a combination of techniques in their determined effort to fulfil it, together with the intriguing evidence of Soviet-Bloc defectors who knew of the operation, have only just come to light as a result of a libel action settled last year. This information from sources inside the Kremlin and its offshoots constitutes the first fine-focus description of a major active-measure operation conducted at the highest and most secret levels. It will, therefore, be presented in some detail as a classic instance of the effective use of active measures against an individual, to assassinate his character and destroy his career, just as the manipulation of the British Labour Party is a text-book example of their use against a democratic institution.

On 9 October 1984 Sir James Goldsmith, a businessman of international repute, took full-page advertisements in British and German newspapers to give prominence to the results of a libel action in which he felt that he had been fully vindicated.[1] For many years Sir James, whom I know through long friendship to be unusually perceptive politically, has been deeply perturbed about Communist and pro-Soviet manipulation of the Western media. In that context he had been invited to give evidence on 'The Communist Propaganda Apparatus and Other Threats to the Media' to the Media Committee of the Conservative Party of the British House of Commons and had done so on 21 January 1981. His statement briefly described the Soviet machinery used for active measures, and in connection with the way that newspapers and magazines are utilized, often unwittingly, he quoted Major-General Jan Sejna, an important defector from Czech intelligence who claims to have first-hand knowledge of active-measures operations and has satisfied his CIA debriefers to that effect.[2] Sir James said, 'General Sejna, the high-ranking Czech intelligence defector, admitted that the campaign by the German news magazine *Der Spiegel* to discredit Franz Josef Strauss was orchestrated by the KGB.' Strauss, a flamboyant figure who had been West Germany's Defence Minister and is currently Prime Minister of Bavaria, had been subjected to a bitter campaign of vilification by *Der Spiegel* (The Mirror), a weekly publication with a wide and influential circulation.[3]

Though made in the precincts of Parliament, Sir James's statement was not legally privileged, but it was not until his full speech was published in the British magazine *NOW!*, which he had founded, that the owners and editors of *Der Spiegel* took exception to it. Solicitors acting for *Der Spiegel* issued a writ for libel on 6 March 1981 and demanded a retraction and apology with damages and costs. The writ also claimed that Sir James had suggested that *Der Spiegel* and its management 'either were owned or had been subsidized by, or on behalf of, a foreign power; had been penetrated by journalists sympathetic to Communist propaganda or, alterna-

33

tively, had been bought by Soviet agencies in the most direct sense of the word'.

In fact, all that Sir James had done had been to quote the Soviet dissident Andrei Sakharov, who, in a testament smuggled out of the Soviet Union, had written, 'People in the West have been bought by Soviet agencies in the most direct sense of the word. . . . These include political figures, businessmen and a great many writers and journalists, government advisers and heads of the Press and TV.'

As the evidence presented in this book should convince the reader, there can be no doubt about the truth of Sakharov's general statement and Sir James did not, in any way, indicate that he believed or suspected that *Der Spiegel* or anybody connected with it fell into that category. It would have remained for the court to decide whether any such allusion could have reasonably been implied by any reader of *NOW!* magazine, for Sir James immediately decided to defend the libel action. Using his very considerable resources and resourcefulness he assembled the maximum possible amount of reliable evidence about Soviet active-measures operations from the most reputable sources, including high-level Soviet and Soviet-Bloc defectors.[4] I have discussed his motivation with him at length and it is clear that his purpose was not simply personal vindication but to perform an international service by providing a platform on which the secret offensive against the true democracies being waged by the Soviet Union could be subjected to worldwide publicity and scrutiny. Sir James is convinced, as I am, that the threat to our freedoms from the active-measures campaigns is far more serious than even British and European secret services, with all their knowledge, are prepared to accept, while the general public awareness of it is almost negligible. He made this point at length when addressing an international audience at the Defense Strategy Forum in Washington on 22 May 1982.

In the result, however, the libel action was settled out of court on the initiative of the lawyers acting for *Der Spiegel* and with Sir James Goldsmith's consent. In the High Court of Justice, Queen's Bench Division, on 8 October 1984, barristers representing the owners and publishers of *Der Spiegel* and Sir James Goldsmith made mutually agreed statements which will be reproduced later. Lord Rawlinson, the former Attorney-General, acting for Sir James, outlined the general contention that the Soviet Union makes use of unwitting Western media, through well-placed agents of influence, to pursue its campaign to undermine free Western societies and political systems. In particular, he stated Sir James's conviction that the Soviet Union had used active measures to defame and discredit Franz Josef Strauss and had made use in that campaign of the fact that *Der Spiegel* was well known as opposing Dr Strauss's political views and regularly published articles expressing that opposition. Lord Rawlinson stated that, had the case continued, high-level defectors would have given evidence of meetings at which plans were approved to seek to discredit Strauss and to use *Der Spiegel* in the process.

Mr John Wilmers, QC, representing the owners and publishers of *Der Spiegel*, then stated that his clients fully accepted that, broadly speaking, Soviet Intelligence seeks to operate in the way stated by Lord Rawlinson, though they had not been shown the mass of evidence which Sir James had secured. It was also stated that the owners and publishers of *Der Spiegel* were 'conscious of the dangers to press freedom posed by Soviet covert propaganda' though they were 'not conscious of having been used in the manner mentioned by Sir James'.

With the agreement of his lawyers Sir James felt that with the full agreed statement, which could be given wider publicity, he had been sufficiently vindicated to agree that the libel action should be withdrawn. This, presumably, occasioned some relief in the International Department and Service A of the KGB in Moscow, which could not have been relishing the prospect of a detailed exposure of their methods of character assassination by Soviet-Bloc defectors in a court case which was bound to attract widespread media interest. I therefore contacted Sir James with a view to securing the evidence which would have been given in court, so that it could be placed on public record as a reminder of a classic case of character assassination by the media – one that brought major advantage to the Soviet Bloc which had, unquestionably, begun the process years before *Der Spiegel* administered the knock-out blow in the autumn of 1962. After a meeting Sir James agreed to provide the affidavits, research reports and many authoritative statements he had acquired and the evidence is presented here and in the source notes along with results of my own investigations. Much of it is also highly relevant to the general manipulation by Soviet active-measures operators of the media, information services, agents of influence and Communist front organizations and will be utilized in the separate sections dealing with those themes.

Strauss, whose career was disrupted and permanently diminished by the *Der Spiegel* Affair, was Minister of Defence in the coalition government headed by Chancellor Konrad Adenauer. A butcher's son from Munich, he was a jovial Bavarian of distinguished intellect who had earned his position in the Christian Social Union Party as a politician of such charisma and leadership that, at the age of forty-seven, as he was in 1962, he was regarded by many as the likely successor to the ageing Chancellor. I met him at various NATO functions while he was Defence Minister and found him to be a most formidable figure. He was staunchly committed to West Germany's membership of NATO, to which his country had been admitted seven years previously, and to the close alliance with the US which that membership entailed. As Defence Minister, which he had been appointed in October 1956, he had striven to ensure that the West German forces would make the essential contribution to the defence of Europe required by NATO membership and was in no doubt that a dangerous and continuous threat was posed by the Soviet Bloc in pursuit of the Politburo's ultimate aim of world Communist domination. In particular, he was convinced that America's nuclear weapons had been instrumental in preventing much more determined intimidation of Western Europe, and possible invasion, by the Soviet Bloc. Believing that appeasement is the enemy of peace, he strongly supported the stationing of American nuclear weapons on German soil for use in NATO's defence against Soviet-Bloc aggression and promoted that view, which prevailed, resolutely in the Bundestag.

This stance which was, perhaps, fortified by his fervent Roman Catholicism, had made him hated by Moscow's atheistic regime and the strong possibility that such a dynamic, dedicated and young anti-Communist might become Chancellor had marked him out as a target for elimination from the political scene by active measures of special intensity.

From the moment of the West German commitment to American support and the start of the 'economic miracle' wrought through Marshall Aid, Moscow had been pursuing a hate campaign against West German government leaders and their officials, who were continually accused of plotting revenge for the recent defeat. The decision that German forces should be re-established and rearmed as part of NATO inflamed these accusations of 'revanchism' and, in line with the policy then favoured by the KGB's Colonel Agayants, the Soviets sought to promote the fears of another war by smearing the personalities involved. Strauss was the obvious target and from the time of his appointment as Defence Minister a major propaganda campaign against him had been launched and was being pursued relentlessly by the East German Communist Party and its main newspaper, *Neues Deutschland*.[5]

A penetrating survey entitled 'The East's defamatory campaign against F. J. Strauss' was undertaken by a high official of the West German secret service (BND), who is required to remain anonymous but has provided a summary of it. It shows that once Strauss had become Defence Minister, in 1956, the entire press and propaganda apparatus of the Soviet zone of Germany carried out systematic attacks on him. The author says that an internal instruction from the East German Politburo, dated 16 June 1957, expressed dissatisfaction with the campaign which needed to be continued, making use of what the instruction described as 'the well-timed release of new, and already prepared, damaging material'. Strauss was always to be referred to as the *War* Minister and his Ministry as the *War* Ministry or, even more forcibly, as the *Atomic War* Ministry.[6]

The campaign was intensified in 1958 with Strauss being described as 'the chauvinist agitator against the Soviet Union and the initiator of plans for launching war against the USSR, East Germany and the satellites'. A fake 'Study Group of Former German Officers' living in the Eastern Zone was brought into play to claim that Strauss was following in Hitler's footsteps.[7]

In April 1959, according to the former BND officer who had access to such information through his intelligence work, the Agitprop Chief of the East Zone Communist Party (then euphemistically known as the Socialist Unity Party) gave new orders for the defamation of Strauss at every opportunity in the East German media which, it was hoped, would exert some influence in West Germany and elsewhere in the world through the impact of the Soviet media, which recycled much of the defamatory material for both domestic and overseas consumption.[8] Further scurrilous articles appeared in *Neues Deutschland* and, towards the end of 1959, the campaign was extended to the Czech press, using East German material.

In January 1960 the Soviet-Bloc propaganda machine concentrated on suggestions that the West German Government, and Strauss in particular, were anti-Semitic. The intention was to imply that he was a neo-Nazi and he was, in fact, accused by the propagandists of being the 'initiator of Nazi excesses'. In a brochure called 'Action Gallows Cross', Strauss was accused of having organized the profaning of synagogues and Jewish graveyards when that had been accomplished by Soviet-Bloc active-measures agents. To quote Count Hans Huyn, a member of the Bundestag who has made a study of Soviet disinformation,

> On Christmas Eve 1959, the synagogue in Cologne was defaced with painted swastikas. The next few days saw similar anti-Semitic manifestations in other German cities. As a result, a wave of anti-German indignation swept through the entire Western world. Adenauer was compelled to issue a public apology. The demand for appropriate steps to be taken was heard from sources ranging from the House of Commons to the Zionist General Council. The loudest sounds of indignation came from *Pravda* in Moscow. The damage was done and it was not until years afterwards that the West learned the whole truth from KGB defectors: the entire campaign had been planned by General Ivan Agayants, Director of the Department of Disinformation in the First Directorate of the KGB, and carried out with the assistance of East Berlin's State Security Service.[9]

Detailed evidence is also available from some of the most reliable defectors that the whole programme of vilification against Strauss was instigated in Moscow and passed to the satellite agencies for execution. General Sejna, whose sworn statements on these matters have been made available to me, claims that he was present at briefings by Soviet intelligence officers and heard, at first hand, that Strauss was high on the Kremlin's 'hit-list'.[10] Though Sejna heard no evidence that this animosity might even extend to physical assassination, General Reinhard Gehlen, the West German intelligence chief, acting on intelligence information or gut-feeling about the KGB, warned Strauss that he might be murdered and to take precautions.[11] To Sejna's personal knowledge the defamation campaign dated back at least to 1957 when he had been Executive Secretary of the Czech Communist Party's Defence Council, a position which made him privy to many KGB activities. Sejna recalls that all possible measures were being pressed into the service of discrediting the leading members of the Adenauer government to help the Social Democratic Party to gain power because the Soviets had penetrated it so heavily.

Clearly, saturation denigration in the Communist-controlled media would not be sufficiently effective even though some of it was spilling over into the Western media. What was needed, on routine active-measures principles, was a campaign of vilification in important organs of the Western media where, ideally, it should appear to have arisen spontaneously. Sejna claims that, in the eyes of the Soviet Bloc, the best and most obvious target for that purpose was *Der Spiegel*, which had originally been modelled on the American magazine *Time*, and had the same wide appeal and impact.[12]

Der Spiegel had been set up with the support of the Allied Control authorities in 1946 and from its inception had been controlled by an exceptionally able journalist, called Rudolf Augstein, who has stamped his personality on to the magazine giving it saleability through liveliness, surprise and, above all, controversy.[13] Like most editors in search of large circulations, Augstein realized that reports of serious matters are most likely to have impact and influence when projected through the medium of the personalities involved, and the more such people can be 'humanized', especially through their personal weaknesses, the more readable the story is likely to be and the more talked about. That, of course, was the policy of Lord Beaverbrook; it made his London *Daily Express* not only the world's largest seller but read by all sectors of society.

Being young himself – he was born in 1923 – Augstein began by admiring the young thruster, Strauss, and *Der Spiegel*'s cover-story, when Strauss became Defence Minister, showed him in a heroic pose. This friendliness quickly turned to animosity, however, and, whatever the reasons, Augstein and his staff began a relentlessly sustained campaign of vilifying the man and his policies. The campaign was to achieve all the objectives of the tasks which the Kremlin leadership has set its active-measures departments, perhaps more spectacularly than even they had thought possible. Augstein and his colleagues insist that this was coincidental but Sejna and other defectors involved in the Kremlin's campaign against Strauss believe that it was not. Sejna, in his sworn statement, says that *Der Spiegel* was specifically selected as the medium whereby Strauss would be vilified to the point of political destruction, one of the reasons being that the magazine had already been conducting a vicious anti-Strauss campaign and could be encouraged to do more.[14]

In the autumn of 1958, for instance, Augstein, writing under the pseudonym 'Jens Daniel', published an article in *Der Spiegel* that bore remarkable similarity to views that had been expressed, shortly before, by Khrushchev, then the Soviet leader. He urged recognition of the East German Communist régime, the evacuation of foreign troops, meaning the Americans in particular, and the establishment of an atom-free zone in Europe – all much desired by the Politburo as a means of eventually intimidating West Germany into submission. 'Daniel' used the word 'revanchism', a Soviet invention implying neo-Nazi revenge against Russia, as though it were a word in the German language which, until then, it had not been. Augstein and *Der Spiegel* generally had also taken to describing Strauss as the Minister for War which, as is now known, was a requirement of the Soviet active-measures planners.[15]

As *Der Spiegel* grew steadily in readership and influence – it now prints more than 900,000 copies weekly – it became increasingly hostile to the US, to NATO and to nuclear weapons in particular. An analysis of its relevant articles carried out by a West German specialist, and made available to me, has shown that the magazine's policy seemed to be reflecting the Soviet-Bloc propaganda against West Germany and that many of its attacks on Strauss and other targets coincided with occasions when they appeared to assist the Communist cause. Articles painted a picture of Strauss – 'the elephant from the Bavarian backwoods', a reference to his portliness – 'lusting after atomic weapons at any price'. He was consistently accused of disregarding right and law.[16]

Throughout 1960 the Soviet-sponsored campaign in the Communist-controlled media was intensified, with the Polish press and radio being brought into the attack. In the following year a book was published justifying comparisons between Strauss and Hitler.[17] In March 1961 Strauss was accused in the Communist *Berliner Zeitung* of complicity in the mass murder of Jews and Poles at Lwow in July 1941 when he had been in the German Army.[18] Inside the Soviet zone of Germany the campaign was extended by the mass distribution of copies of an article which had appeared in *Der Spiegel* and, according to the former BND officer, sought to portray Strauss as a second Hitler.[19] During 1961 alone, Strauss was headlined in seventy-two prominent antagonistic articles in *Neues Deutschland* and given further prominence in 420 other items.[20] The Czech defector Ladislav Bittman has recorded in his memoirs that Soviet-Bloc disinformation activities were intensified in the 1960s to reinforce the image of a West Germany being the heir to the Nazis and, therefore, a potential threat to all the people of Europe.[21] When Strauss visited Norway in 1961, the active-measures machinery went into action and demonstrations were organized against him.

The Soviet need for its disinformation to be picked up by the Western media continued to be fulfilled. A false rumour, first published in *Neues Deutschland*, that Strauss was planning to train German troops in the use of nuclear weapons in the Libyan desert was repeated in *Der Spiegel*.[22] A particularly bitter attack, entitled 'The Final Conflict', appeared in *Der Spiegel* in July 1961 at a high point in a fresh Berlin crisis concocted by Moscow and only five weeks before the erection of the Berlin wall. In the previous month the political sympathies of *Der Spiegel* writers had been demonstrated, beyond doubt, by Augstein, again writing as 'Jens Daniel': 'It was the policies of the Federal Government which left the Soviets only the choice either to put the screw on Berlin or to wait until Federal Chancellor Strauss had nuclear weapons at his disposal. Now he will not have them at his disposal but only because the Soviets put the screw on Berlin.'[23] That statement is evidence that Strauss might have succeeded Adenauer, but it was based on the false premise that the West German Chancellor could have had nuclear weapons 'at his disposal' when, in fact, under American law the weapons would, necessarily, have been under US Government control, as they still are.

Der Spiegel delivered a more personal attack on Strauss by alleging that he had used his political influence to help a close friend, Hans Kapfinger, to profit from a huge deal to build more than 3,000 houses for American troops and their families in West Germany. The firm concerned was called Fibag, and Gehlen, in his memoirs, states that, to his knowledge, Strauss was unaware of its existence.[24] According to the study by the former BND officer, *Der*

Spiegel had published an article at the end of January 1962, under the title 'Kapfinger's Stories', bringing together and commenting on material from Eastern-Bloc media. As a result, the officer claims, West German Intelligence was able to establish that the Central Committee of the East German Communist Party had issued an urgent internal instruction to produce yet more 'documentation' about Strauss. It was to be printed in several languages, should concentrate on allegations of corruption and should include charges of sexual dissipation. Information available to the BND showed that Soviet diplomats were to be told to do all they could to bring Strauss down, damage the West German Government and disillusion its allies.[25] The Communist organizations and fronts worldwide intensified their anti-Strauss propaganda, sensing that they were cornering their quarry.

In summarizing his analysis of *Der Spiegel*'s articles, the West German specialist wrote: 'It has been my experience over many years that the same terminology, the same style, the same malicious intention to stir up sedition and demoralization could and can be found in Communist publications and other pronouncements from the Communist side.' His views are supported by Dr Hans Mathias Kepplinger, a distinguished German scholar who has also analysed the content of *Der Spiegel*'s news coverage.[26] He notes that the magazine advocated policies which were right on the Soviet line – the dissolution of NATO and the Warsaw Pacts, American disengagement from Western Europe, both militarily and politically, with nuclear weapons renounced and the assumption of a neutral stance. While the Kremlin's foreign policy was portrayed as informed, rational and calculable, that of the US was uninformed, irrational and incalculable and, therefore, a danger to world peace. As Dr Kepplinger puts it, the guilt for the arms race was predominantly attributed to the USA.

In fairness to *Der Spiegel* and to Herr Augstein it must be conceded that any publication is entitled to take a stand on defence policy and, should matters arise in the Communist press which happen to suit that policy, to follow them up in the normal practice of journalism. Many newspapers in the free world were genuinely concerned about the rearming of West Germany so soon after the destruction wrought by the Nazis and none more so than the paper for which I worked, the *Daily Express*, and its proprietor, Lord

Beaverbrook. With some difficulty I and others convinced Beaverbrook that, unless the West Germans were encouraged to re-form an army and air force, the enormous cost of defending them against a Soviet take-over would fall on the British, American and French taxpayers. He remained concerned, however, as I did, about the provision of battlefield nuclear weapons to the new German forces, especially while there was uncertainty about the control over them. Believing that only the deterrent effect of nuclear weapons based in West Germany could counter the Soviet threat, Strauss was determined to secure such weapons under terms which gave West Germany equality with other NATO members. It seemed, in the early 1960s, that NATO had a sufficiency of nuclear weapons in the hands of the American and British forces in Europe, but Strauss insisted that if West Germany was to pay a major share of NATO's costs and provide what would be its largest army she must be treated as a full NATO partner. If there were to be NATO fingers on the nuclear trigger, West Germany's had to be one of them, especially as most of the destruction caused by their use would be on West German territory.

Beaverbrook and the *Daily Express* came to terms with the nuclear situation in West Germany after the NATO conference in Athens in May 1962, which I covered. Strauss was successful in obtaining assurances that West Germany would be defended by nuclear weapons which would be under American control but could not be removed without West German consent. Further, like any other NATO nation, West Germany would have a finger on the nuclear trigger in respect of the Polaris missile submarines assigned to NATO, though the final control over these would rest with the US President.[27] Augstein and *Der Spiegel*, on the other hand, were incensed by Strauss's success and stepped up the campaign. Writing about Augstein's general attitude, in *Der Spiegel* itself and presumably without any objection from Augstein, its editor, Gerd Schmuckle, a former press officer in the West German Defence Ministry, wrote: 'Augstein was eaten up by his loathing for Franz Josef Strauss. With sparkling pen he revelled in an over-heated feud. He had taken up arms against rearmament, NATO, military strength, emergency regulations and atomic weapons. And, above all, he was against Strauss. His imagination in the public carving-up of his opponent was inexhaustible.'[28]

Augstein wrote like a militant left-winger, especially when appearing under the pseudonym 'Jens Daniel', and there is no doubt that he employed militant left-wingers among his writing journalists – men who were likely to use their writing opportunities to promote their political opinions. One of these, Berndt Engelmann, was awarded an East German prize in 1984 for his 'defence of the democratic rights of West German citizens', for the fight against Monopolism, Militarism and 'Revanchism', and for the 'Peace Struggle'. He received the prize in East Berlin from the East German Minister for Culture. During the time that he was employed by *Der Spiegel*, from 1956 to 1962, as an editor and special correspondent, he concentrated on investigative journalism discrediting Strauss, so much so that in 1980 he produced a 'Black Book on Strauss' which was intended to remind readers how dangerous it would be for 'peace' should Strauss ever become Chancellor after all.[29]

In the article about Augstein's feud with Strauss, written by Gerd Schmuckle, Strauss's former press officer, and printed in *Der Spiegel* itself, it was stated that General Gehlen told Strauss that there was a Communist espionage cell in the editorial staff of the magazine, though Schmuckle chose not to believe it.[30] The most significant statement attributed to Gehlen, however, appears in the British version of his own memoirs, where he is shown as recounting how his counter-intelligence men recruited an officer of the East German secret service as a double agent. The memoirs state that, to maintain this officer's credibility with his East German masters, Gehlen permitted him to carry out some of the missions entrusted to him on the Communists' behalf and that one of these was to carry certain documents from East Berlin to *Der Spiegel*. The recruitment of this double agent is dated at around 1962. Neither I nor other investigators have been able to confirm the existence of this double agent but *Der Spiegel* did not require the removal of the statement in the British edition of the Gehlen memoirs when they were published in 1972.[31]

The notorious KGB officer, Vitali Lui, who writes under the name Viktor Louis, is known to have provided material used by *Der Spiegel*, *Stern* and other German media as well as the British press. As the defector Shevchenko pointed out recently, Louis, 'a wealthy tipster for the Western press', writes only when Moscow authorises him to do so, implying that there must be some advantage to the Kremlin from the publicity.[32]

It would have been normal practice for members of *Der Spiegel*'s staff to have been in contact with Soviet-Bloc intelligence agents, using them as possible sources. Even the link with the alleged East German double agent would have been no professional crime so long as the recipients of documents checked the information being provided and satisfied themselves that it was not disinformation before making use of it. Most defence and political correspondents in Fleet Street maintain contact with Soviet-Bloc press and cultural officials knowing them to be intelligence officers, the hope being that they might provide some reliable information or leads. In fact, as my own experience quickly convinced me, such officials are interested only in gleaning information from well-informed sources so they can relay it to Moscow for intelligence or active-measures purposes; in using journalists for the planting of disinformation and propaganda and, where possible, in recruiting journalists as paid agents as described in Chapter 7.

Hermann Renner, a former journalist on *Der Spiegel* during the time of the campaign against Strauss, maintains that Augstein's dislike and distrust of Strauss and his policies were so fierce that there was no need for any specific material from the Eastern Bloc, the conflict between the two men being 'rooted in their natures'. He regards any orchestration of the *Der Spiegel* Affair by the Eastern Bloc as being no more than 'amplified background music', reinforcing it.[33]

Whatever the full truth, which may never be known, no journalist, and certainly no journal, is entirely immune to sophisticated active measures ingeniously, and often indirectly, applied by masters of the craft. In view of the proven fact that there were at least two full-blown Soviet agents on the writing staff of the *Daily Express*, Peter Smolka and Wilfred Burchett, and others of whom MI5 were aware on other highly respected Fleet Street papers of Conservative bent, it would not be remarkable if an organ as potentially useful to Moscow as *Der Spiegel* had been penetrated.[34]

Chapter 4

Mission Accomplished

'The Der Spiegel *Affair has been Strauss's Chappaquiddick.'*
Wm. F. Buckley Jnr

Whatever political intentions may have inspired *Der Spiegel*, the magazine's publishing policy was clearly susceptible to active-measures influence if only because its demands were so similar to those of Moscow's International Department. In view of what is definitely known about Soviet active-measures techniques, it is axiomatic that devious efforts would be made not only to conceal any link between Moscow and the magazine but to prevent its staff from becoming aware that any foreign effort was being made to influence or manipulate them. The International Department's first move, in such a situation, is to distance itself from the operation by delegating the action to a satellite agency and there is reliable defector evidence that Czech intelligence was chosen to spearhead the operation against Strauss and, specifically, to make use of *Der Spiegel* as a medium for active-measures material if it could.

General Sejna states that the person who gave the specific order to Czech intelligence to escalate the use of the Western media in general to discredit opponents was none other than Boris Ponomarev, the chief of the International Department himself.[1] He says that Ponomarev visited Prague a few days after the twenty-second Congress of the Soviet Communist Party, in October 1961, bringing directives, one of which required Czech intelligence, which then had its own disinformation department, to help in discrediting the West

German ruling parties and, especially, Strauss, whom one of the directives described as 'a most dangerous revanchist and the Number One anti-Communist'. Sejna states that he was present when Ponomarev spent ten minutes talking about Strauss, stressing that every effort had to be made to prevent his becoming Chancellor.

Sejna's evidence about the level at which the operation was being directed, and the extreme importance attached to it, is strongly supported by that of Ilya Dzhirkvelov, a former KGB officer who defected to Britain in 1980. I have a copy of a statement made by Dzhirkvelov and have interviewed him at length. I have also established that when he made his statement he had no knowledge of the statement made by Sejna and that there has been no collusion between them. Dzhirkvelov, a most personable Georgian, had joined the KGB in 1944 and, later, had served as Deputy Secretary General of the Union of Journalists of the USSR which, he states, was set up by the International Department with the prime purpose of acting as a vehicle to feed disinformation to foreign media. He attended many secret meetings and through KGB friends, one of whom was on Khrushchev's secretarial staff, he learned about most of the major active-measures operations while they were still in the planning stage.[2]

Dzhirkvelov attended a top-level secret meeting convened by the International Department at the beginning of 1960 and chaired by Ponomarev with the Party's chief ideologist, Mikhail Suslov, present and other senior officials. Ponomarev stressed that the Soviet 'journalists' could do a great deal to discredit 'undesirables' like Strauss and Dzhirkvelov and the other 'journalists' present were instructed to work out, urgently, practical proposals to 'improve the situation'.

The possible measures which the Union of Journalists might take were then discussed with Khrushchev's son-in-law, Alexei Adjubei, then editor of *Izvestia* and whom I met, around that time, when he visited the *Daily Express* as part of a London tour. Adjubei named Strauss as being 'most dangerous' and remarked, 'With West Germany in our hands we would control the whole of Western Europe and could liquidate NATO.'

As part of the softening-up process of the Western media, a group of West German journalists, mainly the editors of papers supporting the Social Democrats, were invited to Moscow to be given exceptional hospitality and to be taken on trips never previously available to foreigners. Before they arrived, Dzhirkvelov and the other Russian 'journalists' who were to serve as hosts were given pep-talks about the great opportunity which the visit presented. The talks were given by the KGB specialist in character assassination, General Agayants. He insisted on infiltrating senior KGB officers into the Journalists' Union for the operation, one of them being a German specialist who was to accompany the visitors on their tour in the guise of a journalist working for the Soviet magazine, New Times.[3]

In a further meeting with Ponomarev the hosts were instructed to tell the visitors, quite openly, that the Soviets viewed Strauss as 'a revanchist and a Hitlerite who is very harmful to Europe'. This was followed by a further summons to Dzhirkvelov to see Agayants who gave him some precise instructions concerning Strauss. He was ordered to hint to the visiting Germans, at every opportunity, that the KGB had evidence that American intelligence had recruited Strauss while he was a prisoner-of-war and that he retained links with the CIA, which continued to pay him large sums. Agayants said that if the visiting journalists demanded to see the evidence they were to be told that it could be produced, if they would guarantee to reproduce it in West German papers without disclosing the source. Presumably, forged documents had been prepared but were never issued, so far as is known. Dzhirkvelov records that he did his best to convince the head of the visiting group that Strauss was a dangerous American agent.[4]

According to Sejna, the intervention finally chosen, about a year later, for the ultimate discrediting of Strauss was to involve genuine secret documents procured from NATO through Soviet agents operating inside that organization. Sejna claims that Czech intelligence had a steady stream of NATO documents and this has been confirmed by the conviction of two Soviet agents – Georges Pâques, a Frenchman who was deputy head of the French Section of NATO's information department in Paris, and Hugh Hambleton, a Canadian economist also working in Paris.[5] In his sworn affidavit Sejna states that, in January 1962, the Czech Minister of the Interior, Lubomir Strougal (who is Prime Minister at the time of writing), told him that Soviet advisers had approved a plan whereby

48

secret NATO documents should be leaked to *Der Spiegel* from Strauss's Defence Ministry. The selected documents would have to be so newsworthy that a campaigning magazine like *Der Spiegel* would be unable to resist printing a major story about them, and it was believed that the magazine's feud with Strauss would make publication almost certain. Strauss would then be discredited for the leakage of secret information, not only with the public but with his NATO allies. According to Sejna, a study of Strauss's personality – a KGB routine for subjects it selects for defamation treatment – had indicated that he would over-react angrily and make his situation worse.[6]

Neither Sejna nor Dzhirkvelov knows any further detail of the plan or whether it was put into effect as required, but their evidence leaves no doubt about the intentions of the active-measures chiefs and the particular methods whereby they hoped to achieve them. There is also the uncorroborated statement in Gehlen's memoirs that a courier for the delivery of documents to *Der Spiegel* existed in the form of the East German double agent.

Further, both Sejna and Dzhirkvelov insist that they were later informed, quite separately, that an active-measures operation involving *Der Spiegel* had taken place and had been highly successful. Dzhirkvelov recalls a meeting with Ponomarev, early in 1963, at which the International Department chief proudly boasted that successful use had been made of *Der Spiegel* to undermine Strauss. He says that he personally heard this claim repeated by Suslov, the Politburo ideologist, at a confidential meeting of Party newspaper editors. Later, in 1974, an old KGB friend, Colonel Arkady Boiko, who had personally conducted active measures against West Germany, told him that the biggest coup he had heard of was the use of *Der Spiegel* to compromise Franz Josef Strauss. For good measure, Dzhirkvelov, who is an impressive witness, claims that he heard Khrushchev's son-in-law, Adjubei, describe the *Der Spiegel* Affair as 'one of the best jobs ever'.[7]

None of these people ever suggested that Herr Augstein or any other member of the magazine's staff was aware that it was a target for Soviet attention and, in the final paragraph of his affidavit, Dzhirkvelov makes the point of saying that 'many respectable and politically impeccable publications fell victim to the KGB active measures without knowing by whom they had been used'.

49

Whatever the actual effectiveness of the active-measures operations, the event which has gone into political history as the *Der Spiegel* Affair was more successful than Ponomarev and his minions could have expected. This is what happened.

On 10 October 1962 *Der Spiegel* published a long article, entitled 'Bedingt abwehrbereit' (meaning 'Conditionally Prepared for Defence'), which gave accurate details about a NATO exercise code-named Fallex '62 together with secret NATO assessments of its consequences. The exercise, which had been carried out in Western Europe during the previous month, was the first to be based on the assumption that an attack by the Soviet and Warsaw Pact forces on Central Europe would initiate a Third World War. The Soviets were supposed to have made the first use of nuclear weapons and, in the ensuing exchange, large parts of West Germany and Britain were deemed to have been destroyed with up to 15 million killed there and the US mainland suffering even larger casualties.[8]

In disclosing the NATO commanders' conclusions about the lessons to be learned, *Der Spiegel* took the view that West Germany's defence policy should be in line with that of the US, where the Kennedy administration wanted to increase NATO's conventional forces so that the use of nuclear weapons could be delayed and possibly eliminated. Strauss, who with Adenauer was in some conflict with Kennedy's views on several issues, was said to have disagreed with the American policy for NATO and, in spite of the appalling lessons of Fallex '62, to be continuing to insist on the quick use of nuclear weapons, since otherwise the deterrent would lose its credibility. He was described as refusing to comply with NATO's demands for an increase in conventional forces and of acting contrary to the wishes of the German Army commanders themselves. The Luftwaffe chiefs were said to be supporting Strauss in being in favour of a NATO capability to make a pre-emptive nuclear air strike against the Soviet Bloc.

The impact of the article was unprecedented. The Federal Criminal Police were called in to investigate the breach of security and what seemed to have been a leakage of secret information. On 26 October the offices of *Der Spiegel* in Hamburg and Bonn were searched and sealed off. Several members of the staff were arrested, including Augstein, Dr Klaus Jacobi, a managing editor, Hans Schmelz of the editorial staff and Hans-Detlev Becker, acting editor.

The magazine's defence correspondent, Dr Conrad Ahlers, who had written the article, was detained while on holiday in Spain, was extradited and then arrested. Like the others, he was held in prison pending trial on suspicion of having committed treason.[9]

The Federal Prosecutor-General claimed that during the search of *Der Spiegel*'s offices a copy of the secret minutes of the West German Parliamentary Defence Committee had been discovered along with other documents. Apart from 'State secrets of the first importance' he said that there were also photographs of 'military objects' which were classified. General Gehlen, who was well placed to know, told the Defence Ministry that Augstein possessed secret documents from NATO, while Strauss himself was later to state that *Der Spiegel* had received information from his Ministry giving the total number of American atomic warheads based in Germany, their explosive power and potential targets.[10]

While these documents were being examined, three more people were arrested, one of them being a Defence Ministry official, called Colonel Alfred Martin, who was suspected of having passed military secrets to the magazine. Another was Colonel Adolf Wicht of the Federal Intelligence Service, headed by General Gehlen. The Federal Prosecutor-General claimed that Wicht had warned the *Der Spiegel* management of the forthcoming action and that, as a result, other secret documents which had been used in the offending article had been removed from the magazine's offices. This involvement of the Federal Intelligence Service was to damage its reputation and that of Gehlen himself, inflicting further injury on the Government and its machinery.[11]

Inevitably, the arrests led to the widespread assumption that they were a reprisal for the consistent attacks by *Der Spiegel* on Strauss and his administration. *Pravda*, *Izvestia* and other Communist newspapers were quick to speak out on behalf of Augstein, claiming that his arrest recalled the actions of the Nazis when Hitler had seized power. General credence to the belief that Augstein was being victimized was given by the fact that an article similar to that published by *Der Spiegel* had appeared in the West German newspaper *Deutsche Zeitung und Wirtschaftszeitung* in the previous month without causing any official protest.[12]

Soon, there was a well-orchestrated outcry from behind the Iron Curtain which was mirrored in West Germany from academics, including some Soviet agents of influence, and from other newspapers which sided with *Der Spiegel* because of what seemed to be an unwarranted interference with the freedom of the press. There were accusations of censorship, which is illegal in West Germany, and, ironically, the Iron Curtain Communist press, which is totally censored and has no freedom whatever, made the most of it. As could be guaranteed, Strauss's political opponents joined in the furore.

In a speech on 2 November 1962 Strauss insisted that he had not been responsible for initiating the arrests and that it was no act of revenge on his part. This turned out to be true, as the action had been taken on the initiative of the Federal Prosecutor-General, as was to be stated later in the Federal Supreme Court.[13] Few were inclined to believe Herr Strauss, however, or Chancellor Adenauer when he was questioned. Strauss's resignation was being widely demanded along with the immediate release of Augstein and his colleagues who were seen as media martyrs languishing in prison for bringing the truth to the people, as British journalists would have been in a similar context.

A Bundestag debate, in which Adenauer intervened to justify the arrests, ended in uproar, and the political wheels which were to crush Strauss were soon turning and could not be stopped because of the nature of the West German Government which, at that time, was a coalition of three parties – the Christian Social Union Party, the Christian Democrats and the Free Democratic Party – all of whom had ministers in the ruling administration.[14] The leader of the Free Democratic Party, Dr Erich Mende, has put his account of the immediate events on record.

When *Der Spiegel*'s offices were raided and the arrests made it was naturally assumed that the Federal Minister of Justice, Dr Wolfgang Stammberger, who happened to be a Free Democrat, must have been deeply involved. He had not been and he intensified the general resentment, and the political anger of his party, by declaring on television that he had been completely by-passed and that the first he had heard of the *Der Spiegel* episode was through the radio. It was widely assumed that Strauss must have been responsible for this unconstitutional behaviour, his fear being that Stammberger might overrule him. Dr Mende and his colleagues then learned that Stammberger had been further insulted because his top civil servants had been instructed not to tell him what was going to happen. Stammberger's facts were correct but it transpired that it had not been Strauss, but Adenauer, the Chancellor himself, who had issued the order for the Justice Minister to be by-passed, though, later, Adenauer was to lie, publicly, about this.[15]

Mende visited Adenauer and told him that the coalition was in serious danger because the leaders of the opposition party, the SPD, seemed to have even more damaging information about Strauss, which they had secured from some secret source, and were preparing to use it. At a meeting of the leaders of the three coalition parties, on 17 November, it was agreed that there would have to be a reshuffle, with Strauss moving from the Defence Ministry, and the five Free Democratic Party ministers, including Stammberger, resigned office to enforce it. Meanwhile, Augstein had written an article in his prison cell accusing Strauss of numerous misdeeds and asking, 'Shall the State go to ruin for the sake of one man?' It reached *Der Spiegel* somehow and was published on 14 November.

On 26 November Adenauer told Strauss that he could not remain in the Cabinet and this was announced four days later, though, in his native Bavaria, Strauss had won an overwhelming electoral victory on the previous day, 25 November, this being, in part, a protest at the way he was being treated in Bonn.[16] A new coalition of CDU, CSU and FDP members was announced on 11 December. It excluded Strauss, marked the end of his chances of becoming Chancellor in the foreseeable future and permanently blemished his political career.

According to Dr Mende, Chancellor Adenauer admitted to him, in confidence, that he, not Strauss, had been responsible for excluding Stammberger from the operation against *Der Spiegel* and he had taken the action because he suspected that the Justice Minister had been in regular touch with the magazine, which seemed to be unusually well informed about events in the Justice Ministry. He said that he understood that Stammberger, who was also dropped in the reshuffle, was afraid of *Der Spiegel*, for it had damaging information about him in its exceptionally compendious filed records. Stammberger, who died in 1982, had allegedly been involved in fraud and forgery while in the German Army during the war.[17]

The *Der Spiegel* Affair, therefore, led not only to the resignation of Strauss and his removal as a candidate for Chancellor, just as Moscow had wanted and for which the active-measures operators had worked so patiently, but caused the reorganization of the Federal Cabinet with extensive repercussions lasting into the middle of 1963, when Adenauer retired. It also caused a secret rupture of relations between Adenauer, during the remainder of his office, and his intelligence chief, Gehlen. Since damage to adversary intelligence agencies is a permanent high-priority target for active measures, this represented a most welcome additional bonus and illustrates the International Department's axiom that active measures, patiently pursued, will create their own opportunities provided that their effects can be monitored by reliable feed-back. (This assault on Gehlen and the BND continued, being particularly severe in 1971.)

When the Fallex '62 article was being prepared by *Der Spiegel*, the journalist Hans-Detlev Becker had put certain questions to the spokesman for the Federal Intelligence Service based in Hamburg, Colonel Adolf Wichts. The reasons for the questions were not given but Wichts decided that they could be answered without damage to security. The notes which Becker made of these exchanges with the Intelligence Service were found in his desk when the *Der Spiegel* offices were raided. When this became known several of Gehlen's numerous enemies and detractors saw an opportunity to involve both him and his organization in the scandal. They projected the whole Fallex '62 article as really a CIA plot to overthrow both Strauss and Adenauer and painted a picture of Gehlen as an extremely sinister figure.[18]

This damaging publicity had its impact and, from that time, Adenauer seems to have become disenchanted with his intelligence chief which, of course, was a bonus for the KGB. There is even evidence that Adenauer ordered the arrest of Gehlen, though the latter denies this in his memoirs.[19]

The extent to which active measures were involved in this collateral exercise may never be known, but the blaming of the CIA looks like a routine use of the upside-down ploy. Active Soviet espionage may well have played a role as it is certain that Gehlen's organization was deeply penetrated by the KGB with agents well placed to report on weaknesses and how they might be exploited.

The *Der Spiegel* Affair, in all its facets, was widely reported throughout the world and dominated the Western media for several weeks. There were hints that the Soviets might have been involved somehow in initiating it but, at that stage, there was no substantial evidence to support the suspicion, from defectors or anyone else, and with the mission so thoroughly accomplished, investigation of its causes was too academic to appeal to anyone.

That, of course, was exactly how the Politburo and its active-measures practitioners wished it to remain.

Chapter 5

Kremlin Conspiracy Exposed

'Tactical campaigns, such as those aimed at defamation of an individual, are often based upon complex falsifications and virulent slander whose Soviet origins are difficult to trace.'

John Barron

In May 1963 the Federal Supreme Court ruled that there was insufficient evidence to justify charges of treason against Augstein and the other journalists and they were released. The Court reserved its decision about whether to proceed against Colonel Martin, the Defence Ministry official, for breaching official secrets but, eventually, on 25 October 1966, the charges were dropped on the grounds that they 'could not be continued without endangering the security of the State'.[1]

What this danger was still remains officially secret, but in 1980 Herr Strauss gave some indications to the West German *Deutschland-magazin*, which quoted him as saying, 'What *Der Spiegel* published . . . was relatively harmless in comparison with what Martin also told Conrad Ahlers and what Ahlers put down on paper. This information was deposited by Rudolf Augstein . . . in his safe. It was found there during the search of *Der Spiegel*'s offices. Martin leaked, among other things, the total number, the explosive power and the potential targets of American atomic warheads based in West Germany.'[2]

The secret papers taken from Augstein's safe containing information which was not used by *Der Spiegel* are still held at the Bundeskriminalamt (the Federal Ministry for Crime) in Wiesbaden. My inquiries suggest that several former members of the Federal Intelligence Service could throw considerable light on the contents of these papers which are still held secret, but they are not being permitted to do so, even at this stage, for general security reasons.[3] These reasons would seem to be linked with the decision that it would be against West Germany's security interests to continue with the prosecution of Martin, *Der Spiegel*'s informant. Such decisions are usually taken to avoid having to make damaging admissions which could be valuable to the intelligence service of an adversary. It would certainly seem that the information which remained secret related to the behaviour of Colonel Martin, who is still alive but remains tight-lipped on the issue.

The collapse of the case against *Der Spiegel* was not the only triumph for the magazine, which was widely regarded as a champion of press freedom and to have been victimized by the wrongful application of political power. The circulation soared by about 50 per cent and continued to rise until it now exerts great political influence, especially on young Germans. With its continuing left-of-centre stance, it is held to have been partly responsible for the growth of the peace movement in West Germany and the widespread anti-American feeling among the young there.

In October 1966, the Federal Supreme Court in Karlsruhe decided, after examining all the facts, that the police action against *Der Spiegel* had been lawful and constitutional. It also ruled that the Defence Ministry, and Strauss as Minister, had not played a decisive part in initiating the raid on the offices of *Der Spiegel*. The head of the department of public law in the Federal Ministry of Justice had already testified, on 26 January 1966, that it was the Federal Prosecutor-General and not Strauss who had initiated the police raids, the Defence Ministry's report on the security aspects of the case having been sent to the Prosecutor-General while Strauss was on holiday.[4] Later, Gerd Schmuckle stated in his article in *Der Spiegel*, already referred to, that, while serving as Chief Press Officer at the Defence Ministry in 1962, he had taken the offending article about Fallex '62 to Strauss, who was on holiday in Bavaria, and that after he had misguidedly assured Strauss that it seemed relatively harmless, Strauss had not even bothered to read it![5]

In the meantime Strauss had taken Augstein and *Der Spiegel* to

57

court on two occasions and each time the judgment had been in his favour.[6] The damage, however, had been done and was beyond repair, demonstrating that other principle of active measures that, whatever the facts may indicate, people are generally prepared to believe the worst about a public figure, especially if he has previously had more than his fair share of good fortune.

Strauss not only remained out of the Federal Government but continued to be hounded by *Der Spiegel*, which had the apparent purpose of eliminating him from political life completely. In June 1963 the magazine observed, in reference to Strauss's leadership of the Christian Social Union in Bavaria, 'One might have thought that no one who withdrew from ministerial office under shameful circumstances could become or remain Chairman and Parliamentary leader of such a party as the CSU.' The former Defence Minister was falsely accused by *Der Spiegel* of being involved in the Lockheed bribes scandal, of having removed incriminating documents from his Ministry and of having been supplied with women.[7] (Attempts were even made by the East German radio to implicate him in a double murder, the allegation being that one of the victims knew too much about profits which Strauss had made from arms deals.)[8]

Strauss took his detractors to court again on five occasions and the judgment was always in his favour.[9] No Western politician has been defamed so systematically on both sides of the Iron Curtain. Strauss's successor as Defence Minister, Kai-Uwe von Hassel, received far less attention though pursuing essentially the same policies. He was not such a charismatic figure as his predecessor and had no chance of becoming Chancellor.

In spite of the continuing offensive, Strauss remained resilient and good-humoured, being confident that, as the truth became officially established, he would be able to regenerate his career. His enemies were greatly displeased when he returned to the Federal Government as Finance Minister in 1966, holding the post for three years. In 1978 he left the Bundestag to become Prime Minister of Bavaria, a post he retains, and was the CSU's candidate for the Chancellorship. As has been said, in America, the *Der Spiegel* Affair was Strauss's Chappaquiddick, and his only realistic chance of becoming Chancellor had been effectively demolished in 1962.[10]

Having disposed of Strauss, *Der Spiegel* continued to harass General Gehlen and the Federal Intelligence Service which, whether

58

coincidental or not, was very much in Moscow's interest. Gehlen records in his memoirs that a man known to be a KGB officer, Vladimir Karpov, summoned *Der Spiegel*'s Moscow correspondent to his office and gave him a damaging story about the Federal Intelligence Service dating from 1955 and which was published in a disinformation form. The accusations were refuted by the West German Government which dismissed them as a deliberate attempt to discredit Gehlen and shake the confidence of West Germany's allies.[11]

In September 1969 *Der Spiegel* admitted that material it had printed about the alleged intended use of nuclear, chemical and biological weapons by American forces in Europe had been circulated to it, and to other Western media, as part of a KGB disinformation operation. In June of that year the editors of several periodicals in West Germany, France, Britain and Italy had received copies of an anonymous letter sent from Rome by someone claiming to have been a friend of Major-General Horst Wendland, who had been Deputy Director of the West German Federal Intelligence Service until he was found dead from a gun-shot wound at his desk in October 1968. The letter, which *Der Spiegel* printed (as did the *Washington Post*), claimed that Wendland had sent the letter-writer copies of classified documents which he wanted distributed after his death. He claimed that Wendland had been particularly disturbed by the fact that the Americans could use atomic, chemical and bacteriological weapons without prior consent of the US Congress or President. It was claimed that this knowledge was, perhaps, a reason why Wendland had committed suicide. Photocopies of authentic top-secret NATO documents were enclosed to support the contention, which was false so far as the use of atomic weapons was concerned.[12]

There can be little doubt that the documents and the forged letter had been circulated by the KGB's Service A as an active-measures operation quickly devised to take advantage of Wendland's suicide. The documents were out-of-date material which had been supplied, years previously, by one of the KGB's NATO spies, probably Sergeant Robert Lee Johnson, an American who had had access to a vault in Paris used by couriers transporting NATO documents between allies until his arrest in 1965. The documents described contingency plans, and all nations draw up such plans to cope with every conceivable situation, whether likely or not.[13]

59

The *Der Spiegel* Affair might have been relegated to the German history books, where it must surely always figure, but for the defection of General Sejna from Czechoslovakia in 1968. During his long debriefing by the CIA Sejna volunteered that he had first-hand evidence of KGB activity in connection with the *Der Spiegel* Affair and the defamation of Franz Josef Strauss. This information remained secret to the CIA until the autumn of 1977 when Dr Walter Hahn, a distinguished American authority on intelligence issues and a senior staff member of the US Strategic Institute, happened to mention Sejna in an article in the Institute's *Strategic Review* of which he is editor-in-chief.[14] Hahn then received a telephone call from a friend in the US Defence Intelligence Agency (DIA) to tell him that Sejna, who was in Washington, wished to meet him. Hahn then attended a classified briefing of Pentagon officials given by Sejna and has reported as follows:

> Sejna gave a run-down, among other things, of Czech intelligence operations in the 1950s and 1960s. Among them, he mentioned Franz Josef Strauss and the *Spiegel* Affair. I could not pursue the matter at the briefing but, several months later, I was tipped off that Sejna was no longer under DIA wraps. I arranged a meeting with him in the early summer of 1978. He told me then what he knew about the *Spiegel* Affair.
>
> According to Sejna, the calculation was that the publication by *Der Spiegel* of NATO documents would have the effect, at the very least, of triggering a scandal, which would put Strauss under fire for his failure to prevent leaks from the Defence Ministry. At best, given his volatile nature, Strauss might overreact and thus get himself into deeper difficulties. Sejna said that he was present when the Czech Minister of the Interior, Rudolf Barak, presented the plan for the *Spiegel* operation to the Czech Central Committee. Barak had to get approval at the highest level because it represented a 'strategic operation' involving the transfer of documents.
>
> Sejna told me also of a sequel to the story. In 1965, a meeting of high-level Warsaw Pact officials took place in Prague. The meeting was given a briefing by Vladimir Koucky, the Secretary of the Czech Central Committee in charge of foreign affairs. Koucky gave a run-down of Czech covert operations in Western Europe. He bragged at length about the success of the operation against Strauss.[15]

Two years later, in October 1979, Hahn met Strauss in Munich and told him what Sejna had said. Strauss remarked that he found the story plausible and that he himself had received certain indications that outside forces had been at work in the *Der Spiegel* Affair.

Dr Hahn arranged for Sejna to give his information directly to a member of the staff of the *National Review* published in Washington. The *Review*'s editor, William F. Buckley, accepted Sejna's account as factual and published it on 8 February 1980 in an article entitled 'The Vindication of Strauss'. The article contained the following passage:

> For a period in the early sixties it looked as if Strauss, then serving as Defense Minister for Adenauer, might be tapped to succeed the old man. This the Soviet Union could not countenance and, accordingly, the boys hatched a plot. It turned out to be successful beyond their dreams. Within a matter of months Strauss had quit office in disgrace. And now a Czechoslovak defector, General Jan Sejna, has given details of how the KGB manipulated the future of Europe. The Soviet plan, executed through Czech and Communist agents, was to discredit Strauss. Accordingly a mole in the Defense Department headed by Strauss leaked to the magazine *Der Spiegel* highly secret and tendentious details of unsuccessful manoeuvres by the fledgling German army. The publication of the report proved a sensation, both in tending to discredit the work of Strauss professionally, and in suggesting that he could not even maintain the security of his own office.

Clearly the Buckley article indicated that Colonel Alfred Martin, the official in the West German Defence Ministry who passed secrets to *Der Spiegel*'s defence correspondent, had been the mole. Four months later, in June 1980, a German periodical, *Deutschland-magazin*, went further in commenting on the alleged KGB connection:

> According to Sejna the KGB directed the affair of *Der Spiegel* to the extent that it allowed its agents within West Germany's Defence Ministry to pass secret information to *Der Spiegel* – anticipating that Augstein would publish it. . . . The chief mole for *Der Spiegel* inside the West German Defence Ministry was Colonel Alfred Martin. He supplied Augstein's magazine with classified material.

Neither Herr Augstein nor Colonel Martin took any action

against *Deutschland-magazin*, which they must surely have seen, or against the *National Review*. It will be appreciated that what those journals had printed was more direct and more detailed than Sir James Goldsmith's statement to the Conservative Party Media Committee a few months later. In fact, no evidence that Martin had any involvement, direct or indirect, with Soviet-Bloc sources was ever discovered. He may have been motivated by his extreme opposition to Strauss's policy and, perhaps, by personal dislike of his Minister, a circumstance which I have seen mirrored in the British Defence Ministry more than once. Like any other West German, his views could have been influenced by the overt Soviet and covert pro-Soviet anti-Strauss campaign.

The crucial aspect of Dr Hahn's evidence is that it dates back to 1978, three years before there was any suggestion of any libel action based on Sejna's statement. This disposes of any possibility that Sejna was recalling information specifically in support of Sir James's case when that was eventually joined. Sejna provided Sir James's lawyers with an affidavit confirming Hahn's recollections of events and in a book entitled *We Will Bury You*, which he authored in 1982, Sejna wrote:

> Our broad approach under Soviet direction was to help the Social Democratic Party to gain power and hold it. We did all we could to discredit the Christian Democrats and compromise their leaders, especially Franz Josef Strauss: for instance we had excellent channels to certain prominent West German magazines which we used for smear operations.

Extracts from the book were serialized in the widely read German newspaper *Welt am Sonntag*, apparently without public rebuttal from *Der Spiegel* or any other magazine.[16]

The evidence of a single defector, such as Sejna, can always be challenged in court on the grounds that he is a traitor to his own country and, therefore, not necessarily to be trusted. It can also be claimed that defectors, notoriously, embroider their information to enhance their reputations as sources. Sejna's evidence, however, was first given in secret with no apparent motivation for blackening the reputation of *Der Spiegel* or any other West German publication. His evidence was also supported in detail by Dzhirkvelov who has no particular grudge against the West German press. Bittman fully confirmed the general use of the Western media as targets for Soviet disinformation exercises and a mass of further evidence in that respect will be presented in Chapters 7 and 8, dealing with the manipulation of the media worldwide.[17]

The libel action was settled by statements in the High Court of Justice, Queen's Bench Division, before Mr Justice Caulfield. Acting for Sir James Goldsmith, his counsel, Lord Rawlinson, QC, said that he was happy to state, publicly, that 'it was never intended by Sir James to imply that the plaintiffs or their paper were controlled by or co-operated with Soviet Intelligence or knowingly employed any journalist who was a KGB agent'. In a preceding paragraph, however, the court was told, 'It was and remains Sir James's position that many Western publications were and are unwittingly used by the Soviets in their campaigns conducted by the KGB and other Soviet organizations. So, in Sir James's view, *Der Spiegel*, in common with other Western publications, can themselves fairly be described as victims of KGB propaganda techniques.'

Lord Rawlinson also said:

In addition to the overtly controlled Communist press – the value of which is limited since the sources are publicly known – there is a major and continuous effort to plant propaganda covertly through well-placed agents of influence who, themselves, may be either conscious or unconscious of the role that they are playing. The media thus used are not intended to realize that they are participating in KGB-orchestrated campaigns.

It is Sir James's position that, in pursuance of these policies, the Soviets made a conscious decision to seek to discredit the West German politician, Dr Franz Josef Strauss, and mounted a campaign of defamation, disinformation and provocation against him. Franz Josef Strauss was Minister of Defence in Chancellor Adenauer's government when he made a speech in the Bundestag calling for the deployment on German soil of US-controlled nuclear weapons so as to counterbalance the growing Soviet threat. It is Sir James's position that against that background the Soviets decided to make use in that campaign of the fact that *Der Spiegel* was well known as opposing Dr Strauss's political views and regularly published articles expressing that opposition.[18]

63

All these statements, and the fact that the court was told that Sir James could have called witnesses, who would have given evidence of meetings at which plans were approved to seek to discredit Dr Strauss and to use *Der Spiegel* in the manner Lord Rawlinson had indicated, were agreed to in advance by counsel for *Der Spiegel* and its owners who remained concerned to refute and deny any suggestions that the magazine was under the control of the KGB or employed journalists who were Communist intelligence agents.

Following the statement by Lord Rawlinson, *Der Spiegel*'s counsel, Mr John Wilmers, QC, said that his clients 'fully accept that broadly speaking Soviet intelligence seeks to operate in the way stated by my Learned friend [Lord Rawlinson], although they themselves are not conscious of having been used in the manner mentioned by Sir James Goldsmith. My clients are conscious of the dangers to press freedom posed by Soviet covert propaganda.

'I am happy to say that the parties, upon the basis of this agreed statement, have agreed that the action should be withdrawn'.

Each side agreed to pay its own costs.

No indication was given to the court as to who had taken the initiative to end the action but, according to Sir James, in a letter published by *The Times* on 18 October 1984, the request for an out-of-court settlement came from *Der Spiegel*'s side: '*Spiegel*'s British counsel contacted my counsel, Lord Rawlinson, to propose such a settlement.' Legal documents leave no room for doubt that it was *Der Spiegel*'s lawyers who sought the settlement. After the German magazine published a fallacious statement indicating that it was Sir James who had capitulated, he took action in the German courts and, as a result, *Der Spiegel* was restrained from restating the suggestion that Sir James had instigated the settlement and was ordered to publish a statement by Sir James that it was *Der Spiegel*'s counsel who had made the approach. This statement was published, with obvious reluctance, on 24 December 1984.[19]

While Sir James Goldsmith regarded the agreed statements in court as a vindication of all that he had said about the use and effects of Soviet active measures in the Strauss case, and took full-page advertisements in leading newspapers to make them widely known, *Der Spiegel*, understandably, declined to print the advertisement and played down the settlement which, it must be stated, is standard practice by the media in general in such circumstances. On 15

October 1984 the magazine carried a brief, unsigned editorial which attempted to ridicule the evidence of the defectors by pointing out how Oleg Bitov, whose peculiar behaviour is described in Chapter 7, had re-defected back to Moscow where he retracted statements he had made on other matters. Bitov had no inside knowledge of the *Der Spiegel* affair and any contribution he could have made to it would have been minimal. *Der Spiegel* also reprinted an article published by *Die Zeit* which claimed that, while the KGB certainly spreads false information, there is the protection of responsible editorial staffs between the KGB and the readership. Sadly, as most of us who have spent many years in journalism know, editors, however distinguished, are occasionally gullible and buy 'gold bricks', the most recent example being the acceptance by *Stern* magazine and the *Sunday Times* of the fake Hitler diaries.

Sir James insists that had he not been vindicated to the extent that he was he would not have agreed to any settlement of the libel action.[20] The most telling criterion of the degree of his vindication is the fact that the words complained of by *Der Spiegel* can now be repeated with impunity by anyone, fairly, in context, of course.

It would be highly instructive to know the reaction inside the Kremlin to the exposure of its active-measures operations achieved as a result of Sir James's robust defence of the action brought against him. The evidence he accumulated so resourcefully provides the first really detailed account, from inside sources, of the Politburo's evil intentions and its continuing involvement in outrageous activities. It also exposes the extreme vulnerability of free and open societies to active measures of all kinds, especially when insidiously applied in combination to achieve a cumulative effect. Some future defector may provide the West with a first-hand account of the anger and hostility generated in the International Department, Service A and the Politburo itself by the service which Sir James has performed. Meanwhile it can be imagined from this brief summary.

There can be no reasonable doubt from the defectors' statements, the documented evidence of the actions of the Communist-controlled media and from intelligence sources that the Kremlin's International Department, making use of the KGB and its satellite agencies, was intent on destroying the reputation of Strauss, so that he would cease to be Defence Minister and never become Chancellor. In this purpose, according to the defectors' evidence, they rated themselves to have been totally successful.

Der Spiegel pursued a line of policy and journalistic action which coincided, it seems, with the aims of the active-measures operations. It pursued hostility to NATO, the US, nuclear weapons in Europe and, above all, Strauss, portraying him as corrupt and as a second Hitler. It often praised Soviet foreign policy, with discrimination, supported the 'peace' movements and pinned the guilt for the arms race on the US. Without *Der Spiegel*'s activities Strauss might well have remained in Federal office and have become Chancellor.

Defector evidence suggests that *Der Spiegel* was a prime target for the active measures being planned in detail by Ponomarev and his aides with the continuing agreement of the Politburo, which has to sanction each stage of any operation designed to discredit a Western political figure.

There is evidence that *Der Spiegel*'s journalists had received documents originating behind the Iron Curtain and which might have been expected to contain disinformation.

While Colonel Martin was never convicted there seems to be little doubt that he was a source of information originating in classified documents and passed to *Der Spiegel*. His motivation could have been sheer opposition to Strauss's policies and no evidence that he was a 'mole' for the Soviet Bloc was ever found. Following Defence Ministry inquiries, which lasted until January 1969, he was not dismissed or censured and retired shortly afterwards on full pension. Nevertheless, what he did suited the Politburo's purpose perfectly and, even if entirely unwittingly and without realization of the consequences in that direction, he advanced the Soviet interest. The article about Fallex '62, which Martin facilitated, was the terminal event in a sustained defamation campaign against Strauss promoted by *Der Spiegel* and consistently supported by overt Communist propaganda orchestrated by Moscow.

If, as Sir James Goldsmith maintained, and as *Der Spiegel*'s lawyers admitted to have been possible, the magazine was the unwitting vehicle for active measures, then it was an example of the perfect operation – one which accomplishes all its aims without even the medium concerned being aware that it is being used. The case, in fact, demonstrates how difficult it is to unravel a really well-conducted active-measures operation.

The removal of Strauss from the political scene was rightly lauded in the Kremlin as a major triumph for active measures but, as the next chapter will show, it was only a thrust in an offensive being waged on a broader front, and continuing today, with the objective of achieving and maintaining Soviet nuclear supremacy.

Chapter 6

The Great Missile Deception

'The Soviet approach is to build military superiority and then to use it whenever and wherever they can to their advantage. They recognize that usable superiority can be achieved only if the West acquiesces in the process, or better still if it assists.'

Dr Joseph D. Douglass

In the spring of 1970 I attended the formal opening of the Strategic Arms Limitation Talks (SALT) between the Soviet Union and the US in the marble hall of the splendid Belvedere Palace in Vienna. As the Russian and American delegates posed for photographs they happened to be flanked by two large oil paintings, which seemed to me to be highly symbolic of their respective attitudes and of their consequent behaviour, should any agreement be reached, as it eventually was two years later. The painting on the left where, appropriately, the Soviet delegates were standing, was of a hyena, the epitome of patient cunning and rapacity. That on the right, by the Americans, was of an ostrich, a less aggressive creature with a legendary reputation for adopting a trusting posture which blinds it to circumstances it would rather not face. I reported this oddity in a dispatch to my newspaper, remarking that it might prove to be prophetic.[1] As will be seen, my suspicions, which were already well-founded, have turned out to be completely justified. What has since transpired and what had been going on before, dating back to the 1950s, constitute an active-measures operation of stupendous magnitude, planned with extraordinary foresight and utilizing every device and ploy, including the deliberate breaking of solemn agreements. Its purpose was to establish the nuclear superiority which the Politburo believes to be essential to its ideological purposes and has proved to be so successful that the Great Missile Deception is no exaggerated title for it. The operations against Franz Josef Strauss and against the British Labour Party, already described, are part of this gigantic jigsaw, as are manipulation of the 'peace' movements and the media and other measures to be dealt with later. The Great Missile Deception, which began effectively under Khrushchev, has given the Politburo nuclear superiority over the West and has led to the rushed American programmes to restore the balance, with all the political problems they entail. It continues under Gorbachov, who is as determined as his predecessors, maybe more so, to maintain the superiority which represents such a colossal effort in money and resources.

To understand the Politburo's motivation it is necessary to appreciate that, while it is ostensibly a civilian body, its power-base, like that of any totalitarian tyranny, is a massive military machine of which the Communist Party Secretary is Commander-in-Chief. This is needed to maintain control of the Soviet peoples and of the satellites, for which combat-ready forces are required, as demonstrated by the invasions of Hungary and Czechoslovakia. Military might is also basic to the ideological belief that a showdown with capitalism may, ultimately, be necessary and, whether that ever occurs or not, superior military power alone provides the means for intimidating Communism's adversaries and of sapping their will to resist by implanting the belief that they cannot win. To quote General Sejna, 'The ultimate victory of the Communist revolution is the red thread that runs through all Soviet policy, no matter what new chieftains rise or fall. It is a precise, long-term commitment to which all planning, whether economic, military, cultural or whatever, is harnessed, just as are all activities in the intelligence and propaganda fields.'[2]

Another factor of prime importance is the attitude of the Politburo, and the Soviet military chiefs, to nuclear missiles, an issue underlying almost every important decision it takes. The two convulsive post-war military developments, the giant long-range missile and the H-bomb warhead which, with its huge area of devastation, offsets the inaccuracy of the early rockets, profoundly affected defence planning in the West but in the Soviet Union it engendered an immediate revolution in military and political thought. In a way that would never be possible in a true democracy, the Politburo decided in the mid-1950s to build a strategic nuclear missile force in a crash programme in which there was to be 'high-speed development of various types of rocket and nuclear weapons, electronics, automation. . . . This made it possible, in a relatively short period, to supply the Soviet Armed Forces with the most modern combat equipment, including such formidable weapons as intercontinental ballistic rockets with powerful thermonuclear charges.'[3]

Such a massive programme could be achieved only at the expense of the material well-being of the Soviet people, with consumer goods being in the discard. The Politburo was unhesitant in deciding its priorities.

A most impressive study of Soviet military thinking, based on official statements in Soviet military manuals and other technical literature, undertaken by Dr Joseph Douglass of System Planning Corporation, in Virginia, has disclosed a fundamental difference between East and West in the concept of nuclear armaments.[4] From the beginning, the horrors of atomic war have been fully appreciated by Western military chiefs and the accent has been firmly on the value of nuclear weapons as a deterrent to war. It has been the consensus of the many military men with whom I have discussed defence over the last forty years that if atomic weapons ever have to be used then they have failed in their purpose. In the Soviet Union, on the other hand, the attitude has been quite different and remains so. In the first place, the basic characteristic of Soviet military doctrine is its 'offensive' nature. Soviet officers are taught that a side that only defends is inevitably doomed to defeat. To quote Dr Douglass, 'The Soviets do not regard nuclear war as apocalyptic but rather as involving great destruction that can and will be survived and result in the triumph of Communism and the defeat of capitalism.' This view is confirmed by two Soviet military authorities writing in the journal Questions of Philosophy in October 1980: 'Marxist-Leninists decisively reject the assertions of certain bourgeois theoreticians who consider nuclear missile war unjust from any point of view.' To the Politburo, then, nuclear weapons were an essential requirement for a 'fighting strategy' rather than for deterring the West, though they would serve that purpose too. They were given such emphasis that, in addition to the supply of nuclear weapons for battlefield purposes, an entirely separate arm, the Strategic Missile Force, was established and is perhaps the single most important component of the Soviet military organization.[5]

Dr Douglass's study stresses the extreme secrecy with which the 'nuclear revolution' was to be accomplished. It would be impossible to conceal certain aspects of the developments because of the need to stage very large nuclear blasts and to fire big missiles over long ranges, but the maximum effort was to be made to deceive the West about the true strength of Soviet nuclear power.

Established deception techniques to confuse the West were put in hand immediately, but the Great Missile Deception as a fully conceived active-measures operation derived from the conference of senior KGB officers organized by Aleksandr Shelepin in May 1959 and which I have described in Chapter 2. The basic ploy was to lull the Western powers, and the Americans in particular, into believing that they held a substantial lead in both the nuclear and missile fields which the Soviets were unlikely to overtake, provided that American research and development proceeded at a steady pace, because Soviet technology was so far behind. Meanwhile the Soviet effort to achieve superiority would be given absolute priority in scientific man-power and material resources.

During the mid-1950s the Soviet deception plans suffered a setback because the Americans had convinced themselves that the Russians had, somehow, leaped ahead in the development of intercontinental nuclear missiles capable of attacking the US mainland. This is now known to have been a mistake, due to the faulty analysis of intelligence data, but it caused the US Government to stage a crash programme to bridge this missile-gap by producing a literally stopgap nuclear bombarding rocket, called Thor, which could reach Moscow if it were sited on the east coast of Britain. It was conceived entirely as a deterrent weapon which, hopefully, would never have to be used.

I was closely involved with these developments through high-level friends in the Defence Ministry and visited Washington for briefings and visits to the Thor factories as well as witnessing a firing trial. I therefore know the degree of desperation which enabled the Americans to produce the weapon from scratch in three years, instead of ten, which is usual, and to have it operational in Britain by 1958, as it was. There could, of course, be no secrecy about the development and deployment of Thor, particularly as announcements had to be made to the British Parliament and people. Indeed, the Americans organized the widest publicity to help to ensure that Thor would act as a deterrent to the Soviet Union. This attitude reflected the fundamental difference between the Western and Soviet approach to long-range nuclear missiles. The West has always believed that publicity about its nuclear weapons is an essential aspect of their deterrent capability. The Soviets, with their essentially offensive approach, maintain maximum secrecy about all their weapons of war.

A series of Soviet tests of nuclear devices, which were radioactively 'dirty', involved explosions with the unprecedented power of 30 million tons of TNT.[6] These produced a mixed reaction among Western defence analysts, for while they suggested backward nuclear technology they also implied that the Soviets had the capability to build enormous missiles to carry such heavy warheads. The analysts felt they were on much safer ground, however, after April 1961 when a high-ranking intelligence officer of the GRU, the military counterpart of the KGB, approached the British Secret Intelligence Service (MI6) through a courier who had commercial reasons for visiting Moscow. This officer, Colonel Oleg Penkovsky, offered to supply secret information in his capacity as deputy head of a combined KGB/GRU operation to collect and collate scientific intelligence on the grounds that he had become totally disenchanted with the Soviet system.[7] During two visits to London and one to Paris, and through contacts in Moscow, Penkovsky provided a huge amount of information about Soviet military missiles. While most of the intelligence officers involved in debriefing Penkovsky are convinced that he was genuine, there is no doubt that either he was 'turned' soon after the debriefings began or that he was detected by KGB counter-measures and then fed with false information which he then passed to MI6 and the CIA, either wittingly or unwittingly. What he provided in 1961 now seems to have furthered the Politburo's objective of convincing Western defence and intelligence chiefs that Soviet scientists were lagging far behind the US in nuclear missile technology. The missiles about which Penkovsky had provided training manuals had ranges of only about 1,000 miles. In

72

fact, his information was instrumental in convincing the US National Security Council that the missile gap, which had been responsible for the crash programme on Thor, had never really existed. Later examination of the Penkovsky material showed that the data he had provided about Soviet rockets was several years old and therefore expendable. He had produced very little information about intercontinental missiles though he had been in a position to know a lot about them. With hindsight, some Western intelligence officers suspect that Penkovsky had been a plant from the start, deliberately sent to assure the West that it was way ahead in nuclear missilry.[8]

In the previous year an American U2 spy-plane had been shot down over the Soviet Union and its pilot had been captured.[9] In the resulting international row between President Eisenhower and Khrushchev, the President had forbidden any further spy-flights over Soviet territory, so the West remained blind to Soviet missile developments until the first reconnaissance satellite was launched at the end of 1962. This situation, which meant that the West lacked any reliable means of checking Penkovsky's assurance that there was no missile gap, may have been accidental. It is a fact, however, that the U2 was by no means the first American reconnaissance plane to be shot down by the Soviets and it had not suited them before to create an international incident. Before the shooting down of the U2 the Soviet military chiefs had devoted much attention and resources to what they call *maskirovka* – deception by the ingenious camouflage of objects and projects visible from the air – together with other measures intended to deceive, such as the use of dummies and misleading manoeuvres. It may, therefore, have suited their plans for the American reconnaissance flights to continue until the Penkovsky 'defection' caused a change of strategy.

The installation of intermediate-range missiles of the kind described by Penkovsky on Cuba in 1962 tended to confirm the American view that the Soviets were being driven to install them there, as the US had installed Thor in Britain, because they lacked enough reliable operational weapons of intercontinental range. This hunch seemed to be supported by the degree of deception being practised by the Soviets to complete the installations on Cuba, as though the Politburo considered them essential. Khrushchev himself used an influential Soviet journalist, who was secretly a GRU colonel, to give Pentagon officials an assurance that the Soviets would not place offensive missiles on Cuba, when they were already doing so.[10] At a higher level, Gromyko, the Foreign Minister, and Dobrynin, the Soviet Ambassador to Washington, made official denials that missiles were being installed, which they knew to be lies. As declassified American intelligence estimates show, these denials were accepted until reconnaissance photographs showed them to be false.[11]

The subsequent arrest and public trial of Penkovsky and the announcement of his immediate execution may have been calculated to convince Western intelligence services, further, that what he had told them was true.

By 1963 the Americans had fully convinced themselves that there had been no missile gap and had made sufficient progress with their first intercontinental missile, the Atlas, for the Thors to be withdrawn. According to defectors, the Soviet deception planners were greatly relieved.

Disinformation had been spread widely, mainly through the Western technical media – which the popular media used as sources – that Soviet technology was far inferior to the Western and that progress there was slow in spite of the Soviet success in orbiting the first Sputnik and putting the first man into space. Indeed, these events were manipulated to give the impression that the Soviet scientists were concentrating their missile programme on the peaceful exploration of space with a view to being the first to place a man on the moon, a ploy which the Western press, including myself, 'bought'.

During that period I attended several international astronautics conferences at which Soviet scientists gave a firm impression that a man on the moon was a prime Soviet intention, though it almost certainly never was. While considerable resources were set aside for the exploration of space, and particularly for its reconnaissance and espionage aspects, the Soviets' rapidly expanding industrial, scientific and technological facilities, all firmly under the Politburo's control, were concentrated on establishing an offensive military capability at a rate and on a scale which would have been quite impossible except in a dictatorship where talent, as well as money and resources, can be made to do whatever the rulers decide. Research and development on a quite astonishing range of sea-borne, air-borne and ground-based missiles were set in motion.[12] From the start, the ground-based missiles were to be given the maximum degree of mobility, a decision which continues to yield offensive dividends.

Among the first moves made by the KGB, in its requirement to delude the West, had been the infiltration of highly professional officers trained in deception to serve as false defectors and to feed the American security and intelligence authorities with disinformation supplied to them, almost daily, by Moscow through various KGB 'residents' in the US. The most effective of these had been intruded into the service of the Federal Bureau of Investigation (FBI) in March 1962, when it was headed by J. Edgar Hoover.

This KGB 'plant', whose real name is still uncertain, was given the FBI code-name 'Fedora', the next name on an approved list devised from types of hat.[13] 'Fedora', who held a fake post with the United Nations Mission in New York, told the FBI that he was really a KGB officer specializing in scientific and technical work and was in rebellion against his KGB masters because of some altercation over expenses. He claimed that he had been posted to the US to set up a spy-ring to secure technological secrets without which Soviet military scientists would never be able to solve their problems. Hoover accepted 'Fedora' without proper checks, probably because most defectors offered their services to the CIA, the rival agency, and he felt that his catch might give him an edge regarding new intelligence which he could feed directly to the White House and so gain prestige for his agency and for himself. What is remarkable – and appalling – is that over the ensuing twelve years 'Fedora' handed a mass of cleverly designed disinformation to Hoover and, in return, received a great deal of true information to feed back to Moscow. This was provided, reluctantly, by the CIA at Hoover's insistence as 'chicken-feed' – material to assure the KGB that 'Fedora' really was working for them and was not doubling with the Americans. 'Fedora' was regarded as being especially valuable because he was allowed to visit KGB headquarters in Moscow, when on leave there, and – so Hoover thought – could make specific inquiries on the FBI's behalf, even consulting files. What 'Fedora' really did in Moscow was to provide a more thorough feed-back debriefing of the results of his penetration of the FBI and consult with his managers about the next stages of the operation.[14]

The disinformation supplied to 'Fedora' from Moscow deliberately covered various fields but was cunningly concentrated on providing assurance that Soviet scientists were in deep technical trouble with new missiles because of the backward technology available to them. 'Fedora' specifically stated that his spy-ring was required to buy or steal certain components of American missiles so that Soviet scientists could copy them.[15]

As a back-up and to provide collateral support for 'Fedora's' fake information, the International Department arranged for the GRU, the military arm of Soviet intelligence, to send one of their officers to the US as a false defector. When this man approached the FBI with an offer to work for them he was given the code-name 'Tophat' and received rapturously because, being GRU, he was likely to know even more technical detail about the Soviet missile situation than 'Fedora'.[16]

'Tophat' did not disappoint and he and 'Fedora' were exceptionally influential because Hoover was passing their most important disinformation to the President, the Defense Secretary and other high-level policy-makers in the Pentagon. The degree to which their false information was accepted was a tribute to Lenin's foresight and perception when he said, soon after the revolution, 'The West is full of wishful thinkers. We will give them what they want to believe.'

To keep the deception going and to allay suspicion an important disinformation agent was planted with the CIA in the shape of Yuri Nosenko, a KGB officer who established his apparent good faith by 'blowing' the burned-out British spy, John Vassall, as I have described elsewhere.[17] The Soviet deception planners have always been prepared to make sacrifices to establish or preserve the cover of a particularly important infiltration agent, even to the extent, on one well-attested occasion, of permitting a shipload of Red Army soldiers to be sunk. When Nosenko finally defected to the US in June 1962 he effectively backed up 'Fedora's' claims and convinced Hoover and the CIA that he was genuinely working against the KGB.

During the early 1960s both the British Secret Intelligence Service (MI6) and the Security Service (MI5) were penetrated by KGB agents and they too may have contributed to the knowledge which enabled the Great Missile Deception to succeed. Some of these, probably including the Director General of MI5, Sir Roger Hollis, had access to top-secret intelligence appreciations interchanged between Britain and America and which, on occasion, were likely to have included assessments of the East–West nuclear missile balance.[18] As will be seen, a particular traitor in the most sensitive British agency of all, GCHQ, was to play a crucial role in the final stages of the operation.

In 1964 it was discovered that KGB agents had been regularly entering the most secret room in the British Embassy in Moscow in between the two-hourly patrols of the guard. The room, which was allotted to GCHQ for its radio-intercept operations, was screened off by thick steel bars with a door secured by an unpickable lock. The Russians had not needed to deal with the lock because the bolts securing it had never been properly installed. They were only finger-tight and the Russian intruders had kept them oiled. At regular intervals they had entered to examine the GCHQ machines and check readings. Later it was found that by tunnelling under the new GCHQ room the Russians had been able to read messages being encoded by cypher machines by recording and analysing the clatter they made.[19] Such intrusions were also likely to have yielded information about the extent to which the missile deception exercise was succeeding and whether it needed modification.

GCHQ and its larger American counterpart, the National Security Agency (NSA), played a role in the day-to-day 'confirmation' of Soviet backwardness in missile and nuclear research. Because it is so difficult to plant agents on the ground in the closed society of the Soviet Union, with its ubiquitous secret police, the West has had to rely, increasingly, on intelligence derived from interception and other electronic means. The Soviet deception planners saw to it that their messages to out-stations or to agents like 'Fedora', which might be intercepted, matched the remainder of the disinformation. For their part, the British and American interceptors took the view that if the information already in their possession checked positively with the new intercepts then it was almost certainly reliable. They did not have the advantage of any inside information from penetration agents in the Soviet version of GCHQ.[20]

Reliance on the veracity of Soviet intercepts was intensified in 1969 after a special analysis of those made before and after the Soviet invasion of Czechoslovakia in the previous year. It showed that there had been no attempt by the Soviets to use their coded radio messages as a means of deceiving the West, though deception techniques had been used, heavily, against the Czechs. Later, however, it was deduced that the Politburo had simply been contemptuous of any Western knowledge of the invasion plans, being completely convinced that NATO would never intervene.[21]

An example of the degree to which the Pentagon was misled is provided by its record of the performance of the large Soviet SS9 missiles, known in the West as Scarp. On the basis of an intelligence analysis supplied to him, the US Defense Secretary, Robert McNamara, was satisfied that Scarp was incapable of being used to knock out the American force of Minutemen rockets which were being built and hidden in underground launching silos. In fact it has since been learned that Scarp, which was 35 metres long and 3 metres wide, could deliver an enormous 25 megaton warhead at ranges up to 8,000 miles and with an accuracy of a quarter of a mile.[22] It went into service in 1965 and by 1975 there were 288 of them. These were backed up by SS11, Sego, long-range missiles of which about 960 were in position by 1973. By early 1970 the Soviet Union had surpassed the US in numbers of operational intercontinental ballistic missiles and they were more accurate than the West appreciated.

Meanwhile McNamara had recommended that, as the US had enough nuclear missiles, the best course was to let the Soviets catch up and he had assured President Johnson that he saw no evidence of aggressive intent on their part.

The International Department had made the fullest use of the May Day parades to further this successful deception. Several large missiles which were really prototypes or transition missiles never intended for deployment were prominently displayed. At one of these parades Western defence attachés had been subjected to impressive fly-pasts of new heavy bombers to give the appearance that the Soviet military chiefs were still relying on aircraft to a great extent. In fact there were only small numbers of bombers which regrouped and flew over the viewing stand several times.[23]

To support this particular deception, the KGB made use of a 'mole' it had placed inside the West German Federal Intelligence Agency, a German traitor called Hans Felfe. Through East German sources, with whom Felfe was known to be in contact as part of his work, the KGB gave him exaggerated estimates of the number of free-fall nuclear bombs being held in Soviet stockpiles for manned bombers. The West Germans passed this information to the CIA's Directorate of Science and Technology where it was evaluated as useful collateral evidence of Soviet backwardness in missile development.[24]

The false impression about Scarp and other Soviet missiles, the existence of which could not be hidden, had been promoted by special 'information' which 'Fedora' had provided about the accuracy of weapons under development. The accuracy against a distant target is rated by what is called the circular error probable (CEP), denoting the size of a circle in which the warhead of the missile can confidently be expected to fall and explode. The CEPs provided by 'Fedora', after what he alleged to have been special inquiries in Moscow, were so large that the Western scientific analysts concluded that the Soviet scientists must be experiencing serious trouble with the special item of equipment controlling the range, which is called the accelerometer. This meant not only that existing missiles, like Scarp, must be inaccurate and therefore not dependable for knocking out specific targets, but that the Russians would be seriously hampered in progressing to the next stage, known as *mirving*.[25]

In the early American missiles like Thor, Atlas and Polaris, the warhead, which separated from the main rocket and proceeded to its target under its acquired momentum, contained three nuclear packages which separated over the target area and arrived at three separate points, thereby blanketing it. The Soviets had successfully tested such MRVs (multiple re-entry vehicles) in 1968 but the much more sophisticated system MIRV (Multiple Independently-Targeted Re-entry Vehicle) was thought to be beyond them. A MIRV warhead contains up to fifteen separate packages which are ejected at pre-determined times and, as each is separately guided by a small jet-engine, they can be directed at separate targets many miles apart. Some of the packages are decoys, but this advance, which the Americans accomplished in the late 1960s, meant that one large missile could engage up to ten targets. The American authorities, who had produced operational MIRV systems by 1971, were led to believe that until the Soviet scientists solved the MIRV technology any surprise attack on the American mainland was remote and that a continuing fairly relaxed attitude to research and development was in order.

This belief was fortified by independent information funnelled to the FBI by 'Tophat', using his alleged GRU sources, and further collateral, and equally false, evidence was acquired through the activities of another KGB agent infiltrated into the deception network who called himself Vadim Isakov.[26] The KGB had instructed this man to go through the motions of trying to buy, or otherwise acquire, an accelerometer. Knowing that he was under surveillance he approached an American dealer in surplus government equipment, asking him to supply an accelerometer and other devices used in missile guidance. The trick worked so perfectly that the FBI asked 'Fedora' to find out why Isakov had been so interested in acquiring an accelerometer when he was next on leave in Moscow. As might be expected, he brought back the secret information that it had been a desperation move because there had been more failures with Soviet accelerometers in missile tests.

Meanwhile the Soviet scientists were, in fact, pressing ahead with MIRV research and accomplished the hurdle with ease and speed so that MIRVed SS17, 18 and 19 intercontinental rockets were fully operational by 1975.[27]

By early 1972, after a campaign in the Western media stressing the dangers of the arms race, it suited the Russians to enter into discussions with the US to limit the further expansion of long-range missile production. These were the SALT talks in Vienna, to which I have referred, and the Soviets entered them with a distinct numerical superiority. The Politburo also wished to concentrate more of its effort on the development and production of battlefield missiles. Believing that it had a marked technical superiority which would not easily be surpassed, the US signed the SALT 1 agreement in 1972 which left it with 1,054 intercontinental land-based missiles, the number it had reached five years previously, while the Soviets were permitted to place up to 1,500 in position. The Soviets were also to be allowed to have 950 strategic missiles carried in up to 62 submarines while the US was to be constrained to 710 missiles on 44 submarines. Again, the Americans were relying on the technical superiority of their missiles.[28]

Under the agreement both sides were permitted to improve the quality of their missiles, so long as they kept within the numbers, and the Soviets moved ahead rapidly with a major operational advance called the cold-launch concept. In this system the missile is expelled from its underground silo by compressed air and does not ignite until it is clear. This means that the silo can be reloaded with another missile and used again and, because there is no problem with the escape of hot gases from the silo, bigger missiles can be accommodated. In this way the Russians were quickly able to increase the size and weight of their nuclear warheads as well as, secretly, multiplying the number of warheads they could project in a surprise attack.

Since SALT 1 the build-up of the Soviet strategic force has continued at a pace which former US Defense Secretary, James Schlesinger, described as 'unprecedented in its breadth and depth'. The Soviets tested 371 large rockets in 1973 alone.[29]

Once the Americans had effective photo-reconnaissance satellites in orbit over the Soviet Union, their suspicions were aroused in the early 1970s when pictures of some of the craters made on the ranges by impacting inert warheads became available. The craters seemed to be more accurately placed than would be likely if the problems with the accelerometers had been genuine.[30] In late 1974 the CIA therefore began a long back-track examination into the possibility that they had been deluded, but Soviet deception agents were soon employing a most ingenious tactic to neutralize the suspicion and to continue the deception on a truly advanced technological scale.

Just as agencies like GCHQ and NSA have been able to intercept coded KGB radio messages, and to decipher some of them, so they have been able to intercept messages transmitted by Soviet missiles during tests. When any experimental missile is test-fired, the propulsion unit and the dummy warhead send back a mass of information about their performance to scientists on the ground monitoring the missile's progress. Devices fitted in them to measure velocity, acceleration, engine performance and aerodynamic details, altitude, sideways drift and other parameters are linked with radio-transmitters which send the information to ground receivers, the system being known as radio-telemetry. Interception of this information by Western listening posts can, of course, reveal the same details of the missile's performance. Both the British and Americans quickly learned how to insert false signals into the telemetry in the hope that it would fool the Soviet scientists trying to interpret it, but

81

the opposing deception experts responded with great ingenuity.[31]

To further their successful accelerometer ploy the Soviet scientists began to fit their test missiles with three accelerometers instead of the usual one and each of them sent back signals to the ground receivers. This was intended to convince the Western analysts that the Russians could not trust a single accelerometer and were being driven to average the results of three to secure anything like an accurate figure of a missile's performance. As a telemetry expert testified later to a Senate Select Committee on Intelligence, using the three accelerometers also enabled the Soviets to distort their signals and to 'under-represent the accuracy of their intercontinental missiles'.[32] In fact, any one of the accelerometers had been thoroughly reliable. The International Department was then presented with a quite extraordinary opportunity, as a result of a double coup by the KGB, and exploited it to the full.

Early in 1973 the Americans secretly launched a satellite with reconnaissance capabilities far in advance of anything previously available. Code-named 'Rhyolite', it hovered in stationary orbit 22,300 miles above the missile test-ranges of the Soviet Union and, when its folded dish aerial was fully extended to its width of 70 feet, it could pick up the telemetry signals from missiles and transmit them to ground stations. The Soviet scientists knew that it was there but were not supposed to know any of its secret details.[33]

Under the UKUSA agreement between the US and Britain, signed in 1947, the information gleaned by Rhyolite was shared with the British radio-intercept organization, GCHQ, centred on a large headquarters at Cheltenham and with many out-stations. Regrettably, one of the technical officers there, Geoffrey Prime, had been recruited by the KGB while serving with RAF signals in West Berlin in 1967 and in the spring of 1975 he was cleared for access to Rhyolite's secrets. He had secured a post in GCHQ because of his signals experience and ability as a translator of Russian and was then given an additional course in espionage by his Soviet controllers, who also supplied him with espionage equipment as well as money. From 1975 onwards, until he left GCHQ in September 1977, he supplied the KGB with everything he knew about Rhyolite – what it did, how it worked and improvements being made to it. The Soviet scientists involved in the Great Missile Deception quickly saw how the information might be exploited.[34]

Prime knew only those details necessary for his work and the KGB was deficient in other secret information essential to their deception purposes. Whether by luck or skill on the part of the KGB recruiters, they managed to acquire exactly what they needed from two young Americans. One of these, called Christopher Boyce, was employed in the code-room of the company which had built Rhyolite and was deeply involved in its operations. Further, though only twenty-two, he was cleared for regular access to the strictly guarded code-room to perform his job of changing the code-settings on some of the machines. Boyce photographed key-cards, which revealed the codes being used to operate the satellite, and a mass of other material including a manual giving mechanical details. He then passed them to another young American who handed them to the KGB for money. This regular service, coupled with Prime's, gave the Soviet deception specialists all they needed to know. From mid-1975 they were able to feed false information about their missile firings into the antennae of the Rhyolite satellite and others which had been orbited to boost the reconnaissance operation, exaggerating the technical problems they were facing and underrating the true capabilities of their weapons.[35]

In 1977 the two American spies were caught and imprisoned and, presumably, the US analysts must have wondered whether there had been Soviet interference with the satellite information, but, as they did not know of Prime's treachery, it is possible that they concluded that the Russians did not have enough information to carry out a deception exercise. This would seem to be indicated by the extreme American anger in 1982 when Prime's treachery was discovered, only because of his sexual offences against little girls. Prime had left GCHQ, somewhat mysteriously, and so was unable to continue his important role as a feedback agent, but there is a suggestion in the Security Commission's report on his case that there may have been other Soviet agents inside GCHQ.[36]

Meanwhile the framework of a further agreement on the control of strategic arms, to be known as SALT 2, had been agreed by President Gerald Ford and the Soviet leader, Leonid Brezhnev, in November 1974. As this was developed, leading to the formal signing of a SALT 2 Agreement by President Carter and Brezhnev in July 1979, Russian advances made it clear that the Politburo intended to press ahead with undiminished speed to improve its missile capability and increase its total throw-weight – the number and power of the nuclear warheads it can deliver in a given time. New and more accurate intercontinental missiles were introduced with major advances in submarine-launched missiles, research in the latter field culminating in the production of a colossal ballistic missile submarine, the 25,000-ton Typhoon.[37]

In 1977 the Soviets also began to deploy an intermediate-range missile of outstanding capability called the SS20. This consists of the upper two stages of the three-stage SS16 intercontinental rocket and therefore has a MIRVed warhead. As its range of 3,000 miles is just too short to reach the US, it is not subject to the SALT agreements and has therefore been produced in large numbers, the current deployment being more than 400 launchers. As each launcher, which is mobile, can be quickly reloaded and refired the number of SS20s available for action is not known, though the Soviets are known to be stockpiling refire missiles.[38]

The Carter administration, having accepted the Rhyolite information and other deception material, had been so misled that it felt safe to cut back on the development and production of long-range missiles, believing that it had lead-time. It cancelled the B1 bomber while the Soviets pressed ahead with their Backfire and Blackjack bombers.

As a result of a deception and propaganda campaign, so successful that it will be considered separately in Chapter 15, Carter also cancelled production of a new American battlefield weapon, the neutron bomb.

In 1978 a Soviet intelligence officer defected from the United Nations in New York and finally identified 'Fedora' as a disinformation agent.[39] For that and other reasons the FBI and the CIA were finally convinced that their splendid source had been a plant who had hoodwinked them for twelve years until he returned to the Soviet Union in 1974, still insisting that he hated the KGB. Understandably, the FBI and the US Government preferred to keep the exposure secret and did so until it was revealed by an investigative writer in 1981.[40]

In the previous year, at an intelligence conference in the US, a former CIA strategic analyst, David S. Sullivan, publicly disclosed the extent to which American national intelligence estimates had underestimated Soviet strategic force deployments and how Soviet

84

deception during the SALT decade, 1969–79, had undermined the US negotiating positions. The US intelligence authorities misinterpreted the Cuban missile situation and accepted the myth that Khrushchev had favoured a doctrine of minimum deterrence when, in fact, the missile build-up of the late 1960s is the principal source of the Soviet Union's present status as a super-power. They fell for the 'missile-gap' deception and permitted the Soviet leadership to perpetrate 'massive negotiating deceptions in both SALT 1 and 2'.[41]

In the published report of his disclosures Sullivan stated that the Soviets had made a false statement in May 1972 about the size of their new heavy SS19 missile and suggested that it could be banned when, in fact, they were planning to deploy it widely. They gave a false pledge not to build mobile intercontinental missiles when they intended to go ahead and do so. They gave a false range for the Backfire bomber, denying its intercontinental range and refuelling capability and falsely claimed not to have cruise missiles with a range greater than 600 kilometres. Sullivan stated, 'The practical effects of these strategic underestimates have been very grave. The US is still paying for them in its woeful strategic posture for the 1980s.'

When Ronald Reagan was elected President in 1981 he learned the truth of the extent to which the Soviet Union had achieved a dangerous degree of superiority in both intercontinental and battlefield nuclear weapons and decided to restore the balance as quickly as practicable. The arrest and confession of Prime, early in the following year, confirmed the staggering degree of the Soviet deception, the Pentagon putting the cost of the damage he had inflicted at 1,000 million dollars.[42] With the usual caution imposed by the intelligence authorities, it was not until April 1982 that the US Defense Secretary, Caspar Weinberger, officially admitted that the Soviet Union had achieved nuclear missile superiority. It was also admitted, by Senator Daniel Moynihan, that the discovery that the Russians had been able to cheat on the strength of their missile forces was largely responsible for the American reluctance to ratify the second SALT treaty. Since then the Reagan administration has released a report covering various Soviet violations of treaties and declarations bearing on arms control and disarmament.[43]

The Western effort to restore the missile balance, about which there can be no secrecy or cheating because of the democratic requirement to secure the agreement of parliaments, has caused a violent reaction from the Politburo which is determined to maintain its superiority and protect its colossal investment. So, in tandem with the positive deception effort to prevent the West from knowing the truth about the Soviet build-up of nuclear armaments, there has been an even more strenuous campaign to dissuade the West from doing anything which would make inroads into the Soviet superiority. This aspect of the secret offensive has concentrated its cunning and resources on the various 'peace' movements in the world, with the fear of nuclear war being stage-managed so deceptively that millions are being persuaded that it is not only pointless but reprehensible to make the necessary investment to defend themselves. The insidious techniques which are making this strategem so successful will be the subject of several chapters, but for a proper appreciation of the Soviet exploitation of the universal yearning for peace in the nuclear age it is necessary, first, to examine the worldwide manipulation of the media, without which it could never have been accomplished.

Chapter 7

The Long March through the Media

'The foreign journalistic community in any country of the free world is continuously targeted by the KGB.'

Stanislav Levchenko

The Bolshevik revolutionaries, and Lenin in particular, were quick to appreciate the power of language, both written and spoken, as a political weapon and especially as a means of deception. And since deception, intrigue and clandestine activity of every kind had been such successful factors in their illegal seizure of power in 1917, the Politburo has turned to such measures, almost automatically, ever since, having steadily refined their use in the process. If the first casualty of war is the truth, then it founders continuously in the cold war operations run by the Soviet Union. Words in common international parlance have been deliberately distorted in Soviet definition so that, to the unsuspecting, they have become a potent form of deception in themselves. Table 2 shows how key words used in the political 'struggle', the 'class war' and the active-measures offensive have been so twisted to suit the Soviet purpose that the Kremlin's vocabulary is utterly different from that of those Western countries which have to negotiate with them. The Soviet interpretation of words like 'peace', 'democracy', 'détente', 'freedom' and 'human rights' is so different that treaties and agreements using them can have no safe validity for the West.

This abuse of language to suit the Politburo's nefarious purposes received peculiar prominence in April 1985 when it became known that special editions of English dictionaries prepared for sale in the Soviet Union by the Oxford University Press had been required to present the definitions of certain words on 'Marxist/Leninist' lines. 'Socialism', for example, was defined as 'a social and economic system which is replacing capitalism', an untruth intended to deceive the Russian reader. While 'capitalism' was defined in the normal *Shorter Oxford Dictionary* as 'The condition of possessing capital or using it for production; a system of society based on this; dominance of private capitalists', it had to be redefined for the Soviet reader as 'An economic and social system based on private ownership of the means of production operated for private profit, and on the exploitation of man by man'. 'Communism', normally defined in the dictionary as 'A theory of society according to which all property should be vested in the community and labour organized for the common benefit', had to be presented to the Soviet people as 'A theory revealing the historical necessity for the revolutionary replacement of capitalism by Communism'.[1]

When these and other tendentious examples of political redefinition were exposed the executives of the Oxford University Press expressed regret and promised that it would not happen again. The 100,000 printed copies of the 'doctored' dictionary on sale in the USSR remain as evidence of the degree to which the agents of the Politburo interfere to ensure that everything the Soviet people read is angled to support the deception which keeps them in total subjection. Such actions complement the wholesale deception foisted on the Soviet people, from the cradle to the grave, by works in Russian such as the *Great Soviet Encyclopaedia* published by the 'State Scientific Agency' and kept up to date with annual supplemental volumes. It is a falsification of world history on an unprecedented scale in which Soviet Communism is trumpeted for its achievements and free enterprise is castigated for its inhumanities. Scientific advances and inventions made in the West are claimed for Soviet science. No mention is made of the failures of the Soviet system in providing material benefits and welfare or of the iniquitous privileges of the ruling élite. These perfidies are duplicated in the stringently controlled books provided for the educational system and for general reading, any literature challenging the 'Party line' being banned from the USSR.

Table 2

Term	What it means in the West	What it means to the Politburo and its supporters
Aggressive circles	Groups intent on committing some form of aggression	Any Western groups opposed to the aggressive policies of the Soviet Union
Anti-fascist	Opposed to the form of dictatorship practised by Mussolini and Hitler, which was originally known as a form of socialism	Pro-Soviet
Armed aggression	An attack by a foreign country or a group	When practised by the Soviets, 'making the world safer for socialism'
Ballot box	A device whereby the mass of the population can secretly record its support for or opposition to a political party, institution or individual	A device through which the mass of the population is required to record its support for the Communist Party and its leaders
Correct	True and accurate	Conforming to the current Communist Party line
Democracy	A form of government in which the ultimate power is in the hands of the people, who elect competing political parties by secret ballot	Totalitarian rule by the Communist Party, which elects itself for all time and can never be subjected to possible defeat by secret ballot

Term	What it means in the West	What it means to the Politburo and its supporters
Détente	A relaxation of international tension	A situation in which an adversary is lulled into believing that there is a relaxation of tension and which can, therefore, be exploited to promote Soviet aims
Direct action	Something done in a direct manner	Violence
Fascist	A member of a Fascist (National Socialist) party	A term of abuse for anyone opposed to Communism or far-left socialism
Freedom	Liberty within the law, including freedom of speech, writing and association	Totalitarian enslavement
Freedom fighters	Patriots resorting to armed force to free their country from an occupying power or from a tyranny	Terrorists and rural and urban guerillas including alien troops, often trained, armed and financed by the Soviet Bloc
Government	A group elected by the people to carry out the wishes of the electing majority and subject to re-election at regular intervals	An assembly to rubber-stamp decisions taken in secret by the Politburo
Imperialism	Territorial aggrandizement	Territorial aggrandizement by any nation other than the Soviet Union which acquires territory only 'to protect its borders'

Term	What it means in the West	What it means to the Politburo and its supporters
Industrial organizer	Someone connected with the organization of an industry	A fomenter of industrial strife in an adversary country
Justice	The independent administration of laws laid down by democratically elected parliaments and open courts, usually with independent press coverage so that justice is seen to be done	The administration of laws laid down arbitrarily by the dictatorship and its offshoots and with only controlled press coverage
Media	Vehicles for the printed word, for sound and visual images either independently owned or with safeguards for their independence if owned by the State	Newpapers, magazines and journals; radio and television stations all owned by the State and operated to the Politburo's rigid requirements
Peace	The absence of war, and friendliness towards other countries	A situation in which every offensive measure short of shooting-war should be pursued to further the Politburo's long-term aim of world Communist domination
People's democracy	A true democracy with the people able to expel the government at a general election	A pseudo-democracy where the people are expendable ciphers, every facet of their lives being under tight control

Term	What it means in the West	What it means to the Politburo and its supporters
Police brutality	Brutal behaviour by the police	Any attempt by the police of a true democracy to prevent violence or to protect themselves from it
Progressive	Moving forward in an improving way	In favour of Soviet-style Communism
Reactionary	Opposed to revolutionary change	A term of abuse for anyone opposed to Soviet Communist-style revolution
Socialism	The subordination of the individual to the interests of the community but undertaken through the wishes of the majority as expressed in a secret ballot	A euphemism widely used by the Soviets as a deception-word for Communist government by the Politburo
Tolerance	Recognition of the rights of others	(Not in the political vocabulary)
Trade union	An organized body of workers for the protection and promotion of their common interests and with various legal rights, including the right to withdraw their labour	An organ for Party control over the workers to force them to fulfil production requirements and to prevent strikes or other disputes
Truth	Conformity with reality	A distortion of reality and events in every conceivable way that can strengthen the Politburo's hold on the Soviet people and further its foreign aims

One of the first moves made by the Bolsheviks in their drive to hold power was the seizure of the Russian press, which has been under the complete control of the Communist Party ever since, with radio and television being in the same captive situation. This has enabled the Politburo to continue to distort events continuously, a deception of the 'masses' which has been widely extended abroad through Soviet publications on sale there but, more effectively, through the organs of the foreign Communist parties under Moscow's control. In addition, as was highlighted by the intensive research into the background of the *Der Spiegel* Affair conducted by Sir James Goldsmith, unremitting efforts have been made to manipulate the Western media in the Politburo's interests. The Western media, in fact, constitute one of the major institutions through which the Soviet Communists and their supporters are dedicated to making their 'long march'. While all the instruments of active measures are regarded by the International Department as being complementary, the manipulation of the foreign media is the most important and most productive in exerting mass influence because the media form the main channel through which the public receives information.

It is no coincidence that active-measures operations against the West have intensified as the 'communications revolution' has progressed, the effect of television on demonstrations, picket lines, speeches and other events which would otherwise receive scant notice being fully appreciated by the planners of the International Department and the exploiters of the KGB. Tremendous efforts are made by active-measures operators to plant propaganda and disinformation in Western media so that there does not seem to be any Soviet-Bloc involvement. This is achieved in a variety of ways which will now be considered in some detail.

A former Director General of MI5, the British counter-espionage and security service, has gone on record as warning that the KGB, and the Soviet-Bloc intelligence services generally, are 'very active in the press world in Fleet Street'.[2] They are similarly active not only in every other Western country but in the East and throughout the Third World, as the evidence of defectors like Stanislav Levchenko proves beyond question. Writers, commentators, editors, producers and other media figures are prime targets for active-measures operations not only because they are potential channels for Soviet propaganda and disinformation but because they are also powerful agents of influence on others of their kind.

Of the many methods of planting Soviet propaganda and disinformation in regular use the most continuously reliable is through journalists who are already committed ideologically to the Communist cause. Such men and women tend to be totally dedicated irrespective of any risk to their jobs and if they are talented professionals, as they often are, they can achieve a great deal quite openly. If their material is highly readable or entertaining they are likely to be given space for their views, especially by an editor who prides himself on his objectivity or 'liberalism'.

There are many such people in influential positions in the British and American media and, no doubt, elsewhere in Europe. The laws of libel make it difficult for some of the most blatant to be named but perceptive readers will have their own opinions.

One of the most dedicated and successful agents of influence used as a channel for Soviet disinformation and propaganda for almost forty years was the Australian journalist Wilfred Burchett, who died in 1983 at the age of seventy-two. His career merits a brief survey as an example of what one able writer born in a free society can achieve on behalf of a repressive tyranny.

Burchett, who had been a secret member of the Australian Communist Party, which his father had helped to found, began his clandestine career by volunteering information to the Russians following a trip he had made to the German rocket centre at Peenemunde in 1947. A KGB officer working under the cover of being a Soviet journalist reported to Moscow that Burchett wanted to 'sell himself' and Moscow was quick to 'buy' him.[3] Burchett had previously been in touch with the Soviet Ambassador in London, Maisky, who had chosen him to run the Intourist Office there at the early age of twenty-six. He soon became known to MI5 as a dangerous Communist, my evidence for that being a personal contact which I made with Burchett in October 1946, while he was working as a foreign correspondent for the London *Daily Express*. The incident offers a telling example of the extent to which a trusted journalist can become a source of information of the highest order of secrecy.

I chanced to meet my distinguished colleague Sefton Delmer, then chief foreign correspondent of the *Daily Express*, in the bar of the Players Theatre Club, in London, and he introduced me to his companion, Wilfred Burchett, whose name I knew from his dispatches but whom I had never met because he had been based abroad. Knowing my interest in atomic weapons, Burchett told me that shortly before the first atomic bombs had been used against Japan, in the previous year, he had been with the American forces on the Pacific Island of Tinian, from which the bombers that delivered the bombs had operated. He described how the commander there, General Kenny, had taken several correspondents, including himself, to see the first bomb, though they were instructed not to describe what they had seen. During the brief time that the tarpaulin over the bomb was withdrawn, Kenny told them the weight of the bomb and the current production rate. At that time the all-up weight of the bomb, four tons, was one of the most important military secrets because it determined which type of aeroplane could carry it and how many one plane could carry. It was also decisive in determining whether such a bomb could be delivered by a missile, the V2 being capable of carrying only a one-ton warhead. I doubted that this information, which Burchett had made no effort to publish, could safely be released so I discussed my knowledge of it with the D Notice Secretary, to whom I submitted a news article for vetting by the security authorities. On the following day I was told that, while my information was correct, the release would not help the Russians much because Burchett, whom I had named as the source with his permission, had almost certainly given the information to Moscow as he was dedicated to the Communist cause, a fact of which I had been entirely unaware as, presumably, had General Kenny.[4]

After leaving the *Daily Express* Burchett covered the trial of Cardinal Mindszenty, indicating his guilt, and performed similar pro-Communist tasks when reporting other show-trials in Hungary and Bulgaria. During the Korean War he reported from the Communist side as correspondent for the French Communist newspaper, *L'Humanité*. Among the disinformation he purveyed was the false claim that the Americans were using germ warfare in both North Korea and northern China. He appeared in a prisoner-of-war camp in North Korea, interrogating British and American prisoners and editing 'confessions' extracted under harsh treatment to 'prove' the germ warfare lie.[5] One prisoner testified that Burchett, who wore a Chinese military uniform, warned him that he could have him shot and that it would be a 'good thing' if he were shot.[6] Some of this evidence became public during a libel action which Burchett brought in Australia after it had been alleged that he had been in the pay of the KGB. Burchett lost.[7]

According to the Soviet defector Yuri Krotkov, Burchett did receive money from the KGB, but in good 'conspiratorial practice' he always insisted on being paid through the various Communist parties so that he could deny being employed by any government agency.

One of his foreign correspondent colleagues, the Canadian journalist William Stevenson, has recorded that Burchett revelled in a 'spurious sense of power' because of the privileges bestowed on him by the Communist régimes he supported.[8] After living in Moscow, writing in praise of the alleged reforms being made by Khrushchev, he reported from the Communist North Vietnamese side in the Vietnam war with the US, becoming a fervent admirer of Ho Chi Minh. He was able to insinuate much disinformation into his own dispatches and also to induce some Western correspondents to write from an anti-American angle. The reward was Burchett's influence in securing visas for journalists to visit Hanoi.

Burchett, who was married to a Bulgarian, remained an active disinformation agent until he died in Sofia in September 1983. In a fulsome obituary in the Guardian, the far-left journalist John Pilger described him as a journalist who 'did not believe objectivity was a holy grail, an end in itself, but only one means to the truth'. The American writer Reed Irvine more accurately described him as:

> a prime example of the success the Communists have had in insinuating their propaganda into the media of the Free World. Even though he had been exposed as having been on the KGB payroll and had, notoriously, served the Communists during both the Korean and Vietnam wars, Burchett had many friends among the Free World journalists and was able to get his articles placed in influential publications such as the New York Times.[9]

I would describe Burchett as a full-blooded Soviet agent who had no option but to make his political allegiance clear. There have, of course, been many journalists who were much more insidious

Soviet agents and who were required to keep their real function totally secret. Among these, Harold (Kim) Philby, who operated under journalistic cover in Spain and France before joining MI6, is probably the best known, though even he is probably placed below the German journalist Richard Sorge in the Soviet hierarchy of foreign intelligence agents.[10]

In a previous book I have described how a KGB officer posing as a press attaché at the Soviet Embassy in London tried to recruit me to work for him with the promise of money.[11] This officer, who used the name of Anatoli Strelnikov, failed, but he and those like him who were cultivating British journalists were more successful with others who happened to be already motivated ideologically in the direction required. In the late 1970s a major Fleet Street reporter was exposed as an established KGB agent of influence and, possibly, as a potential spy, when the proprietor of his newspaper was approached by MI5 to be told that the man was a secret Communist who had been in the regular pay of the Soviet Bloc for several years. An East European defector had given clues to the man's identity, including his code-name, and MI5 had identified him after some difficulty. When confronted with evidence from his bank accounts he chose to resign from his prestigious post, and from Fleet Street, without fuss. As the proprietor did not want it known that he had harboured a Soviet agent of influence, whose reports had been given such prominence, the case was stifled. This very able reporter had been prepared to use his freedom as a journalist in a free society, with access to important figures in Whitehall, to assist in the hopeful imposition of a régime which would immediately deny those freedoms to him and to all others. He could not have been unaware that for comparable behaviour in the country of his dreams he would have been given a long prison sentence or possibly executed.[12]

Though the source of the information about that potential traitor was no longer in danger, MI5 was as keen as the proprietor to avoid any publicity about the case. By such conspiracies of silence, dangerous subversive agents are protected from public censure, the laws of libel making it impossible for his name to be given here.

The United States has had its share of secret Communists, as well as open Communists, among journalists in a position to exercise far-reaching influence. One of the most notorious was Whittaker

Chambers, who worked on *Time* magazine and was to state that, for a long period, the *Time* unit of the New York Newspaper Guild was tightly controlled by a small group of Communists. Indeed, there were so many Communists and sympathizers in the *Time* organization that a newsletter, called *High Time*, was circulated to every staff member at intervals and bore the statement 'Published by the Communists at *Time* Inc'. Chambers, who achieved international notoriety in 1948 by his exposure of Alger Hiss as a Soviet spy, said that, once he had decided to defect from Communism following Stalin's obscenely cynical pact with Hitler in 1939, the remaining Communists in *Time* tried to freeze him out of news-writing and slandered him whenever possible.[13] The Chambers case is old – he died in 1961 – but the continuing controversy over Alger Hiss – now known to have been a spy from KGB intercepts – has kept it alive and, in 1984, President Reagan awarded Chambers a posthumous Medal of Freedom for his exposure of Soviet agents.[14]

While Chambers eventually became disenchanted with Communism, several influential American journalists did not. Some, like Joseph F. Barnes, a former foreign editor of the *New York Herald Tribune* and, later, executive editor of the book publishers Simon and Schuster, remained active until exposed. In 1951 he was identified as a Soviet agent of influence and a secret member of the Communist Party with close ties with Soviet Intelligence by two self-confessed KGB agents, Whittaker Chambers and Hede Massing, giving evidence to the Senate Subcommittee on Internal Security. One of his former Communist friends, Dr Karl Wittfogel, testified that he tried to induce Barnes to break with Communism after Hitler and Stalin signed their pact, but he described Barnes as a 'fanatic who didn't care about the facts'.[15]

Other American journalists, like Cedric Parker who had worked for the *Capitol Times* of Madison, Wisconsin, for forty-three years, were exposed as life-long Communists only after their deaths. When Senator Joe McCarthy branded Parker as a Communist the charge was ridiculed but, as Reed Irvine has observed, Parker could be relied upon to help spread the Soviet propaganda line through his paper.[16] Winston Burdett, a correspondent for CBS television, admitted having been recruited by Soviet intelligence and to being in touch with a senior GRU spy, while Alden Whitman, who was on the staff of the *New York Times*, after serving on a newspaper in

Buffalo, confessed to having been a secret Communist when he appeared before a US Senate Committee. During his later years at the *New York Times*, where he remained until his retirement in 1977, he was involved in the production of obituaries when deceased Communists seemed to receive favoured treatment.[17]

With the intensification of active measures and the recruitment of foreign journalists to promote them it remains a matter for conjecture as to how many secret Communists are currently in the US media, and particularly in television, as it does in the UK. Detailed evidence of the extensive spread of the Soviet secret offensive was provided, however, in 1980 by the arrest of a leading journalist in France. This was Pierre-Charles Pathé, the son of the cinema pioneer, who was convicted of having served as a paid spy and agent of influence for the Kremlin for twenty years. Pathé had been recruited in 1959 and was thenceforth controlled by a series of KGB officers working under the diplomatic cover of being delegates to UNESCO headquarters in Paris or being diplomats in the Soviet Embassy there. During the first three years, while Pathé was being 'developed' in the KGB's thorough and patient way, the meetings had been open, but after he had been fully recruited as an agent they became clandestine and remained so, the usual 'conspiratorial practices' being observed.[18]

Pathé provided information which came his way from well-placed contacts, but his main function was as a journalistic agent of influence. Writing under his own name, or under the pseudonym Charles Morand, he published articles angled in the Soviet interest in many French newspapers and launched a confidential newsletter for private circulation. The KGB provided ideas and disinformation for the articles and often vetted them before publication, as well as giving financial assistance. The newsletter, called *Synthesis*, launched in 1976, pursued similar lines and circulated among many members of the Chamber of Deputies, the Senate and the diplomatic community, as well as reaching most of the French newspapers. In subtle ways it defended the stance of the Soviet Bloc and undermined the Western alliance, pouring particular scorn on any French submission to American influence. The newsletter regularly attacked the CIA and suggested that the FBI had been involved in the assassination of President Kennedy.

Pathé was a particularly valuable agent of influence because he

had an established reputation among politicians and other journalists who tended to follow up his stories. Being a member of an
exclusive club, made up largely of French politicians, he was in an
excellent position to act as a talent scout for 'willies' and other possible auxiliaries for active-measures operations. His activities came
to the notice of French security in 1978, during the routine surveillance of a KGB officer, Igor Kuznetsov, and in the following year he
was caught handing over a document to the Russian and receiving
money. After trial, Pathé, then aged seventy-one, was jailed for five
years but, after serving only one year, was released and pardoned,
presumably because of his age.[19]

Rarely daunted by any setback, the active-measures campaigners
continued their efforts in France. In June 1980 the French Interior
Ministry deported Simon Malley, the editor of the magazine
Afrique-Asie, which had a large circulation, mainly in Africa and
Latin America, and pursued a strong pro-Soviet line. Malley, who
had been born in Egypt and had helped to found the Egyptian Communist Party, had lived in France for eleven years but, in spite of
protests, was ordered out of the country for political activities
against France's interests. In the French Parliament the Interior
Minister accused him of inciting people to assassinate foreign heads
of state. As he held US citizenship he was deported there but soon
managed to obtain a Swiss residence permit and continued to edit
Afrique-Asie from that country.[20] On the advent of the Mitterand
Government in 1981 he was allowed back into France.

While Pathé and Malley were on the point of being exposed in
France, KGB active-measures operators were effectively busy in
Denmark through the activities of a Danish journalist called Arne
Herlov Petersen, who had been suborned and then recruited as a
paid KGB agent of influence several years earlier. In 1979 he published a pamphlet, in English and Dutch, entitled 'Cold Warriors'
and consisting of scurrilous attacks on Margaret Thatcher, Joseph
Luns, the NATO Secretary General, Senators Henry 'Scoop'
Jackson and Barry Goldwater and Franz Josef Strauss. He followed
this, in 1980, with 'True Blues – the Thatcher that couldn't mend
her own roof', a 23-page pamphlet attacking the British Prime
Minister in personal and political terms calculated to cast doubt on
her competence and accusing her of a pro-American belligerency
which could only worsen East–West relations – a tirade reminiscent

of the campaign against Franz Josef Strauss eighteen years earlier.[21]

Petersen's treacherous career came to an end early in November 1981 when the Danish Government expelled his current KGB controller, a so-called Second Secretary of the Soviet Embassy in Copenhagen, one Vladimir Merkulov, for 'activities inconsistent with his diplomatic status'. Petersen was arrested and charged with being an agent for Merkulov. The Danish security service had established that Petersen had been in contact with at least three Russians known to be KGB officers and had worked as an active-measures agent, planting articles supplied by Moscow and rejigged in his own style, as the 'True Blues' pamphlet had been.[22]

He had purveyed forgeries, moved funds to support 'peace' movements and served as a talent scout to supply the KGB with information about other Danish journalists who might be recruited as agents of influence. While he had once been an overt Communist he had been required to end all contact with the Party when he had been recruited to active-measures operations. The KGB had paid the expenses of his publications and given him extra cash, gifts and free travel facilities. He had been assured that, in the event of imminent war, he and his family would be evacuated to the Soviet Union.

In the spring of 1982 the Danish Ministry of Justice decided against prosecuting Petersen on the grounds that Danish interests had not been sufficiently damaged, but it put the main charges and evidence against Petersen on public record. Interviewed on Danish television, the Danish Foreign Minister challenged Petersen to sue for libel, but he declined to do so.[23] This action by the Danish authorities offers a sensible example to other Western governments who are disinclined to become involved in court cases and, in the past, have allowed such subversive behaviour to go uncensured.

I have described the Petersen case in some detail because it is an attested example of a journalistic agent of influence under regular KGB control. He took repeated orders and reported back. As a CIA officer told a US Congressional Committee, 'They used him in various parts of their game-plan and he did their bidding fully, even when he got a lot of flak from his colleagues. He just took it.'[24]

Regrettably, there are journalists who are even more mercenary than Petersen and who take regular bribes from the KGB to pursue active measures through the columns at their disposal. The most graphic evidence of such cases has been provided by Stanislav Lev-

101

chenko, the Soviet active-measures specialist who defected to the US in 1979, after service in Japan.

Levchenko, then aged thirty-eight, has been a major source of information on active-measures operations and there can be no doubt about the accuracy of it. Before his information was accepted by the CIA, the agency made a thorough background investigation and subjected him to intensive interrogation, including polygraph tests, in case he might be a KGB plant. Further confirmation of his authenticity has been provided by the CIA's identification of other active-measures officers and agents on evidence which he provided. His disclosures have also been confirmed by the Japanese security authorities and the Soviet authorities have sentenced Levchenko to death in his absence, making him a prime target for assassination.[25]

The details of his career not only demonstrate the high priority given to active measures by the Politburo and the latter's intimate involvement, but prove the close association between the apparently innocuous International Department and the KGB. Born in Moscow and the son of a major-general, Levchenko was among the élite, the *nomenklatura*, those families manning the enormous bureaucracy which underpin the leadership and continue to do so because they are given privileges denied to the 'masses' for whom the revolution was supposed to have been accomplished. After studying the Japanese language and culture at Moscow University he entered the Institute of People of Asia and Africa, which is controlled by the International Department, to complete a thesis on the history of the Japanese 'peace' movement. He was sent to Japan in April 1966, officially as an interpreter for the Soviet Trade Delegation but under orders from the International Department to meet with leading figures of the Japanese 'peace' movement and to report back on their activities. He visited Japan twelve times in similar guises and, while an active-measures career in Japan was clearly in line for him, he was required, as a reserve army officer, to do three months' training, in 1966, as an illegal intelligence agent to be infiltrated into Britain in time of an emergency to report on the state of readiness of the nuclear strike forces there. He was one of many trained to join the existing fifth column of British Soviet agents who would rise during the emergency to carry out sabotage operations and assist the Soviet commandos landing at various points in advance of the main assault.[26]

In 1971 Levchenko joined the First Directorate of the KGB and, after a year at the KGB Intelligence School, was assigned as a case-officer to the Japanese desk in Moscow Headquarters, handling files on Japanese agents working for the KGB. Prior to being posted as a field officer to Tokyo, he was attached to the international Soviet magazine *New Times*, to give himself credible cover for his clandestine work. He was taught journalistic skills and the magazine published several long articles in his name. In February 1975 he arrived in Tokyo with his family as the *New Times* correspondent. In reality he was what the KGB calls a 'Line PR' officer with the rank of captain and, later, major. As Levchenko explained, inside the KGB 'Residency' in any major city there are various sections or 'lines' responsible for various subversive activities. The section responsible for active measures is called Politicheskaya Razvedka (Political Intelligence Service), abbreviated to Line PR, and in many countries, such as the US, it is the KGB's biggest branch.[27]

Being accredited with the official Japanese Press Office, Levchenko was able to attend off-the-record briefings with Japanese defence officials and, with twelve of the fourteen 'correspondents' attached to *New Times* being KGB staff officers, he was soon describing Japan as 'a paradise for spies'. He inherited some committed Soviet agents among Japanese journalists from his predecessor and was soon recruiting others so successfully that by 1979 he was running ten agents with whom he had about twenty clandestine meetings a month.

A KGB manual, seen by John Barron, recommends that the best way to 'hook' new journalistic recruits is to persuade them to write harmless analytical articles for mythical Soviet journals and newsletters for payment and to proceed from there, once signed receipts for the payments have been obtained.[28] Levchenko began that way and then virtually blackmailed his prey into writing Soviet-inspired articles in the Japanese media for which they were working. Four of the journalists he was running were prominent newspapermen with high-level political contacts so that the KGB received useful information as well as planting propaganda containing much disinformation. To quote Levchenko, one of these journalist-agents 'was a close confidant of the owner of a major Japanese newspaper with a daily circulation of more than 3 million copies and had been used to implement a variety of active measures'.

According to several interviews given by Levchenko, one of his most effective agents was already a secret Marxist who edited the conservative newspaper *Sankei*. This was Takuji Yamane, whose KGB code-name was Kant. In addition to planting reports and articles virtually dictated by the KGB he influenced his publisher as well as his subordinates, who had no idea that they were serving the Soviet interest. *Sankei* was an ideal medium since it was unlikely to be suspected by its readers of being Soviet-inclined, much less Soviet-controlled. When Levchenko publicly exposed Yamane after his defection, the too-willing agent of influence was fired.

Another of Levchenko's puppet Japanese journalists was well placed inside *Kyodo*, the national news-service. There were, in addition, the agents being run by the other KGB officers in the 'Residency'. Only the chief, the 'Resident' himself, would know the total number but Levchenko claims that there were agents on almost every major Japanese newspaper as well as on television. According to John Barron, through an agent who was a television executive the KGB bribed a Japanese network to air Soviet propaganda and slant the news in return for exclusive rights to telecast the 1980 Moscow Olympics in Japan.[29]

While concentrating on clandestine activities, Levchenko and his KGB colleagues kept their cover going by writing dispatches and sending them back to *New Times* and the other Soviet media they served. The articles appearing under their names were then relayed back to Tokyo by the press attaché of the Japanese Embassy in Moscow in his normal line of duty. Often, however, the Soviet 'journalists' in Japan were too busy with active measures to have time for writing, and articles written for them, either in KGB headquarters or in the International Department, were sent to them via the diplomatic bag so that they could go through the motions of filing them back, by telephone or cable, to Moscow where they would be printed under their names.

In his debriefing by the CIA and, later, in interviews, Levchenko listed his main active-measures functions in Japan as provoking distrust between Japan and the US to weaken their political and military cooperation; preventing improvements in relations between Japan and China; preventing any anti-Soviet collaboration between Washington, Tokyo and Peking; creating a pro-Soviet lobby among Japanese politicians, especially in the Socialist Party, leading to the eventual signing of a treaty of friendship between Japan and the USSR; penetrating the Japanese Socialist Party and Liberal Democratic Party to these ends; and inducing the Japanese to abandon all hope of recovering the Kurile islands which the Soviets had seized after the defeat of Japan, to which they had contributed little.

Levchenko claims that after his promotion to major and his appointment to acting chief of active-measures operations in Japan, he had come to realize that the Soviet régime was a 'totally corrupt dictatorship', having already been harbouring doubts and resentment. His wife had relatives in the Soviet Union and his son was at school in Moscow, so he defected without them. They have since been systematically persecuted by the KGB.[30]

Further first-hand evidence of how the KGB utilizes journalists has been provided by Ilya Dzhirkvelov, who defected to Britain in March 1980 after thirty-six years' membership of the KGB or close association with it, and who has already been quoted as a witness in connection with the *Der Spiegel* Affair. From 1947 until 1980 Dzhirkvelov was involved in aspects of active measures and has stated:

> In the KGB itself I worked for the Foreign Journalists Development Department, 'development' being a KGB euphemism for the surveillance, influencing, misinforming and possibly recruiting of journalists. From 1957 I was Deputy Secretary-General of the newly created Union of Journalists of the USSR. Officially I handled international relations of the union; unofficially I was responsible for cultivating foreign journalists and feeding them information given to me by the KGB.[31]

Details of how he accomplished these special functions have been given in the chapters dealing with the defamation of Franz Josef Strauss.

In further confirmation of this evidence concerning the KGB's exploitation of journalists, the Czech defector Ladislav Bittman, who specialized in applying active measures in West Germany, told a US Congressional Committee that he was personally in contact with several agents for whom he acted as case-officer and that nearly all of them were journalists.[32] More evidence of a similar nature has been provided by Tomas Schuman, the Soviet journalist from the Novosti agency who defected to the West in 1970 and whose story is recounted in Chapter 8.

The most recent Soviet journalist of note to appear in the West and to have been involved in active-measures operations is Oleg Bitov, whose defection to Britain occurred in September 1983 while he was, ostensibly, on a visit to Venice on behalf of the *Literary Gazette*, the Soviet weekly of which he was 'foreign culture editor'. He was based in Britain for eleven months, during which time he wrote several articles castigating the Soviet system and also travelled abroad, and it transpired that he had been sent to Italy as a substitute for a 'journalist' colleague who was really a KGB colonel and had been denied a visa. His mission was to pick up any gossip that might be used by Moscow's disinformation experts to implicate the CIA in the attempted assassination of the Pope in May 1981. The Bulgarian secret service and the KGB were widely suspected of being involved in the attempted murder which had been perpetrated by a Turkish terrorist, Mehmet Ali Agca, and the active-measures experts were anxious to use the upside-down ploy by claiming that it had all been a CIA plot. With the arrest of certain Bulgarians by the Italian authorities there was an obvious possibility that Bitov might appear as a witness against the KGB. So it was clearly in the KGB's interests to secure his return to the Soviet Union.[33]

To the amazement of those who had been dealing with him, Bitov gave himself up to the Soviet Embassy and disappeared back to Moscow where, under KGB 'guidance', he announced that he had been kidnapped and drugged by the British and held in England against his will until he eluded his captors and 'escaped' back to Moscow. The possibility that any Russian, and especially one so unimportant as Bitov, would be kidnapped in an allied country by British intelligence is negligible, especially when violence of any kind has been denied to MI6 and MI5 for thirty years. The evidence, including Bitov's behaviour since his return, when he has continued to peddle disinformation about Britain in the *Literary Gazette*, make it near-certain that such pressure was applied to him that he was forced to return, leaving behind some £40,000 which he had earned from his writings during his 'defection', and other assets including a motorcar. The only credible alternative explanation is that Bitov was a plant from the start – a false defector sent to pose as an anti-Soviet and then to return to claim to the Soviet people that life in the West had sickened him so much that he could not tolerate it.[34] This is the view of Dzhirkvelov, with whom I have discussed the case, and it is supported by the fact, extraordinary for any real defector, however contrite, that Bitov has been promoted to a columnist on the *Literary Gazette*.

Whatever the truth, the Bitov affair demonstrated, beyond doubt, the continuing use of Soviet journalists by the KGB in its campaign of deception and lies.

While media active-measures specialists like Levchenko and, possibly, Bitov, took conspiratorial precautions to cover their real work, some have managed to operate openly with great success. The outstanding exponent is the affluent Vitali Lui, known to the West as Viktor Louis, who has enjoyed spectacular success in planting angled stories in Western newspapers under his assumed name. His involvement with *Der Spiegel* and other West German journals has already been mentioned, along with his regular use of the now defunct London *Evening News*. Louis is also believed to have been instrumental in triggering off the damaging Profumo scandal by anonymously telephoning the Labour MP George Wigg to alert him to the political potential in publicizing the War Minister's predicament.[35]

An even more successful operator than Louis, and one who works at a much higher level, is Georgy Arbatov who heads the Soviet Institute for the US and Canada, ostensibly a branch of the Academy of Sciences but really controlled by the International Department and used by it as a means of enabling its agents to travel widely in the West on what appear to be academic missions.[36] Arbatov, who began his career as a journalist, writing for journals like *New Times*, makes regular visits to the US, Britain, West Germany and other countries, seeking material for articles and books which are widely read because he is not only a full member of the Communist Party's Central Committee, but close to the leadership. His true role was recently blown by the defector Shevchenko, who described his Institute as 'a front used by the Central Committee and the KGB for collecting information, promoting the Soviet position, recruiting Soviet sympathizers in the US and disseminating disinformation'. Shevchenko claims that many of his articles, such as those dealing with arms limitation, are prepared by the Foreign Ministry or the International Department. Arbatov retains close contact with the KGB, liaising with the various 'Residents' on his visits abroad, and has several KGB 'advisers' in his Institute. Pudgy and rather lugubrious, he is quick and engaging in conversation and has, therefore, appeared many times on Western television where he is what Shevchenko calls 'a vigorous drummer for the Soviet system'. He is also regularly interviewed by newspapers and magazines and has become a major outlet for disinformation concocted by the International Department and the KGB 'advisers' on his staff. No comparable Western operation would ever be permitted in the Soviet Union.

Another regular visitor posing as an academic but in reality a colonel of the KGB, is Radomir Bogdanov whose cover is that of being a Deputy Director of the Soviet Institute for the US and Canada. He is known to use his visits to talent-spot and suborn prominent American and Canadian academics for use as agents of influence. Bogdanov, who was the KGB Resident in New Delhi for ten years, even managed to address US Congressmen on Capitol Hill![37] No senior CIA officer has yet managed to harangue Soviet politicians in the Western interest during any visit to Moscow.

Most of the editors, television producers and writers who publicize the views of active-measures agents like Arbatov and Bogdanov in the Western media probably fall into the category of 'willies' and would sincerely deny that they are being used. They are most often the victims of contacts whom they trust but who are Soviet-inclined agents of influence such as left-wing politicians, diplomats, trade-union leaders, scientists, civil servants and ecclesiastics. Various factors affecting daily journalism are conducive to the exploitation of 'willies'. Regarding the publication of Iron Curtain information which cannot be easily confirmed or disproved, both writers and editors are often driven by the fear that if they do not use it some other paper will, the need for exclusivity in newspapers having been intensified by the severe competition from television. If such a 'good story' is exclusive it then tends to be copied by other papers which are all in the habit of 'lifting' each other's material late at night to avoid being 'scooped' in the final editions, and its appearance in more than one paper gives it additional credibility. When a planted story appears in a paper of repute it tends to be sent out worldwide on the agency tapes and then to appear in many other journals and may be quoted on foreign radio. Further, once a story has appeared it is then automatically stored in the clippings libraries of all newspapers and tends to be repeated when a related issue arises in future and journalists are searching for collateral information.[38]

Western journalists, particularly in Britain and the US, have a well-deserved reputation for inflicting propaganda injuries on their own countries by printing information damaging to national prestige. A few of these are deliberate agents of influence but most are 'willies' working on the principle that a 'knocking' story or a scandal is always more interesting than a success. The attacks on various nuclear weapons, particularly as regards their effectiveness and cost, which have greatly assisted the Soviet campaign against them, are current examples while the classic instance will always be the treatment of the Vietnam war by the American media, which, for whatever motive, was instrumental in undermining the nation's will to win. (It could – and probably will – be argued that I have been a 'willie' during my journalistic career, through my frequent criticism of weapons and defence policy, though I doubt that my efforts were welcome to the Kremlin, as my purpose was to ensure that the nuclear deterrent situation, in particular, was strengthened. The same applies to my continuing criticisms of the British security services which, while perhaps immediately welcome in Moscow, are intended to increase their efficiency against Soviet penetration and so reduce not only the quality of KGB espionage but the effectiveness of its active measures.)

One of the KGB's most successful subjects for media manipulation is that of defamation of individuals considered to be hostile to the Soviet interest. The case of Franz Josef Strauss is the classic instance, but there have been many others in which Western media have been crucial to the operation, that of the former Conservative MP Commander Anthony Courtney being one in which KGB involvement was proved.[39]

Courtney was a Naval Intelligence officer who had learned to speak Russian and had been involved in missions against the Soviet Union before he entered Parliament in 1959. He was an inveterate critic of the weakness of the Foreign Office in permitting the Soviets to send so many KGB officers posing as diplomats to Britain and allowing so many others to have diplomatic immunity. After he urged increased restriction of the activities of Soviet-Bloc officials working in London under various covers and repeatedly claimed that Moscow had asserted a psychological ascendancy over the Foreign Office, he was warned by the Russian ambassador's wife and by an Embassy KGB officer that his efforts were being badly received by the Kremlin. In the spring of 1961, when Courtney had recently been widowed, he was taking part in a British industrial exhibition in Moscow and, on the initiative of an attractive woman he had met during a previous visit, she visited his bedroom in the National Hotel. There the KGB took surreptitious photographs which they filed for possible use, as they do with every visitor whom they can inveigle into a compromising situation.[40]

In August 1965 the KGB struck by sending a printed broadsheet carrying compromising photographs to his new wife, various Ministers, MPs and, of course, newspapers and magazines. As only the KGB could have taken the photographs, most news-editors realized that it was a Soviet character-assassination exercise and, to their great credit, took no action. The story was, however, effectively blown by *Private Eye*, the scurrilous magazine, which also commented that the KGB had been stupid not to send a copy of the broadsheet to it in the first place. Using a crude and ruthless device, the KGB effectively destroyed not only the political career of an able MP, courageous enough to attack the Politburo, but ended his marriage.

Private Eye can hardly be described as a 'willie' as it is thoroughly aware of what it is doing when it pursues its many campaigns of vilification against selected individuals. This has been well established in various libel actions brought against the magazine and, in particular, by an action brought by Sir James Goldsmith and settled in the High Court on 11 July 1983.[41] The magazine was forced to admit that it had pursued a campaign of vilification 'relentlessly and continuously' and that a libel which it admitted to be 'a complete fabrication' had been totally untrue. The extent to which *Private Eye* is susceptible to any damaging story planted by any individual or agency was revealed in a recent biography of *Private Eye* written by the *Private Eye* journalist Patrick Marnham, who recorded that the magazine's editor, Richard Ingrams, has said that 'checking many stories is a waste of time, since they are simply denied and that is the end of the matter. Instead he relies on "the ring of truth"; does the story have it or not when rapped lightly and placed next to his ear?'[42]

Explaining some of *Private Eye*'s so-called journalistic methods, Marnham revealed that 'the journalist decides what the story is and then shepherds the facts, or such of them as are convenient, carefully towards the story'. As Sir James Goldsmith remarked, 'Goebbels could not better have described the technique of propaganda.' *Private Eye*'s main sources are various discreditable Fleet Street journalists who use it as a medium for the publication of stories which have been rejected by their own editors or are regarded as so certain to be rejected that they are not even submitted. This makes the magazine particularly vulnerable to use by politically motivated journalists, as well as by those pursuing vendettas, and it would seem to be no coincidence that one of *Private Eye*'s former staff was Paul Foot, a one-time leading propagandist for the Socialist Workers' Party, a revolutionary Trotskyist organization. It may be no coincidence, either, that the *Private Eye* column dealing with financial matters specializes in the blackening of leading capitalists and the City in general, though personalities of any persuasion can be pilloried.[43]

There are magazines comparable to *Private Eye* in other Western European countries and these do not go unnoticed by the International Department. One of these, a West German publication called *Konkret*, regularly publishes disinformation on anti-American and anti-NATO themes and continues to support anti-NATO demonstrations. Its founder, Klaus Rainer Rohl, eventually revealed that he had been a secret member of the Communist Party and that the cash needed to set up the magazine had originated in Prague and reached him via East Berlin. One of *Konkret*'s former editors was Rohl's wife, Ulrike Meinhof, who, after separating from him, became one of the murderous leaders of the Baader-Meinhof terrorists, these, in their early days, being financed by the KGB through East Berlin.[44] C. A. Weber, the editor of another magazine, *Die Deutsche Woche*, was actually convicted of espionage for the Russians, as General Gehlen records in his memoirs.

The Soviet-inspired defamation of an Indian politician, Moraji Desai, the leader of the opposition to the pro-Soviet Indira Gandhi, has been exposed by Tomas Schuman who, as a former official of the Novosti press agency, had inside information about it. Schuman states:

> With financial and ideological encouragement from Novosti, collaborators in the leftist-liberal media poured gallons of venom on that person, describing him as a reactionary, fascist, ultra-right-wing fanatic, lackey of Western imperialism etc. Novosti-sponsored tabloids published bits and pieces of rumours, half-truths and pure fabrications designed to discredit this politician.[45]

The International Department and the KGB have also been successful in inducing Western media to slander and discredit dissidents and defectors. Igor Gouzenko, for example, was – and still is after his death – repeatedly denigrated in the Canadian press, even being accused of having started the Cold War, deliberately.

Though I may be small fry on the books of the KGB, they have done their best to discredit me by statements in *Pravda*, *Izvestia* and other publications which they control, claiming that I am a British secret agent, perhaps in the hope of making it difficult for me to obtain visas for travel abroad, as well as suggesting that I am peddling official British disinformation. While the Soviet Union was friendly with Egypt a Cairo newspaper 'revealed' that not only was I a spy but I was making an illicit fortune out of mining arsenic in Sweden for use in poison-gas weapons. It was an example of the active-measures technique which attempts to persuade the ignorant by the sheer wealth of detail. More recently my name has appeared in a fake KGB list of paid CIA agents.[46]

Some journalists who would refuse money from a Soviet agent might be induced to print material in return for promises of future exclusives or of visas to visit the Soviet Union with special facilities for visits or access to forthcoming Kremlin officials. My own experience shows how easy it is to fall victim to this ploy in good faith. Lord Beaverbrook was most keen that I should be the first to see a space-shot firing in the Soviet Union and made personal representations with the Soviet Ambassador. As a result of this interest, and of my own, the Soviet press attaché, Strelnikov, later to turn out to be a KGB officer, told me that a Russian astronaut had been successfully fired into the lower areas of space in a high-trajectory rocket that did not go into orbit – what was known as a lob-shot.

112

The *Daily Express* printed the story in good faith and it turned out to be untrue. To repeat what should be a golden rule for all journalists – nothing a Soviet official says can be taken at face value.

Wise journalists will also realize that Soviet-Bloc officials are, at all times, dangerous and utterly ruthless in their pursuit of recruits. Not long ago a celebrated American journalist, who has homosexual tendencies when in drink, found himself unable to resist going to bed with a Russian who happened to be a KGB officer and later made it clear that he expected the American to use his very considerable influence to the Soviet purpose whenever possible.[47]

There have been many other attempts to blackmail journalists and I know of one former defence correspondent on a now defunct national newspaper who fell for the crudest trick in the KGB book. He accepted several invitations to the Polish Embassy in London and the wife of one of the attachés there made it clear to him that she would be a more than willing partner in a seduction. The husband invited him to his residence, and when the journalist appeared, the wife apologized for her husband's absence saying that he had been sent out of town. They were in an intimate situation when the husband returned 'unexpectedly' and said that unless he received some professional service in the way of a flow of information he would lodge a complaint. This particular journalist was sensible enough to seek advice from a Defence Ministry official and suitable moves were made to solve his problem.

While there are many instances of journalists who become agents, some like Philby using the profession to become full-blown spies, cases where agents become journalists to pursue a pro-Soviet line are rare. They do exist, however, and the classic instance is the former CIA officer Philip Agee, who defected from American intelligence in 1969, claiming to be disillusioned with its activities. Since then, while remaining in the West, he has been a particularly pernicious purveyor of disinformation against his old employer and functions as a Communist revolutionary propagandist. As Sir James Goldsmith told the Conservative Party Media Committee, 'The causes which he promotes closely parallel the campaigns initiated by the International Information Department in Moscow.'[48]

Agee had spent seven years in the CIA, mainly as an undercover agent in Latin America, and in 1964, while serving in Montevideo, he made contact with the KGB. He remained inside the CIA for five more years and, after resigning, went to Cuba. Moving to Britain in 1972 he settled in Cambridge, becoming assistant editor of the American journal *Counter-spy*, which was dedicated to the denigration of the CIA and the exposure of its secret agents, thereby laying them open to assassination by terrorists. He is known to have had many clandestine meetings with Cuban intelligence officers in Britain and with KGB officers posing as diplomats. The fact that he was able to pursue such activities, so clearly inimical to British interests, demonstrates the tolerance shown to such subversives by British law – an inherent weakness of most true democracies in protecting themselves against Soviet active measures.[49]

Agee's name became widely known through his exposé of the CIA called *Inside the Company*, which he published in 1975 as a paperback.[50] It purported to be the diary of his experiences with the CIA from his recruitment in 1957, through his service in South America starting in 1960, to his resignation. He visited the Soviet Union for two months in 1976 to discuss further revelations about the CIA and was involved in the launching of yet another British extremist magazine called *The Leveller*. In 1975 he was reported as telling a Swiss newspaperman, 'The CIA is plainly on the wrong side – the capitalist side. I approve KGB activities in general, when they are to the advantage of the oppressed. . .' When addressing rallies in Jamaica, at the invitation of the Jamaican Commission for Human Rights, he claimed that the CIA was trying to destabilize the country and turn the people against the 'social-democratic' government of Michael Manley.

It was not, however, until 1977, when further evidence of dangerous subversion – including regular contact with foreign intelligence officers – became available that the Labour Government's Home Secretary, Merlyn Rees, had Agee deported. As could have been predicted, many on the left wing defended Agee during the ludicrously generous six months he was allowed in which to lodge an appeal. Left-wingers in the media joined in and, as Sir James Goldsmith stated to the Media Committee, 'British TV subjected us to a programme of propaganda and special pleading in his favour.' There were debates in Parliament and attention was drawn, in particular, to an ITV 'World in Action' programme 'which seemed specifically designed to further the interests of Agee' and in which far-left witnesses were paraded on his behalf.[51] Merlyn Rees, who is eminently fair-minded, became the target of violent criticism and abuse. The cries from the hard left and those promoting 'civil liberties' which, to the cynical extremists, include the freedom for aliens to conspire against the liberties of their host country, recalled the reaction to the previous Conservative Government's decision to deport a West German pro-Soviet revolutionary called Rudi Dutschke in January 1971. Dutschke, who was dedicated to the overthrow of true democracy, had been allowed into Britain for one month's medical treatment but, at the repeated request of Michael Foot to the Home Office, had been allowed to stay for two years. He had regularly broken his pledge not to take part in political activities, and a tribunal inquiry, to which MI5 officers gave evidence, showed that he had met with other revolutionaries both in Britain and during travels abroad for which the financing remained mysterious. The tribunal was in no doubt that Dutschke had been exploiting the freedoms allowed to him in Britain in order to destroy them.

Britain had barely got rid of Agee when one of the most wanted members of the Baader-Meinhof terrorist gang, Astrid Proll, was arrested in London where she had been working under a false name. Though she had entered Britain on a false passport and was visited by known terrorists while in prison, civil liberties groups and left-wingers fought against her extradition to Germany, even throwing flowers into the dock at her hearing. When she was finally deported the Government was again censured by the extremists.[52]

Agee's subsequent behaviour has demonstrated the wisdom of ejecting such an active-measures operator. He tried to continue his subversive work in France, Holland, Sweden, Switzerland and Italy and eventually gained entry to West Germany where he obtained a residence permit by a subterfuge. In December 1979 his American passport was revoked and when his lawyers appealed the Supreme Court stated, 'Not only has Mr Agee jeopardized the security of the US, he endangers the interests of countries other than the US.' Agee still manages to travel extensively. In Nicaragua he urged the people to take over the American Embassy or burn it to the ground. In 1983 I appeared on a Spanish television programme about espionage, in Madrid, and was surprised to find that Agee, who speaks fluent Spanish, was on it too, promoting anti-Western themes.

While the West German authorities have no illusions about the damage which Agee is trying to inflict on hard-won freedoms, they seem powerless to follow the action of other countries – however reluctantly taken – by ejecting him. Activists like Agee are quick to exploit their 'human rights' and 'civil liberties' and have no difficulty in finding lawyers to battle on their behalf. One wonders if they ever think about the treatment they would receive for comparable activities inside the Soviet Union or in any of its satellites.

One wonders, too, if Western writers and journalists who abuse their precious freedom of expression ever seriously consider what would happen to them if the Soviet cause which they espouse or assist unwittingly should ever triumph. It would be pathetic if the media were to be seen, historically, as having been responsible, if only in part, for the destruction of their own freedom.

Chapter 8

The Agencies as Agents

'We have to influence non-Communists if we want to make them Communists or if we want to fool them. So we have to try to infiltrate in the big press, to influence millions of people.'

Igor Bogolepov
A Soviet Foreign Ministry defector, in evidence to the US Senate Internal Security Subcommittee

Among the prime targets for the encouragement of unwitting 'willies' and the planting of conscious Soviet agents or agents of influence are the press agencies, on which newspapers are far more reliant than the public generally appreciates. Many of the provincial newspapers and national papers, on occasion, publish a dispatch sent out by a reputable agency as it stands and with the attribution, e.g. 'Reuter', 'Press Association' or 'Associated Press', under the headline. In addition, almost all agency reports are 'followed up' by the nationals which then project stories of their own with their own reporters' names on them, having checked out the information as far as they can. A reporter who is given an agency dispatch to check and develop by his news-editor fails if he cannot make the story 'stand up'. There is also a general requirement to 'harden' a story, if possible, by removing the qualifying phrases which might be in an agency dispatch, and this often leads to the presentation of what started as speculation as fact. A zealous reporter anxious to please is therefore under internal pressure to 'stand the story up' and see both the story and his name in print.

I can testify from my own Fleet Street experience that the specialist reporter who is likely to reject a dispatch or any other report of interest to the news-editor or editor, because it cannot be confirmed or is patently untrue, soon becomes unpopular. The all too common news-room attitude, 'Don't show it to him; he'll only knock it down', has led to the printing of many false stories, some of them based on original agency reports which have not been properly checked or have been hardened beyond justification. There is the additional factor that some editors and their immediate subordinates, such as news-editors and features-editors, have an inborn gullibility which drives them to buy 'gold bricks'. False and planted stories are often the best from the point of view of readability and excitement and the creation of envy in other papers which have 'missed' them. Such editorial tendencies are, by no means, confined to the popular tabloids. The acceptance of the fake Hitler diaries by both the German magazine *Stern* and the *Sunday Times* would seem to have owed a lot to the yearning for the sensational exclusive that will increase circulation and demoralize rivals.[1]

It is understandable, then, why the press agencies should be such prime targets of the International Department for the planting of disinformation and the surfacing of forgeries, because one success will reach so many readers. The reputable agencies of the West are, of course, fully aware of their vulnerability and do what they can through editorial judgment, which is generally of a high standard, and through checking to ensure that no false information is transmitted, but they occasionally fall victim, especially with dispatches from foreign sources which are difficult to check, especially when time for doing so is usually very limited.

To give a worldwide service the international press agencies need to issue reports about the Iron Curtain countries, and because all news there is so tightly controlled and so heavily censored there has to be much reliance on official Soviet sources. One of these sources, which exerts effective active-measures influence, especially in the Third World, is the main Soviet press agency, called Novosti.

The Novosti Press Agency (*Agentstvo Pechati Novosti*) was set up in 1961 allegedly as an independent, non-governmental information agency 'to promote and consolidate international understanding, confidence and friendship by widely circulating abroad true information about the Soviet Union and acquainting the Soviet

118

public with the life of other peoples'. This looked like a laudable purpose but the prospectus was completely fraudulent and, from its inception, Novosti was an agency for disseminating lies and deceptions to the Soviet people and to the world at large. Its true nature has been fully exposed by defectors from its ranks or those closely associated with it, including the KGB. The most knowledgeable of these is Tomas Schuman, who defected to the West in 1970 and whose evidence has been made available to me as part of the material acquired by Sir James Goldsmith.[2] Schuman, whose name before defecting was Yuri Bezmenov, was born in Moscow in 1939, the son of a high-ranking military officer. Showing aptitude for foreign languages, he was already being employed by the KGB as a translator in 1960 and began his eight-year connection with Novosti in 1962, working closely with the International Information Department which utilizes the press agency for active-measures operations.

Schuman states:

From the moment of its foundation Novosti was subordinated to the Department of Agitation and Propaganda of the Central Committee of the Communist Party and to the Department of Disinformation of the KGB for the purposes of planning, coordinating and conducting active measures. It is now subordinated to the International Department and works in close liaison with the KGB.[3]

According to Schuman, who works in both Canada and the US, the editorial headquarters of Novosti, in Pushkin Square, Moscow, employs more than 3,000 journalists, editors, translators and public relations specialists. These are subservient, however, to a Chief Editorial Board, located separately and staffed mainly by KGB officers who receive briefs from the International Department and work through the foreign media looking for openings for active-measures operations which Novosti can initiate or foster. This KGB involvement has been confirmed by the defector Ilya Dzhirkvelov, who has first-hand knowledge of a special disinformation group working in separate offices from Novosti to fake up stories for issue to the agency.[4] This group includes the Novosti political observer Mikhail Bruck, who has such excellent English that he often appears as a spokesman on British and American television. The

British defectors Donald Maclean and Kim Philby, who both spied for the KGB, are believed to have worked for Novosti as advisers on the type of disinformation likely to be believed in Britain.

The Moscow headquarters controls Novosti bureaux in major foreign cities and has direct links with the press departments of the Soviet Embassies which assist in the free distribution of Novosti concoctions. These press officers, who have diplomatic status, assist in the planting of the material in foreign media through contacts whom they are expected to develop among journalists and other media people. As Schuman describes the techniques:

> When I was concocting stories and backgrounders for the foreign media, sitting at my desk at the Headquarters of Novosti in Moscow, I simply refused to believe that my boring stuff could be of interest to anyone in the free world, least of all convince anyone about the 'advantages of socialism'. I was wrong. I did not realize at that time that, before my article reached the page of a foreign newspaper, it had to travel a long way through the Novosti-KGB system and then, nicely packaged, be presented to an editor or a commentator in a foreign capital after a long process of cultivating that editor.

The cultivation of sympathizers and media likely to use Novosti material is extended by the inviting of foreign guests of Novosti to the USSR. These tours are an exercise in deception, for the guests are taken only to places and areas where the surroundings have been carefully contrived to give a false picture of real life under Communism. As Schuman describes the system:

> By skilfully isolating foreign correspondents and other visitors from any sources of information and any important people in the USSR, Novosti and the KGB artificially create what we called 'a deficiency of newsworthy information', whereby a foreign guest would gladly swallow a 'bite' offered by a Novosti PR man. After all, a correspondent of an influential newspaper has to file some story on his arrival in Moscow.

In securing foreign collaborators the Novosti men are advised to concentrate on people ready to compromise moral principles for personal advantage. Schuman recalls that those who ideologically believed that Communism is the best solution for mankind formed the smallest group of collaborators. Most of those who were 'prepared to help' did so because they got some reward for their services. 'In most cases Novosti is only too happy to pay in roubles, dollars or pounds to anyone who agreed to publish its crap,' he says. He lists a series of services for which Novosti is prepared to pay large sums: defamation and slander campaigns against Soviet dissidents and other citizens who are out of favour, including defectors; defamation and slander of foreign politicians or writers opposed to the Soviet Union or Communism in general; the orchestration of defamation and disinformation operations against law enforcement and intelligence agencies of target countries.

An extraordinary incident in which Novosti disinformation was *bought* by the West, literally as well as figuratively, came to light in 1975 when articles about the Soviet Union printed in the fifteenth edition of the *Encyclopaedia Britannica* were subjected to Western criticism. As Schuman was able to prove – and as the editors and publishers of the internationally authoritative encyclopaedia later confirmed – the new edition contained fifteen articles about the Soviet Socialist Republics which had been concocted by Novosti writers under the guidance of Party hacks. They described the so-called republics in what Schuman calls 'mythical terms' with false information and many omissions, including the ways in which some of them had been forcibly seized, with millions of people being transported and many killed. They were full of praise for Soviet political organizations and larded with propaganda clichés. Similarly misleading articles had been acquired about East Germany and the other Soviet satellites. The publishers explained this considerable active-measures triumph as due to their normal practice of commissioning articles from writers in the countries concerned, but critics wondered if they would have applied that principle to the Nazis when they were in power, especially as all the articles supplied by the active-measures machine had been printed verbatim. In spite of the outcry the articles remain in every major library.[5]

Like all other Soviet agencies with offices abroad, Novosti is regularly used as cover for KGB agents involved in frank espionage and subversion as well as other kinds of active measures. Indeed, according to John Rees, one of the reasons it was set up was because TASS, the official Soviet telegraph agency, had been exposed so often as a haven for KGB agents that some new, untarnished cover was required.[6] The defector Levchenko, who had close connections with Novosti over many years, states that each of its foreign bureaux usually has up to six 'journalists' of which three will be KGB men while two are likely to belong to the GRU, the only 'clean' person being the bureau chief who does all the genuine journalistic work, the rest busying themselves with active measures and espionage.[7]

Novosti journalists have been expelled from many countries for subversive activities. In 1966 a Novosti man was expelled from Kenya for plotting to overthrow the government there and in the following year another, together with a reporter from *Pravda*, was thrown out of Kenya for similar activities. In 1967 a Novosti correspondent and a *Pravda* man were also expelled from Ghana for plotting the restoration of Nkrumah, who had been well disposed towards Moscow.

When the British Government finally decided in 1971 that the level of subversion by Soviet agents had become insupportable and expelled 105 of them, several of those who had been active were 'journalists' assigned to Novosti and TASS. The subversion was of such an impudent and dangerous nature that it involved links with senior KGB officers and British 'Fifth Columnists' committed to carrying out sabotage, as will be described in Chapter 18. In April 1983 the Novosti bureau in Berne was shut down because of hard evidence that it was a centre for Soviet subversion. 'Journalists' there were printing anti-nuclear tracts even against Swiss power-plants in an attempt to undermine the economy in Moscow's general active-measures campaign against prosperous capitalism without poverty, which so powerfully demonstrates the failure and bankruptcy of Leninist Communism. In closing down the bureau the Swiss Government said that Novosti had served as a centre for 'disinformation, subversion and agitation' and for the 'political indoctrination of young members of the Swiss peace and conscientious objector movements'. The promotion of conscientious objection against service in the Swiss forces was seen as an attempt to undermine Switzerland's modest defences by a super-power which practises conscription on the most massive scale ever seen in peacetime.[8]

Novosti also operates a separate publishing house, turning out thousands of books, magazines and pamphlets in many languages with special accent on suborning the young. These publications, suitably larded with disinformation and propaganda, reach many Western shops, some of which are run by Communists specializing in left-wing literature. No comparable Western publications are allowed to enter the Soviet Union and the penalties for introducing them surreptitiously are severe.

Novosti is staunchly backed up in the secret offensive by TASS, the official Soviet telegraph agency, which, according to Levchenko and Dzhirkvelov, who used it as cover, is just as heavily penetrated and misused, the number of its operatives who have been expelled from various countries being evidence of this. TASS is also used by the International Department for damage limitation operations when active measures have gone awry or some unforeseeable event occurs. Thus, after the expulsion of the 105 KGB and GRU agents from Britain in 1971 TASS quickly circulated wire-service dispatches, believed to have been written by Philby, accusing three prominent Lebanese of being British spies. This rather crude attempt to switch the international spotlight on Britain's spying service backfired, however, for the Lebanese sued TASS for libel and were awarded heavy damages, though TASS claimed immunity from the libel laws because it was the official agency of the Soviet Government, an interesting admission in the circumstances.[9]

Through its agency correspondents working overseas, the International Department was able to conduct a more successful damage limitation operation, or, at least, to recoup some propaganda benefit from a major disaster after a crack Soviet Air Force pilot, Lieutenant Viktor Belenko, flew his ultra-secret Mig 25 fighter to Japan in September 1976 and sought asylum in America. The loss of this advanced aircraft, known in the West as the 'Foxbat', with its aerodynamic, radar and weapons secrets, was severe, but the main Soviet problem was to explain how any élite officer would risk his life to escape from the Communist paradise to the 'capitalist jungle'. The active-measures agents peddled stories that Belenko had been in the pay of the CIA and, as John Barron has reported, 'The West German magazine *Stern* promptly published an article saying the same thing. The Soviets were then able to cite the article in a reputable capitalist publication as proof, to their own people, that Belenko was a mercenary traitor who sold out his country for money.'[10] The accent, of course, was on the appalling crime of bribery practised by the CIA when the Soviets would never dream of resorting to such underhand measures which are, in fact, in daily use by them. A Japanese news-service was induced to recycle the story in a different form in 1982, embroidering it by claiming that Belenko had been originally spotted as a CIA agent when he flew at the Farnborough Air Show in Britain, which he had never done. When the senior wire service, Reuters, picked up this fabrication it was republished by leading American newspapers and remains on their records as 'history'.

Being almost totally restricted to Soviet-controlled hand-outs of 'news', the representatives of foreign wire-services resident in Moscow are driven to report widely from the contents of *Pravda*, which, being the official organ of the Soviet Communist Party, is thought to be less misused as a vehicle for deception and disinformation than other publications. As Levchenko has testified, however, and as the evidence of cases in which *Pravda* journalists have been expelled from various countries proves, there are occasions when the active-measures operators cannot resist making use of its facilities and of the added advantage that the material is likely to be transmitted worldwide by the wire services of the West in addition to TASS. *Pravda* means 'truth' in Russian, but only as defined in Table 2 – a distortion of reality and events in every conceivable way that can strengthen the Politburo's hold on the Soviet people and further its foreign aims.

Another mine of disinformation much used as source material by foreign agencies is the Soviet magazine *New Times* which is published in Russian, English, German, Spanish, Polish, Czech and Arabic and, as Levchenko has exposed in sordid detail, is at the complete disposal of the International Department and the KGB. The activities of *New Times* journalists in Tokyo, as described by Levchenko, are probably typical of those in all major capitals. One of the three Soviet agents expelled from Britain in April 1983 with much publicity, Igor Titov, was listed as a correspondent for *New Times*. As he did not enjoy diplomatic immunity, Titov, who had been involved in active-measures operations rather than frank espionage, was warned that he would be prosecuted if he failed to leave the country within a week. Though proclaiming his innocence, he left.[11]

As the propaganda and deception content of all Soviet publications and agency dispatches has become more widely appreciated by the independent Western media, much of Moscow's patient output is ignored by them. It still receives prominence in the Communist publications of foreign countries, however, and so is rarely completely wasted. In some countries, such as France and Italy, the domestic Communist newspapers and periodicals have wide circulation and considerable influence and so provide very worthwhile outlets for active-measures disinformation and deception. The British Communist paper, the *Morning Star* (formerly the *Daily Worker*) has a tiny circulation, yet, for reasons which are difficult to follow, it is frequently quoted in the BBC's daily accounts of what newspapers are saying, while provincial newspapers with comparatively huge circulations are ignored. It is also regularly quoted by Labour Members of Parliament and by trade-union leaders who do not admit to being Communists, though they use the paper's columns to expound their views, which are then often republished behind the Iron Curtain. The *Morning Star* which is constantly threatening its faithful readers with its closure unless they send donations, claims to receive no money from the Soviet Union, though the daily sale of nearly a third of its circulation to the Soviet Bloc represents an effective hidden subsidy, but its American counterpart, the *Daily Worker*, has been substantially funded by KGB officers on money provided by the International Department, according to the FBI.[12]

There are, of course, many other publications open to Communist propaganda and disinformation in all Western countries, two of the best known in Britain being *Marxism Today*, the theoretical magazine of the Communist Party, and *Straight Left*, run by trade-union leaders and certain far-left Labour MPs. *Straight Left* seems to me to be clearly aimed at the establishment of a 'dictatorship of the proletariat', which in Moscow has ended up as a dictatorship by a small, self-perpetuating, power-hungry clique.

A set of organizations which provide the world's press agencies and the media with much of their raw material and function very much like press agencies, through their hand-outs, background documents and official announcements, are the information departments of government ministries, and international bodies. The penetration and manipulation of these prime source services may, therefore, be even more productive than subversive action against the press agencies and media themselves, and information departments have been major targets for Soviet active measures over many years. They tend to be staffed by men and women who have been in journalism, so they can be penetrated by people who have already been recruited to the Soviet cause or by the recruitment of staff already in position. Such information officers see and hear a great deal more than the material they are permitted to announce or issue as hand-outs and may have access to highly secret data when serving in defence or foreign service departments. When senior enough to take part in deciding what should be released they are perfectly placed to serve as agents of influence and can also leak to other known agents of influence or to media people likely to act as 'willies'.

The most recent case involving the suborning of an information officer in the Soviets' 'long march through the institutions' is that of the Norwegian Arne Treholt, who was a section head of the Information Department in Norway's Foreign Ministry and was sentenced to twenty years' imprisonment on 20 June 1985. The court also ordered the confiscation of £99,000 which, it decided, he had been paid by his Soviet spy-masters. According to the evidence, Treholt had been recruited to the KGB service through blackmail after taking part in a sexual orgy and being surreptitiously photographed in 1975. He told the police that, when faced with compromising photographs he had no option but to help the KGB, though he later withdrew that statement, alleging that it had been made under pressure. The court decided that for almost ten years, while he was a civil servant and later a diplomat and deputy Minister, he had loyally followed the instructions given by his KGB contacts. He had handed over classified documents about NATO's plans to defend northern Norway in the event of a Soviet attack. He had also informed the Kremlin about oil developments in the North Sea which were of strategic interest, apart from supplying a mass of information covering secret Foreign Ministry briefings, NATO intelligence assessments and details of confidential meetings between Norwegian Ministers and foreign political leaders including Lord Carrington, Henry Kissinger, Helmut Schmidt and Pierre Trudeau.[13] Norwegian security authorities are said to have suspected the existence of a high-level 'mole' for several years, but it seems likely that Treholt was finally detected as a result of information from a Soviet defector.

Treholt, then aged forty-one, was arrested on his way to meet Russian agents in Paris and was caught with a mass of classified documents which he had no proper reason to be taking out of the country. Among his contacts named at the trial was a KGB general, Gennadiy Titov, who had posed as a diplomat in the Soviet Embassy in Oslo and had been expelled in 1977.

Before Treholt, the classic case of an information officer using his sensitive position in the Soviet interest was that of the Frenchman Georges Pâques, who performed so many treacherous services that in 1964 he was sentenced to life imprisonment, later reduced to twenty years. Pâques, an intellectual, then aged fifty, was deputy head of the French section of NATO's press and information department at the headquarters, at that time in Paris. He had made contact with the Russians while in Algeria in 1944 and from then on supplied information of the greatest value. He fell under suspicion only when Marcel Challet, an officer of the French counter-intelligence service, the DST, went to Martinique for a secret meeting with the KGB defector Anatoli Golitsin, who was living in the US. Golitsin, known to the French by the code-name 'Martel', revealed that the KGB had obtained French military budget secrets, details of an American radar network to be set up in Turkey, de Gaulle's intentions regarding Algeria and his coming disengagement from NATO, and other valuable secrets. Golitsin did not know the name of the French spy who had supplied all the information, but Challet narrowed the suspects down to Pâques, who had held an important defence post, and he was convinced that Pâques was one of the French ring of senior Soviet spies known to Golitsin by the KGB code-name, 'Sapphire'.[14]

Pâques had become most productive when in his position in the NATO information service, and in the seven months before his arrest had provided details of NATO intentions as well as potted biographies on some 200 people for the KGB's files. He was put under surveillance and was seen to meet regularly with Vladimir Khrenov, an attaché in the Russian delegation to UNESCO. When arrested, on 10 August 1963, he was carrying a number of classified documents in a brief-case. Under interrogation Pâques confessed that he had been under continuous KGB control for nearly twenty years. In 1956 he had given the KGB details of the combined British-French-Israeli attack on Suez, and in 1961, details of French policy in the Berlin crisis, while in 1963 he had supplied NATO's overall plan to defend Europe against a surprise Soviet attack. Pâques gave so much about NATO files that the Moscow Centre was able to provide another of its agents with access to them with file code-numbers in the NATO Registry so that he could get them out and photograph them.[15] This other spy was the Canadian Hugh Hambleton, sentenced to ten years' imprisonment by a British court in December 1982.[16]

While Pâques had been busy on the Soviet Bloc's behalf in Paris, another information officer had been hard at work in London, though in a much less sensitive position. He was Arthur Bax, who had been head of the Labour Party's press department for sixteen years and was a close friend and confidant of some of the Party leaders. In 1961 information was received from a defector that he had been in regular receipt of substantial sums of money from the Czech Embassy, which was acting as a surrogate agency for the KGB. As I have related in more detail in my previous books, Bax was put under intensive surveillance and it was noticed that he paid regular visits to the entrance hall of a block of flats where there were pigeon-holes for the occupants' letters. A Czech intelligence officer was also in the habit of visiting the entrance hall and it was soon established that they were leaving envelopes for each other. A further watch established that Bax was part of a ring involving a New Zealander and the wife of a Swedish diplomat. Eventually, the Labour Party's deputy leader, George Brown, was supplied with records of telephone conversations, bank statements and evidence of meetings between Bax and Czech agents. When confronted, Bax initially denied all the allegations but, fearing exposure, he then confessed to Brown that he had been passing information about internal Labour affairs for at least four years. If Bax had not been detected he could have been a most valuable agent of influence when Labour came to power in 1964.[17]

Instances in which the KGB and the GRU have used their own information services, both in their Moscow ministries and their embassies abroad, to plant their agents are legion. In 1984 the US Government denied entry to Oleg Yermishkin, a so-called counsellor in the Information Department of the Foreign Ministry who was known to be a KGB officer. He had been selected to live in Los Angeles as head of the advance party supposed to be making arrangements for the arrival of Soviet athletes taking part in the Olympic Games there (from which Moscow eventually withdrew). The attempt to infiltrate Yermishkin is evidence that the International Department and the KGB will seize on any opportunity to infiltrate an agent into a sensitive area, Los Angeles being a centre of advanced technology.[18] In the same year, 1984, the Irish Government expelled three Russians for active-measures operations. One of them, Guennadi Saline, had been listed as a press attaché.

The United Nations Educational, Scientific and Cultural Organization (UNESCO) churns out an enormous amount of literature and, to a considerable extent, functions as a giant information department. Since it was first set up, with headquarters in Paris, in 1946 it has attracted left-wingers and crypto-Communists, many of them failed journalists. Over the years it has become so heavily politicized against the West, through penetration of its ranks by pro-Soviets, that the US has decided to withdraw its support and Britain looks like following suit at the time of writing. As could have been predicted, the projected British withdrawal has been bitterly opposed by the British far-left.

Because of the protection and cover they afford, all the major United Nations institutions have been heavily penetrated. Vadim Isakov, the KGB agent who played an active-measures role in the Great Missile Deception, was located in the United Nations Children's Fund (UNICEF) and when the proven KGB spy John Cairncross, who had worked in MI6, had to resign he fled to Italy and quickly found a refuge in the Food and Agriculture Organization.[19] Whole books have been published listing the abuse and manipulation of the United Nations by the Soviets.[20] The area most blatantly used for active measures and espionage is the main headquarters in New York. Arkady Shevchenko, who was an Under Secretary General there before his defection in 1978, has described the UN as a 'gold mine for Russian spying'. He estimates that of the 800 Soviet representatives working in New York, as many as 50 per cent operate in some way or other for the KGB and other intelligence organizations. Indeed, he has stated publicly that he renounced his membership of the Communist Party because of the 'monstrous abuses carried out by the KGB'.[21]

In spite of this and other exposures, the International Department and the KGB have not reduced the scale of their operations out of the United Nations and its offshoots, being unable to resist the facility, denied to ordinary diplomats, that renders UN staff free to travel, without restriction, in the countries where they are based. With its right to appoint so many Soviet officials, including such key personnel that even a special assistant to the Secretary General himself, over many years, was a KGB colonel, the Soviet Union is likely to increase the thrust of the secret offensive it wages through the medium of an organization designed to foster peace, goodwill and mutual assistance between all nations.[22]

Chapter 9

Seeing Red

'The medium is the message.'

Marshall McLuhan

A survey published by the BBC in April 1985 stated that 46 per cent of a random sample of people questioned thought that television 'sometimes deliberately misleads' while only 38 per cent regarded it as 'generally honest'.[1] In view of the anti-establishment, anti-American and generally pro-left attitude of certain programmes and certain presenters and producers one is, perhaps, surprised that the figure for those believing that television deliberately misleads was not much higher.

Reliable evidence of what goes on in the preparation and presentation of television documentaries – the main vehicles for imparting left-angled information and images – is available from several highly reputable and experienced professionals. One of these, who is sufficiently established to afford the luxury of being able to disclose his experience, is Alan Whicker who is, I believe, essentially non-political and has no axe to grind. In a book of memoirs Whicker is especially forthcoming about two particular programmes likely to exert considerable influence, especially on the young and the unquestioning. Writing about Granada's regular programme, 'World in Action', and Thames Television's 'TV Eye' (formerly 'This Week') he states:

These topical programmes, which presume to give objective truth unalloyed by the personal idiosyncrasies of a reporter, are in fact the most opinionated and politically slanted of all television series. 'World in Action' is usually a sort of Marxist party-political; 'TV Eye' is the predictable protest of the militant Left. On occasion they lay aside their political message and produce powerful and enterprising investigative journalism. More often they peddle the same old repetitive line and struggle to knock the pillars down: ridicule the Establishment, show the police as stumbling buffoons or brutal fascists, support the wreckers working to bring down our freedoms, to whom any riot or strike is a victory, attack all Centre and Right governments anywhere, avoid a constructive word about the US or a hurtful comment on a Communist state.[2]

These two programmes are far from being the only offenders. The BBC's 'Panorama' is frequently politically slanted, especially in programmes concerning nuclear weapons. Programmes written and presented by the left-wing Australian, John Pilger, sound and look like straightforward pro-Soviet propaganda, while those put out under the name of Jonathan Dimbleby usually have a strong militant-left flavour. After Pilger projected a programme called 'The Truth Game', in favour of unilateral nuclear disarmament, and which was lavishly praised by the Communist *Morning Star*, the journalist Max Hastings suggested a programme putting forward the multilateralist argument. Pilger is said to have objected on the grounds that the idea of balance was an 'old chestnut', a remark which brought the comment that in his 'Truth Game' only one side is allowed to play.

The difficulty of securing any retraction of false or distorted statements from the BBC or other television companies is even greater than with newspapers, which is problematical enough. This was demonstrated, most dramatically, in a now historic BBC 'Money Programme' in which Sir James Goldsmith declined to continue for something like half an hour until he had secured a most reluctant admission that a previous issue about his business had contained lies.[3]

The British Army's Director of Public Relations, Brigadier David Ramsbotham, was even less successful in securing any redress in 1982 after Granada Television had screened a programme called 'Private Darkins' Army' which, to the viewer, was heavily prejudiced against the Army, suggesting, in particular, that it was racially biased against black soldiers. Fearing an angled presentation, the producer was offered the opportunity to interview a coloured Regimental Sergeant-Major and other black NCOs but refused, restricting his discussion to black private soldiers who were likely to complain. Brigadier Ramsbotham's complaints served no purpose, for the damage to the Army had already been done.[4]

American television seems to be just as susceptible to political slanting to the Soviet advantage. A nationwide programme about the Russian Orthodox Church transmitted by NBC in 1980 misled the American public by what an academic critic called 'a large dose of propaganda'. The Russian Orthodox Church and its leaders in the Soviet Union are used by the active-measures operators to reach and subvert foreign religious groups, which is one reason why its existence is tolerated by the atheistic authorities. As will be seen, it is involved in the 'peace' offensive. The programme gave the impression that it is much freer than it really is and gave no indication of the discrimination and harassment to which its members are subjected or the severe restrictions imposed on its clergy.

British television and other media performed a most valuable service for the Politburo after a Soviet fighter pilot shot down a Korean airliner with the loss of 269 civilian lives in September 1983. The airliner had strayed into Soviet territory during an ordinary passenger flight and should have been instructed to leave or have been conducted away, as would have happened in any truly civilized part of the world. But such is the Soviet attitude to infringement of its borders and its readiness to use military force, that the pilot was given firm instructions from the ground to destroy the intruder. The Politburo and the International Department were quick to see the need for an immediate active-measures operation to limit the international damage resulting from the almost universal horror at such ruthlessness and lack of concern for innocent life. The response was a claim that the Korean machine had been deliberately involved in a highly irresponsible espionage venture by the CIA which was, therefore, totally to blame for the disaster. This patently absurd thesis, which could have been promulgated only by an organization hardened by years of official lying, and which in no way excused the callousness of the Soviet behaviour, would have been seen for what it was but for the fact that it was swallowed and elaborated by Western media. It was presented as a likely explanation by a journal called *Defence Attaché* from which the argument was picked up by broadcasters and writers who repeated it, some with apparent glee, and embroidered it to such an extent that even the American space-shuttle was brought into the plot.[5] The British TV programme 'TV Eye' advanced the American espionage proposition at length and with clear belief, leaving in the minds of many viewers the probability that the Russians had been provoked into the only possible response. Since then Communist newspapers and agencies have replayed the totally unfounded allegations as established fact.

In November 1984 the spurious basis of the Western publicity was exposed when Korean Airlines sued *Defence Attaché* for implying that it was willing to disregard the welfare and safety of passengers and staff to involve itself in such an exercise.[6] It received substantial damages and a public apology, but the lengthy argument and the doubt it sowed greatly assisted the Soviet authorities to ride the outcry long enough for it to recede in the public memory, along with the other atrocities perpetrated in Afghanistan, Czechoslovakia and Hungary. The brevity of the Western reaction to the deliberate murder of 269 passengers in a civilian airliner provided the International Department with further evidence that it can safely work on the principle that, however outrageously the Soviets behave, the West will soon forgive them or come to terms with the fact that they have won and that nothing can be done about it. The Western attitude to the barbarous behaviour of the Soviet troops in Afghanistan, who have killed thousands of men, women and children and forced four million into exile, has confirmed Moscow's cynical attitude that a sufficient degree of forgiveness will always be forthcoming from freedom-loving peoples yearning for peace at almost any price. Given only a little time, the West can be guaranteed to forgive and forget and even to solve the Politburo's recurrent crisis by providing cheap grain and butter, thereby releasing roubles for the next stage of the offensive.

The Politburo, under its new-look leader, Mikhail Gorbachov, has signalled its continuing ruthlessness through its uncompromising attitude to the cold-blooded murder of an American military liaison officer, Major Arthur Nicholson, after he was shot by a Soviet sentry in March 1985 while carrying out duties to which the Soviets had agreed.[7] Again, the Kremlin offered no apology and showed no remorse. Major Nicholson's purpose, like that of Soviet counterparts operating on NATO territory, was to watch for any signs of clandestine mobilization.

The television survey which I have already mentioned disclosed that Channel 4 of British television was 'most often expected to be anti-establishment'. While that channel, which is wholly owned by the Independent Broadcasting Authority (IBA), occasionally permits some anti-left views to be expressed, nobody who watches it regularly can be left in doubt that some of those in command there are left-inclined and, in some cases, extremely so. This has led to comments by political observers, such as George Gale of the *Daily Express*, who wonder why Lord Whitelaw, who set up Channel 4, should be so content with its success when it is such a 'subversive influence' against the Government's policies.

In the spring of 1985, when Channel 4 produced an essentially anti-British series called 'End of Empire', the venom was injected even into the heavy advertising which accompanied the programmes. In relation to the episode covering the fall of Singapore someone injected the question in a full-page newspaper advertisement, 'Would you stand up for the National Anthem after tonight's episode?' Little opportunity to promote anti-establishment and anti-patriotic thought seems to be missed.

In 1983 there was strong reaction to a Channel 4 programme called 'Ireland – the Silent Voices', which included an interview with an IRA terrorist and scenes of street fights in Ulster from a film previously banned by the BBC and ITV. The IBA, which, since its inception, has been loaded with members from the left, considered the programme to be 'satisfactory'. The IBA had been equally unrepentant about a previous programme screened by Thames Television in September 1977 called 'Life Behind the Wire'. It showed detainees inside the Long Kesh prison receiving instructions on the use of firearms in preparation for their release or their escape. It contained interviews with IRA sympathizers. Under the Independent Broadcasting Authority Act the IBA has powers to ban such programmes but regularly fails to use them, as it also does concerning the foul language and smut which characterize many of the programmes it controls.

The IBA took no action to prevent the screening of a programme in November 1983 which attacked Britain's role in the Falklands war and had been made by an Argentinian film crew. It contained interviews with Anthony Wedgwood Benn and others who could be guaranteed to criticise the British Government.

In February 1985 the IBA did move to ban a Channel 4 programme about the involvement of MI5 in phone-tapping and surveillance of suspect trade unionists and members of the Campaign for Nuclear Disarmament (CND), but all the ban did was to intensify the interest in the programme when the ban was lifted and it was screened in the following month.[9] I was involved in the programme, and in a subsequent film made by the same producers, and my own experience confirmed to me the left-wing bias which had led to its production in the first place. The programme arose out of a letter sent to the progressive magazine *New Society* by a former woman member of MI5 called Cathy Massiter.[10] Miss Massiter made it obvious in her letter that she had been disenchanted with certain aspects of her work in MI5 and she was visited by the two eventual producers of the programme, who recorded her views on film. I was then interviewed concerning my general views about MI5 and, while only a fragment of the material recorded at my home was used, I was permitted to state that MI5 was performing the task required of it when it covered the activities of certain suspects in CND and, in view of CND's practice of spying on cruise missile convoys and interfering with their movements, they should be neither surprised nor angry. The remainder of the programme centred on Miss Massiter's allegations that MI5 was exceeding its duties and infringing what she referred to as its 'charter'. The second programme, which allowed Miss Massiter to repeat her main charges against MI5, was also pre-recorded and almost everything of consequence which I said during the discussion with three others and a chairman was deleted by the producers. I made a point of saying that Miss Massiter should never have been recruited to MI5 because the work required cannot be effectively performed by anyone so concerned with 'civil liberties'. I pointed out that what CND supporters did was to assist Soviet active measures, whether wittingly or not. I explained that it was a hopeless situation if MI5 had to wait for someone to commit a criminal act before surveillance became possible and that the security service had to work on suspicion, when this had been aroused. I mentioned that Quisling and others who became traitors to their countries had committed no criminal acts to begin with. None of this appeared in the programme, but

136

those who were hostile to any surveillance of trade-union leaders or CND people seemed to have been allowed their full say.[11]

Another way in which television is frequently 'loaded' in the left-wing political interest is by the rigging of the audience in discussion programmes where there is to be audience participation. Such an audience is supposed to be representative of the majority but, all too often, extremists are planted in it with prior instructions as to when to intervene, or the chairman may ensure that they are called. Nicholas Winterton, the Conservative MP for Macclesfield, has put on record an extreme case in which he took part in Bradford, a town with many coloured immigrants, in June 1981 when the Nationality Bill was passing through Parliament. Referring to the programme put out by Yorkshire Television, Winterton wrote:

> It was clear to me, as it must have been to any reasonable viewer, that the preponderance of people in the audience were biased against any dispassionate discussion . . . and deaf to all entreaties for reasonable dialogue. In short the audience had been 'rigged'. . . . The ugly scenes of near riot, not witnessed by the TV viewers, which occurred before the programme could even begin, and the scenes of vituperative anger and abuse which were broadcast could have been nothing but prejudicial to the advancement of good race relations. . . .[12]

The programme, which was broadcast nationwide, was prefaced by a newsreel suggesting that there was a major general problem of racism in Britain. When an Asian suggested that only a small minority of activists and agitators were responsible for unrest in some coloured communities he was abused and two members of the audience advanced on him, threateningly, and his point of view was not pursued by the presenter of the programme.

Television producers and presenters may argue that their purpose is simply to generate the maximum degree of discord to make the programmes exciting, but, whether this be true or not, it serves the left-wing purpose and the Soviet purpose when they stimulate violence and any ensuing riots and disorders are rescreened abroad, including in the Iron Curtain countries.

If the television documentary provides scope for political slanting, the 'drama documentary', with actors playing contrived scenes allegedly representing reality, offers even wider opportunity to the writer and producer. Typical of this device was 'Death of a Princess', made for ATV in 1980, which inflicted enormous damage on Britain's trade and other interests in the Middle East. It was presented as a dramatized reconstruction of the love-affair and death by execution of a Saudi Arabian princess and her lover which had occurred in 1977. Written by Anthony Thomas, it was described by Alan Whicker, who admires him as a brilliant handler of cameras, as 'one of the least truthful pictures to be transmitted on television . . . a collection of unsubstantiated gossip and hearsay'.[13] *The Times* called it 'a salacious detective story fallaciously presented as fact'.[14]

When the programme received advance publicity, a lawyer acting for the Saudi Arabian Embassy asked to see it and the Saudi Foreign Minister expressed his deep concern. Saudi Arabia is one of Britain's biggest overseas customers, an employer of British labour abroad and a creator of employment in Britain. Yet when it was suggested that some particularly offensive and untrue scenes should be removed, ATV rejected the proposal on the grounds that it would infringe the freedom of the media and the artistic integrity of the producer.[15] It became obvious that the showing of the programme would be likely to damage Britain's trade links and friendship with the Saudi Royal Family on which they depend. In the event it wrecked relations not only with Saudi Arabia, which could have withdrawn its huge financial assets from London, but with the Gulf states, which felt that the programme was an insult to Islam as a whole. Contracts worth many millions were cancelled, the British Ambassador was expelled, and a Royal visit had to be postponed.

Programmes projected as fictional drama are also frequently angled to produce a political effect on the viewer, the commonest, perhaps, being those which show the police or prison authorities as being excessively hostile and violent, especially against coloured people. Even the situation comedy may be charged with political content by the left-wing writer or producer.

Normally television news bulletins are presented objectively and ITN seems to be particularly punctilious in that respect. They do occasionally fall victim to what appears to be political slanting, the most recent example being the treatment of the over-sensationalized discovery that the father of Princess Michael of Kent had been a member of the Nazi Party and had held the rank of major in the SS. The source of this information turned out to be a left-wing

138

sociology lecturer who had been a branch secretary of the International Socialists, a revolutionary group now called the Socialist Workers' Party.[16] He had dug up a document in a library and on that slender evidence, which proved to be highly misleading, television news bulletins presented the discovery along with old pictures of concentration camps with piles of emaciated bodies being hauled off to the gas chambers. No apology seemed to be forthcoming when further documents proved that the Princess's father, Baron von Reibnitz, had never been connected in any way with crimes committed by the SS, in which he had been given honorary rank in the cavalry section. He had even been expelled from the Nazi Party in 1944 for what must have been a courageous disagreement about its policies.

Count Hans Huyn has recorded how, after a group of far-left demonstrators in Berlin had attempted to convince the public there, in September 1981, that the US was planning a limited nuclear war in Europe, he had flown to Washington on business. There on radio and television a main item was the burning of an American flag in Berlin, shown three times in the space of an hour. As Huyn comments, the effect could only have been to cause Americans to think that if that was how Berliners responded to the way American troops had preserved their freedom from Soviet take-over, then the forces should be brought home.[17]

What appears to the viewer to be the straightforward television coverage of events can be highly advantageous to active measures being pursued by the Soviet Union. The interest generated by the 'peace women' at the Greenham Common cruise missile base owes a great deal to the zealous, nationwide exposure of their activities by television news bulletins and documentary programmes. Television cameras seem to be present at almost every 'demo' and are well placed where the most militant attempt to enter the base using wire-clippers or are lying down to prevent the entry or exit of vehicles. The demonstrations seem to be staged essentially to secure the television coverage which has stimulated the growth in CND membership and elevated people with modest attributes to national figures.

It is largely through television that militant trade-union leaders, who would otherwise have remained known only for their normal duties, have been overblown into national figures whose comments are sought on various political issues and who invariably use the opportunities for their own purposes. The coverage given to Arthur Scargill during the miners' strike was unprecedented. Day after day – often several times each day – he was given the opportunity to promote his false claims and his anti-government, militant-left propaganda in what was, without reasonable doubt, an effort staged by him to depose the democratically elected government.

Such Western coverage of events of political significance, and especially those showing the police in action against miners or 'peace' women, are recycled on Soviet television after suitable treatment in the way of cuts and commentary. It greatly assists the International Department in its routine requirement to show the Soviet people how fortunate they are to be caged in a country where such demonstrations are never allowed.

While producers and senior executives of the BBC and the independent television companies can arrange for programmes to be angled in their political interest, they can also exert powerful left-wing interest in another way – by ensuring that performers who would like to present the anti-Communist or anti-Socialist view are not allowed to do so. That delightful entertainer, Michael Bentine, who breathes sincerity, has put on record how, in 1963, he was approached by a senior official at the BBC and was plainly told that it would be a fine thing if he used his programme 'It's a Square World', for 'bashing the Establishment' meaning the Macmillan Government. In his memoirs Bentine wrote, 'I was told that I would be backed up to the hilt by the hierarchy if I complied. My unexpected refusal made me most unpopular and my BBC career came to an abrupt halt.' As a former intelligence officer who maintains some contact with sources, Bentine may be more sensitive than most to the motivation behind such attempted manipulation. He remains convinced that he was blacklisted for insisting that his show should remain apolitical.[18]

A casualty from similar causes and one whose case is more closely documented is Hughie Green, the creator and presenter of the highly popular programme 'Opportunity Knocks', which ran for sixteen years and discovered much new talent in the entertainment world. Hughie Green is in no doubt whatever that his programme was brought to an abrupt end in January 1977 because he had showed himself to be too patriotic. Patriotism is regarded as 'reactionary' and 'right-wing' by the left-wing producers and executives of television who prefer 'internationalism', a Soviet active-measures catch-word with the accent on the catch. For its part, the IBA regards patriotism as 'political' though it has demonstrated no objection to the consistent angling of documentaries and other shows in the political interest of the left.

While the steady take-over of the television channels by the left-inclined had become obvious to Hughie Green, it did not affect his programme seriously until December 1972 when he staged 'Opportunity Knocks' on and around a Polaris missile-carrying submarine.

Because of the huge audiences attracted by 'Opportunity Knocks', Hughie Green was asked by the Royal Navy, in 1972, to present a programme on the Polaris missile submarine, *HMS Revenge*. The Navy's purpose was to secure some publicity for its part in maintaining the nuclear deterrent policy which, at that time, had helped to preserve peace in Europe for twenty-seven years. The venue was so unusual and so inviting that Green agreed and a script was prepared in collaboration with a Royal Navy team headed by Rear-Admiral Tony Troup, Flag Officer Submarines. Close Naval scrutiny was essential because of the security problems with cameras aboard what was then an extremely secret vessel, but an agreed script was prepared and Green and his team travelled to the Polaris base at Faslane in Scotland.[19]

Two hours before the filming was due to take place aboard the submarine, Green and his director were telephoned from Thames Television's headquarters in London to be told that the IBA had cut two-thirds of the script, which had been approved in detail by the Navy and also had the approval of the Secretary of State for Defence. In attempting to do this the IBA was in breach of its governing regulations which clearly state that it may not censor 'items inserted at the request, or under the authority, of a Minister of the Crown'. Green was told that he was not to say or indicate that he was on a Polaris submarine and was not to suggest that such submarines were needed because others, meaning the Russians, had them too.

As the agreed script had been available to the IBA for at least a fortnight it was clear that someone had taken a late look at it and had not liked the publicity in favour of Britain's deterrent. There was no Labour Party objection to it because it had not only accepted the necessity for the Polaris fleet but within two years, when Harold

Wilson became Prime Minister again, his government would invest a further £1,000 million in the weapon system. It would seem to me, as it seemed to Green, that somebody in the IBA, an official or a member, had a personal objection to the publicity.[20]

In view of the effort which the Navy had already put into the programme and the involvement of Navy and Defence Ministry officials at the highest level, Green was extremely embarrassed when he had to tell the Commodore in charge at Faslane of the IBA instructions he had just received. The Commodore telephoned Admiral Troup and after consultations with the Defence Ministry the IBA was told that it had no right to interfere with a script already approved by a Minister or under his authority. The programme then went ahead with virtually no cuts, to the great satisfaction of the Navy and millions of viewers who were given an insight into the intricacies of the Polaris missile system which had not been disclosed before. Admiral Troup congratulated Green in a letter on a fine show, 'in spite of the IBA's efforts'.[21]

A year later Green staged another 'Opportunity Knocks' programme on and around the Concorde supersonic airliner at a time when a mass of false accusations and disinformation about the machine was being given wide publicity in newspapers and on radio and television. It was being alleged that the machine would permanently damage the upper atmosphere and create unacceptable pollution and noise at airports, all of which has been proved false by its remarkable record in service. Green's programme, which took cameras on to the flight-deck, in flight and for the landing, gave millions of viewers an armchair ride in the exciting aeroplane, and gave experts the opportunity to rebut the damaging accusations which were being strongly supported by the Labour Party, which had never approved of the Concorde project.

Several months later Green, accompanied by his manager, met a senior executive of Thames Television who immediately told him that he would have stopped the Concorde programme had he been given the opportunity. He criticised Green for failing to 'kill' Concorde. Green's contract had three years to run but, after that meeting, he told his manager that he felt sure that his contract would not be renewed.[22]

The last straw for the left-wingers was Green's presentation of 'Opportunity Knocks' on 3 January 1977 in which he spoke up stir-

142

ringly, and perhaps somewhat emotionally, for freedom under true democracy and for a drive to restore Britain's economic greatness through a renewed will to work in industry and commerce. Making his final speech a 'farewell to 1976', he tried to convince his 7 million viewers of the indisputable fact that the only way to prevent the continuing foreign loans, which could have bankrupted Britain, was through hard work and a regeneration of independent spirit. The programme brought 23,000 letters of praise but from the IBA it brought condemnation which seemed to be welcomed by many in Thames Television. Green was told that 'Opportunity Knocks' was finished and he claims that he has been barred from British television ever since.

There was an immediate sequel when the Philips record company decided to issue a recording of a patriotic song called 'Stand up and be Counted', with which he had ended the final 'Opportunity Knocks' programme. The record was made and Green announced that any royalties accruing to him would go to charity, but it never made the charts because radio programmes were barred from playing it. Both the IBA and the BBC denied that they had issued any instructions banning the record, but I have seen a memorandum, originating from a representative of the IBA, to Radio Clyde in Glasgow, effectively barring any playing of the record and with an admission that the IBA was 'anxious to prevent any trade press publicity' about it.[23]

The television executives can argue — and probably will — that those like Hughie Green and Michael Bentine who have been forced out of television had simply had their day and had to make way for 'new blood' with a different appeal, but the viewing figures for their programmes would hardly support that contention. In any case there can be no doubt that television and radio in Britain today are deeply infiltrated by the left and the far left who are exerting deliberate political influence on the nature and content of programmes. The extent of the publicity given to Arthur Scargill during the miners' strike was convincing evidence, and it became very difficult for the most objective listener and viewer to avoid the conclusion that questioners and interviewers were hostile to the National Coal Board, the Government and the police. In my experience Alan Whicker was not exaggerating when he wrote, 'Industriously they scour the world for some enemy of Britain to encourage, lavishing sympathetic understanding on the masked man with the rocket. No hostility to the West is too obscure or wrong-headed for their attention, yet some off-screen reporter will fearlessly heckle a stunned 19-year-old trooper who has just been blown up.'[24]

The cause of every illegal immigrant is championed, often repeatedly, and when some of these have been proved to have been appalling liars little or nothing has been done to put the record straight. Publicity usually seems to be forthcoming for legal immigrants with a grouse or grudge and support is given to the deliberate promotion of social and financial goals for blacks – usually referred to as 'aspirations' – which are clearly unattainable and are calculated to engender disappointment and anger among those who fail to achieve their so-called 'just demands'. During the riots and disorders of 1981 and on other occasions when there have been confrontations between blacks and the police, claims of 'police brutality' have been given prominence while little if anything has been said about the extent to which the disorders were encouraged by revolutionary groups like the Socialist Workers' Party and the Militant Tendency.

Has the infiltration and the political slanting any direct connection with the Soviet secret offensive being waged through active measures? I have no doubt that much of it is home-grown. Many of the infiltrators and the slanters are Communists, crypto-Communists and other left extremists pursuing their own political purposes with no need of any assistance or guidance from overseas. They are the modern equivalent of what Lenin is said to have called 'useful idiots' – those who do the Kremlin's work for it on their own initiative and, in some cases, without realizing the fact. Nevertheless there is evidence that the KGB, and its previous equivalents, have always rated the penetration of the BBC as being a high-priority objective. The evidence of defectors and of some British spies who were recruited as Soviet agents shows that the BBC has long been high on its target list, and this must also apply to the independent networks.[25] Agents of influence recruited there or infiltrated after recruitment can perform cumulative services, and the BBC, in particular, has been regarded by the KGB as a good jumping-off ground for service in more sensitive departments. Guy Burgess, for example, worked in the BBC before serving as an agent-runner in MI5 and as a full-blown spy in the Foreign Office.

144

This KGB interest is confirmed by the decision by MI5, the counter-espionage agency, to set up a special desk to deal with subversion in television, radio and the other media and by MI5's long-standing arrangement to vet candidates for BBC posts which are politically sensitive. MI5 may have no power to apply similar precautions to senior staff of the independent television companies, but, if it hasn't, I am satisfied that security and accuracy would benefit if it had.[26]

Chapter 10

The Disinformation Game

'Disinformation is not just lying; it is expected to serve as a subtle means of inducing another government to do what the Kremlin wants it to do or to frighten or bluff a foreign government into inaction or into making a concession to the USSR.'

Statement by a former KGB officer, cited in
The US Military Review

Disinformation, a translation of the Russian word *dezinformatsia*, is an ancient technique of deception comprising various ways of disseminating false or misleading information to discredit or undermine adversary governments, individuals or institutions. Ever since Lenin enjoined his followers to 'induce the West to believe what they want to believe' it has been refined by the Soviet Union into one of the central components of its active measures. To be credible, a disinformation operation should be based on some degree of reality, and the material involved should, in part, be genuine. It is also more likely to be successful if the target wants to believe it. Disinformation operations therefore offer great scope for ingenuity and the game has become a speciality among KGB and International Department officers.

False rumour, slander and innuendo can be disseminated orally with great effect, especially when reinforced by radio reports transmitted either by radio stations under Soviet control or by stations prepared to broadcast planted material. Thus when Saudi Arabian dissidents seized the Grand Mosque in Mecca in 1979, Soviet diplomats stationed in many capitals, working to an order from the International Department, used their agents of influence to spread the rumour that the CIA was behind it, thereby stirring up profound anti-American feeling among the millions of devout Muslims who felt affronted. This totally false allegation received support when the American Embassy in Islamabad was burned. Soviet agents spread the rumour that the Pakistani Army had justifiably set fire to the Embassy as a reprisal for the CIA's part in defiling the Grand Mosque.[1]

Examples of the direct use and indirect manipulation of television to spread disinformation have already been given. Most Soviet disinformation, however, is still generated in written form, through the controlled Communist media and journalistic agents of influence elsewhere, as already described in connection with the character assassination of Franz Josef Strauss and other cases, and through forgeries, which will be considered in some detail later in this chapter.

Whenever possible, active-measures agents aim for a 'multiple sell' – the printing of the material in more than one reputable newspaper or magazine. A 'double sell' is often achieved simply through the habit of some journalists of hunting in pairs. When specialist writers, and especially those on foreign assignments, have to cover a large field, two of them may share their information to reduce the risk that either of them will be scooped. If one 'buys' some disinformation then the other is likely to print it too and this gives the story added credibility, especially if the newspapers are reputable, as they often are. As very much a 'lone wolf' operator in Fleet Street, I was surprised at the extent to which the sharing of information is practised, though all editors frown on it. When doubt exists in the mind of the reporter who first receives the information, the agreement of a colleague that it is a 'good story' is likely to strengthen his courage in writing it as news.

A successful disinformation plant can exert a long-lasting effect through the cuttings libraries maintained by all newspapers. The first thing a good journalist does when pursuing a lead is to send for the relevant cuttings to see whether the story is new or, if it is not, what help the cuttings can provide in developing it. When false stories are not effectively denied they remain in newspaper offices as part of the historic record. As Sir James Goldsmith put it to the

147

Media Committee, 'Once the press cuttings have been polluted by propaganda the false information will be repeated quite innocently and, as it is repeated, will gather further credibility and momentum.'[2] Formerly, when cuttings were stored in envelopes, a false story might be marked with a red card stating that it had been effectively denied, but this has become more difficult with the switch to the storage of cuttings on microfilm. Among Soviet disinformation stories likely to exert continuing effect are the lie that the shot-down Korean airliner was conducting a CIA espionage operation, the blaming of the Nazis for the execution of 4,000 Polish officers by the forerunner of the KGB at Katyn, near Smolensk in 1940, the false description of the neutron warhead as a capitalist bomb which kills people but saves buildings and the fiction that the Strategic Defence Initiative, the so-called 'Star Wars', is an American plot to threaten people with nuclear weapons in space.[3]

Some disinformation exercises are short-lived because they quickly achieve their main objective. The KGB defector, Dzhirkvelov, has described how, while working as a 'journalist' in the Sudan, he received articles which had been concocted by the KGB and revealed apparently scandalous connections between the East African branch of the US Peace Corps, a body of social workers set up by President Kennedy to work in undeveloped countries, and the CIA. He was able to pay local journalists to run the articles, which were then reprinted elsewhere, and the Peace Corps became so discredited locally that it withdrew its services.[4] Most disinformation operations, however, are long-lasting and rely on cumulative effects rather than spectacular actions. The continuing active-measures campaign to limit the damage to the Soviet image abroad from the Politburo's failure to implement the human rights aspects of the Helsinki Accord is an example. The International Department has used the upside-down ploy by arguing that Communism provides the only human rights that matter in the form of employment, housing, food and medical care – all inadequate by Western standards – and that the freedoms by which the West sets such store, such as freedom of speech, movement and worship, home ownership and civil liberties in general, are 'bourgeois' and therefore irrelevant. The same ploy is invoked to suggest that it is the British and the Americans who are violating human rights by using the police to control riots and violence on picket lines. Soviet propaganda has found a rich seam in the anti-apartheid campaign against South Africa while blanketing, as far as it can, human-rights violations in Afghanistan and Soviet racism against Jews, Balts and other ethnic minorities in the Soviet Union itself. To quote a further example, suggested by Hans Huyn, 'To spread disinformation on Chile, Moscow has mounted a campaign costing hundreds of millions while hardly anyone gets to know about the tens of thousands killed and the atrocious conditions in punishment camps in the Marxist state of Mozambique.'[5]

A detailed example of the trouble which Soviet-Bloc disinformers will take to achieve a success is provided by the first-hand experience of Major Ladislav Bittman, who defected from the Czech intelligence service in 1968 after fourteen years of specializing in such operations. In a complicated operation in May 1964, code-named 'Neptune', four chests filled with blank paper were lowered into a lake in Czechoslovakia where a television crew was on hand in connection with a troop exercise which had been specially staged to get them there. Frogmen, allegedly taking part in the exercise, 'discovered' the crates and the television team photographed them, though they remained unopened. Meanwhile, the KGB had supplied the Operation Neptune team with a mass of genuine Gestapo and SS documents which had been captured during the war. The documents had been selected to show the Germans at their worst, and Operation Neptune's purpose was to provide an excuse for resurrecting the anti-German feeling generally and among NATO's allies in particular. The Czech Minister of the Interior, Lubomir Strougal, and the Party Secretary, Antonin Novotny, approved the operation and after the initial publicity about the 'discovery' Strougal gave a press conference about the documents which led to widespread publicity in both the West and East. The tone of the reporting was suitably anti-German and the operation was judged to have been particularly successful in Italy, France and Austria. As Bittman has recalled, the media projected the line – 'look what those German bastards did to us during the war and there are so many of them still living in Germany'.[6]

Bittman has also revealed how the Soviet Bloc will deliberately mislead its own press to plant disinformation in the West, especially about the true strength of military forces. The Czech press was given distorted information about the true military strength of the Czech

Army in the hope that it would be picked up by Western analysts, as it was. At the same time double agents were pressed into service to confirm these false facts and figures by feeding in similar data from their 'secret sources'.[7]

As already indicated, in connection with the Great Missile Deception, such double agents are essential for any ongoing disinformation operation to feed back the results so that the planners can judge how the operation is progressing, make any modifications to keep it on track and capitalize on any unforeseen opportunity. The KGB and International Department field officers are expected to perform this function, but detailed and accurate feed-back often depends on spies and moles planted in government departments of the target countries, as Geoffrey Prime was planted in GCHQ and 'Fedora' in the FBI.

The active-measures chiefs do not neglect the value of books as prime sources of disinformation in view of their ongoing influence through libraries and paperback editions. The few defectors from the West, like Philby, and Soviet spies recovered through exchanges of prisoners, such as Gordon Lonsdale, are pressed into service. Philby's best-selling memoirs, *My Silent War*, for instance, are loaded with disinformation, some of it subtle but some obvious to those with knowledge of his true treacherous activities while in the service of MI6.

In addition to the criminal activities of murder, robbery, blackmail and slander, to which the KGB descends to serve the Politburo's purposes, it also regularly indulges in forgery. From the start of the Cold War the Soviet Union has made use of forged documents to blacken its Western adversaries and has used its satellites, especially East Germany and Czechoslovakia, to do such work for it under KGB supervision. Soviet experience in the production and issue of forgeries dates back to the 1920s but this chapter will deal only with recent, proven forgeries; of the large number available for study I have selected some two dozen to show the extent and variety of this method of deception, which is branded as criminal in all civilized countries.

Service A of the KGB has some autonomy in the production of forgeries but there is usually consultation with the International Department before any are circulated and, in the case of those involving major political figures, the agreement of the Politburo must be obtained. It is as though the British Cabinet met round the table to discuss the manufacture and placement of forged documents to blacken their adversaries. Yet, remembering that the same men of the Politburo gather round the table to decide whether particular adversaries should be assassinated, one should not be too surprised.[8]

In recent years the use of forgeries has increased as they have become more sophisticated and therefore more difficult to expose. Some are total forgeries of imaginary documents which look official and may have been reproduced on official paper supplied by KGB agents of influence with access to the necessary stationery. Others are genuine documents which have been doctored to give a false impression. In most instances the documents eventually circulated are photocopies in which the alterations are difficult to detect. In the mid-1970s, for unknown reasons, the Soviets refrained from using forgeries but in 1976, perhaps after a protracted examination of their value, they resumed their use as an integral element of their active-measures operations. Since then there has been a marked improvement in the quality of the forged documents. There has also been a concentration of the effort to use them to disrupt relations between the US and its Western European allies. In 1982 the FBI was detecting such forgeries at the rate of about one a month.[9]

The most common method of surfacing a forgery is to post it anonymously to a newspaper or individual journalist and hope that it will be projected as a news story without verification, as sometimes happens. The reporter's interest may be stimulated by a false stamp of 'Top Secret' on the document. A covering letter to enhance authenticity may be included, the spurious author usually giving personal outrage as the reason for his action. It may carry a fictitious signature or the author may pretend that he is an official who dare not risk exposure by signing the letter. To secure rapid publication without time for verification, the sender may hint that other newspapers have the document.

The Soviets try, above all, to entrap highly respected publications which are not tainted as being sympathetic to the left, as a forgery planted there is much more likely to be believed and to be recycled by other papers. To quote John Barron, who has made a special study of active-measures forgeries:

151

In the Federal Republic of Germany the prestigious magazine *Der Spiegel* has served as an outlet for blatant disinformation, as has the popular magazine *Der Stern*. In September 1969 both magazines published articles based on documents purporting to outline Top Secret U.S. contingency plans. The documents suggested that, should Soviet forces overrun Western Europe, the U.S. would devastate the continent by waging bacteriological and nuclear warfare. They were mailed from Rome by an unknown source whose signature was illegible. They were copies rather than originals and therefore not subject to technical tests that would prove their fraudulence. *Der Spiegel* did, subsequently, acknowledge that the documents were fruits of a KGB disinformation operation.

Der Stern in its issue of 1 September 1970, published another incendiary fabrication ostensibly based on a secret American *Handbook of Nuclear Yield Requirements* which the magazine claimed came from a 'Big Unknown'. This fabrication alleged that in wartime the U.S. intended to blow up more than a thousand civilian targets in Western Europe as well as in Egypt, Syria, Irak and Iran.[10]

The perpetrators work on the principle that no denial will ever completely offset the damage inflicted by news stories based on a forgery, especially as there are so many people who want to believe the worst. Indeed, once a forgery has been published, especially by a reputable newspaper without Communist connections, it acquires a credibility of its own and will be filed in the cuttings libraries of newspapers where it remains permanently available to be used again. Forgeries are also circulated privately to reach political leaders, agents of influence and opinion-makers and these are difficult to neutralize by denial.

As with all active measures, the main target for forgeries is the US. Presidents, Vice-Presidents and other very senior officials of the American Government have been victims. A forged tape-recording of a telephone talk between President Reagan and Margaret Thatcher which allegedly took place during the Falklands conflict surfaced, along with a transcript of it, shortly before the British general election in June 1983. It was sent to two Dutch newspapers in the hope that, having been published by them, the story would be picked up by the American and British press and radio. The tape carried the true voices of Mrs Thatcher and President Reagan and examination showed that they had been spliced together from various speeches, the joins being covered by intrusive ringing telephone tones and other contrived interference. The transcript, which was in Dutch, claimed that the tape confirmed suspicions that the Argentine cruiser *Belgrano* had been torpedoed on the express instructions of Mrs Thatcher after it was moving away from the battle zone. Analysis of the tape left little doubt in the minds of CIA officials that the whole forgery was the work of the KGB's Service A.

Between the contrived interference Reagan's voice could be heard saying, 'If there is a conflict we shall fire missiles at our allies to see to it that the Soviet Union stays within its borders.' Mrs Thatcher could then be heard saying, incredulously, 'You mean Germany?' The President then replied, 'Mrs Thatcher, if any country endangers our position we can decide to bomb the problem area and so remove the instability.' The forgers' intention was to suggest that radioactive areas would be deliberately created in West Germany to stem a Soviet advance. At the end Mrs Thatcher could be heard saying that she had organized the sinking of the *Belgrano* to prevent any possibility of an agreement with Argentina to which Reagan, allegedly, responded with 'Oh God!' Reagan's words had been extracted and doctored from a long address on nuclear strategy. His 'Oh God!' was really the beginning of his quote from a hymn, 'O God of love, O King of Peace'.[11]

The forgery was too overdone to fool the Dutch journalists who received it and it was not printed. Its contents were, however, widely circulated verbally and may have contributed to the Labour Party's repeated accusation that the *Belgrano* had been sunk to sabotage peace negotiations with Argentina and may also have helped to damage relations between Argentina and the US. The deception was a follow-up operation to a totally forged newsrelease from the Pentagon, dated 5 May 1982, which had been widely circulated in the following month. It purported to be remarks by Caspar Weinberger, the US Secretary for Defense, regarding support for Britain during the Falklands crisis, its prime purpose being to damage relations between the US and the Argentine and those South American states supporting Argentinian claims to the Falklands. Weinberger was shown as referring to 'Argentine's stubborn and selfish attitude' and defending 'military assistance to . . . our British ally'. It mentioned the sharing of intelligence information and alluded to Anglo-American combat planning. Copies had been sent to the Argentine Ambassador in Washington and to Argentinian officials in Buenos Aires. They were denounced as a total fabrication by the Pentagon and, almost certainly, the work of Service A.[12]

Weinberger has been a frequent target. In 1984 a Beirut newspaper published a fake transcript of a meeting between him and the Saudi Arabian Defence Minister. Weinberger was quoted as offering advanced weapons, like new tanks which were not then in service with the US Army. Mayor Ed Koch of New York, a Jew who supports Israel, used the transcript to attack Weinberger who is thought to be pro-Arab.[13]

In July 1983 the left-wing Italian weekly, *Pace e Guerra*, reprinted a fake telegram alleged to have originated from the American Ambassador in Rome, Maxwell Rabb. The telegram was alleged to have stated: 'As was to be expected, our operations on Bulgaria's connection with the attempt on the Pope's life has led to complete success. European mass media have enthusiastically developed the preliminary worked-out thesis.' The telegram, which was, clearly, part of the KGB's active-measures operation to involve the CIA in the shooting of the Pope, was denounced as a forgery but this did not prevent the *Morning Star* from using it two months later in an article denouncing Mr Rabb.[14]

1983 was a big year for Soviet forgeries planted in many different countries. In February the Madrid news magazine *Tiempo* published excerpts alleged to be from a memorandum of the American National Security Council dating from 1978 in which the presidential adviser, Brzezinski, was said to have given President Carter details of a destabilization campaign against Poland. In the following month a press conference was called in Accra to accuse the American Embassy of trying to bring down the government of Ghana. The evidence was a report by the West German Embassy which the West German Government denounced as a complete fabrication. There were comparable anti-American operations in India.[15]

Earlier, in April 1982, the Belgian leftist weekly *De Nieuwe* published a copy of a forged document while numerous anti-nuclear demonstrations were in train. It purported to be a two-page letter from the NATO Supremo, General Al Haig, to the NATO General Secretary, Joseph Luns, discussing the possibility that NATO might

The anti-Communist West German politician Franz Josef Strauss addressing a meeting of the Christian Social Union Party. The Kremlin was determined to eliminate him from the political scene (*Camera Press*)

A photograph of the former KGB officer Ilya Dzhirkvelov on the false identity card issued to give him cover as a TASS agency correspondent while carrying out subversive work in the Sudan in the 1970s (*Associated Newspapers Group*)

ТАСС ТЕЛЕГРАФНОЕ АГЕНТСТВО
СОВЕТСКОГО СОЮЗА

УДОСТОВЕРЕНИЕ № 454

Тов. Илья
ДЖИРКВЕЛОВ
корреспондент

Телеграфного Агентства Советского
Демократической
спублике Судан
Москва 20 ноября 19 70.

энеральный директор

DER SPIEGEL

7. NOVEMBER 1962 · NR. 45
16. JAHRGANG · 1 DM
ERSCHEINT WÖCHENTLICH
IN HAMBURG · C 6380 C

Rudolf Augstein

Rudolf Augstein, the Chief Executive of *Der Spiegel* magazine, being arrested on charges of security breaches following publication of an article which was critical of the NATO exercise Fallex '62 (*Der Spiegel*)

The 'Whiskey' class Soviet submarine No. 137 which ran aground while illicitly probing the defences of the Swedish naval base at Karlskrona in 1981 – one of many callous infringements of a neutral neighbour's sovereignty (*Associated Press*)

Major General Jan Sejna (centre), the Czech soldier and politician who was intimately briefed on Soviet plans for the undermining of Western Europe when he defected to the West in 1968. He had first-hand knowledge of the Kremlin conspiracy to destroy the political career of Franz Josef Strauss

A deliberately misleading photograph of Prime Minister Margaret Thatcher, produced by left-wing photographers to associate her with the idea of war. The slogan behind her really reads 'Forward Together' and its misuse demonstrates how, by what the propagandists call 'cropping', a photograph can be subversive (*Sheila Gray/Format*)

Boris Ponomarev, the long-term head of the International Department and directly responsible to the Politburo for the active-measures offensive (*Syndication International*)

Wilfred Burchett, the ardent pro-Communist Australian journalist who functioned as an agent of influence and, when opportunity offered, acted as an agent of subversion (*Syndication International*)

How we stop the Cruise launcher

Here the TEL is shown parked in the firing mode with the quad missile box elevated. The LCC seen below contains all systems needed for a two-man crew to target and fire

The basic GLCM combat unit comprises 16 missiles loaded on four TELs (transporter/erector launchers) and two LCCs (launch control centres) for command and control

Part of a detailed document issued to 'peace' protesters to explain how they should try to stop the deployment of cruise missiles from their bases, either on practice runs or in an emergency

A letter forged by the KGB on stolen White House notepaper, purporting to be from President Reagan to King Juan Carlos of Spain. Its purpose was to damage American relations with both Spain and Britain

THE WHITE HOUSE
WASHINGTON

October 23, 1981

His Majesty
The King of Spain
Madrid

Your Majesty:

Permit me to bring to your attention a delicate and confidential matter which, I deeply believe, is highly important for both of our countries.

After our private talks, I learned that some persons close to you oppose Spain's entry into the North Atlantic Treaty Organization and have voiced new conditions for the membership of Spain. The highly secret information I have received indicates that members of this group come from Spain's armed forces, political parties, the government, and even the Catholic Church. It is my good fortune to be able to enclose the draft text of a memorandum the group prepared for you, which I was given by a strictly confidential source.

I believe Your Majesty agrees that it is totally important to the United States for Spain to enter NATO without delay, in fact, in 1981. Spain, after all, faces major tasks in this context. Suffice it to mention the role of the Canary Islands after the NATO Southern Command is set up. So, it is understandable that the United States is concerned about these doubts coming from influential and reliable individuals we regard as our friends. I believe in sharing conviction. We cannot permit another objectionable posture like the attitude of the French, which constantly creates problems for NATO in elaborating its new conceptions with reference to Latin America, Africa and the Mediterranean area. I have always believed Spain's absence from the Western system of defense to be a mistaken step, because your esteemed country would hardly feel at home among the self-styled "non-aligned" nations.

I respectfully ask Your Majesty to help disperse the uncertainty regarding Spain's NATO membership, created by the group influenced by the OPUS DEI pacifists. I believe it would help by granting those demands which do not directly conflict with NATO interests. For instance, my advisers inform me there are good grounds for destroying the leftwing opposition. In that event, the friendly relations between our two countries would improve. It would also neutralize the efforts aimed at creating difficulties for Spain's entry into NATO.

In such an instance, Your Majesty, I believe it imaginable that America might consider the final solution to Gibraltar in favor of Spain.

If necessary, the United States would undertake to dispel any anxiety in connection with Spain's new note which may arise, on the one hand, for the Mediterranean powers, and, on the other, on the part of the over-sensitive North African states with reference to Spanish territories in Africa and the Canary Islands.

I hope this message will strengthen Your Majesty's belief that Spain will benefit immensely by joining NATO. Such an act would enable Spain to once again assume the place she merits in history among the major World Powers. I urge Your Majesty to act, therefore, with dispatch to remove the forces obstructing Spain's entry into the NATO.

Yours truly,

Ronald Reagan
Ronald Reagan

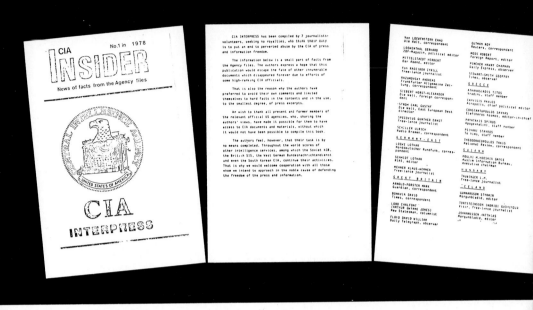

A Soviet-Bloc forgery showing part of a long list of journalists who have allegedly been recruited, for payment, by the CIA. The author's name is included

An artist's impression of Soviet SS20 missiles – part of a force of more than 400 – ready for launching from a forest clearing at West European targets. The missiles have a range of up to 3000 miles (*Soviet Military Power*)

Sir James Goldsmith, the international businessman, whose concern about Soviet active measures led to his involvement in the *Der Spiegel* Affair (*L'Express*)

Part of the disinformation pamphlet circulated on the KGB's behalf by the Danish agent, Arne Herlov Petersen. Its purpose was to show Mrs Thatcher as being so belligerently pro-American that she endangered the peace of Europe

ARNE HERLØV PETERSEN

TRUE BLUES

The Thatcher that couldn't mend her own roof

JOE HILL PRESS
1980

MS. THATCHER AND HER POLICIES

»Whatever you won't hear (about Thatcher) in casual conversations: A terrible ogress ... I'm fond of her obstinacy ... She has a nice hair-do. An energetic wench ... A nasty woman ... I'll never vote for a woman at the menopause age ... I'll vote for her to annoy men ... A charming, well-educated woman, but a Prime Minister? She is an impudent woman ... We already have a woman at the head of the kingdom, that's enough[1]). That is how a correspondent of the impartial French daily *Le Monde* reported conflicting, ironic and even insulting remarks, which, he says, the Britons made about Margaret Thatcher when she was running for the job of the Prime Minister of Great Britain at the Parliamentary elections in May 1979.

This diversity of views, however, did not prevent Thatcher from coming to power. The Conservatives won an impressive victory, getting an absolute majority of 339 seats. The Labor won only 268 seats, that is, even with the support of all other parties that are not represented in the Government the Conservatives would still have a 43-seat majority.

Thus, the Parliamentary elections of May 1979 gave the Conservatives a sufficiently stable majority for the next five years, when Parliamentary elections are to be held in May 1984.

Although all political observers share this view, they are far from being unanimous in that the present Conservative leader – Margaret Thatcher – will be able to stay in power through this term. And not without reason.

First, many Britons associated Margaret Thatcher with the attractive

[1]) Que n'entend-on pas au hasard des conversations: Terrible ogresse ... Je l'aime pour son obstination ... Elle est si bien coiffée ... Une pouliche rapide ... Une sale bonne femme ... Je ne voterai jamais pour une femme qui a l'âge de la ménopause. Je voterai pour elle, rien que pour embêter les hommes ... Une femme charmante, bien éduquée, mais premier ministre? Elle a du toupet ... Nous avons déjà une femme à la tête du royaume, cela suffit. (*Le Monde*, 24.4.79. page 5).

Gunther Guillaume (right), the Soviet-Bloc agent who was planted inside the private office of the West German Chancellor, Willy Brandt, and who became a close confidant. Guillaume had access to many diplomatic and NATO secrets (*Press Association*)

Stanislav Levchenko, the most informative of all Soviet defectors concerning active measures. He was a major exponent in Japan where he ran many agents of influence on behalf of the International Department and the KGB (*AFP*)

make a nuclear first strike. Stamped 'NATO Secret', it called for 'action of a sensitive nature' to jolt 'the faint-hearted' and its prime purpose was to stimulate opposition to the modernization of NATO forces and the demand for nuclear disarmament. It was denounced as a forgery by NATO officials after being reported on Belgian radio and television yet was reprinted in the Luxemburg Communist Party newspaper, *Zeitung*, a month later.[16]

Luns has been the subject of several defamation operations involving Soviet forgeries. One letter purporting to be from Luns to the American Ambassador to NATO stated that Luns was compiling a list of journalists opposing the neutron bomb with the implication that those supporting it, and NATO generally, might be given payments.[17]

Early in November 1981 copies of a completely fabricated letter allegedly sent by President Reagan to the Spanish King, Juan Carlos, were received by several Spanish journalists and by all the delegations to a Conference on Security and Co-operation in Europe being held in Madrid. Dated 'The White House, 23 October 1981' and signed 'Ronald Reagan', it was accompanied by a forged memorandum supposed to have been prepared by the Spanish Foreign Minister and his officials. The letter told the King that several of his advisers were opposing Spain's accession to NATO and it urged him to move against them, hinting that, in return, the US would support Spanish efforts to recover Gibraltar from Britain. The Soviet objective was to show that the US, and Reagan in particular, were interfering in Spanish affairs and to damage the position of the King. Its timing may also have been associated with the possible discussion by the conference of Soviet responsibility for the imposition of martial law in Poland.[18] There can be little doubt, from the evidence of defectors like Levchenko and Dzhirkvelov, that a forgery of this nature involving heads of state would have been sanctioned by the Politburo itself.

Levchenko has confirmed that in 1976 the KGB forged the 'last will and testament' of the Chinese Premier, Chou En-lai, who died in that year. It was an active measure directed against China and worded to cause dissension and unrest there by encouraging political rivalries. The forged will was surfaced by a KGB officer in a leading 'moderate' newspaper in Tokyo, *Sankei Shimbun*, where he had a well-placed agent of influence, and other Japanese papers followed up the story. TASS then replayed it worldwide, quoting *Sankei Shimbun*. KGB headquarters regarded the operation as being highly successful, Levchenko recalls.[19]

Many of the documents emanating from the Soviet-Bloc forgery factories are directed at institutions and organizations rather than individuals. Readers may recall that, after the Soviet Union decided to boycott the 1984 Olympic Games in Los Angeles, there were press reports that the racialist American organization called the Ku Klux Klan had sent abusive and threatening letters to African and Asian countries planning to take part. Examination of the letters has shown that they were not produced or sent by the KKK but by the KGB.[20]

Members of the US Strategic Air Command (SAC) responsible for the operation of nuclear bombers and missiles have been portrayed in KGB forged documents as being mentally unstable and so irrational that they could trigger off a nuclear war at any time. A fake letter from a Pentagon official concerned with the health and medical aspects of the forces alleged that two-thirds of the SAC's air crew were psychiatric cases. This letter which, allegedly, had been sent to the Secretary for Defense, was followed up with bogus letters said to have been written by some of the 'psycho-neurotic' pilots.[21] It has been my privilege to fly with SAC pilots and other representatives of the US Air Force, and a more stable and dedicated group of people would be hard to find.

The CIA has, inevitably, been a prime target for KGB forgeries and in 1978 Service A issued a totally fake 26-page document entitled 'CIA Insider – New Facts from the Agency Files', listing scores of foreign journalists alleged to be paid agents of the CIA who print planted information and provide intelligence.[22] My own name was included among the list of Britons so employed and I can state, emphatically, that at no time have I ever been approached by the CIA about any matter whatsoever. The Czech defector Ladislav Bittman has provided first-hand evidence of how Soviet-Bloc intelligence concocted a complete book to blacken the CIA. It began with an agreement between the Czech and East German intelligence services, made at the KGB's behest, to label the maximum number of American diplomats, politicians and cultural representatives serving abroad as CIA agents. Eventually the book appeared in 1968 allegedly authored by Julius Mader, a tool of the East German intelligence service, and entitled *Who's Who in the CIA*.[23] The book, which was intended to discredit the US diplomatic service throughout the world, has been described as 'an impeccable source' by the CIA defector, Philip Agee.

Mader was also the author of an article which appeared in March 1982 claiming that the CIA was waging chemical, bacteriological and meteorological warfare against Cuba. It cited an alleged official American document, entitled 'Basis for bacteriological attacks in the Caribbean', and was illustrated by a CIA map which had been doctored to show 'sites for agriculture epidemics'. The allegations were so unlikely that the Soviet Bloc had little hope of surfacing it except in some unsophisticated country with a Marxist régime and it first appeared in the *Ethiopian Herald*, being then repeated, with modifications, in the pro-Communist Portuguese paper, *Diario de Lisboa*. The operation's purpose was to back false claims by Fidel Castro that major epidemics in Cuba, affecting crops, animals and people, had been deliberately initiated by the CIA.[24]

The KGB has made a habit of using doctored CIA maps in forgery operations. It buys maps which are freely published by the CIA and its forgers change them and then issue photocopies in which the alterations are difficult to detect. In September 1981 the Austrian Communist Party newspaper published an article claiming that a secret CIA map showing targets inside Austria earmarked for attack by nuclear missiles and neutron bombs had been found in a 'secret service building' in West Germany. Again the author was Julius Mader. The Soviet press picked up the article and gave it prominence in the Soviet Union and abroad through TASS. A month later another freely published American map of Afghanistan was used to create a scare story in the pro-Soviet Indian paper, *Patriot*. It was alleged to show targets inside Afghanistan selected by the CIA for the tribesmen fighting the Russian invaders.[25]

In the summer of 1977 I received two long letters, with the promise of a third, from Tenerife allegedly from an American intelligence officer on retirement leave there. They were filled with intriguing information – enough for many sensational newspaper stories – including details of American operations against British politicians and trade-union leaders with allegations of tax evasion by ministers. Being convinced that they were a plant I handed them to Sir Maurice Oldfield, the head of MI6, but, short-sightedly on the part of MI6 regarding future co-operation, I received no information as to whether they were forgeries or not.

Failure of a particular active measure does not deter the KGB from attempting it again and again. According to John Barron:

> In 1975 Service A fabricated a US Army manual bearing the forged signature of General William Westmoreland. It contained two sinister themes: wherever U.S. military forces or advisers are stationed they are to interfere in the internal political affairs of the host country to ensure anti-Communist and anti-leftist policies and, in extreme cases, are to manipulate and incite ultra-left groups to violence so as to provoke the host government into militant anti-Communist actions.[26]

The KGB circulated the bogus manual in Turkey, Thailand and Japan, but nobody paid any attention. After Red Brigade terrorists murdered the former Italian Premier, Aldo Moro, in 1978 the KGB decided to try again. A Cuban intelligence officer peddled the manual to a Spanish newspaper together with an article by a KGB agent who cited the fabrication as proof that the CIA sponsored leftist terrorists and, hence, was probably responsible for the murder of Moro. After the newspaper published excerpts from the manual and the article, the Spanish magazine *El Triunfo* reprinted both. Immediately, Italian newspapers replayed the Spanish stories and, soon, the press in twenty countries published the fabricated manual or excerpts with allegations against the CIA. A chorus of overt propaganda from the Soviet Union quoted the stories in the non-Communist press as unbiased evidence that the US really was the force behind international terrorism and the actual murderer of Moro.[27]

The KGB staged a re-run of this successful active measure in January 1982 when various Soviet periodicals carried the accusation that the CIA had really been behind the kidnapping of the American Army General Dozier by the Italian Red Brigade in the previous month. They claimed that the operation was a double-take to undermine the left-wing opposition to the Italian Government and to NATO by discrediting the Red Brigade. Though the story sounded incredible it was repeated until the Western media began to print it.

On 27 November 1981 Moscow Radio accused the US Government of being behind the unsuccessful coup which had been staged on the previous day against the President of the Seychelles, Albert René. It alleged that the US had collaborated with the South African Government in order to secure more military bases in the Indian Ocean. TASS repeated the accusations and these were picked up by African and Indian papers. After President René denied that there had been any American involvement the KGB surfaced a fabricated letter from an official of a New Orleans company, which appeared to have been written to a general in the South African Air Force, about the recruitment of combat-trained helicopter pilots. This letter, which was intended to confirm American complicity in the failed Seychelles coup, appeared in several African newspapers.[28]

With South Africa under worldwide condemnation because of its apartheid policy, repeated efforts have been made to present the US Government as aiding and abetting it. In the autumn of 1980 a completely bogus document, purporting to be a Presidential Review Memorandum dated 17 March 1978, during the presidency of Jimmy Carter, called for American support for South Africa's stand and for the surveillance of black leaders in the US. It also suggested that the FBI and CIA should monitor the activities of black African representatives. The document, which was first surfaced in September 1980, was intended to undermine relations between the US and black African states. Articles citing it appeared in several Soviet publications, in some black African journals and in the left-wing Dutch paper, *Volkskrant*.[29]

Such forgeries have the additional purpose of branding the US as being 'racialist'. Originating, as they do, in a viciously anti-Semitic country, where there are no blacks apart from those potential terrorists being trained at the Patrice Lumumba 'Peoples' Friendship' University, they are an example of the upside-down ploy, standing reality on its head. The KGB employed the same technique to excuse its assassination of the Afghan leader, Hafizullah Amin, in December 1979 after the Politburo had ordered his murder and the installation of its puppet, Babrak Karmal. A forgery was circulated to support the claim in the Soviet press that Amin had been a CIA spy. The American Embassy in Islamabad had been burned, so Service A fabricated a partly burned document claiming to be a copy of a cable sent by the US Ambassador in Islamabad to his counterpart

159

in Kabul. It reported that a regular CIA courier to Amin had disappeared and requested that previously agreed emergency arrangements should be reactivated.[30]

With good reason, the Politburo is especially sensitive about the truth concerning its invasion of Afghanistan and the appalling atrocities being inflicted on the inhabitants in its drive for yet more territory. Service A has been instructed to hound anybody presenting the truth, especially in neighbouring countries like Pakistan and India. A particular victim of forgeries and false reports has been George Griffin, an American diplomat who had been stationed in Kabul and had visited Delhi once a week to brief the press there about events in Afghanistan. Having failed to induce the Indian Government to prevent the visits, the Soviets surfaced false reports, accusing him of being involved in undercover CIA operations against India. The attacks were renewed when Griffin was posted to New Delhi with articles and radio statements alleging that he was promoting the Punjabi Sikhs in their bid for a separate state.[31]

The most notorious forgery of all, and one of the most successful, judging by the number of times it has been surfaced, is known as the 'Holocaust Documents', a collection of doctored American military planning papers purporting to show targets for nuclear attack by American defence forces in the event of a Soviet invasion. The main purpose was to show that the US was preparing for nuclear war and to sacrifice Western Europe in the process of defeating the Soviet Union, for its own political purposes. This contention has been the essential element in the sustained nuclear campaign against NATO. The story about the documents first surfaced in the Norwegian magazine *Orientering* in 1967 and has since appeared more than twenty times in other countries, though repeatedly denounced as a forgery. Between 1967 and 1971 copies of the 'Holocaust Documents' were sent to many newspapers and magazines in at least ten West European countries. It appeared in London in a 'developed' form in June 1980 when the British Government announced a decision about the sites for cruise missile bases. In September 1982 a letter appeared in Finland's largest-circulation newspaper, *Helsingin Sanomat*, signed by three doctors with no known Communist connections, indicating that they accepted the authenticity of the Holocaust Documents. Three months later the story surfaced in Austria and will probably be resuscitated as the campaign continues against NATO's attempt to redress the Soviet superiority achieved by the Great Missile Deception.[32]

As a *Times* leader commented, succinctly, on 16 October 1984, 'It is the nature of journalism that a sensational forgery is likely to win wider coverage than its later retraction and Moscow makes the most of this fact.'

The most persistent and most massive Soviet disinformation effort, utilizing every form of deception, including wholesale forgeries, is, of course, against the Soviet people themselves and others under Kremlin control. Rigorous restrictions and penalties are imposed to prevent them from learning the truth about life in the free countries and any news advantageous to the West is withheld from them. The recent example of the Kremlin's behaviour over the Live Aid concerts for African famine relief provides a telling example. A selected audience of Communist trusties was invited to a Moscow television studio to respond rapturously while a Russian rock group called Autograph broadcast two songs to the outside world. The announcer, Vladimir Posner, claimed to be 'proud to be part of the gathering of millions of people' and implied that the Soviet people were joining in to help the starving Africans. In fact, the authorities were not prepared to permit the collection of a single rouble for the fund and the Soviet public was kept in ignorance of the event. Clearly, the purpose of the active measure was to deceive the outside world into believing that the Soviet Union was participating in the great charity, while the Soviet people could not be permitted to know anything about an event enhancing the prestige of the 'imperialist, capitalist, money-grabbing' West.

Chapter 11

Agents of Influence

'If you have an individual who is an adviser to a minister or a president, or if you have a minister himself as your agent of influence, you can do a tremendous amount in a country as far as active measures are concerned. One only has to recruit that agent and tell him what to do and he will go do it.'

John McMahon
Deputy Director of the CIA

From its inception, the Politburo has always devoted resources and effort to the recruitment of agents of influence – men and women who, through their positions and authority, can influence events in the direction of the Kremlin's interests, both immediate and long-term. The influence which can be exerted by foreign politicians, journalists and trade-union leaders is obvious; the influence of others who are less overt or even totally secret may be greater.

While people like Kim Philby, Donald Maclean, Anthony Blunt and Guy Burgess were primarily spies reporting secret information to their Moscow controllers, they were also able to function as important agents of influence by virtue of their position as advisers on policy. As a senior diplomatic official, highly regarded by his colleagues, Maclean was in a position to influence issues like nuclear relations with the US and the British attitude to the Korean War.[1] In March 1985 it was revealed, in the House of Lords, that Burgess and Philby, the latter as a representative of MI6, sat in at meetings of the Russia Committee, a post-war group of senior officials whose deliberations were so secret that its first chairman, Lord Gladwyn, is currently barred from consulting the records of them. The Russia Committee was examining ways of 'loosening the Soviet hold on the orbit countries and ultimately enabling them to regain their independence'. Presumably the two spies were there to be consulted for expert advice as well as being in a position to give Moscow information which led to the rapid liquidation of anti-Communists infiltrated into their home countries.[2]

Financed by the KGB, Burgess entertained Government officials and businessmen at lunches and dinners in the Dorchester Hotel and, apart from picking up scraps of information for Moscow, would be required to exert influence where he could and to talent-spot those who might be recruited as further agents of influence.[3]

In the US, during the months leading to the Japanese attack on Pearl Harbor, one of the drafters of the hardline policy towards Japan, Harry Dexter White, was a Soviet agent.[4] In the office of the Foreign Secretary, Alger Hiss, a person of considerable standing and influence, was also working for the KGB, as deciphered KGB radio messages have proved.[5] The extent to which President Roosevelt's trust in Stalin was influenced by well-placed Soviet agents of influence in the American government machine is still being studied by historians.

As that of a high-grade intellectual, the advice of Anthony Blunt was widely sought during his six years in MI5 and he could have influenced security policy in many directions as well as serving as a penetration agent inside the KGB's top-priority target. His colleague who became the longest-serving Director General of MI5, Sir Roger Hollis, was almost certainly a long-term Soviet intelligence agent and in that position would have been able to exert enormous influence on many aspects of intelligence.[6]

Agents operating in such secret departments run less risk of exposure since they are above suspicion, and instead of using public channels of influence, like the media or Parliament, they use what Moscow calls 'private channels of communication'. One well-tried ruse for influencing Ministers to soften or abandon a line disliked by the Politburo is to suggest that the new line being recommended is 'reflecting public opinion'.

The KGB secured a succession of brilliant coups in planting agents in such sensitive positions but, surely, the greatest was the insinuation of a professional spy and agent of influence as an adviser to the West German Chancellor, Willy Brandt. He was an East German 'refugee', called Gunther Guillaume, and both he and his wife were KGB agents trained for their special mission as 'illegal' intelligence officers, meaning that they would work under deep cover with no diplomatic immunity.

Guillaume, who was born in Berlin in 1927, had been a young member of the Nazi Party and this fact may have enabled East German Intelligence to blackmail him into joining them. He and his wife, Christl, were instructed to flee to West Germany as refugees from Communism to serve the cause of true democracy. After a brief period in a West German refugee camp, they both joined the Social Democratic Party (SPD) and Mrs Guillaume became secretary to one of the district organizers. Her efficiency led to promotion to the Bonn headquarters along with her husband who, in January 1970, became an adviser in the Chancellor's office, specializing in economics, finance and social policies. Through diligence, efficiency and charm he became a close confidant of the Chancellor, Brandt. At that stage, if not before, the operation must have been taken over by the KGB and, because of the unusual political potential involving the leader of a foreign government, the Politburo must have been intimately concerned.[7]

Throughout their time in the SPD the Guillaumes reported back to East Berlin, Christl being the one who met the couriers and serviced the dead-letter boxes. They reported on the confidential policy-making and personnel of the West German Government, on security operations against the West German Communist Party (DKP) and NATO issues. Guillaume had become so close to Brandt that he was able to report on personal matters concerning him. There seems to be little doubt that, apart from spying at this exalted level, which must have been of the greatest value to the Politburo in its diplomatic relations with West Germany, Guillaume influenced policy during the years when it went very much to Moscow's liking through Brandt's pursuit of 'Ostpolitik'. Brandt, a former journalist who had always played down the threat from Moscow, accepted the Soviet war gains, the division of Germany and the sovereignty of East Germany, which was formally recognized by him as a separate state in a treaty which he signed with the Soviet Union in August 1970.[8]

The Guillaumes were exposed only because of an extremely stupid habit on the part of the East German intelligence service which sent regular birthday greetings in code to its more important agents. Birthday greetings were sent to both the Guillaumes and to their son, and Britain's GCHQ, which intercepted the messages, was able to determine the true identities in May 1973. The Guillaumes were watched, fed with false information for a while and arrested in April 1974. During this interval Guillaume accompanied Brandt and his wife on a holiday in Norway, where Brandt had operated in the anti-Nazi resistance.[9] In his memoirs Brandt indicates that he had not been told about the suspicions concerning Guillaume and makes little mention of the 'Guillaume Affair' even though he felt that his position had been so compromised that he resigned as Chancellor after his former adviser had been sentenced to thirteen years' imprisonment and Christl to eight years.[10]

In September 1981 Guillaume was exchanged for several political prisoners and several West German agents held in East Germany. He was then aged fifty-four and was said to be suffering from severe high blood pressure. His wife had already been released in a similar exchange six months earlier.[11]

The Norwegian government adviser Arne Treholt, who has already been mentioned as a KGB agent in Chapter 8, also served as a useful Soviet agent of influence. He played a major role in ensuring that Norway's Labour Government rejected the deployment in Norway of any cruise or Pershing missiles in the programme to modernize NATO's battlefield nuclear weapons. The missile proposal was rejected by only one vote. He had also been an adviser in negotiations about how Norway and the Soviet Union should divide the Barents Sea, where there could be large oil and gas reserves.[12]

As the evidence of the defector Levchenko shows, the Soviets attach almost as much importance to securing agents of influence in the Far East as they do in Europe and they meet with comparable success. 1981 saw the arrest of a political secretary of the Prime Minister of Malaysia, followed by the quick expulsion of three members of the Soviet Embassy staff there.

Another example of a well-placed spy being able to double up as an agent of influence is provided by the recent case of the Canadian economics professor Hugh Hambleton, who was sentenced to ten years' imprisonment in Britain in 1982. He had spied actively for the Soviet Union over thirty years but, while serving as an economics adviser inside NATO headquarters in Paris from 1951 to 1961, he had been able to influence policy. His continuing importance in that respect, once he had secured a professional post in Canada, was recognized by Yuri Andropov, then KGB chief. According to Hambleton himself, the KGB gave him a dinner during a clandestine visit to Moscow in 1975 and Andropov attended it. The KGB chief, who was soon to become Soviet leader, told him that his potential for influencing opinion in North America was so promising that the KGB would finance his career, especially if he was prepared to enter Canadian politics.[13] In the past the Kremlin has been able to secure agents of influence – and even of information – among people as powerful as heads of non-Communist governments and even heads of state. Perhaps the most damaging of these known Soviet agents was Eduard Benes, the President of Czechoslovakia immediately before the Second World War. Benes' frank espionage and assistance to Stalin has been proved by the deciphering of wartime KGB radio traffic. He was partly responsible for Stalin's purge, in which hundreds of Red Army officers were executed. He was the courier through whom a faked report that senior Red Army officers were collaborating with the Germans was passed to Stalin.[14]

According to the high-level defector Sejna, Urho Kekkonen, the President of Finland from 1957 to 1981 and previously Prime Minister, was a Kremlin collaborator. While creating the impression of standing his ground against the Russians he is accused of promoting the fiction that it is possible to be neutral and friendly with the Soviet Union without any sacrifice of national sovereignty when, in fact, the Kremlin secured all it wanted. Sejna claims that Marshal Grechko, the Soviet Defence Minister, told him, in 1966, that Kekkonen had agreed that, in the event of war, Finland would declare its support for the Warsaw Pact and make its territory and ports available to the Soviet armed forces. Kekkonen also promoted the Politburo's concept of a Nordic nuclear-free zone and was crucial in promoting the Helsinki Agreement which enabled the Soviets to improve their military and political position while conceding virtually nothing.[15] It is, perhaps, significant that Western journalists are forbidden to see Kekkonen who, at eighty-four, is required to follow his own ruling that nothing should be said or written that might be embarrassing to Soviet–Finnish relations.

Among the high-level prey sought by the active-measures predators are diplomats, right up to the level of ambassador, whom they hope to secure as agents of influence. When the former Chilean Ambassador to the US, Orlando Letelier, was murdered in 1976, papers found in his brief-case revealed that Cuban intelligence, which is controlled by the KGB, was financing his 'human rights' activities and that his true purpose was to install a Cuban-style Communist government in Chile. Letelier, whose address book included KGB officers, had previously been associated with the World Peace Council and had been very successful in inducing American journalists to project the Chilean Government of General Pinochet as a monstrous violator of human rights.[16] A report by the US Accuracy in Media organization showed that, in 1976, the *New York Times* printed sixty-six articles about human rights in Chile but only three on human rights in Cuba where violations may be worse. The record for the *Washington Post* was similar – fifty-eight about Chile to four about Cuba.

Perhaps the best attested case of the Soviet suborning of a foreign ambassador is that of John Watkins, the Canadian Ambassador to Moscow in the middle 1950s. I have been given first-hand information on this case by British and Canadian intelligence officers involved in it. Watkins, a homosexual, was subjected to blackmail after being set up and photographed in compromising situations while on a tour of the Soviet Union. A Soviet Foreign Ministry man with whom Watkins had become friendly and who was really the KGB officer in charge of internal intelligence operations, General Oleg Gribanov, told Watkins that he could prevent any exposure of his homosexual exploits provided he agreed to be helpful to the Soviet Union in a new high-level post in Ottawa, to which he was being promoted. Gribanov urged Watkins to go out of his way to be friendly to the Soviet Ambassador in Ottawa, to help to 'liberalize' circumstances for Soviet citizens residing in Canada – making it easier for them to serve as spies and subversives – and generally to 'steer things' in the Kremlin's interests. Watkins was warned that his Soviet friends would be 'watching'. Canadian security officers, who were warned of Watkins's position by a Soviet defector, could find no firm evidence that this blackmail attempt had been successful, but it was a bold attempt and Watkins had failed to report it.[17] Another secretly Communist Canadian ambassador in positions to serve as an agent of influence was Herbert Norman, a friend of Anthony Blunt at Cambridge University. Norman served as Ambassador to Japan, High Commissioner to New Zealand and Ambassador to Egypt where he committed suicide after he knew he was under deep suspicion.[18]

The French Ambassador to Moscow, Maurice Dejean, was ensnared through his weakness for beautiful women. With his chauffeur and his wife's maid both being KGB agents, he was set up for the trick in which the husband returns 'unexpectedly' to find his wife in a compromising situation with the lover. Dejean did not report his dangerous position, in which the KGB required him to serve as an agent of influence, but the plot was exposed by a defector and Dejean was summarily dismissed by de Gaulle.[19]

The British Ambassador to Moscow in the late 1960s, Sir Geoffrey Harrison, was also severely compromised through photographs of intimate details of his affair with a KGB prostitute, who had been infiltrated into the Ambassador's residence as a maid. He was sensible enough to report his predicament and was withdrawn from the Soviet Union; the British authorities preferred to suppress the case rather than complain to the Kremlin. The sordid details did not prevent the award of the GCMG to the erring envoy and the treatment of such cases, which means that few come to light, suggests that the suborning of high-level diplomats may be commoner than imagined and not only in Britain.[20]

It is extremely difficult for Western democracies to suborn Soviet ambassadors or other high-level diplomats. In Moscow Soviet personnel are under regular surveillance by the KGB while in their foreign embassies and trade delegations they are watched by the SK (Soviet Kolony) security officers stationed there to prevent defections or any unauthorized association with Westerners. In contrast to the highly dangerous practice of having Soviet citizens as servants, chauffeurs and local officials in Western embassies in Moscow, the KGB ensures that its embassies and other missions abroad are staffed entirely by Russians so that no willing ladies or homosexuals can be infiltrated, as they have been into the foreign embassies in the Soviet capital, often with disastrous results for the West. In any case, British intelligence officers have been forbidden for many years to make use of sexual blackmail and this may apply to other Western agencies.

The same difficulties apply to the recruitment of Soviet civil servants in Moscow whereas MI5 is in no doubt that some senior British civil servants, apart from those who have been prosecuted, have served as Soviet agents of influence.[21] A civil servant who may become senior enough to advise a Minister, or even a Prime Minister, is clearly a prime target for recruitment for active-measures operations. One such was subjected to searching inquiries in the 1970s and remains suspect.[22]

Ministers and other MPs are not immune to the active-measures talent-spotters, and parliaments of the Western democracies are high on the list of institutions through which the Soviets continue their 'long march'. The former MI5 officer Peter Wright has described, publicly on television, how in 1955 MI5 secured a full list of the secret Communists in Britain. In a surreptitious entry operation, code-named 'Party Piece', MI5 officers broke into a Mayfair flat where the Communist Party's files of the secret membership were stored. While the owner of this 'safe house' was away for the night, some 55,000 files were removed, photographed and returned so carefully that nobody could detect that they had been disturbed.[23] It was found that thirty-one serving MPs were on the list and there is no reason to believe that the figure is any smaller now. Indeed, because of the high degree of 'entryism' it may be much higher. The Czech defector, Bittman, told a Congressional Intelligence Committee that in the mid-1960s the Czech intelligence service had several paid agents of influence among British MPs, serving as mouth-pieces for disinformation and the planting of invidious Parliamentary questions and comments. He claimed that there were also paid agents in the West German Parliament and that one of them was Alfred Frenzel, who had been a member of several Parliamentary Committees and received a seventeen-year sentence for espionage in 1960.[24] Bittman's claims have been independently confirmed by two other Czech intelligence defectors, Josef Frolik and Frantisek August, who have written memoirs and given evidence to US investigating committees.[25] Frolik's evidence resulted in the exposure of the Labour MP Will Owen in 1970 and the naming of others, including the former Labour Minister John Stonehouse, as targets for Czech active measures. Frolik has since

169

named a Cabinet Minister in the Callaghan government as one of the reasons why he remains afraid to revisit Britain, while August has recorded that, during his time in London in the early 1960s, 'the staff of Czech Intelligence believed that, of all their British targets, Members of Parliament were the most vulnerable'.[26] As the Director General of MI5, Sir Martin Furnival Jones, stated the problem in 1971, 'If the Russian Intelligence service can recruit a back-bench MP and he climbs to ministerial position, the spy is home and dry.'[27]

The problem has almost certainly been intensified by the contacts between the Labour Party and foreign Communist régimes resulting from the decision in 1973 to lift the ban on membership of Communist front organizations. Since then the Labour Party has sent many delegations on friendship visits to Moscow and Eastern Europe. It is the view of MI5 that the Conservative and other parties are by no means immune to Soviet-Bloc penetration. There have certainly been attempts to recruit some of the women secretaries and the army of advisers who work for MPs or have regular access to them.[28]

Journalists are frequently used as advisers to political committees in confidential or even secret roles, as I have been myself. The impact on Labour Party policy of the left-wing journalist Duncan Campbell, for example, has been considerable. He was a potent member of the Labour Party study group responsible for the discussion document laying down what the Party proposed to do by way of legislation to control MI5, MI6, GCHQ and other aspects of the security and intelligence services.[29] Campbell is also an official adviser to the very left-wing Greater London Council on civil defence issues. While there is no suggestion that Campbell is, in any way, linked with the Soviet Union, there can be little doubt that the measures he supports and the various detailed disclosures he makes about security, intelligence and American defence activities in Britain are welcome to Moscow.

Scientists have been avidly sought by the Soviets as agents of influence because they tend to be held in high regard and are widely used as advisers to government departments. They are regarded as soft targets because they tend to be fundamentally internationalist in outlook, scientific knowledge knowing no boundaries, and need to consult with scientists of other nations on a regular basis which gives plenty of opportunity for foreign travel. So many of them are so specialized and withdrawn in their work that they are politically naive and surprisingly gullible, especially when visiting the Soviet Union as selected guests of academicians. Albert Einstein and Bertrand Russell, while geniuses in their fields, were incredibly gullible. The late Lord Blackett, while officially a member of the Labour Party, was regarded with such suspicion in Whitehall, following his pro-Soviet book *The Military and Political Consequences of Atomic Energy*, that he was barred from membership of Defence Ministry Committees while the Conservative Government was in office.[30] Blackett delighted Moscow with his claim that 'the dropping of the atomic bombs was not so much the last military act of the Second World War as the first act of the cold diplomatic war with Russia now in progress'. Blackett predicted that when the Soviet Union became more industrialized and had nuclear weapons of its own it would be interested in genuine disarmament – a prophecy which has proved to be completely false.[31] Blackett and other left-wing scientists who may have been essentially 'willies' were supported by open Communists like Professor J. D. Bernal and Professor J. B. S. Haldane who wrote regularly in the Communist press for many years.

In France the Communist lead was taken by Professor Frédéric Joliot-Curie who, with his great reputation, proved to be a cogent agent of Soviet influence. The US, too, had a sizeable post-war crop of scientists – some recent immigrants from Europe – who pursued 'internationalism' in a way highly acceptable to Moscow.

Several of these left-wing scientists attended the so-called World Congress of Intellectuals for Peace, held in Poland in 1948, which spawned the most potent Communist front to date, the World Peace Council. Accompanying them was the self-styled scientist Ritchie Calder, who became a founder member of the Campaign for Nuclear Disarmament, took a generally anti-American line and, eventually, was made a life-peer by Harold Wilson for his advisory services.

Cynically, but with increasing success, Moscow's atheistic régime has secured the services of leading ecclesiastics as agents of influence. The World Council of Churches, founded in 1948 to further the ecumenical movement of uniting Christian believers, should be the voice of Christendom but has widened its scope to the concept of 'unifying all mankind'. It has, inevitably, become penetrated by

171

Marxists and radical theologians who, being anti-capitalist, are easily exploited by active measures. They have become particularly anti-American and pro-Soviet in their support of liberation movements and appear to condone the use of violence by so-called freedom fighters. With grants to African terrorists, which began in 1970, with the founding of the Programme to Combat Racism, the World Council of Churches has, in fact, subsidized murder. In 1978 it gave £45,000 to the violent Patriotic Front of Zimbabwe, led by Mugabe and Nkomo, only three weeks after the Front had massacred nine British missionaries and their children. At the time the grant was made, 450 Anglican bishops attending the Lambeth Conference voted to 'reaffirm support and strengthen their understanding of the World Council of Churches'.

The Soviets have even managed to sponsor a religious front organization to promote Communist aims in the form of the Christian Peace Conference, founded in 1957 and with headquarters in Prague. As a declassified CIA report on the Conference comments, 'There are few more useful instruments than an international, purportedly religious body that can, with guile and deception, advance Soviet disarmament policies and justify terrorist wars of liberation.'[32] It is no coincidence that the Conference's chief executives always appear to have indisputable loyalty to the Kremlin. Like other fronts, it is controlled by the International Department which selects its officers and has close links with the KGB. At a meeting in Kiev, a major Soviet participant, posing as an academic, was the notorious KGB officer Radomir Bogdanov.

The degree to which the Russian Orthodox Church is controlled by the KGB and is required to operate on its behalf is heinous. Many of its priests are KGB officers and, as a West German intelligence report of 1977 concluded, all candidate priests are checked by the KGB before being admitted to theological studies, and the Moscow Patriarch's main duty is to support Soviet policy where he can and especially through 'peace' propaganda. Details of the KGB's penetration of the Russian Orthodox Church have been given by the KGB defector Anatoli Golitsin, and in CIA reports which name the present Patriarch, Pimen, as a KGB operative.[33]

Few ecclesiastics show themselves as overt Communists, one notorious exception being the late Dr Hewlett Johnson, the Dean of Canterbury, who was awarded the Stalin Peace Prize. The 'Red

172

Dean', who claimed that Soviet Communism under Stalin was nearer to Christianity than was Western capitalism, wrote several pro-Soviet books which sold very widely and could have influenced the naive.[34] Most of those who give comfort to Moscow deny being pro-Communist, claiming that any assistance which the Politburo derives from their activities is purely coincidental. The current leader of this genre in Britain is Monsignor Bruce Kent, the Catholic priest at the forefront of the Campaign for Nuclear Disarmament, who preaches unilateral nuclear disarmament and advocates mass protest on a scale ideally suited to the International Department's aims. Other prominent clergymen were vocal in support of the leader of the miners' strike when they were stimulating violence on picket lines and manipulating their members for political ends.[35]

While the pulpit has obvious appeal for disinformation experts, greater concentration is focused on the classroom and university lecture-theatre in pursuit of the Communist belief that those who are recruited when young are likely to be life-long disciples. Teacher-training establishments are obvious targets and the type of person functioning there was vividly illustrated by the head of Media Studies at London University's Institute of Education, Robert Ferguson, who in March 1985 complained about the nature of the long-running children's programme 'Blue Peter' on BBC television. He wanted it changed to 'Red Peter' because it is 'pro-capitalist, royalist, racist and sexist'. He believed that its very successful charity appeals should be used for publicity about nuclear disarmament and as a vehicle for people like the Communist leader Mick McGahey to appeal on behalf of miners with lung disease.[36]

The 1960s saw a proliferation of 'social science' departments in universities and teaching institutions which attracted Marxist staff and have produced many more Marxists for similar posts. They have been a vocal source of continuing criticism of the evils of capitalist society which must have been music to the Politburo's ears. One lecturer in sociology at Mid-Cheshire College of Further Education, John Penny, was jailed for fifteen months for organizing and operating a hit-squad of left-wing extremists to attack the National Front. An activist of the Socialist Workers' Party, he had previously been convicted for disorderly conduct on a picket line but had managed to keep the conviction secret from his college.[37]

Not surprisingly, so-called 'peace studies' have mushroomed as a discrete subject in universities, teacher training colleges and schools, especially in the Labour-controlled areas. They have a marked bias in favour of unilateral nuclear disarmament, the Campaign for Nuclear Disarmament (CND) and pacifism in general – all helpful to the Soviet active-measures offensive. CND propagandists are being invited to address senior pupils and expound their one-sided views with no speakers to present the opposing argument. Teachers openly wear CND badges, hand out CND membership forms to pupils and require essays on such tendentious questions as 'Which do you prefer, swords or ploughshares?' Graduates in 'peace studies' now form a pressure group in favour of introducing the subject into more schools so that they can secure jobs in teaching it. This is furthering the trend towards politicizing education and undermining traditional values, which is being fostered by the far left and especially by those with influence on education through local government. While teachers should not try to indoctrinate children in any particular political direction, a vote intended to affiliate the National Union of Teachers to CND in 1982 was defeated by only a narrow margin.

Extremist students, who are often members of revolutionary parties, make a point of joining picket lines in disputes with which they have no direct connection simply because they offer opportunities for 'direct action', meaning violence. Arrests made on picket lines have shown that among the most vocal shouting 'The workers united will never be defeated' are louts who have never done a day's work and have little intention of doing so. Indeed, one of the follies of the Welfare State is that it provides money, in the form of social security benefits and student grants, to people who spend almost all their time on revolutionary activities intended to destroy the system that makes such benefits possible. The classic instance of this occurred at the Polytechnic of North London during the 1970s when Marxist 'students' belonging to revolutionary parties like the International Socialists corrupted the college during a sustained four-year siege which has been fully documented by some of the staff who suffered.[38] The students' union there, which was supposed to represent the interests of its 4,000 members, disrupted lectures, broke up governors' meetings, vilified the teaching staff and viciously flouted all authority in a programme of wrecking designed to turn the Polytechnic into a revolutionary base. In the process the staff was penetrated by Marxist militants who openly supported the wreckers.

The wrecking has continued with 'occupations' of buildings, meetings being disrupted and participation in industrial disputes like the Grunwick factory affair in 1977, when the students' union van was used as a mobile 'troop-carrier' to transport violent student-activists to vantage points in the battles with the police.

The Polytechnic case has exposed a monstrous abuse of public money in the revolutionary interest which is also occurring at some other colleges and universities. Each student union receives a substantial annual sum from the public purse to support various social activities and amenities as well as administrative costs. The amount is based on the number of students because membership of the union is compulsory and automatic. Once the union falls into extremists' hands, most of this money can be diverted to revolutionary ends. At the Polytechnic, for example, much of the annual budget of about £200,000 has been spent on funding an excessive number of full-time officials, with secretarial help, who spend most of their time on political activities. Gifts have been made to striking miners, to the defence funds of militants under arrest and to finance 'demos'. The student militants have their own media financed at public expense. Virulent publications, circulated free of charge, are used to indoctrinate and intimidate new students. The staff and governors of this and other institutions seem to have been too intimidated to take any effective action and the Government has preferred not to interfere.[39]

The campuses of the American universities went through a phase of political activism and violence, but the undermining of authority there seems to have subsided while in Britain it continues with the left-wing battle for minds being extended into the classroom, where it embraces even the youngest children. Left-wing militants are deliberately trying to destroy the image of the schoolmaster and schoolmistress as law-abiding figures held in respect and to change them into untidy, aggressive agitators dedicated to creating a militant generation prepared to use violence for revolutionary ends. Events like those at the William Tyndale school in Islington, North London, in 1976 demonstrate the degree to which such people can gain control of a school and sabotage the existing system.[40] The Inner London Education Authority is riddled with extreme left-wing militants, one of whom was recently appointed to oversee the teaching of politics in schools 'to ensure that children are taught to think politically', meaning in a revolutionary, Marxist way. Communists and Trotskyists reject traditional education because it is aimed at teaching the young to think for themselves after examining the various aspects of an argument. They insist on indoctrination of Marxist dogma with the pursuit of truth being set aside in favour of the acceptance of slogans and revolution being demanded in place of gradual change. Children are being required to take a Marxist stand on political and sociological issues long before they are mature enough to do so with any degree of independent thought. The undermining of their natural will to defend their country is a major aim.

Racial literature of an extreme left-wing nature is being distributed in schools and 'racism' has intruded into mathematics with children being required to work out the differences in wages between black and white workers in South Africa or to compare the wages paid to Sri Lankan tea workers with the price of tea in British shops. English literature is being systematically purged and long-standing classics are being removed from school libraries and curricula because they are 'politically unacceptable'. Infants are being encouraged to despise and distrust the police, with teaching aids like anti-police video-recordings being supplied free.

At the time of writing twelve left-wing Labour MPs are supporting a national school strike instigated by militants, and schools are being picketed. Youngsters, softened up by extremist pamphlets, have been urged to stay away from school and, in Merseyside, two hundred did so. They were harangued by the Militant Liverpool MP, Terry Fields, who urged them to 'strike for their future'. The occasion was well covered by television and the sight of Fields addressing the chanting, fist-clenching children and waving his grateful acknowledgement was reminiscent of the Politburo on the podium in Red Square. What such children are capable of doing when roused was viciously demonstrated a few days later when girls and boys, aged between eight and ten, rampaged and wrecked a community centre at Bridgwater, Somerset.[41]

While much of the subversive work in the schools and universities is being done for the Politburo without need for direct support, or even encouragement, the International Department has taken direct

176

action in infiltrating Britain's schools by offering to send them free Russian books which are blatant propaganda with titles like *Privileged Class*, *The Great Vital Force of Leninism* and *The Liberation Movement*, the later two being written by Boris Ponomarev![42] Comparable books extolling the virtues of true democracy are not allowed into the USSR, which continues to maintain strict censorship – in clear breach of its undertakings under the Helsinki agreement.

The militant stance being taken by an increasing number of teachers has been reflected in the attitude of their unions and especially of the National Union of Teachers (NUT). While the majority of teachers remain politically moderate, the union has to a considerable extent become a left-wing pressure group with Communists and Trotskyists in influential positions. In the early 1980s the Communists claimed a 'considerable strengthening' in the NUT, indicating that infiltration had been deliberate, and lauding the decision of its annual conference to campaign for 'unilateral renunciation by the British Government of the use and development of nuclear weapons', with which the Politburo must have been pleased. The existing peace lobby in the NUT has been strengthened by the appearance of a special organization called 'Teachers for Peace', which means the type of peace being promoted by the active-measures operators.

As an aspect of education and influence those operators have not ignored the theatre, where promoters of revolution like Vanessa Redgrave and her brother Corin have been termiting away for years. Currently there is a move to oust anybody who acts in South Africa even if they do so only for multi-racial audiences. The travelling theatres which visit schools have been heavily infiltrated, as their repertoire proves. Theatre Centre, which is funded by the Arts Council, the Greater London Council and the Inner London Education Authority, has entertained many secondary schools with *Susumu's Story* – a play about Hiroshima which makes no attempt to explain why nuclear weapons were used to enforce the surrender of the Japanese, who had behaved with extreme ferocity and cruelty. Another play, called *Red Letter Days*, gives a totally false picture of life in Moscow.[43] In June 1985 a Conference of Third Form Children was held in Sheffield to commemorate the Soweto massacre. According to the *Morning Star* (27 June), it began with a 'rivetting theatrical experience provided by actors from the local Crucible Theatre Company. A young black woman played the part of a football enthusiast who is killed.'

The extent to which actors, film stars, writers, poets and painters are deliberately used as agents of influence by the Soviet Bloc was indicated in detail by the Czech defector Josef Frolik in his evidence to the US Senate Judiciary Committee. He said that the intelligence services of all Communist countries make use of 'all available means to penetrate and influence the ranks of artists, cultural workers, writers and journalists' and that many Soviet artists performing abroad are employed by them, sometimes on specific tasks.[44] 'Cultural attachés' are commonly used as covers for KGB officers, and 'cultural exchanges' are encouraged to assist their subversive operations.

While pictorial artists tend to be less influential, politically, than writers, cartoonists are assiduously sought as agents of great influence with apparent success in all countries of the West. They are particularly effective in character assassinations and in campaigns ranging from that staged against Franz Josef Strauss in the 1960s to those currently being waged against Ronald Reagan and Margaret Thatcher, who are consistently portrayed as war-mongers who can hardly wait to start a nuclear 'holocaust'. The television puppet show 'Spitting Image' portrayed Reagan as a brainless idiot week after week in a campaign which was as disgraceful as it was untrue.

Photographers can be equally valuable either as deliberate agents of influence or 'willies'. They can – and do – angle their pictures to show 'police brutality', the exploitation of poverty, military 'imperialism' and racialism against blacks. Whenever Gerald Ford slipped, as all people occasionally do, there always seemed to be a camera on hand to record it and such pictures were used to suggest that he was accident-prone and, therefore, unfit to be in charge of nuclear weapons. Throughout the recent miners' strike left-wing photographers and television cameramen could be seen stalking the police to secure angled pictures of 'police brutality'.

The most consistently powerful agents of influence are those who control organizations which they can utilize as agencies of influence, exerting pro-Soviet pressure and furthering active measures on an international scale. Such agencies, which try to mask their subversive activities as much as they can, are known, collectively, as

Communist fronts and the most effective have been set up by the Soviets specifically for their purposes. Others have been infiltrated and taken over when their potentialities became apparent. Many people may join or associate with such fronts in good faith without being aware of their secret purpose, which is usually vehemently denied. The various Soviet Friendship societies are supposed to be non-political but are widely exploited by the International Department, so much so that the British version was proscribed to members of the Labour Party until 1973.

In a House of Lords debate in April 1985, Lord Orr-Ewing listed thirteen major Soviet fronts operating on an international scale.[45] Most of them will be described in the chapters dealing with the 'Peace' Offensive, because, currently, their efforts are being concentrated in support of it, but it is convenient to name them here, as they exercise pro-Soviet interest in many other directions: the World Peace Council and its offshoots, the International Institute for Peace and the Christian Peace Conference, the World Federation of Trade Unions, the World Federation of Democratic Youth, the International Union of Students, the International Association of Democratic Lawyers, the Women's International Democratic Federation, the Afro-Asian People's Solidarity Association, the International Organization of Journalists, the International Federation of Resistance Fighters, the World Federation of Scientific Workers and the International Radio and TV Organization.

There are many others such as the so-called Labour Research Department, which has nothing to do with the Labour Party, claims 2000 trade-union bodies as affiliates and specializes in undermining free enterprise and capitalism. It gives a round-the-clock service to agitators and strikers, providing damaging details, which may be inaccurate, about the target company's finances. In June 1985 it produced a story-book for children entitled *Union Farm*, explaining how to strike, do picket duty and organize union meetings.

In the US there is the Institute for Policy Studies which has established exchange arrangements with Soviet organizations such as the Institute for the US and Canada, which is used by the International Department for active-measures operations. Delegates in these exchanges have been identified as senior KGB and GRU officers, some of them having been refused visas. There is even an organization called Generals for Peace, a group of former NATO officers who, in 1984, produced a booklet called *The Arms Race to Armageddon* containing wildly inaccurate statements about NATO's plans and purposes and described by a distinguished reviewer as 'indistinguishable from normal Soviet output in this field'.[46]

No 'Innocents' Clubs', as such groups of well-meaning people have been cynically called, escape the attention of the International Department, which is under standing instructions to effect the Communist penetration and manipulation of any Western organization offering possibilities for active-measures operations. Of those which were founded with the worthiest motives, the most persistently penetrated and most effectively manipulated have been the trade unions, particularly those of the United Kingdom, in the Politburo's 'long march through the institutions'.

Chapter 12

Active Measures and the Trade Unions

'We must be able, if needs be, to resort to all sorts of tricks, slyness, illegal methods, evasion and concealment of truth so as to get into the trade unions, to remain in them and to carry on Communist work at all costs.'

Lenin

Recent defectors have confirmed the high priority which the Kremlin continues to give to the penetration of British trade unions by open Communists, by secret Communists and by other agents of influence who are instructed to pretend that they are acting out of personal conviction and in the interests of their members. The Czech defector Frantisek August has recorded how, during his service as an intelligence officer in London, from 1961 to 1963, he was required to concentrate on trade-union leaders with the object of recruiting them as paid agents, their purpose being to 'exert political leverage on the British Government' in various ways.[1] This has been confirmed by Josef Frolik, another Czech defector to the West, who has given details of his efforts in a biography, in evidence to the CIA, to the US Senate Judiciary Committee and in a long affidavit of which I have a copy.[2] I also secured copies of tape-recordings of private interviews which Frolik gave in Washington and passed them to Sir Maurice Oldfield, then Chief of MI6. As the names of trade-union leaders given as Soviet-Bloc targets were not privileged under

British law, and could lead to libel actions, I took steps to have them privileged by getting them mentioned in Parliament. According to *Hansard*, the official Parliamentary report, Folik had named four living trade-union leaders as special targets – Jack Jones, the powerful leader of the Transport and General Workers' Union, Britain's biggest, Hugh Scanlon (now Lord), leader of the Amalgamated Union of Engineering Workers, Ernie Roberts, now a Labour MP and then also of the AUEW, and Lord Briginshaw (by then already Lord), a former leader of one of the newspaper unions. Frolik also alleged that the late Ted Hill of the Boilermakers' Union had been a secret Communist and an agent of influence for the Soviet Bloc.[3] Frolik did not claim any success with these or other targets. After suggesting to Prague headquarters that he should try to capitalize on this acquaintance with some trade-union officials he was curtly told to concentrate on NATO because the trade unions were the preserve of the KGB.

General Jan Sejna, a third Czech defector, stated in his sworn affidavit made in connection with the *Der Spiegel* Affair that 'through manipulation of the trade unions we proposed to exacerbate existing causes of social and industrial unrest and stimulate new sources of confrontation'. In Britain 'progressive' forces were encouraged to penetrate both the trade unions and the Labour Party, which they supported and, to some extent, controlled. The first objective was to help strengthen the British trade-union movement so that it would become an accepted pillar of government, as indeed it did under the Wilson and Callaghan administrations. Then, a power-base on the left wing of the Labour Party and in the trade unions was to be organized to challenge for the leadership of the whole trade-union movement, with the help of the Communists. This 'progressive' movement had instructions to agitate for changes in the laws governing trade-union rights and responsibilities in order to increase the importance of the unions and their prestige, to give them a greater say in industrial management and to help establish them as a power-base. Sejna records, 'The Russians saw this issue as a means of pushing not only the trade-union movement but also their supporters in the Parliamentary Labour Party further to the left.'[4]

The trade-union laws were, in fact, greatly improved in their favour when Michael Foot was Employment Secretary from 1974 to 1976, with the Trade Union Congress (TUC) working in collaboration in framing the new pro-union legislation, and would have been 'improved' still further had Foot become Prime Minister at the 1979 general election.[5]

It could be significant that as the left-wing penetration of the Labour Party and the trade unions gathered momentum, the Communist term 'comrade' replaced the former social-democratic 'brother'.

The defector August has recorded how a particular aim of the Czech intelligence service in London in the early 1960s was to infiltrate the Civil Service unions with the object of penetrating various sensitive government departments to which officials of those unions had access.[6] I can testify that the top target in that category was the Institution of Professional Civil Servants (IPCS), to which the most senior civil servants, including high-level defence scientists, belonged. As I have described in a former book, I had a hand in exposing a highly influential secret Communist who was General Secretary of the IPCS for many years, Stanley Mayne. Through his branch officials Mayne had access to a great deal of secret information about establishments responsible for radar, atomic weapons, aircraft and anti-submarine research and almost all other defence research. He was not only a member of the Party, unknown to the Whitehall authorities with whom he had to deal, but took part in meetings of Party committees. There was no suggestion of any disloyalty but he had ensured that on his retirement he would be replaced by a man of similar persuasion. The Conservative Government eventually declined to negotiate with Civil Service Union officials who were Communist or pro-Communist.[7]

While the IPCS has since remained free from penetration at the top, other Civil Service unions have been besieged by the far left, this being particularly true of the largest, the Civil and Public Services Association with more than 180,000 members. Its left wing ran a strike at a social security computer centre in Durham, in 1984, which hit pensioners badly and achieved nothing for the strikers.

Following serious disruptions to the intelligence-gathering operations at GCHQ in 1979 and 1981 by Civil Service unions representing the staff there, the Government became gravely concerned about the dangers of such action during a serious military emergency. It therefore decided to bring GCHQ into line with MI5 and MI6, where membership of any union has always been forbidden, and to require the staff to abandon their unions. This move, which was long overdue on security considerations, caused a political uproar, which continues, with union leaders claiming that it is a slur on the loyalty and integrity of the GCHQ staff as a whole. In fact the Government's real fear is that the unions concerned might fall into extremist left-wing hands, when a politically motivated strike at a crucial time could paralyse the nation's defences through lack of up-to-the-minute intelligence.[8]

The effect of similar politically motivated strikes by trade unionists concerned with the operation of the radio and television services during a military emergency has also been carefully considered by the security authorities. The West German Government has a special force trained to take over and operate the radio and television services there in the event of pro-Soviet action by left-wing trade unionists. British defence chiefs have, so far, avoided taking similar precautions, but the Home Office has organized means for keeping the public informed of events should normal services become unusable through trade-union action.[9]

The evidence of the Soviet Bloc's recruitment of trade-union officials provided by defectors has been steadily supplemented by MI5's active penetration of both the Communist Party and the trade unions. For many years MI5 has had a special section devoted to the study and surveillance of the Communist Party and of leading Communists, both overt and covert. It is long-established practice that such organizations and people, who are potentially subversive, should be subject, on occasion, to being watched, having their telephones tapped and their letters opened, and the need for this has been amply justified by the number of Soviet agents, intent on damaging their country, who have been detected as a result.[10] As many trade-union leaders are overt Communists, while others who call themselves social democrats have the same intentions, they fall into the category of suspects. Though the surveillance has been widely known about for years and the Communist Party has even displayed MI5 microphones inserted in its headquarters, mock outrage was generated when a former MI5 officer, Cathy Massiter, publicly claimed on television in March 1985 that trade unionists were having their telephones tapped. She claimed that she left MI5 because such surveillance was breaching MI5's 'charter', though, following an inquiry, this was denied by the Home Secretary. Miss Massiter confirmed that MI5 introduces 'moles' into some trade unions, and had even surreptiously entered the home of the Communist trade-union leader, Ken Gill, to search it.[11]

I have made continual inquiries into the surveillance of extreme left-wing trade unionists over many years and am convinced that it is justified and necessary in the national interest. As early as 1947 Whitehall's Joint Intelligence Committee produced a secret paper entitled 'The Spread of Communism throughout the World and the extent of its Direction from Moscow'. An informant who was involved in producing it has told me that it dealt with the techniques of the penetration of the British trade unions by Moscow-trained agents.[12] I have already referred to the Templer Committee of 1950, which produced further evidence of the Soviet manipulation of the British trade unions to convert them into Trojan horses.

When MI5 secured the list of crypto-Communists in the surreptitious entry operation, Party Piece, already described, it was found that several top trade unionists were on file as secret members taking their orders from Moscow via the Party, as well as many lesser officials.[13] Other operations have been successfully undertaken in the more recent past so that MI5's knowledge of the secret Communist trade unionists and others posing as straightforward members of the Labour Party is reasonably up to date.[14]

As the Communists are aware, however, the security authorities make very little practical use of the information they obtain by clandestine means because they are so fearful of exposing sources and methods. Governments have also been extremely reluctant to capitalize on information which could have exposed many pro-Soviet active measures being promoted through the unions. Even when the Party Piece operation and further inquiries showed that one particularly influential trade-union leader was a fully fledged Soviet agent, successive governments forbade MI5 to interrogate him because they feared political repercussions in Parliament and charges of 'union-bashing'. Even when another senior trade-union leader was observed having meetings with KGB officers in London, interrogation was forbidden.[15]

An exception to this general policy of silence was made by Harold Wilson during the very damaging seamen's strike of 1966. Wilson, then Prime Minister, was provided with convincing evidence by

MI5 that the strike was being orchestrated by a few Communists imposing their will on the rest and hoping to bring the country to an economic standstill by bringing out the dockers and others in support. He frightened the Communists by stating in Parliament that the moderates on the Seamen's Union executive were being terrorized by a professional gang of Communists who planned their tactics 'with outside help'.[16] Within twenty-four hours the militants backed down after taking advice which convinced them that the extent of their Soviet involvement would be exposed if the strike was not ended. George Wigg (later Lord) told me that the evidence which Wilson could have produced would have been 'sensational'. I argued then, and still do, that, while a full disclosure might have upset the Foreign Office, which sets such store by Anglo-Soviet relations, an exposure of the Soviet Union's 'active measures' on that occasion would have served the national interest.

In 1973 two senior officers of MI5 called to see the late Maurice Macmillan, while he was Minister at the Department of Employment, to complain about the inroads being made by Communists into the unions and the extent to which these were being promoted by the Soviet Bloc. They said that MI5 would welcome legislation to curb these subversive activities, and Macmillan, who agreed with them, reported the visit to the Prime Minister, Edward Heath, who said that he would do what was necessary.[17] No legislation ensued, however, and the penetration of the unions has intensified.

MI5 took matters into its own hands in 1975 when it penetrated a secret meeting in West Germany of Communist trade-union leaders from Britain and Europe to discuss tactics for disrupting industry throughout Europe in the ensuing five years. The meeting, which was sponsored by Moscow, decided that the automobile industry was the most vulnerable to disruption and sabotage and that the British sector offered the softest target. The results, at British Leyland and Ford in particular, were extremely damaging and continued even though MI5 leaked its knowledge to a journalist who exposed it in *The Times*.[18]

The continuing concern of the present government with Communist infiltration has recently been demonstrated by two developments. The first is the issue by the Home Office of a new definition of 'subversive activities' which has been widened to mean 'those which threaten the safety or well-being of the State and which are intended to undermine or overthrow Parliamentary democracy by political, industrial or violent means'.[19] The second is the issue of new instructions to the Three Advisers, a standing group set up to advise Ministers when evidence exists suggesting that someone employed in connection with work 'the nature of which is vital to the security of the State' has or has had Communist connections. The instructions also apply to officials of any union involved with secret establishments who are suspected of Communist connections.[20] Both developments are the result of the steady intensification of Soviet active measures.

Once the trade unions have been successfully penetrated, a process which has to be continuous as people retire and must be replaced, what is expected of them by Moscow? A major requirement is the general undermining of the capitalist system to hasten the day when, according to Soviet ideology, it must collapse through its own inherent instability. This is achieved by so-called 'industrial action' aimed at wrecking – the promotion of unrest and dissatisfaction by agitators who are often the 'shop-floor' union officials, the shop stewards, many of whom have been, and still are, open or secret Communists. They create the unrest by stimulating unreasonable and often impossible demands which the management cannot accept and remain in competitive business. They seize on excuses for 'demarcation' disputes, arguments about which workers can do which tasks, and exaggerate minor arguments with the management into issues of high principle. The manufactured conflict often results in walk-outs and local strikes which bring the business to a standstill. These are often called unofficial strikes but, frequently, they are tacitly approved by the national union authorities. Once a group has abandoned work every effort is made to widen the dispute by bringing in other unions.

Another restrictive practice designed to make any business unprofitable and liable to collapse is the trade-union insistence on over-manning, which has been steadily applied to every major British industry. Nowhere has this been used more damagingly than in the union-ridden newspaper industry, the print unions being the major culprits. A relatively trivial incident at the old *Daily Mirror* building, Geraldine House, typifies the technique. Two chutes were erected so that bundles of newspapers could be slid down to waiting vans, but it was soon found that one chute was adequate. The union

187

concerned nevertheless insisted that both chutes must always be manned, and they were.[21]

As happens so often with Communist subversive measures, the over-manning strategy pays a double dividend. It undermines the capitalist system and then, when the inevitable shake-out of excess labour is forced on the firms if they are going to survive, there is a sudden surge in unemployment which can be exploited as a failure of the system.

On occasion the print unions have gone to the extreme of demanding payment for doing nothing as a means of forcing a damaging dispute. Shortly before its demise, the London *Evening News* started a colour supplement which was printed by an outside company. A few days before it was due to appear the print unions demanded that their members should be paid for producing it because, they claimed, they could have done so had they been asked. The management's refusal to be blackmailed into payment led to a delay in the issue of the supplement with picket lines at the news-paper's door, and successive disputes brought about the permanent closure of the paper with the loss of many jobs.[22]

Various members of the militant print unions are overt Com-munists or follow the Communist line, supporting the *Morning Star* and promoting the breaking of 'bad laws' which limit the power of trade unions.

The National Union of Journalists, which covers the writers and sub-editors, has been steadily penetrated by Marxists and militants who have staged many damaging strikes. When union meetings are called the militants tend to choose the most damaging time in the evening when minutes are precious for meeting edition schedules. The meetings are mandatory and are kept going by trivial issues and points of order to inflict maximum disruption. Militant sub-editors are powerfully placed to spike reports which are not to their politi-cal taste.

Strikes and disputes are invariably supported by the Communist press and by the Communist Party, which has often been involved in their initiation and orchestration. Many trade unions have their own publications with wide circulations, like the National Union of Mineworkers' *The Miner*, and they lend their support. Strikes and disputes also provide occasions for picket-line demonstrations and violence in contrived confrontations with the police, the deliberate flouting of the law being designed to bring it into disrepute, especially when television is on hand, as it usually is.

The other major requirement of the Communist-penetrated trade unions is the use of their power to move the Labour Party increasingly to the left so that in the event of its election to power it can be manipulated in the Soviet interest.

The whole Soviet-inspired effort by the Communists has been extraordinarily successful over the years. Though probably only about 0.1 per cent of Britain's trade unionists are members of the Communist Party, some 10 per cent of all officials of the major trade unions are Communists or far-left revolutionary Marxists. These include figures like Ken Gill, the General Secretary of the Technical, Administrative and Supervisory Section of the Amalgamated Union of Engineering Workers (AUEW), Mick McGahey of the National Union of Mineworkers (NUM), James Milne, General Secretary of the Scottish TUC, Terry Marsland, Assistant General Secretary of the Tobacco Workers' Union and Ray Alderson of the Civil and Public Services Association, who are all overt members of the Communist Party.* In addition there are many whose attitude and activities are difficult to distinguish from those of overt Communists. These include Arthur Scargill, President of the NUM, Ray Buckton, General Secretary of the Associated Society of Locomotive Engineers and Firemen (ASLEF), Jimmy Knapp, General Secretary of the National Union of Railwaymen (NUR), Alan Sapper, General Secretary of the Association of Cinematograph, Television and Allied Technicians, Jim Slater, General Secretary of the National Union of Seamen, Ken Cameron, National Secretary of the Fire Brigades' Union and Campbell Christie, Deputy Secretary of the Society of Civil and Public Servants.

Small as it is on paper, the Communist Party has cells in every major factory, port and shipbuilding yard receiving instructions on how to stimulate and exacerbate disputes, and the extent to which Communists and pro-Communists can manipulate a mass-membership which may be opposed to their aims and activities is one of the most disturbing peculiarities of true democracies. Except for the

* Gill and Marsland were among twelve prominent Communists expelled from the Party in July 1985 following an internal squabble. They retain their Communist views.

extent to which votes taken by show of hands are rigged, the Communists have achieved their wrecking successes largely by 'legitimate' means – by exploiting the apathy of trade-union members, most of whom do not bother to vote on contentious issues. The tactics have been well documented by authorities like Frank Chapple (now Lord) who took over the Electricians' Union after years of Communist domination sustained by a criminal degree of ballot-rigging. Meetings are called suddenly and at awkward times and places by left-wingers who know that their followers will attend. Any opponents who do turn up are then bored into premature departure by interminable points of order when the important, and binding, votes are then taken.[23]

The continuing use of ballot-rigging to ensure the election of far-left candidates was exposed in the spring of 1985 in connection with the election of the new General Secretary of the Transport and General Workers' Union. The voting system was shown to be wide open to abuse. Ballot papers had been forged with whole branches voting for the left-winger because one official had filled in all the ballot papers. Members who were listed as having voted for him had been given no chance to vote. The ballot was re-run, but only because of a continuing public outcry following exposure of the malpractices by newspapers.[24] A secret postal ballot overseen by an independent body is, obviously, the fairest way of conducting any major vote, but many of the union leaders oppose it because, once elected, often for life, they like to be entirely responsible for what they do. Their shop stewards support them because they prefer a show of hands at open-air meetings when the counting can be fraudulent, with intimidating thugs on the podium noting names.

The stoppages and strikes in the London docks, led by the militant Jack Dash, accelerated the end of London as a major port with the loss of thousands of jobs and a consequent increase in the prosperity of competing continental ports. Similar subversive activity helped to ruin the port of Liverpool and, more recently, of Southampton. The shipyards have been systematically devastated by demarcation disputes, sit-ins and similar industrial activities which have achieved nothing except the loss of trade and jobs.

The antics of the Communist shop-steward Derek Robinson ('Red Robbo') were to be seen regularly on television and the results are to be seen in the loss of jobs and commercial opportunities in

British Leyland, then a nationalized organization. The British Leyland factory at Speke, in Liverpool, was forced to shut down by unacceptable action by the revolutionary workers who then organized a 'sit-in' in the hope of inducing police action so that they could make allegations of police brutality. The factory no longer exists and the extremist action helped to force up unemployment in Merseyside, where the whole work-force has been labelled as undependable so that new businesses want no part of it. The exceptionally high unemployment rate on Merseyside has been largely inflicted on the majority by a militant few.

This deliberate creation of unemployment is a major purpose of Communist active measures, for it can then be attacked as evidence of the failure of the capitalist system, and the unemployed become a new target for unrest, demonstration and, hopefully, riot. The situation was put succinctly by Sir James Goldsmith in his evidence to the Media Committee:

> Recently we have seen great companies paralysed by strikes at the very time that they are struggling for their survival. Often these strikes are caused by a handful of men over seemingly trivial issues and we hear the comment, 'They must be mad; they must want to commit suicide.' These small groups do not want to commit suicide. They want to create chaos. They want to create civil strife because only in that way can they bring about the structural changes they seek. Those who are committing suicide are the thousands who follow them blindly. Like the rest of us they have watched this nation being destroyed by a small minority.

The tame acceptance of the leadership of such men by the majority is further evidence of the human gullibility on which the active-measures operators batten, as well as of apathy. This has never been demonstrated so vividly as in the recent miners' strike contrived, against the wishes of most of the members of the NUM, by an overt Communist, Mick McGahey, and Arthur Scargill, who calls himself a former Communist but who follows the pro-Soviet Communist line in all respects, including adulation of the Soviet Union. A well-known Communist, Frank Watters, has described how he was specifically sent to the Yorkshire coalfields to foment strife and strikes and to tutor Scargill, a former Young Communist, in the methods he should use.[25] Scargill learned well. First he contrived to initiate the crippling dispute without a ballot. Then it was pursued by every kind of active-measures technique – deception and disinformation (regarding coal stocks and the imminence of power-cuts), intimidation, violence and denigration of law and order (on the picket lines). The mass picketing had been devised by Scargill who had demonstrated its potential when thousands of 'flying' pickets, whom he had organized, descended on the Saltley coke depot in Birmingham in 1972 and overwhelmed the police. Scargill described to me how elated he was when he saw 'those thousands of men with banners marching towards us'.[26]

Even in defeat, those trained on Communist lines invoke the upside-down ploy and claim victory. On a visit to Moscow, after the striking miners had returned to work in ignominious defeat after a year of severe hardship, Scargill claimed that the strike had been a triumph because it had politicized thousands of young men and women.[27] It had also trained thousands of men in the practice of intimidation, violence and revolt against the law. All this was music to the ears of the Politburo and the International Department, as was Scargill's repeated boast that his efforts had cost the British economy and nation more than £5,000 million, a financial blow which had prevented the Conservative Government from making tax concessions. That political set-back could further another of the Politburo's main aims – getting the Labour Party into office.

To quote The Times, 'One consequence of the coal strike is that Britain has woken up to the much wider involvement of formal and informal Communists in industrial and political life than most people realised.'[28] But how long will Britain remain awake? The forgetfulness factor seems to be operating at its usual rapid rate.

At the time of writing, Scargill is campaigning for a new international organization of miners which would include the Soviet-Bloc countries and could be almost guaranteed to become a Communist front, in line with the other so-called 'international' outfits. He has also secured changes to the NUM's rule book, ensuring his continuing leadership and increasing his power to bend the membership to his political will.[29]

As with other strikes, the militant miners were joined by men and women who had nothing to do with the mining industry. These outsiders were welcomed, not only to swell the numbers and the noise, but to provide scapegoats when violence became excessive and the miners' leaders could claim that their men had not been responsible – another deception ploy. Many of these young extremists, who utilize social security to undermine the system which provides it, claim to be followers of Trotsky or Chairman Mao, or to be anarchists, but their eventual purpose is the same as the Politburo's – the overthrow of true democracy and its replacement by a totalitarian dictatorship which could never be voted out of power. While at loggerheads with the Communist Party on ideological trivia, these new-style extremists, who belong to organizations like the Militant Tendency and Socialist Workers' Party, serve the Soviet purpose by undermining Parliament – there are now several Trotskyite MPs – the capitalist economy, the police, the judiciary and other pillars of true democracy. They display such zeal and ruthlessness that some people have been led to believe that they are more important than the Communists but, in the event of a successful overthrow of democracy in Britain, or any other European country, they would quickly be deprived of any power they might achieve. They would have no military base, while behind the Communist Party, however small its overt membership, stands the might of the Soviet Red Army which could be 'invited in' to 'establish law and order' as was alleged to have happened in Czechoslovakia. The Trotskyists and such like would then be swept away in some modern equivalent of the Night of the Long Knives.

The Politburo must surely be astonished, as well as delighted, when it sees the British trade unions and their extremist auxiliaries inflicting so much damage on the system which provides their members with employment and guarantees their freedom. Once the unions have been penetrated in the Communist interest, the active-measures operators have little to do but sit back and watch their work being done for them. It is surely no coincidence that where the Soviets have generally failed to penetrate the unions, as in the US, there is far less industrial strife, while in places like Britain and Australia, where penetration has been deep and lasting, strikes and disruption are commonplace and so orchestrated that when one ends another is initiated.

The Politburo's wonder at the suicidal tendencies of Britain's trade unionists must be intensified by comparison with the domestic situation, where the Soviet trade unions are mere ciphers with no

193

power and where strikes are 'inconceivable' and would be suppressed with ferocity, as they were recently in Poland. The Soviet trade unions are, in fact, yet another deception, giving the impression that the workers have some control over their lives when, in reality, they are a further lever for the Politburo and the *nomenklatura* to strengthen its power. It was not by chance, for instance, that Shelepin, who headed the Soviet trade-union organization from 1967 to 1973, had previously been Chief of the KGB.

The most forthright description of the Soviet trade unions was given by the American trade-union leader George Meany, in answers to questions about the wisdom of contacts between German and Soviet trade unions posed by the magazine *Der Spiegel*. Meany, the most powerful and most independent American trade-union leader of his day, described the Soviet trade unions as 'nothing but arms of the controlling dictatorship' and could see nothing but danger in any association with them. 'The so-called unions are fronts charged with the task of making the workers more responsive and submissive to the orders and decrees of the dictatorial government,' he wrote. He pointed out that the Soviet trade unions had supported the Kremlin's rulers when they crushed the revolt of the East German workers in 1953 and the Hungarian revolt of 1956 and launched the invasion of Czechoslovakia in 1968. He called them 'counterfeit organizations' of which the officials were chosen not by the workers but by the Communist Party. He accused them of assisting in what would now be called active measures by distorting their findings on their visits to free countries. (These statements were never published by *Der Spiegel*, following a dispute with Meany who refused to agree to cuts which omitted large portions of his answers. A copy of the original questions, answers and cuts has been made available to me.)

The existence of the Soviet trade unions on paper has also enabled the Politburo to set up a major front organization, the World Federation of Trade Unions (WFTU), which serves as a base for infiltrating and influencing the trade unions of the West. Created in 1945, with headquarters in Prague, it began its long reign of disruptive tactics by doing all it could to prevent the rehabilitation of Europe through the Marshall Plan, preferring the ruin to continue so that Communism could be raised upon it. It overstepped the mark in 1949 when the British TUC became unwilling to contribute money to maintain an organization 'intent on propagating Communist views', as the WFTU does through the various magazines and pamphlets it publishes, and there was an overwhelming vote for British withdrawal in September of that year. Its branches in France and Austria were later expelled for subversive activities, but the WFTU has since improved its position and influence, through individual trade unions rather than with the TUC. In 1982 trade unionists from many British unions, led by Alex Kitson, the pro-Soviet Deputy General Secretary of the TGWU, attended the World Trade Union Congress in Cuba, while the Soviets have induced the United Nations to grant the WFTU what is known as 'Category A status'.

The WFTU has been especially active in promoting the 'strike movement' in capitalist countries, and intelligence sources suspect that it was active in trying to prevent an agreement which had TUC support between the NUM and the National Coal Board. More recently it has campaigned against the modernization of nuclear weapons by NATO and the US. In furthering the Politburo's objective of enforcing unilateral nuclear disarmament in the West it has been effectively assisted by British trade unions, which have been instrumental in swinging the Labour Party to a unilateral disarmament policy through their card votes at conferences and general domination of the Labour movement. Certain individual trade-union leaders like Arthur Scargill, Bill Keys, Ron Todd and Jim Slater have given additional services by taking a prominent stand in the front line of the 'peace' offensive.

Scargill has involved himself with the WFTU in moves to set up a 'Miners' International' which would be dominated by Eastern-Bloc countries. His visits to WFTU headquarters in Prague and Moscow have caused concern among other trade unionists, and the Foreign Secretary Sir Geoffrey Howe, has accused him of 'being openly in league with countries which threaten our security'.

Chapter 13

The Offensive Called 'Peace'

'The call for peace is given proletarian meaning only if accompanied by a call for revolutionary struggle.'

Lenin

Of all the words deliberately distorted by the Soviets for mass-deception purposes none has been so debased as 'peace' and no perversion of the language has yielded such political profit. Lenin declared that as an ultimate objective 'peace' simply means 'Communist world control' and his successors have latched on to that concept ever since.

As the KGB spy Anthony Blunt confessed, the word peace was used with great skill in the 1930s to recruit him and other agents to the service of Soviet espionage. He and scores of others were asked if, as good Communist supporters, they would work for 'peace', and they found it difficult to refuse. They did not demur when given the rather exciting news that this work would be clandestine and it was not until months or years later, when they were irretrievably in the net, that they came to realize that they were working for the KGB.[1] When the KGB officer Anatoli Strelnikov tried to recruit me as described, he opened his gambit by declaring that what I was doing in my anti-Soviet articles in the *Daily Express* was 'terrible for peace'. At first I thought that he meant that they were bringing war closer but what he really meant was that my efforts were directed against the march of Soviet Communism and the Kremlin's interests and therefore, in his book, were against 'peace'.

Over the years the Soviet concept of 'peace' and the worldwide yearning for real peace in the nuclear age have been exploited as a determined campaign, using 'peace' as a central feature of the Politburo's active measures. The chief targets of this offensive have been, and still are, the US and its NATO allies, especially Britain, West Germany and Holland.

The basic message of the active measures involved with the 'peace' offensive has been frighteningly effective – everything which the US and its allies do threatens peace while all that the Soviet Union and its allies do promotes peace. As John Barron has put it, 'To support America means to support war, while to support the Soviet Union is to support peace. This is the art of active measures, a kind of black magic of Moscow origin. It is shocking to see how well it works.'[2]

The pseudo-peace offensive was launched in earnest in April 1949 as a major cold-war tactic with the setting up of the grandiosely named World Peace Council by the Kremlin. Its immediate objective was to serve as the centre of the Communist-inspired protest movement against the Marshall Plan and what was then the North Atlantic Alliance. Since then it has remained the fountainhead of the Soviet 'peace' offensive. In 1951 it was expelled from Paris, its original location, for 'fifth-column activities' and moved to Vienna, where, in 1957, it also received an expulsion order 'for activities directed against the interests of the Austrian State'. Currently it is based in Helsinki to distance it from Moscow as part of the pretence that it is independent. It cannot, however, conceal the fact that it is financed by the Kremlin from money allegedly donated voluntarily by Soviet citizens. The ostensible source of the cash is the Soviet Peace Fund to which organizations in the Soviet Union are required to contribute whether they wish to or not. According to an official statement published by Novosti, 'The Soviet Peace Fund has 75 million regular voluntary contributors. It receives box-office receipts of specially organized concerts, stage productions, exhibitions and sporting events.'[3] It is also claimed that 'workers, scientists and figures in the arts in the US, Britain, Italy, France etc. contribute to the Fund'. Foreign businessmen wishing to trade with the Soviet Union are often advised that their prospects will be enhanced if they contribute.

To present a non-Soviet appearance, the leaders of the World

Peace Council are usually chosen from foreigners but they tend to be trusted followers of the Kremlin line and, because of the dependence on Soviet money, the Council's policy can be moulded by Moscow. The Soviet directives to the Council are routed through the so-called 'Soviet Committee for the Defence of Peace', one of its chief officials being a member of the International Department. According to the defector Levchenko, who did part-time work for the Committee, it is 'an active tool of the International Department in manipulating the World Peace Council'.

The current President of the World Peace Council is the Indian Romesh Chandra, who has served on its committee since 1953. He is a long-standing member of the Indian Communist Party and Moscow is confident that he will always promote the objectives of the Soviet Bloc. He has, for example, consistently promoted the view that, while the US is aggressive and threatens peace, the Soviet military build-up is purely defensive, in spite of the rape of Hungary and Czechoslovakia and the invasion of Afghanistan.[4]

A typical British member of the Council was the late Ivor Montagu, a hardline Communist who, according to one of his colleagues, 'never wavered in standing firmly by the side of the Soviet Union as a bastion of peace'. Like other Communists and their dupes he professed to believe that the American possession of nuclear weapons was 'immoral', though Russia possessed more. In a recent debate in the House of Lords, Lord Orr-Ewing named the Labour MP James Lamond as the British Vice-President of the World Peace Council. He also named several leading British trade unionists as members.[5] Lamond denied that the Council is a Soviet front but, until 1973, the true nature of such organizations was so well recognized by the Labour Party that membership of them was proscribed.

The World Peace Council now has subsidiaries in about 135 countries. Among the main offshoots are the US Peace Council, founded in 1979 to promote the Politburo's line on arms control, nuclear freezes and other aspects of the 'peace' offensive; the British Peace Assembly, set up in April 1980 and sponsored by leading trade unionists; the International Institute for Peace, an annexe which the Council managed to leave behind in Vienna after its expulsion, and the Christian Peace Conference, operating out of Prague.

Other major Communist fronts are regularly pressed into the service of the 'peace' offensive. These include the World Federation of Trade Unions, which lends its weight with conferences such as 'Trade Unions for Peace' held in Moscow, where British delegates claimed that their government acts mercilessly against activists of the anti-war movement; the Women's International Democratic Federation, which sponsored a 'World Congress of Women' in Prague in 1981 to co-ordinate women's groups in campaigns against the deployment of American weapons, but not Soviet weapons; and the World Federation of Democratic Youth and the International Union of Students, both based in Prague and under Kremlin control. In addition there is a mass of smaller peace movements such as 'Housewives for Peace', 'Teachers for Peace', 'Parliamentarians for Peace' and even 'Generals for Peace'.

Some British and European peace movements were genuinely pacifist in origin but were speedily exploited by the International Department and the KGB. Many people of goodwill support these organizations but behind them, either actively or, if there is no need for interference, passively, lies Lenin's slogan 'Peace to the people – power to the Soviets'. While some, like the British Campaign for Nuclear Disarmament, which will be considered separately, claim complete autonomy and have no need of money from Moscow, others are under Kremlin influence and control. In April 1981 the Dutch expelled TASS correspondent Vadim Leonov who had involved himself in the Dutch 'peace' movement and had boasted, 'If Moscow decides that 50,000 demonstrators must take to the streets in the Netherlands, then they take to the streets. A message through my channels is sufficient.'[6]

The case of Arne Petersen in Denmark, already described, showed that Moscow was financing his efforts in a campaign for a Nordic nuclear-free zone and other activities on behalf of 'peace'.[7] Two Soviet diplomats were expelled from Norway in 1981 for trying to bribe Norwegians to demonstrate against nuclear arms. In the US, Yuri Kapralov, a KGB officer, is known to have penetrated the peace movement. Posing as Counsellor at the Soviet Embassy in Washington he regularly attended rallies and seminars and spoke at them. In 1982 two KGB officers, Yuri Babaints and Mikhail Morozov, were expelled from Portugal for trying to incite 'peace riots' against NATO. A record number of Soviet-Bloc agents were expelled, worldwide, in 1983, many of them for 'peace' activities, and the catalogue of infiltration and subversion has continued, with the accession of Gorbachov as Soviet leader making no difference. The World Peace Council is more than ever the lynch-pin of the Politburo's great 'peace' offensive, operating through its Trojan-horse front organizations and spending at least $40 million a year on 'peace' initiatives alone, according to an official CIA estimate.[8]

The motives of the 'peace' movements and the ways in which they have been manipulated by Soviet active-measures operators are most vividly demonstrated by an examination of relevant events since the World Peace Council's establishment in 1949. Within a year the Council mounted its first campaign in the form of the Stockholm Peace Pledge, demanding an absolute ban on atomic weapons. It was no coincidence that the US then had a monopoly on usable nuclear weapons while the Soviet Union had a massive preponderance of conventional forces ready and available in Europe. A total ban on nuclear weapons would have left Europe wide open to Soviet intimidation and possible invasion. At the Second Congress of the World Peace Council, held a few months later in Warsaw, it was claimed that 500 million people had signed the Stockholm pledge, yet as soon as the Soviet Union became an H-bomb power in 1953, the pledge was suspended.

Throughout the 1950s and early 1960s the 'peace' movement expressed itself as a 'Ban the Bomb' campaign which was completely unsuccessful except that it recruited people like Michael Foot, who was later to exert momentous effect on British Labour Party policy through his surprise accession to the leadership. From its earliest days the movement has also attracted the peculiar type of clergyman who revels in personal publicity. The first of these was the extraordinary Dr Hewlett Johnson, the Communist 'Red Dean' of Canterbury, who received enormous publicity for his various antics because he was such good 'copy' for the media. He figured, disgracefully, in the promotion of a monstrous deception promoted by the World Peace Council – that American troops were using germ warfare to combat the attempted Communist take-over of Korea by Korean Communist and Chinese troops. Though I have already mentioned this, it merits more detailed description as an example of what a gullible cleric, however exalted, can induce himself or be induced to do.

Early in 1952, before the Politburo had fallen out with the Communist leaders in Peking, who objected to its domination, an organization calling itself The Chinese People's Committee for World Peace issued many thousands of copies of a 52-page booklet containing many photographs purporting to prove that 'the US Government openly resorted to bacteriological warfare in Korea and north-east China in violation of international conventions and against humanity'. To any trained biologist, like myself, the document was clearly fraudulent, and stupidly so, with harmless insects like stone-flies and ground beetles and even spiders being pictured as having been used as the germ-carriers, while the bombs alleged to have contained them were clearly leaflet-bombs. The document was a crude example of active measures, as now applied by Moscow, because the deception involved all manner of high-level authorities from academicians to various political leaders.[9]

In July 1952, Hewlett Johnson, who had been to China, staged a press conference to provide 'proof' of the germ-warfare allegations. I attended the conference and his only evidence was a long scroll signed by various Chinese bishops. He argued that if the allegations were believed by such ecclesiastics they must be true, a crazy generalization still being promoted by his clerical successors in the 'peace' movement. This gaitered buffoon, whose utterances were widely publicized, even believed the farcical claim by Moscow that the British had resorted to 'dropping lepers in the rear of the People's Army in Korea'.[10]

The photographs were quickly proven to be fakes by American and British scientists and nobody, today, believes that any attempt was ever made to wage germ warfare in Korea. It remains a classic example of the readiness of Communist active-measures operators to use the big lie to achieve a propaganda advantage, however fleeting, to exploit the gullible in telling it and to rely on the shortness of the public's memory when such a lie is exposed.

With the Red Army's adoption of a nuclear strategy, once nuclear weapons became available to it, and with Nikita Khrushchev in power, the Politburo switched to a new propaganda thrust called 'peaceful co-existence' and the 'peace' movement was required to promote it once it had been officially launched at the twentieth Conference of the Soviet Communist Party in 1956. The concept of East and West going their own political ways in peace was described in the memoirs of Reinhard Gehlen, the West German intelligence chief, as 'nothing more than the familiar ploy of embracing the enemy and softening him up for the final kill'.[11] What Khrushchev really meant when he assured the Party Conference that 'peaceful co-existence was a fundamental principle of Marxism-Leninism' has been described by General Jan Sejna:

> In the Soviet view 'peaceful co-existence' meant overtly wanting to co-exist with Western countries peacefully but, covertly, to penetrate all Western organs of influence, such as political parties, trade unions and the media, and so weaken them that they become vulnerable to Soviet-controlled Communism, with or without military intervention, for which the Soviets prepared themselves notwithstanding their assertions to the contrary.[12]

The concept that peaceful co-existence might be permanent or even of reasonably long duration has since been repeatedly denounced by Soviet writers as 'unscientific' and in fact, eight months after Khrushchev launched it he also launched the invasion of Hungary to smash the bid for freedom there.

When Leonid Brezhnev succeeded Khrushchev in October 1964 he began a nineteen-year reign characterized by such a degree of duplicity that the Soviet military machine was expanded into the largest ever seen, providing military superiority in both conventional and nuclear arms and making the USSR an undeniable superpower. The specific active measures used so ingeniously to secure this grand objective have already been described in Chapter 6 – 'The Great Missile Deception'. In addition, the Politburo covered its clandestine activities with a new propaganda initiative. It was called Détente.

Chapter 14

The Détente Deception

'Trust us, comrades, for by 1985, as a consequence of what we are achieving by means of détente, we will have achieved most of our objectives in Western Europe . . . a decisive shift in the correlation of forces will be such that by 1985 we will be able to exert our will whenever we need to.'

Leonid Brezhnev
Prague, 1973

Brezhnev, who eventually made himself Commander-in-Chief of the Soviet Armed Forces as well as President and Communist Party Secretary, quickly decided to attack the US indirectly, through a surrogate, by providing North Vietnam with modern weapons which were, eventually, to lead to the American defeat in South Vietnam. In the overt Soviet propaganda against the US involvement, the World Peace Council and its branches were pressed into service and an annual Stockholm Conference offered support to Americans prepared to desert from the armed forces or to refuse to be drafted.

In 1968, after the crushing of Czechoslovakia by Red Army invasion, Brezhnev announced his 'doctrine' claiming the Soviet Union's right to intervene militarily in any 'Socialist' country where 'Socialism' was deemed to be threatened. Then, after this had been tacitly accepted by the West and with West Germany being governed by the Social Democrats with a 'soft' Chancellor, Willy Brandt, Brezhnev suggested a European Security Conference. Its underlying motive was the dissolution of NATO and the Warsaw

Pact which would entail the withdrawal of American forces from Europe, with little possibility of return, so leaving Western Europe at the mercy of the Red Army. After this ploy failed, as Brezhnev must have anticipated, he chose the Twenty-fourth Congress of the Communist Party of the Soviet Union, in April 1971, to launch a 'peace programme' which was the start of détente: ostensibly the diminution of East–West tension, a reduction in the risk of war and the expansion of contacts, especially in trade – all worthy objectives if pursued in honesty.

All truly democratic prime ministers and presidents wish to be remembered, historically, as 'Princes of Peace' and in their striving for this distinction they are prepared to buy 'gold bricks' from confidence tricksters, as Chamberlain did from Hitler, as Roosevelt did from Stalin and as Nixon, Carter and Wilson did from Brezhnev. In this they are invariably supported by their career diplomats and other foreign office personnel who feel that sacrifices are worthwhile to 'improve relations'.

An insider's account of Brezhnev's détente manoeuvre has recently been provided by the most senior Soviet official to defect to the West, Arkady Shevchenko, who was personal assistant to the Soviet Foreign Secretary, Gromyko, from 1970 to 1973 and was then Under Secretary General for Political and Security Council Affairs at the United Nations until his physical defection in April 1978. Shevchenko has revealed that while the Western political leaders were prepared to believe that the Soviets wanted genuine détente, the Politburo regarded it as simply 'a tactical manoeuvre which would in no way supersede the Marxist-Leninist idea of the final victory of the worldwide revolutionary process'.[1]

Brezhnev himself assured his co-conspirators that, like 'peaceful co-existence' in the past, détente would not interfere with the long-term aims of active measures but would, in fact, provide a more favourable operational environment for them. The opening up of trade and cultural relations would facilitate the passage of KGB agents and other operators to the West together with improved access to organizations and agents of influence, including those in the 'peace' movements. Détente would provide the climate for securing the soft loans and advanced technology from the West which the Soviet Union needed for both economic and military reasons. The military chiefs were told that if the West could be lulled into

204

continuing 'détente' until 1985, the Soviet Union would then be so well placed that it could take a much tougher line, especially as regards military intimidation.[2]

The main Kremlin figures involved in the détente deception, apart from Brezhnev, were Ponomarev, the chief architect of the ploy, Suslov, the ideological guru, whose support was essential to pacify any hardline doubters, and Yuri Andropov, then head of the KGB. They saw it as a means of buying time. While détente would not prevent continuation of the campaign to undermine NATO through the 'peace' movement and other active measures, modernization and expansion of the Soviet and Warsaw Pact forces would be able to progress at an accelerating rate.

After the ideological doubters had been assured that détente would enable the Soviet Union to challenge the West in every way short of war, Brezhnev agreed a treaty with Nixon in May 1972, to limit the development of defensive missiles capable of shooting down intercontinental bombarding rockets. This was calculated to avoid any weakening of the mutual deterrent effect of such rockets because it was feared that if one side developed a defensive advantage it might be encouraged to attempt a surprise nuclear assault. The Soviet military planners were to break this agreement.[3] The ensuing SALT agreements, which became possible with the general feeling of relaxation engendered by the détente concept and have already been described, gave the Soviets an agreed slight edge in intercontinental missiles which they proceeded, clandestinely, to exploit into clear superiority.

On the trade and cash side, Brezhnev fulfilled his objectives. In May 1973 he visited Bonn and signed a ten-year agreement for West German industrial and technical co-operation. Two months later, after a visit to France, he secured two ten-year programmes of technical co-operation. In February 1975 Harold Wilson went to Moscow and gave the Soviet Union a soft loan of nearly £1,000 million. As a bonus, the Russians were able to install inspectors in those British factories where contracts were to be placed – to groans from the security authorities who had little doubt that some of them would be used for KGB and active-measures operations and would further strain MI5's limited resources.[4]

Preparatory talks to enshrine détente in a formal treaty – the so-called Helsinki Accord – opened in the Finnish capital in November

205

1972, and after almost three years of discussion by delegates of thirty-five nations, at meetings in Geneva and Madrid, culminated in a summit in Helsinki, the 'Final Act' in July 1975. The Soviets obtained major agreements on technology and trade and some degree of Western disarmament, with both the Americans and British reducing their defence spending afterwards. They also secured agreement that the existing boundaries of the Soviet Empire are 'inviolable', meaning that under no circumstances would the West use force to try to make the Politburo relinquish any territory in its possession or under its control. As Shevchenko comments, 'It does indeed seem that Lenin was right – capitalists are willing to fight for the privilege of selling Communists the rope with which to hang themselves.'[5]

The main apparent achievement of the West was to require the Soviet Union to pay more heed to human rights, especially in respect of dissidents in their own country, and to facilitate the freer flow of outside information to the Soviet peoples. In addition, the US, and Henry Kissinger in particular, had believed that once the West had formally recognized the permanent incorporation of Eastern Europe into the Soviet Bloc, the Politburo would feel more secure, slow down its arms build-up and generally become more conciliatory.

In the event the Kremlin made a few token concessions, such as allowing a certain amount of emigration, moderating the tone of its propaganda and reducing the jamming of some foreign radio programmes, but these were all short-lived and the military build-up and clandestine active measures continued on a steadily increasing scale. To quote Shevchenko:

> My most revealing experience came when I realized that our military chiefs were just laughing their heads off over disarmament. While the talks were going on they were promoting a massive rearmament programme. The start of détente was accompanied by the creation of the most ominous war machine.[6]
>
> One of the great fallacies of détente was the idea that, if the Soviet Union were engaged in economic, trade, cultural and other agreements, the West would be able to moderate the Soviets' voracious appetite for expansion and promote a shift in the USSR's global aims. Nothing could be further from reality. The Soviet Union has never contemplated agreeing to arrangements that would in any way tie its hands in the pursuit of what it wanted.[7]

206

Shevchenko's views are borne out by the facts. President Carter's restraint on US arms developments – his cancellation of the B1 bomber, the termination of Minuteman 3 missile production and the slowing down of the MX missile – had little, if any, effect on Moscow's behaviour. Indeed, soon after America's authority had been sapped by the self-humiliating scourging indulged in by the media after the Watergate scandal, the Politburo began, in 1977, to deploy the ingenious new SS20 missiles in cold violation of détente with a view to swinging the military balance in Europe firmly in its favour. The extent to which this superiority has been achieved and the deliberate deception involved in the process will be discussed in Chapter 16.

On the human rights issue, Vladimir Bukovsky, one of the Soviet dissidents who was allowed to emigrate in 1976 (in exchange for a Chilean Communist imprisoned in Chile), has reported that the Soviet authorities continued to confiscate forbidden books and to prosecute those found in possession of them.[8] They quickly cracked down on other dissidents, subjecting some to psychiatric treatment on the grounds that anyone who was dissatisfied with life in the Soviet Union must be a mental case. When President Carter concentrated his interest on human rights and openly supported Soviet dissidents his action was dismissed by the Kremlin as a challenge to its rule, an interference in Soviet domestic affairs and – unbelievably – 'a violation of the spirit of détente'. The Politburo's active response was to arrest more dissidents.

To quote Lord Home, speaking in the Lords' debate on subversion on 23 April 1985, 'In the Helsinki Final Act the Russian negotiators put their names to two pledges – that they would refrain from any form of armed intervention against other participating states and that Russia would conduct relations with other states in the spirit of the principles contained in the declaration. Within two years the Russian army and air force were in Afghanistan.'

Throughout the so-called period of détente, which effectively collapsed when the invasion of Afghanistan opened even Carter's eyes, the insincerity of the Politburo's commitment has been demonstrated repeatedly by the Soviet support for terrorism and armed rebellion in many Third World countries. When the Soviets were signing the 'Final Act' in Helsinki, they were already planning the use of Cuban troops in Angola, which also breached the Kennedy–Khrushchev deal on the Cuban missile crisis in 1962.

For Brezhnev and the Politburo, détente has never been anything but a tactic in the cold war and the Helsinki Accord was a second Yalta at which the weaknesses and gullibility of the West were cynically exploited. Brezhnev was succeeded by Andropov, the former KGB chief and the hardliner who had organized the savage repression of Hungary in 1956. In his first major speech to the Central Committee, after being appointed General Secretary of the Party, Andropov said that he felt confident that 'détente has a bright future' – as well he might. After Reagan's re-election as President, which disappointed him, Andropov appealed to the peoples of Europe, in a message put out by TASS, to support détente on their own, knowing that Reagan had, long ago, seen through the deception and the active measures supporting it.

In his brief reign, Chernenko talked frequently about the merits of détente in the hope that it would bring about the tacit acceptance by the West of the Soviet Union's occupation of Afghanistan. At the time of writing, the new leader, Gorbachov, has had little time to develop the concept of détente to which, as a Politburo member, he was a contributor as he was to the invasion of Afghanistan, but it would be surprising if such a shining product of the Soviet system failed to try to promote the deception which has delivered such advantages.

An illuminating commentary on détente and the Helsinki Accord has recently been broadcast by Max Kampelman, who was US ambassador to the follow-up meetings of the 'Final Act' held in Madrid over three years. In his first speech he said that, so far as the Soviets were concerned, there had been no follow-up and that all they had done had undermined the whole concept. The hundreds of hours of discussions with Soviet delegates underlined their continuing commitment to Leninism, meaning the Communizing of the rest of the world. 'To have your security depend on the goodwill, the good intentions, of the Soviet régime is to put our own society at risk,' Kampelman said. 'Unilateral concessions by us are not interpreted as acts of goodwill; I believe that unilateral concessions by us are interpreted as a lack of will.'[9]

It was lack of Western will, displayed to an extent which now seems incredible, that secured for the Soviets a particular unilateral concession which they had struggled to engineer through active measures applied on an unprecedented scale. This was the campaign to prevent the US from making the neutron bomb.

Chapter 15

The Neutron Bomb Offensive

'A weapon whose basic design would seem to provide the essence of what Western morality has long sought for waging classical battlefield warfare – to keep the war to a struggle between the warriors and exclude the non-combatants and their physical assets – has been violently denounced, precisely because it achieves this objective.'

Samuel T. Cohen
A senior US neutron bomb researcher

In the 1960s American scientists conceived and partially developed the idea of a nuclear weapon which, instead of relying on blast and fire for its destructive power, would depend mainly on penetrating radiation for its military effect. This radiation would take the form of an intense shower of subatomic particles called neutrons, which have the capacity to pass through metal and, in sufficient concentration, are lethal to living organisms while doing no apparent damage to physical objects. Such a device, known militarily as an enhanced radiation (ER) weapon but colloquially as 'the neutron bomb' carries three major advantages over Hiroshima-type weapons, particularly for civilians caught up in a battle in Central Europe. Firstly, they would be constructed to be of particular use against the massed tanks which the Soviet Union would undoubtedly use in any assault on the West and would greatly help to reduce the massive superiority of the Warsaw Pact in tank numbers. Used as the warheads of precision-guided missiles, they would concentrate their effects on the combat troops involved with the risk to civilians being substantially lessened. Secondly, by exploding these warheads some 100 feet or so above the massed tanks, the blast and fire, which cannot be entirely eliminated from any nuclear weapons, would be greatly reduced, so that the risk of damage to property would be diminished further compared to the devastation certain to be produced by any standard atomic weapons. Thirdly, the neutron weapon produces little radioactive fall-out so the long-term danger to civilians would be very much smaller than with weapons of the Hiroshima type.[1]

The low-yield weapon would have replaced many of the Hiroshima-type warheads and bombs already existing in NATO's defensive armoury and should, therefore, have been more acceptable to the people of Western Europe as being far less indiscriminate and being specifically designed to concentrate its effects on the attacking troops without leaving lasting radioactivity on the ground.

The Soviet military authorities were deeply disturbed by the neutron bomb project because their strategy for a quick thrust into Europe was based on their preponderance of tanks in which they had invested enormous sums and resources. To quote the detailed study made by Joseph D. Douglass, 'The Soviets' preferred operational strategy appears to be to seize and occupy Europe without destroying the prize for which the war is being fought.'[2] The possibility that this could be achieved with a massive tank thrust was clearly threatened by the neutron bomb. After an enormous effort the Soviets had broken the American atomic-bomb monopoly which had prevented their conventional forces from sweeping into Western Europe in Stalin's time, and now the Americans faced them with a new concept to neutralize their ace advantage in tanks.

While there is evidence from intelligence sources that the Soviets were already working on a neutron weapon, it was of less value to them because they knew, at that stage, even if only because of their deep espionage penetration of NATO, that there was no prospect of a surprise assault by NATO tanks on the Iron Curtain. They also saw a stockpile of neutron weapons as posing a much more credible deterrent to a Soviet attack than the battlefield nuclear weapons already in the hands of NATO troops, because the latter would always be held back as long as possible in view of the great damage they would inflict on West German territory.

There was no need for public action by the Kremlin at that stage, however, because, owing to disagreements about the weapon between various US military chiefs and with the election of the liberal President John Kennedy in January 1961, research on the neutron bomb was given low priority, work being concentrated on improving the big megaton warheads for the deterrent intercontinental rockets.[3] Sensing that the weapon might be resuscitated one day, however, Khrushchev, then the Soviet leader, used the concept to attack the American 'war-mongers', claiming that the neutron bomb they had conceived would 'kill everything alive but preserve material assets' and was, therefore, an 'anti-human' weapon. He did not, of course, indicate that within seven months he would shock the world by restarting nuclear tests, after a solemnly agreed suspension, a move of which he must already have been aware because of the time needed to prepare for such tests. He would also have known that the weapons to be tested were the most destructive megaton warheads for bombarding missiles ever devised and that the test-series would be the 'dirtiest', radioactively.[4]

These Soviet tests stimulated further neutron-weapons work, as Khrushchev's advisers must have foreseen, but there was no American decision about making military use of the principle until the middle 1970s when the feasibility of using it in improved battlefield weapons was suggested by the US Army. Some American journalists, sensing a 'good story', took up the theme that the neutron bomb was a 'people killer' and began to campaign against it. Soviet active measures were quickly focused on this promising line of public disinformation so kindly provided by the media, with increasingly effective results.

The Soviet active-measures requirement was to present the neutron bomb as a new and horrendous weapon of mass destruction which would wipe out cities full of 'workers' while sparing buildings and other property belonging to capitalist interests. This was a typical use of the upside-down ploy; for the weapon was of no value for attacking cities and the avoidance of damage to property can hardly be rated as of interest only to 'capitalists' in view of the devastation of residential areas in German cities, such as Hamburg and Berlin, caused by conventional explosives in the last war.

As so often happens, the constant repetition of the lie had its effects on the gullible and on those wanting to believe it for political purposes. Religious groups in several countries swallowed the propaganda line that the neutron bomb was an especially pernicious weapon of a new kind. The campaign was so successful generally that in newspapers and on radio and television in Britain, America and elsewhere in the West, as well as behind the Iron Curtain, the neutron weapon was soon being described as 'the bomb that kills people but spares buildings'. The fact that the 'people' for whom the weapon was intended were invading Soviet troops and not civilians was ignored. Several journals which had initially welcomed the weapon as being less indiscriminate changed their attitude. In West Germany, for instance, *Der Spiegel*, which had criticised the US administration for failing to produce the weapon, began to castigate it as 'immoral, ineffective and a danger to peace'.

American research on neutron weapons continued on a low priority, but by the time that Jimmy Carter became President in January 1977 the military chiefs were recommending its adoption, since the Warsaw Pact was then deploying at least 20,000 tanks against West Germany, the Kremlin's immediate purpose being to intimidate that country and its people into believing that they could not hope to defend themselves. The Soviet active-measures planners were quick to appreciate that Carter, who was essentially pacifist and anti-nuclear by temperament, was uncertain about the political consequences of ordering the production and deployment of the weapon, about which secrecy could not be preserved as it would be behind the Iron Curtain. The Soviet planners also perceived that one way of exploiting Carter's uncertainty was to concentrate their active measures against those countries where the neutron weapons, which would be short-range missiles, would have to be based – Belgium, Holland and, above all, West Germany. West German politicians had been uncertain themselves about the reception of the weapons by the voters, in view of the controversy which had already been stirred up about them, though their military advisers were in no doubt that they would be in their country's interest in providing a powerful new deterrent to the greatest foreseeable danger – a surprise thrust by Soviet armour. The whole apparatus of the 'peace' movement was therefore concentrated on the neutron bomb issue in West Germany and the Low Countries, with others being pressured through demonstrations and the manipulation of the media to give lateral support.[5]

In August 1977 the World Peace Council, acting on instructions from Moscow, declared an international 'Week of Action' against the neutron bomb. In Stuttgart, Frankfurt and Düsseldorf front-groups delivered notes to US consulates and there was a demonstration outside the American Embassy in Bonn. There were demonstrations as far away as Ghana, Tanzania and Peru and anti-American comments in media throughout the world, with a propaganda barrage from the Soviet-controlled radio and newspapers. The Communist Party of the USA was 'mobilized' to mount campaigns at the centre of the Politburo's problem.[6]

Under this propaganda pressure Carter delayed his decision, in September, about the neutron weapon's future to allow more consultation with the NATO allies most involved. Active measures were then intensified and the Moscow manipulators decided to play on the religious faith of President Carter, who is an ardent Baptist. Through TASS they announced that 'Soviet Baptist leaders condemn the production of the neutron bomb as contrary to the teachings of Christ', though what the writer thought about Christ or where the International Department had raised the 'Soviet Baptists' remains a mystery. Fellow Baptists were urged to 'raise their voices in defence of peace' – a strange request from the official organ of an atheistic state – but, as a result, a Sunday service being attended by Carter and his family on 16 October 1977 was disrupted by American demonstrators shouting slogans against the neutron bomb – an event well covered by the media.[7]

The Politburo's campaign was boosted further just before Christmas 1977 when Leonid Brezhnev, then the Soviet leader, attacked the neutron bomb in threatening language, warning that if the Americans went ahead the Soviet Union would have to develop the same 'mass annihilation weapons'. In fact the Soviet stockpiles were then replete with mass annihilation weapons on a scale never conceived by the US – missiles with warheads of 30 megatons or more. The Politburo had clearly seen the value of an initiative by its Party leader, but the move also represented its fear that mass production and deployment of the neutron bomb would, at least, necessitate a complete rethink of the Soviet military strategy with all the expensive and difficult changes it would entail.

The World Peace Council and its many offshoots followed up Brezhnev's lead with a carefully orchestrated assault and early in the

New Year of 1978 Brezhnev responded, as required, by sending harshly worded letters to individual NATO governments warning them that they should reject the neutron weapon. It was a gross interference intended to frighten the Europeans and divide them from the US and, being so sensational, it received heavy media coverage, worldwide, and more was engendered when letters in the same vein as Brezhnev's were sent by members of the Supreme Soviet to various Western parliamentarians and by Soviet 'trade-union' officials to Western trade-union leaders – all at the instigation of the International Department.

Later, in January 1978, representatives of the World Peace Council, headed by Romesh Chandra, appeared in Washington in an attempt to influence the US Congress. Chandra took part in a 'Dialogue for Disarmament and Détente', one of the speakers being the KGB officer Bogdanov, posing as being from the Soviet Academy of Sciences. This pro-Soviet outfit then moved to the United Nations in New York where they had discussions with Kurt Waldheim, the UN General Secretary.[8] In February 'peace' groups gathered in Geneva to denounce the neutron bomb, their expenses being paid by the Soviet Union through the World Peace Council.[9]

The International Department then instructed leading Soviet scientists to write to Carter urging him to scrap the neutron bomb in the interests of humanity, their real interest being in the crews of the Soviet battle-tanks. In March 1978 an 'International Forum on the Neutron Bomb' planned and sponsored by the World Peace Council was held in Amsterdam, with the Dutch Communist Party organizing demonstrators from several countries to march through the city denouncing the neutron bomb as a 'holocaust weapon', with nothing whatever being said about the 30-megaton Soviet weapons.[10]

NATO's Supreme Commander, the American, General Alexander Haig, responded by stating at a press conference in Washington that the neutron weapon would be an important addition to Western Europe's defences, but, yielding to the outside pressures, Carter decided against financing production of it, apparently without consulting his advisers. This decision, which was unilateral, with no corresponding concession from the Soviet Union, was welcomed in London by the Labour Prime Minister, James Callaghan, when, as the author knows from inside sources, he was doing all he could to appease his own left-wing followers in the hope of winning the forthcoming general election which, in fact, he lost to Margaret Thatcher. It was not welcomed by the West German Government which had, courageously, agreed to have neutron weapons on its soil under American control. The West German Defence Minister, Hans-Dietrich Genscher, flew to Washington and, as a result, Carter's decision was converted to another delay but this was to be so indefinite as to be a cancellation.

Lawrence Eagleburger, when US Under Secretary of State for Political Affairs, remarked, 'We consider it probable that the Soviet campaign against the "neutron bomb" cost some $100 million.'[11] To the Politburo it was cheap at the price. It had won a resounding success against its main adversary and against all logical odds by encouraging what were emotional responses to lies and exaggerations disseminated through active measures, and particularly through the manipulation of the media. As the US Congress was told later, 'For the Soviets the real propaganda success lay in the broad adverse treatment given to the neutron bomb by the so-called independent press.'[12]

In strategic terms the most powerful nation in the West had been forced to take a decision which was completely against its own interests and those of its allies. No wonder that in September 1979 the Chief of the International Department of the Hungarian Communist Party wrote, 'The political campaign against the neutron bomb was one of the most significant and successful since the Second World War.'[13]

The triumph also meant that the secret offensive could concentrate on other areas, at least so long as Carter remained in office and with the possibility that he would be re-elected for a further four years. In January 1981, however, when the more realistic Republican Ronald Reagan was elected, the Politburo realised that Carter's ban might be raised and, within weeks, a Soviet-sponsored campaign was resurrected. TASS and *Pravda* were loud in their condemnation of the neutron bomb, claiming that it was particularly barbaric because it was aimed at human beings and, for good measure, the bogey of access to the weapon for German neo-Nazis was included. In February 1981 Chandra, of the World Peace Council, decreed that February would be 'a month of action against the neutron bomb'. *Pravda* followed this with a warning to Western Europeans of the danger that the bomb presented to them, while in Britain the *Morning Star* called for a 'new and second campaign against this most horrible of weapons'. The General Secretary of the Labour Party, Ron Hayward, announced that the Party would also campaign to ensure that this 'foul weapon' would be rejected. It is possible, of course, that he and other Labour officials had no real idea of the weapon's true purpose.

In August 1981 Reagan, who was made of sterner stuff than Carter, made a clear decision to press ahead with production of neutron warheads for battlefield guided missiles, and at the time of writing, in 1985, there is a stockpile in the US, though none has yet been deployed in Europe. Clearly, they could be rushed there in an emergency and almost certainly would be.

The Politburo must have been disappointed, but its active-measures campaign had held up American production of an effective defence against Soviet tank attack for several years, giving the Soviet military authorities time to plan and test, in exercises, different methods of assaulting Central Europe, using tanks operating on a broader front. It had also given them more time to develop neutron weapons of their own.

More importantly, perhaps, the neutron bomb campaign had led to the recruitment of a huge reservoir of gullible people who could be 'called up' again at short notice for further active-measures operations. Even the Politburo must have been surprised at the size of what it could regard as a Fifth Column in almost every country.

Chapter 1 of this book described the highly successful employment of Soviet active measures against an institution, the British Labour Party. Chapters 3, 4 and 5 dealt with their successful use against an individual, Franz Josef Strauss. This chapter has recorded the application of active measures against a weapon – the neutron bomb.

Before the end of 1981 the whole active-measures apparatus and all those involved in it were to be required to repeat the performance on an even larger scale in an attempt to prevent a further improvement in NATO's deterrent power which, like the neutron bomb, threatened to make inroads in the Politburo's hard-won military superiority. This was the offensive against Pershing and cruise missiles which still rages.

Chapter 16

'Cruise' and the CND

'Why should the Soviets go into negotiations and give up the SS20s if the force of public opinion, through the peace movements, was going to compel the cancellation of deployment of the American Pershing and cruise missiles?'

Max Kampelman
*Chief US negotiator at the
1985 Geneva arms talks*

As you read this page, more than 300 Soviet SS20 nuclear missiles are permanently targeted on selected areas in Britain and Europe with launcher crews trained and ready to use them at a moment's notice from the Politburo. They are capable of delivering 900 warheads, each with the power of about 300,000 tons of TNT explosive – on targets that include cities as well as military bases and control centres. The SS20 missiles are mobile and easily moved around the Soviet-Bloc countryside, making them difficult targets for NATO to destroy. The Soviets began to deploy them in 1977, claiming that they were replacing older missiles which had become obsolescent, though in fact many of these remained in service so that most of the SS20s were additional. In 1983 when the Soviets had deployed 351 launchers in 39 bases, some of them located in Siberia and targeted on China, it was understood in the British Defence Ministry that Brezhnev had halted the programme because the military chiefs had enough of these very modern weapons, but in the last two years a further sixty-three SS20s have been added, some of them being an improved version with greater accuracy.[1]

The comparable weapons available to NATO's forces for battlefield use were becoming increasingly outdated by December 1979, when 120 SS20s had already been deployed. It was decided that, on that score alone, they would have to be modernized, but there was an even more pressing political reason for countering the SS20s. The range of the Russian missiles, more than 3,000 miles, meant that all the prime targets in Britain and Europe could be wiped out by SS20s based in the Soviet Union – even from behind the Urals. There were no American missiles in Europe capable of reaching the Soviet Union because those which had range enough had been phased out in the 1960s, having become vulnerable to Soviet attack and obsolete, technologically. The European NATO chiefs therefore feared that the Politburo might convince itself that it could risk a nuclear attack on Western Europe from that position without fear of nuclear retaliation from the US. The American Government would know that if it responded by using its intercontinental missiles to hit the Soviet Union it could expect immediate retaliation against the US homeland and might, therefore, feel constrained to take no action. The immediate danger lay, not so much in the possibility of such a nuclear attack on Britain and Western Europe, but in the probability that the Politburo's thinking might lead it to increase its nuclear threats against the NATO governments, some of which might find them insupportable.

NATO therefore accepted a generous offer of two types of American missile which would soon be ready for service: a Mark 2 version of the existing Pershing rocket and the cruise missile code-named 'Tomahawk'. The Pershing 2 rocket is a very accurate mobile missile with a range of about 1,100 miles. The Tomahawk, which is also carried on mobile launchers which can be moved about the countryside, has a range only half that of the SS20. It is called a cruise missile because it flies at slow speeds being, essentially, a much improved form of the German V1 pilotless plane. As its engine requires air, it needs to travel at low altitude which makes it more difficult to shoot down, though, like the V1, it is obviously vulnerable to anti-aircraft defences which the SS20 is not.

It was agreed by the NATO authorities that a force of 108 Pershing 2s and 464 cruise missiles should be enough to deter the Soviets from using their SS20s, though the Warsaw Pact would still retain a substantial superiority in battlefield nuclear strength. All the Pershings would be based in West Germany along with 96 of the cruise missiles. Of the remaining cruise missiles 160 would be based in Britain, 112 in Italy, with 48 each in Belgium and Holland. The Pershing 2s were to be in place by 1986 and the cruise missiles by 1987.

These decisions were all announced and, inevitably, there was an immediate reaction from the Kremlin and its supporters. The Politburo had again invested huge resources in the SS20 force and, having stolen a march on the West, it was determined to prevent any neutralization of it if possible. With what was then the neutron bomb success under its belt, the International Department was instructed to launch the biggest-ever active-measures campaign with the 'peace' movements being mobilized to the fullest capacity. It was realized that, for maximum impact, the offensive should be concentrated on the NATO countries which were to house the new weapons, and while Belgium and Holland were, politically, the most vulnerable, an intense effort would be necessary in West Germany and Britain where most of the weapons were to be located.

As with the neutron bomb, the cruise missile was to be vilified as something new and particularly horrible, being also of American origin. In fact the Soviet Union had deployed hundreds of cruise missiles, based on ships or carried on aircraft, since the early 1960s and has never ceased to improve on them so that new supersonic versions will soon be available.[2] The apprehensiveness that cruise missiles would increase the risk of nuclear war, when in fact their purpose is to reduce it by deterring Soviet adventures, was to be heightened, especially through the fear that they would create new nuclear targets in the countries which had agreed to take them.

Nowhere has the cruise missile – now abbreviated to 'cruise' by the technically ignorant – been more falsely denigrated than in Britain, where its particular purpose is to prevent Soviet nuclear attacks on the already existing nuclear bases by providing the deterrent protection formerly given by the old Vulcan bombers and other aircraft. 'Cruise' has become the main and most hated target of the Campaign for Nuclear Disarmament and of the 'peace women' associated with it, with little if any criticism ever being made of the Soviet SS20 missiles which made it necessary. For that reason the

CND and its associates will be given special consideration in this chapter.

Even before the NATO modernization programme was announced, Brezhnev made a speech in East Berlin urging NATO to abandon it and threatening consequences if they did not. Offering to reduce the number of Soviet missiles in Europe, he made a unilateral gesture of moving 20,000 troops and 1,000 tanks out of East Germany, to which they could quickly be returned, while the SS20s, if withdrawn to the Soviet Union, could still fulfil their task because of their range. Active-measures specialists were also dispatched to attend a 'European Forum on Disarmament and Security', which had been cobbled together near Ostend. Significantly, they were Vadim Zagladin, Ponomarev's deputy in the International Department, and Valentin Falin, deputy head of the International Information Department.[3]

Two months later, in advance of a NATO ministerial meeting in Brussels scheduled for 12 December 1979, the full active-measures campaign was unleashed. It succeeded to the extent that, after the NATO meetings had dismissed Brezhnev's gestures, both Belgium and Holland declined to accept their share of the cruise missiles. The Politburo had hoped to induce Italy to reject the weapons too, so leaving West Germany as the only continental country to accept them – a situation which could then have been exploited with false fears about 'German fingers on the nuclear trigger', though the weapons were to be under firm American physical control. The Italians, however, robustly agreed to take their allotment.

In the early stage of the campaign the Soviets even offered economic inducements. In late 1979 the Soviet Ambassador to one NATO country suggested that if the host government opposed the introduction of the new missiles the Kremlin might grant more favourable terms for trade.[4]

Under the direction of the World Peace Council and its offshoots the campaign was whipped up into the biggest surge of organized offensive protest ever seen and its motives were widened to exploit the gulf between the US and some of its allies which had been opened up by the neutron bomb campaign. Communists and other left-wing extremists grasped the opportunities for generating anti-Americanism in general with particularly venomous hostility

221

towards President Reagan. In this they have been enormously assisted by the British CND and its offshoot, the 'peace women', who have laid permanent siege to the first cruise missile base at Greenham Common, near Newbury, Berkshire, the concept being that the police and the security forces at the base would be additionally embarrassed if the 'peace camps' were populated by women.

The Campaign for Nuclear Disarmament, which now claims a membership of more than 250,000, includes so many people of good intent, including genuinely religious people like the Quakers, that its leadership is at pains to insist that it is not under any form of political control. This may have been true when it was founded in 1958, under the chairmanship of Canon John Collins, but it quickly attracted left-wing extremists who saw its potential for pro-Soviet exploitation. As the recent evidence of the former MI5 officer Cathy Massiter has established, CND was formerly classified as a subversive organization during the 1950s, 60s and 70s and, while it is alleged that the label has been removed, important people in the movement remain classed as individual subversives so potentially dangerous that they are subject to surveillance. The original classification as subversive arose after MI5 established, by penetrating the movement with agents and informers, that it was being influenced by Communists and Communist sympathizers. Some of its activities were therefore watched, with some individuals being put under telephone and letter check. Files on prominent members and those deliberately keeping out of public attention were built up in MI5's Registry, where they remain.[5]

Critics of MI5's behaviour in this respect, including Cathy Massiter, are loud in their condemnation of the intrusions into privacy and the 'infringements of civil liberties'. The point they miss, or deliberately ignore, is that MI5's actions were a response to the threat created and still maintained by CND and the 'peace women'. CND claims that the 'peace women' are a separate organization, but documents in my possession show that they take instructions from CND headquarters. A full-time official at CND headquarters issued printed instructions of techniques for tracking the missile convoys on their dummy runs to supposedly secret locations, where they would be deployed for action in the event of a military emergency. The movements are logged and recorded by CND activists working on what they call 'Cruisewatch'. Procedures for disrupting such movements in an emergency by what the activists call a 'telephone blockade' – the making of hundreds of calls simultaneously to saturate key Defence Ministry numbers – have also been issued.[6] This is nothing short of fifth-column work of the greatest value to the Soviets in an emergency and particularly to the Russian commandos, the 'Spetsnaz' forces described in Chapter 18. The situation was put succinctly by Jon Bloomfield, a member of the Communist Party and of the CND Council, when writing in *Marxism Today*: 'Direct action and civil disobedience can spotlight key military installations, such as missile sites, and reveal bunkers and plans which the government wants to keep secret.'[7] In sum, CND suits the Politburo's requirements so precisely that it could be better named the Campaign for Nuclear Disaster.

The mass demonstrations at American bases, conventional as well as nuclear, have not only played the Kremlin's game by vilifying all things American but have provided cover for Soviet agents to assess the weakest areas of perimeter fences and to take close-up photographs of prohibited places. Bearing in mind what would happen in similar circumstances in the alien country to which so many of them seem so devoted, it is unlikely that the anger of CND activists at being subject to attention from the security authorities is anything but feigned for propaganda purposes, though some of them may be genuinely deluded. In respect of such CND propaganda the media, and especially television, have been of cardinal value, with many programmes being angled in the 'peace' movement's favour and marked by pronounced anti-Americanism. 'Peace women' are sometimes projected in the media as selfless and gallant campaigners against a war being planned by the US. In fact, in the areas where they operate they are almost universally loathed as a squalid nuisance, being seen to be scruffy drop-outs 'parasitizing' the welfare system. These women, who are hissed in the streets and barred from shops and pubs because of their manner and uncleanliness, live on the social security system in communes which have become a way of life. When they tear down security fences and inflict other damage all that they achieve is to present more bills to law-abiding taxpayers.

The CND and the 'peace women' assist the Communist cause, whether wittingly or not, in another way, by harassing companies involved in defence contracts and by putting pressure on Labour-controlled councils who have 'bought' the 'peace' line to blacklist firms with loss of council contracts if they take part in building defence establishments.[8]

The CND leadership claims that the movement is committed to 'non-violent direct action' but, in practice, this does not bar violence to property. Monsignor Bruce Kent, the current chief CND cleric, is on record as supporting the criminal damage to Defence Ministry property inflicted by CND supporters on the grounds that nuclear weapons behind the security fences are criminal when, in fact, they are legal in every respect. In view of the Government's most recent definition of subversive activities – those which threaten the safety or well-being of the State and which are intended to undermine or overthrow Parliamentary democracy by political, industrial or violent means – a legitimate criticism that can be levelled against MI5 is that it has not devoted enough talent and resources to the threat posed by the 'peace' movement. There is also genuine need, in the interests of public safety, for the security authorities to seek to discover, on a continuing basis, to what extent, if any, the 'peace' movement has been penetrated by agents of terrorist organizations. The 'peace' camps around bases present ideal locations for IRA terrorists, for example, to establish themselves in preparation for an attempt to seize the nuclear core of a weapon which could provide them with devastating blackmail power. The Defence Ministry has spent much time over the years considering such a terrorist contingency and it was the original reason why guards at nuclear establishments were armed.[9]

However sanitized CND may have become to try to rid itself of the Communist stigma, it remains under the influence of highly skilled activists with scant respect for the law. According to Blake Baker, an authority on the extreme left and its activities, nearly a quarter of the national council are members of the Communist Party and there are other committed left-wingers, including fellow-travellers who claim to be ex-Communists.[10] Communists have organized delegations to the various 'peace' camps, where they have been rapturously received, as have pro-Soviet MPs like Anthony Wedgwood Benn. CND delegates have been joyfully welcomed in Moscow, from which they are said to have come away 'with no doubts about the Soviet sincerity for peace', though the KGB was persecuting a small, genuine Soviet peace group while they were there. In May 1982 a CND delegation to Moscow, led by Joan Rud-dock, met the chairman of the Soviet Peace Committee, an agency of the International Department, while, five months later, the Soviet Peace Committee also received a visit from Bruce Kent. In a follow-up interview Kent was reported by Moscow Radio as having said with regard to the deployment of cruise and Pershing missiles, 'the nuclear arms race will enter a new and even more dangerous phase. That is why we take a positive view of the Soviet initiatives. . . .'[11] At a conference in Prague, the British Communist Party's delegate, Baruch (Bert) Ramelson, reported that 'at grass-roots level Communists are very active in local branches of CND'. Leading British Communists and Marxists use CND platforms to attack 'American war-mongers' and praise 'Soviet peace-makers'.

At CND's annual conference in Sheffield in November 1984 the movement backed away from a suggestion that it should also campaign strongly against Soviet nuclear weapons. This was forestalled by a typical Communist ploy put forward by a Communist official and supported by others.[12] Professor Vic Allen, who was elected to the CND Council, protested at any 'anti-Sovietism' and in an article in the *Morning Star* he condemned demonstrations outside the Soviet embassy as 'mischievous'.[13]

In fact the Politburo has nothing to fear from any critical comments on its nuclear strength by any 'peace' movements because they can never be anything but verbal with no impact whatever being allowed on the Soviet people. It might pay active-measures operators to encourage an occasional verbal attack to support the deception that the 'peace' movements are neutral.

What is particularly relevant to this book is the extent to which all the 'peace' movements, including CND, function as agencies of deception and disinformation, making them particularly valuable to the active measures currently pursued by the International Department and the KGB. The anti-Americanism and the particular objection to cruise and Pershing missiles have converted them to anti-NATO organizations, which is right on the Politburo's line.

It is but a short step from violence against property to violence against people and the first often leads to the second, especially when the first proves unsuccessful and generates frustration. Violence of any kind also attracts people who enjoy it for its own sake and these can include the near-insane political activists for whom lethal violence is the instrument of first choice. At the time of writing a phenomenon called in Germany 'The New Terrorists' has arisen, and whether or not they are the result of frustration within the 'peace' movement they are striking the same targets. The left-wing Red Army faction in West Germany, Direct Action in France and the Fighting Communist Cells in Belgium have joined forces to attack NATO installations and other defence targets with bombs and to assassinate those connected with them.[14] Presumably their purpose is to establish the kind of 'peace' they want, the same 'peace' desired by the Politburo, which must rejoice at their activities aimed at 'the foundations of the imperialist empire'.

These terrorist actions are also calculated to create uncertainty and fear and in this they are assisted by the 'peace' movements, including CND, which repeatedly suggest that some dreadful nuclear crisis is imminent when there are no real signs of that. Such fear has been intensified by the production of horrific drama documentaries on the effects of atomic attack and their showing on television, and even in schools, to reach the widest possible audience. The fact that modern conventional weapons would cause equally devastating casualties and damage when used over a longer period never seems to be mentioned.

CND's claim that unilateral disarmament – 'giving a lead' – will result in multilateral disarmament is a fraudulent deception totally negated by Soviet behaviour. When President Carter cancelled the B1 bomber, for example, the Politburo pressed ahead with its production of the Backfire bomber and development of the more advanced Blackjack bomber. CND has been used to spread the disinformation that the British Government has changed its deterrent posture to that of considering a first strike against the Soviet Union. These and other deceptions have so impressed the more gullible and many of the religious that they are likely to vote against a Conservative government in future on anti-nuclear, anti-American principles which are unfounded. This could help Labour to achieve the devastating objectives described in Chapter 1.

While CND claims to be independent, taking no money from Soviet sources and needing none, it is as sensitive as any other 'peace' movement to the political initiatives concocted by the Politburo and the International Department, and the timing of its demonstrations and other activities is often linked with comparable events on the Continent organized by the World Peace Council. Thus when Brezhnev issued a call for a 'freeze' on all nuclear weapons in February 1981 it was quickly supported by CND and all the other 'peace' movements, though it would have allowed the Soviets to keep their SS20s in position while preventing the deployment of American weapons. A Nuclear Freeze Campaign Strategy Conference was even held in Washington while, early in 1982, the World Peace Council and its associate activists concentrated on the United Nations in New York which was holding its Second Special Session on Disarmament. The propaganda for a 'freeze' culminated in a rally in New York attended by more than half a million people. As the FBI was able to report to a Congressional Committee, the KGB was very active in stimulating the 'peace' movement and influencing its direction, with many of its agents operating inside the UN under various covers, as Shevchenko has since confirmed.[15] The concept of comparable activities in Moscow to present and promote the Western argument is no more credible under the present leadership than it was under Stalin.

Under the influence of CND, various left-wing local authorities in Britain declared themselves to be nuclear-free zones. While the hope that this might help to protect them from Soviet nuclear attack could have no possible effect on Soviet nuclear strategy, Moscow cynically urged the World Peace Council to publicize and encourage the nuclear-free zone concept in other countries. From 1981 onwards huge rallies against cruise and Pershing missiles were staged in Europe from Lisbon to Norway. In Amsterdam, in November 1981, an estimated 400,000 people of various nationalities demonstrated against the American missiles, a reflection of the claim by the TASS correspondent Vadim Leonov that a message from Moscow was all that was needed for thousands of demonstrators to take to the streets. In the following January the part played by the World Peace Council in the whole campaign was openly acknowledged by *Pravda* which congratulated it on its efforts in organizing demonstrations. Yet three months later, when seven young European tourists in Moscow hoisted a banner in Red Square, emblazoned with 'Bread, Life and Disarmament', they were seized by KGB men and hustled off to prison.[16]

After Brezhnev's death Andropov stepped up the pressure with threats, like the claim that if NATO installed cruise and Pershing missiles the Politburo would order an immediate retaliatory strike against any incoming missile, even if it had been launched in error or because of a technical fault. He also made it clear that the Soviet Union would never disarm unilaterally, as Britain is being urged to do, because, as he put it, 'We are not simple.' The various offers on nuclear weapons made by Andropov were all intended to bar NATO from deploying counter-missiles to the SS20s, the majority of which were to be retained. For example, when he offered to reduce the number of SS20s in Europe if plans to deploy cruise and Pershing missiles were scrapped it was found, when details were tabled at Geneva, that 'Europe' meant west of the Urals. This left 111 SS20s behind the Urals from where they could strike at prime European targets. Further, there was no suggestion that any of the SS20s he would remove from west of the Urals would be dismantled or destroyed.[17]

The former KGB chief, who was a master of disinformation techniques, must have realized that the Western governments would see through his patent ploys, their purpose being to convince the gullible, and especially those in the 'peace' movements, that the Soviets continue to make generous offers in the interest of peace which the Americans reject because they want war.

Collaterally with the specific offensives against the neutron bomb and the cruise and Pershing missiles the CND has pursued its long-running campaign against the strategic deterrent – the Polaris missile and its designated successor, the Trident. There have been numerous demonstrations at the submarine bases in Scotland, though these are more difficult to mount than those against land-based weapons. While Polaris and Trident have been castigated as horrible weapons of mass destruction, the Soviet Union has launched the first of a fleet of truly monster missile-carrying submarines code-named 'Typhoon'. If there has been any outcry from the peace movement against this development it has been so muted as to be inaudible.

It would seem that, to date, campaigns against both the strategic deterrent and the cruise and Pershing missiles have been unsuccessful. As a result the Soviets have returned to the disarmament talks, from which they had walked out, indicating that they would never return until the Americans and NATO had abandoned their cruise and Pershing missile plans. As Margaret Thatcher told the US Congress in February 1985, 'It is our strength, not their goodwill, that has brought the Soviet Union to the negotiating table.' Nevertheless, in a typical example of disinformation for domestic consumption, *Pravda* claimed that it was President Reagan who had been forced to resume talks under pressure from 'anti-war groups in the West'.

Soon after taking office, Chairman Gorbachov returned to the charge with a new 'freeze' offer aimed, once again, at dividing NATO. On Easter Sunday 1985 he offered to halt the deployment of SS20s and other medium-range missiles in Europe if NATO would do the same. He chose the time when the 'peace' organizations of the West tend to be most active and when more than 400 SS20s had already been deployed, providing a big superiority. He also seemed to be trying to capitalize on the situation in Holland, which had delayed a firm decision on accepting its forty-eight cruise missiles until November. The Dutch Government, which had been under intense pressure from its militant 'peace' movement, had announced that it would deploy its quota of missiles from the following November if the Soviets had more than 378 SS20s on site at that time. All that Gorbachov has to do is to reduce the present total of 414 SS20s by 36 to bring it down to the Dutch threshold. If he does so and Holland declines the cruise missiles, there will be renewed active-measures pressure on Belgium to reverse its decision to take its quota. It would seem to be no coincidence that Gorbachov has set November as the expiry date for his 'freeze' offer.[18]

As he must have expected, the US and NATO rejected the ploy, for the same reasons that they declined a similar freeze put forward by Brezhnev in 1982, but the Soviet Union and its supporters in the West, including prominent leaders of the British Labour Party, were able to criticise their political opponents, and Reagan in particular, for failing to take up the 'good offer', which would largely have achieved the Politburo's military objective.

There will be no let-up in the active-measures campaign against cruise and Pershing missiles, with the 'peace' protesters doing all they can to harass their bases and those serving in them, but the Politburo now has to contend with a more menacing Western development threatening its nuclear superiority to an unprecedented degree and in a way which will tax the ingenuity of the active-measures chiefs: President Reagan's Strategic Defence Initiative. As a result of its irresponsible treatment by the media, this initiative, which involves the placing of totally defensive non-nuclear weapons in space, has become popularly known as 'Star Wars', a term which is not only frightening but suggests that the system is dangerously offensive. As the American media were mainly responsible for the coining and general adoption of this pejorative description, it is a Western 'own goal' which has been gratefully pounced on and exploited by the Kremlin.

Chapter 17

'Star Wars'

'We have within our capability the possibility of developing weapons whose only real role is to kill the things that kill people.'
Senator Malcolm Wallop
US Senate Intelligence Committee

From the earliest days of the nuclear weapons era it has been generally assumed, in the West, that there can be no adequate defence against them. This led to the deterrent concept, the threat of nuclear retaliation to prevent a Soviet assault in Europe, and was reinforced with the emergence of the long-range nuclear missile, which projects a warhead so small that the chance of intercepting and destroying it in flight seemed utterly impossible. Dependence on the deterrent threat, which became mutual when the Soviets developed nuclear missiles, remained so great in the West that protection of the civilian populations, through the provision of shelters and other aspects of civil defence, was virtually abandoned. After forty years of peace in Europe, unprecedented in modern times, there is no doubt, in the minds of Western military and political leaders, that nuclear deterrence has been the success story of the century. Further, the effects of living in a situation with Soviet nuclear missiles targeted on every major city have had little influence on the lives of most people, whatever the 'peace' enthusiasts might pretend.

In the Soviet Union the attitude has been quite different. The military and political leaders there have been contemptuous of the deterrent policy from the start, being opposed to any purely defensive strategy. To preserve the option of waging a 'fighting war', with nuclear weapons if necessary, they have invested heavily in civil defence, and in hardened shelters for both the population and their military equipment. They have paid maximum attention to the mobility of their weapons systems, to increase their capacity to survive in war, and are currently developing a mobile intercontinental missile.[1]

Defence scientists on both sides of the Iron Curtain responded to the challenge of the long-range missile by attempting to devise an anti-ballistic missile which might be able to shoot it down. Some progress was made, but it was quickly realized that the concept could not provide a viable defence for any country, though it might be worth using to protect a few particular targets. The cost-effectiveness of such a crude defence was seen to be so low that in 1972 the US and the Soviet Union signed an Anti-Ballistic Missile (ABM) Treaty which limited the deployment of such missiles to one experimental site in each country and fixed limits on the types and numbers of radar systems used in ABM defence. The strategic philosophers argued that success by either side in anti-ballistic missile defence could be dangerous, because it would reduce the credibility of nuclear deterrence, but the factor most responsible for the ABM Treaty was mutual avoidance of massive spending on defensive systems when it was obvious that technology was not sufficiently advanced to make them effective. As Marshal Grechko told the Supreme Soviet, 'The ABM Treaty does not place any limitations on carrying out research and experimental work directed towards solving the problems of defence of the country against nuclear missile attack.'[2]

In the US, and the West generally, anti-missile missile research was concentrated almost exclusively on methods of destroying the short-range weapons used in battle. It became possible, for instance, for a shell fired from a gun or an air-launched missile to be intercepted and destroyed, but the problems posed by high-altitude nuclear missiles continued to look insuperable. Once launched from the Soviet Union, a missile would take about half an hour to reach the US and ten minutes or so to reach a target in Europe or Britain, but the possibility of detecting, tracking and destroying it looked remote in the extreme. The Soviets, with their huge resources for

232

defence research, continued with ABM developments and have upgraded their ABM missile site, which happened to have been built round Moscow, and have tested two new anti-missile missiles since 1980. They have built radar systems, too powerful to be for any likely purpose but ABM development, at Krasnoyarsk, Pechora, Pushkino and three other sites.[3] These advances are seen by Washington to be in blatant breach of the 1972 Treaty and as clear signs of a Soviet attempt to create a monopoly in 'Star Wars' technology.

Meanwhile, in both the US and the Soviet Union, research has been proceeding on the possible military applications of lasers, highly concentrated beams of light, and beams of electrically charged sub-atomic particles accelerated to enormous speeds – the modern equivalent of the fictional death-ray. Simultaneously there have been spectacular advances in radar-detection communication systems and computer technology.[4]

As a result, a private enterprise study group of scientists and military experts in the US, called 'High Frontier', carried out a feasibility study of marrying the technological developments to produce a system capable of destroying incoming bombarding missiles. It concluded, in 1981, that within a decade a ballistic missile defence system capable of destroying between 95 and 98 per cent of the missiles in a Soviet first strike against the US could be devised at a cost which the US economy could afford. This study stimulated Government defence scientists and by March 1983 there was sufficient agreement about the technological possibilities of an anti-ballistic missile system for President Reagan to be able to announce an official research programme, in which $26 billion was to be invested over the ensuing five years. While there could be no certainty that the research would be successful, in view of the size of the problem, Reagan felt that civilized societies should be given the chance of defending themselves with something better than the threat of retaliatory action with H-bomb missiles which could kill millions.[5]

The system which is envisaged would operate in four stages. The first stage would try to destroy enemy long-range missiles within the first five minutes of their flight, in what is called the boost phase, when the whole missile is still intact and the sections, of which there may be three or four, have not separated. This could be achieved only by having counter-weapons operating in space. They could be giant mirrors which would reflect laser beams sent up from the

233

ground. Stage two would operate in the post-boost phase, after the main rocket section has fallen away but the several separate nuclear warheads remain together in one container. As this also lasts only about five minutes, it, too, would have to be tackled with weapons based in space. Stage three, the mid-course phase, lasts about twenty minutes on an intercontinental flight, but by then the warheads in the container have separated and are on their ways to different targets, greatly complicating the interception problem which may have to be solved with ground-based weapons. The fourth and terminal stage would concern itself with the extremely difficult task of picking off any individual warheads plummeting down after getting through the first three layers of defence. This would have to be achieved with ground-based weapons.[6]

The details remain to be resolved by the research and development, which is likely to take at least ten years, but Reagan has stipulated that the defence weaponry should be non-nuclear, unlike the original weapons covered by the 1972 ABM Treaty which would have created nuclear explosions in space or in the upper atmosphere to destroy the incoming bombarding warheads.

It could reasonably have been imagined that this new, non-nuclear, Strategic Defence Initiative announced by Reagan would have appealed to the 'peace' workers who are so anxious to prevent nuclear explosions on Earth, but, instead, it resulted in an immediate outcry from them and from all other supporters of the Soviet Union as well as from ill-informed 'willies', including some prominent Western politicians. No American initiative can ever suit the Politburo, but the main objection to Reagan's revolutionary proposal was that, if successful, it would seriously erode its vast investment in H-bomb missiles and might negate it totally, eliminating the Soviet option to stage a first strike.

At the Politburo's behest, TASS immediately attacked the reference to the new initiative in the President's inaugural address and the active-measures offensive was switched on to denigrate the whole concept. The US was accused of planning to militarize space, though it has been militarized for years, with the Soviet Union possessing the world's only operational system for shooting down enemy reconnaissance satellites, with scores of such satellites in orbit for military purposes and with the Soviets having amassed twice as many man-hours in space as the US.

The propaganda, echoed by the peace movements and the 'willies', charged Reagan with 'threatening world peace' though the Politburo has been financing work on laser, microwave and particle-beam weapons for many years with over 10,000 scientists and engineers associated with laser developments alone.[7]

The Americans were accused of undermining the concept of mutually assured destruction by long-range rockets, which has kept the peace so far, though the Soviets have never really accepted that concept.[8] In any case, there is no intention of abandoning deterrence, which will be posed far into the foreseeable future. The main thrust of the active-measures campaign against 'Star Wars', however, has been directed, as usual, at America's European allies. While the Politburo has striven so hard to 'decouple' the US from Europe in its previous campaigns, it is currently making use of the Europeans' fear in that respect to induce them to oppose the 'Star Wars' concept. They are being encouraged to believe that Reagan's plan is intended to set up a defensive screen behind which the American people can shelter and leave their European allies wide open to nuclear attack. The truth is that if it proves possible to destroy a bombarding rocket in the boost or post-boost phases, that will also apply to the SS20s targeted on Europe, and the Politburo sees a grave threat to that huge investment in nuclear hardware.

The Politburo chiefs know that the Americans have no intention of retreating from Europe, unless forced out by their allies, a Labour-controlled Britain being the major menace. The only real danger posed by 'Star Wars' is that a frustrated Politburo, under a hardline leadership, might stage a pre-emptive first strike against its Western adversaries before any anti-missile defences become effective. Reagan has said that with his Strategic Defence Initiative he is looking for a means of rendering nuclear weapons impotent or obsolete and that is just what the Politburo does not want, in spite of its 'peace-loving' claims and those of its supporters.

The visit of Mikhail Gorbachov to London in December 1984 – announced by *The Times* as 'Enter a bear, smiling' – seemed to be an attempt to influence Margaret Thatcher and other parliamentarians to support the Soviet concern about the 'Star Wars' development and to exploit any policy differences between Britain and the US. The Prime Minister's subsequent statement to the US Congress suggested that he had failed: 'Wars are not caused by the build-up of weapons. They are caused when an aggressor believes he can achieve his objectives at an acceptable price. . . . If we are to maintain deterrence, as we must, it is essential that our research and capacity do not fall behind.' Gorbachov did have success, however, with Neil Kinnock, the Labour Party leader, who 'condemned' 'Star Wars' on a visit to NATO headquarters in Brussels in March 1985. That great authority on such technical matters told the NATO Secretary, Lord Carrington, a former Defence Minister, that he and his NATO colleagues had not understood the full implications of backing the programme.[9]

Gorbachov has issued warnings about a further Soviet nuclear build-up to a strength capable of penetrating any space shield the Americans could devise if the US goes ahead with its research, and is insisting that the project must be placed on the table at Geneva for negotiations which, he hopes, will result in its abandonment by the West while the Soviets press ahead with their research in secret, continuing the Great Missile Deception. The Soviet Foreign Minister, Gromyko, since promoted to president, has been fuelling European fears about the decoupling of the US in talks in Italy and Spain and with visiting French and West German political leaders in Moscow, in the safe knowledge that 'Star Wars' research presents no such possibility. If negotiations at Geneva can be spun out for a few more years there will be a new American President who may be less enthusiastic for heavy investment in anti-ballistic missile defence and more sensitive to Politburo pressure, as Carter was. Meanwhile, as Mrs Thatcher told the US Congress, 'We shall face a Soviet political offensive designed to sow differences among us, calculated to create infirmity of purpose, to impair resolve – and even to arouse fear in the hearts of our people.'

All this puts the World Peace Council and its auxiliaries throughout the world in the fatuous position of campaigning against a system designed to prevent nuclear devastation and the holocausts which they insist are imminent. The paradox will not deter or even embarrass them if that is the Politburo's requirement. They are used to upside-down ploys.

236

Chapter 18

The Sharp Edge of Active Measures

'Violence in itself is not an evil. It depends on what its purpose is. In the hands of Socialists it is a progressive force.'

Boris Ponomarev, 1977

Since violence is fundamental to the Communist concept of revolution, it is inevitable that active measures, which are intended to promote revolution, should involve violence and they do so in various forms, ranging from fisticuff disorder at demonstrations and on picket lines through assassination and terrorism to full-blooded military operations. Any form of violence in a free, democratic society is welcome to Communist ideologists since the undermining of respect for the law and the agencies for enforcing it, the police, the judiciary and, indirectly, the security services, is destabilizing. A country which has become used to displays of violence is more conducive to the final planned outbreak of riots calculated to overthrow its elected government.

In the past, students and others who join them posing as students have been exploited by left-wing activists with near-success in France, for instance, where, in 1968, protesters took over the Latin Quarter of Paris and spread chaos throughout the city. The danger of the insurrection was so great that President de Gaulle flew to meet General Massu, secretly, to satisfy himself of the army's loyalty if troops needed to be used to preserve the government. Though

237

the driving force of the revolt was a violent left-winger, Daniel Cohn-Bendit, it did not suit the French Communist Party which declared that no revolutionary situation existed and the insurrection petered out, to be replaced, a few months later, by riotous demonstrations in Frankfurt. Campus riots in the US also failed to challenge democratic control, but the tough measures needed to quell them provided photographic evidence of 'police brutality', as did the picket-line violence in the British miners' strike more recently.

With the general decline of student violence, though outbursts are still by no means rare, the professional activists have tended to concentrate on immigrants in the so-called 'deprived' areas. A dangerous degree of success was achieved in 1981 with major riots in Liverpool, Manchester, Birmingham, Preston, Wolverhampton, Hull and several parts of London. Fire-bombs were thrown, as well as missiles, with mobs rampaging and looting. The riots were orchestrated to the extent that agitators were brought in from other areas by vans, fire-bombs were prepared in readiness, look-outs were posted to ferry instructions to the 'street fighters' and vans fitted with Citizens' Band radios were used to counter the police and to create diversions. Pamphlets urging people to join in the disorder were issued by militant groups, who cared nothing that the homes and communal facilities which were burned and looted belonged to the local communities being roused to action. They lived elsewhere.[1]

After the riots had been quelled, with much damage and injury, members of the Militant Tendency, which has penetrated the Labour Party, came out openly in support of the rioters, claiming that the fault lay with white racialists, though most of the rioting and looting was perpetrated by blacks. The real fault lay with the white and black left-wing extremists who exploit the volatility of young blacks. Television has frequently pursued the racialist line, even in the instance where blacks were burned to death at an all-black party in Deptford. No white person was involved in the incident, but the white population was castigated on television and by militants for failing to feel guilty about it. In Scotland, where there is as much unemployment and 'deprivation', there have been no riots, there being too few blacks there for left-wing extremists to rouse to action.

238

Violence against selected individuals considered to be inimical to the interests of the State has been a standard 'cleansing tool' of the Politburo since its inception. To all Politburos, not just to Stalin's, people have always been expendable and the ruling clique sees nothing immoral in eliminating anybody who disagrees with it or has offended it. The great bulk of the victims have been the millions of Soviet citizens murdered inside the Soviet Union or incarcerated until death in 'gulags' there. The Soviet Communist Party's treatment of the people it controls with iron-fisted discipline constitutes one of the greatest crimes of history, amounting to genocide on a massive scale.[2] It has also been responsible for the murder of foreign political leaders who stood in its way, like those of Hungary and, more recently, of Afghanistan. Its assassinations abroad of those whom it considers to be traitors are well documented and prove that when a Soviet citizen has been condemned to death in his absence the Politburo considers it proper that he should be hunted down, wherever he may be living abroad, and killed by any convenient means. The old Chekist adage, 'The arm of the law is longer than the traitor's leg', still conditions the behaviour of the KGB which, unlike the secret services of Britain or America, remains 'licensed to kill'. When Major-General Sejna visited London in 1982 to see his publisher he declined to remain in Britain for longer than six days. With great seriousness he said that if the KGB heard of his visit his assassination might well be required but, since a foreign country was involved, it would require the agreement of Politburo members and that would take seven days to secure.[3] Josef Frolik has given details of two attempts on his life in the US where other important defectors have died in circumstances which looked like suicide but were probably murder.[4] In Canada a long-term KGB 'sleeper', called Anton Sabotka, was activated to try to kill Igor Gouzenko, while in West Germany a KGB assassin,[5] Bogdan Stashinsky, murdered two Ukrainian emigrés using a cyanide spray provided by the special KGB department equipped to produce such devices. The details are known because Stashinsky defected and confessed, being put on trial in October 1962. His confessions revealed that he had been decorated with the Order of the Red Banner for carrying out the murders, the ceremony being performed by Shelepin, the KGB chief, who had other, more important, targets in mind for him.[6]

There are many more examples of criminal Soviet ruthlessness towards individuals who tell the truth about the Communist conspiracy, but in recent years the KGB has turned increasingly to its satellite agencies to undertake the worst and most dangerous excesses so that, in the event of exposure, Moscow can deny all knowledge. In 1972 Ladislav Bittman, the Czech defector who had been an active-measures specialist, gave the inside explanation of an appalling Soviet-Bloc assassination attempt which had killed the wife of the intended victim. On KGB instructions, the Czech active-measures department had created a fictitious organization called the Fighting Group for an Independent Germany and purporting to be so extremely right-wing that Moscow could claim that neo-Nazis were gathering strength in Germany. Its first action, in 1956, when active measures were being concentrated on arousing resentment against Germany's entry to NATO among allies who had suffered from German wartime excesses, was to send out hundreds of letters demanding a unified Germany and the return of all German territories ceded after Hitler's defeat. When this had little effect, the Fighting Group turned to violence and the Czech agents running it selected a target in the form of André-Marie Tremeaud, prefect of part of Alsace-Lorraine which had formerly been German territory. They sent him a booby-trapped box of cigars and, while preparing for a dinner in honour of visiting French parliamentarians, Mme Tremeaud opened the box and was killed. Collateral 'evidence' had been planted elsewhere to make it appear to the police that the box had been sent by the Fighting Group, as was widely believed (until Bittman revealed the truth), especially in France, where the incident generated much anti-German feeling. The anti-German animosity reported in the French press was exploited by the Soviet media as further evidence of German 'revanchism'.[7]

A proven case of Soviet-Bloc assassination occurred in a London street in 1978 when a Bulgarian defector, Georgi Markov, was murdered by a highly sophisticated poisoning technique. The forensic scientists who investigated the murder were in no doubt that a pinhead-sized metal pellet had somehow been implanted in Markov's right thigh. The pellet contained an extremely toxic substance called ricin which is made from castor-oil seeds. Markov's own belief, before he died, was that the implanting had been done with a dart disguised as an umbrella carried by a stranger who had apologized for 'accidentally' prodding him. The discovery of a similar pellet in a Bulgarian defector in Paris, Vladimir Kostov, who survived because the poison had not leaked out, seems proof enough that both cases were the work of an assassination organization with access to advanced techniques. Nor can there be much doubt that the Bulgarian Government ordered the actions because of the attacks made by both men on the régime from which they had fled in disgust. Markov, who worked for the BBC overseas service, had been particularly critical of the Bulgarian dictator, Todor Zhivkov, whose protegé he had once been. According to KGB defectors, the assassination of Markov in a Western country would have needed Soviet approval and the KGB most probably supplied the lethal equipment.[8]

Since then another Soviet-Bloc dissident, a Pole called Boris Korczak, has been subjected to a similar murderous attack in a supermarket in Virginia. He felt a slight sting in his back and a few hours later was delirious and bleeding internally but survived. The cause was another pellet hollowed out to contain poison.[9]

The most notorious attempted assassination in which the Bulgarian intelligence service seems to have been involved is that of Pope John Paul II in St Peter's Square, Rome, in May 1981. The Bulgarian intelligence service (Durzhavna Sigurnost) was set up under KGB supervision and is probably the most closely controlled of all the satellite services. So, if the Bulgarian responsibility is ever proved there could be no doubt that the attempt had Soviet Politburo approval because no satellite organization would have dared to take such an initiative. The Politburo had reason enough to wish to be rid of the Polish Pope, who was openly supporting the Solidarity trade-union movement which, in its eyes, threatened its continuing control of Poland through its puppet, General Jaruzelski, especially after the Pope had issued an open letter declaring his intention to go to Poland to help resist armed Soviet intervention for which the Politburo had firm plans.

The Turkish terrorist who shot the Pope and nearly killed him, Mehmet Ali Agca, has stated that three Bulgarians assisted him and that he had been given special training by the KGB. His evidence is questionable, but, on other grounds, the Italian police arrested the chief of the Rome bureau of Bulgarian State Airlines, Sergei Antonov, and he and four others are on trial. According to Agca, two Bulgarians, Todor Ayvzov, posing as a cashier at the Bulgarian

Embassy, and Major Zelio Vasilev, an assistant military attaché took him to St Peter's Square on a reconnaissance to establish the best position for the shooting.[10]

The International Department responded to Agca's statements with the standard upside-down ploy claiming that Western intelligence agencies were behind the whole story of Soviet-Bloc involvement and that the real instigators were linked with the CIA. To build this up, a Soviet journalist, Ione Andronov, was sent to Italy allegedly to make an objective investigation. His 'findings', establishing the innocence of the Bulgarians and supporting the CIA guilt, were published in the Soviet *Literary Gazette*, in the hope that they would be picked up and published in the West. Though Andronov was widely known to be a KGB officer, making it certain that his account would be a disinformation exercise written to the orders of his active-measures superiors, it was recycled by prominent Western publications such as *Der Spiegel*. Andronov's true role was exposed by another 'journalist' from the *Literary Gazette*, Oleg Bitov, whose strange history is told in Chapter 7.[11]

The Bulgarian–KGB connection with the attempt on the Pope's life has been criticised by Western intelligence observers on the ground that someone more professional than Agca would have been selected for the contract, but Agca had killed people before and he did succeed in pumping two bullets into the Pope. Further, with Agca's Turkish terrorist connections, Moscow could always point in that direction as the reason for the attempt. The death of the Pope, and his replacement by somebody less candid and not associated with any Iron Curtain country, would certainly have been welcome to the Politburo which, under Brezhnev, supported by the cold, calculating Suslov, did not lack the ruthlessness to require it. The reactions of various governments should the Soviet implication ever be proved should be illuminating.

Suspicion still remains inside MI5 and the CIA that Hugh Gaitskell, the right-of-centre Labour Party leader who supported retention of nuclear weapons, was murdered by the KGB, while many students of the assassination of President Kennedy do not accept the official American verdict that the Soviets were not involved in any way. As I have described in previous books, Gaitskell, then fifty-six, felt unwell after returning from Paris early in December 1962 and was admitted to hospital on 14 December, when he was diagnosed as suffering from virus pneumonia. He was discharged on 23 December and, to fulfil an invitation from Khrushchev to visit Moscow, he had to visit the Soviet Consulate, where he was kept waiting for half an hour, being given coffee and biscuits. The same evening he suffered a relapse; he entered hospital again on 4 January and died there on 18 January, apparently from the effects of a dangerous disease called systemic lupus erythematosus. One of the doctors was so suspicious after Gaitskell told him about the visit to the Soviet Consulate that he contacted MI5 which sent a scientific research officer to the Microbiological and Chemical Research Establishment on Salisbury Plain to seek advice. Experts there knew of no way in which the Russians could have induced the disease, but a thorough search of the medical literature commissioned by the CIA produced a startling result. In three separate reports Soviet researchers had described how they had produced a chemical substance which, when administered to animals, produced the fatal symptoms of lupus erythematosus. The fact that no further papers on the subject had ever appeared suggested that publication had been prohibited, possibly because the KGB wished to exploit the chemical. Major-General Sejna, knowing nothing of these suspicions, recorded in his book, *We Will Bury You*, that Khrushchev had hated Gaitskell so much that he had remarked, 'If Communism were to triumph tomorrow, Gaitskell would be the first to be shot outside the Houses of Parliament as a traitor to the working class.' There is no reason to doubt that Khrushchev meant it and would have regarded the assassination as justified in the Soviet interest.[12]

The evidence for KGB involvement in the murder of President Kennedy is more definite. While the circumstances are too complicated to be discussed in detail here, it is certain that the assassin, Lee Harvey Oswald, who shot Kennedy on a motorcade in Dallas, had previously defected to the Soviet Union and had been allowed back with his Russian wife after spending two and a half years there. Previously, as a Marine, he had been stationed on a US air base in Japan from which American U2 spy-planes operated for flights over Soviet territory. It is, therefore, inconceivable that the Russians would not have interrogated him deeply about the flights, in which he had been involved on the ground staff. After his capture, and before he could be fully interrogated, Oswald himself was murdered by someone with no particular motive unless he had been hired or required to do it. Oswald's death before he could talk was certainly in the Soviet interest if there had been KGB involvement.

Oswald had been given some training in espionage methods because he possessed Minox cameras and other spying equipment and knew about microdots, the system for reducing a document to a size little larger than a full stop on this page. He was also known to have been in touch with Soviet agents in Washington and Mexico City. Oswald's initial reactions to police questioning suggested that he had been trained to resist interrogation, and he had not been given such training in the Marines.

There are strong indications that both the FBI and the new President, Lyndon Johnson, were anxious to stifle any inquiries which might prove KGB involvement. The FBI, and especially its chief, J. Edgar Hoover, would have been guilty of gross incompetence in failing to maintain a check on Oswald, if he were proved to have been a KGB agent. President Johnson was keen to cover up any Soviet implication because of the dangerous situation which proof of it could cause in the shape of a demand for vengeance from the American people.[13]

More recently, in 1979, the Politburo gave its full backing to a KGB operation to assassinate the President of Afghanistan, Hafizullah Amin. Originally this was to have been accomplished by a KGB officer infiltrated into the presidential palace. When that failed, a KGB team of assassins stormed the palace and killed Amin and everyone else there.[14]

While the International Department and the KGB prefer to keep individual assassinations under their command and control, even when assigned to surrogates, they are prepared to delegate authority to the terrorist organizations which they supply with money, weapons and ammunition and whose hit-men they often train. All that the Kremlin requires is that the terrorist activities will help to destabilize governments to which it is opposed, create general chaos and uncertainty and, when practicable, liquidate people whom it regards as dangerous adversaries. There can be little doubt, for instance, that the attempt to assassinate Margaret Thatcher and other Ministers at Brighton in 1984, generally attributed to the IRA, would have been welcome to the Politburo, had it succeeded.

The continuing firm support of international terrorism by the Politburo is inevitable because of the very nature of Soviet Communism which regards terrorism – outside the confines of the Soviet Bloc – as just another aspect of the political war against societies which need to be 'smashed' and because of the success it has enjoyed through terrorising its own people. Through the International Department and the KGB, the Politburo has maintained close links with terrorist organizations like the Palestine Liberation Organization, the IRA, the Rhodesian ZAPU, the Egyptian Fundamentalists and many others which are all projected as 'freedom fighters'. Major-General Sejna has recorded how the Russians were quick to see the IRA's potential and agreed that Czech intelligence should train IRA 'delegates' in terrorist warfare and supply the movement with machine guns, hand grenades, explosives and field communications equipment.[15]

To quote the KGB defector, Dzhirkvelov:

> The Palestinian Liberation Organization is certainly used as one of the main tools in the fight against Israel and even against the Western democracies. In the training of the 'fighters' for the Palestinian and other movements active assistance is sought and received from Bulgarian, East German and Cuban special services. The urban guerillas are trained on Soviet territory, in the three above-mentioned 'brotherly' countries and also on the territory of several African states – like Angola, Mozambique and possibly Libya.

Tomas Schuman, the Soviet defector who worked for Novosti, has revealed how that 'journalistic' agency is used by the KGB for spotting and cultivating future recruits for 'national liberation' movements. 'During my career in India, for example, one of my functions was to compile lists of young, "progressively-minded" people who could be recommended later for enrolment in "studies" at the Patrice Lumumba Friendship University in Moscow', he has stated.[16] This so-called university, established by Khrushchev in 1960 and dominated from the start by the KGB, indoctrinates foreign students in the techniques of subversion and revolution. Among its distinguished graduates is 'Carlos', the notorious international terrorist of Venezuelan origin who has murdered many people and served as an adviser to Libyan and other terrorist organizations.[17]

The Soviet authorities are ingenious in distancing themselves from the terrorism they exploit, so that in the event of exposure their involvement can be denied. This has been confirmed by an extensive study undertaken by the CIA which showed that while there are many camps inside the Soviet Union for the training of terrorists, Soviet citizens are not involved in their operations abroad and so can never be caught with a 'smoking gun'.[18] Schuman has also recorded how Novosti staff serving abroad, for instance, are required to act as go-betweens with foreign Soviet agents in touch with terrorists to make the chain back to Moscow as many-linked as possible.[19]

The Cuban intelligence service is being increasingly used to support terrorists, the funds and weapons being supplied by Moscow along with KGB advisers based in Cuba. During the 1960s the United States suffered a serious terrorist campaign from a group calling itself the Weathermen. It was responsible for many bombing outrages and for what it called The Days of Rage, in October 1969, when anti-Vietnam war protesters, urged on by Weathermen agitators, rioted in Chicago, engaging in pitched battles with the police. The Weathermen, assisted by Cubans, were also responsible for terrorist bombings in Quebec, in support of French Canadian separatists, their aim being to support any movement which would create chaos and uncertainty in true democracies. A former member of the Weathermen, Larry Grathwohl, gave first-hand evidence of the movement's ties with Cuba on Canadian television in June 1982. He described how he was always able to establish contact with other terrorists through Cuban embassies. Using Soviet money, the Cuban intelligence service recruited Weathermen volunteers from radical young Americans visiting Havana and then trained them in bombing techniques. On the same programme a former member of the Cuban intelligence service declared that the Soviets were behind the whole involvement with the Weathermen who were not made aware that they were being used in Soviet active-measures operations. This had previously been revealed when secret FBI evidence about the Weathermen movement was made public at the trial of two FBI men in November 1981.

In the late 1960s Mexican students recruited by the KGB but trained away from the Soviet Union, in North Korea, were used in an attempt to plunge Mexico into civil war. The trigger event was an attempt by the revolutionaries to disrupt the 1968 Olympic Games in Mexico City, but this was put down by the resolute use of the Mexican army. According to an official Italian report, which was studied by the Italian Parliamentary Commission set up to investigate the kidnap and murder of Dr Aldo Moro, the KGB has tried to manipulate the Red Brigades in Italy through surrogate organizations believed to have included the IRA, the PLO and West Germany's Red Army faction.[20] Soon after the British Government expelled 105 Soviet agents in 1971 the Kremlin persuaded the Eire Government to agree to full embassy status with the Soviet Union, and Soviet-Bloc agents were quickly in Dublin contacting the IRA with a view to supplying weapons.[21]

In addition to assisting terrorists logistically, the Soviet Union also backs them up with active measures against the governments of the countries where they are operating. From the moment the Russians were expelled from Egypt they made unremitting efforts to disrupt that country's relationship with the US and to undermine the authority and reputation of the Egyptian leader, Anwar Sadat, especially after the Camp David Accords with Israel. The active-measures operators concentrated their attention on the fanatical Muslim Brotherhood which was eventually to assassinate Sadat in 1981. KGB forgeries purporting to be of American origin and suggesting that Sadat was an American puppet, or could easily be disposed of if he offended Washington, were surfaced in Egyptian publications in ways calculated to enrage ordinary Arabs as well as Islamic fundamentalists. It was not difficult to convince Sadat and his government that the 'documents' referred to were Soviet forgeries but they had their effect on the fanatics and are believed, by the CIA, to have contributed to Sadat's increasing unpopularity and eventual murder.[22]

Whenever the governments being attacked by terrorists and 'freedom fighters' take steps to defend themselves and their citizens they are vilified in the Communist-controlled and penetrated media as Fascist butchers using brutal force against heroic 'guerillas', and the photographs in the newspapers and on television are far more likely to concentrate on the slain terrorists than on the defenders. As Sir James Goldsmith told the Media Committee, 'it is very much as though the British Government had been described as criminal butchers because during the Battle of Britain they had brutally shot down German pilots without trial'. This manifestation of the upside-down ploy in which those being indiscriminately attacked by car-bombs, booby traps and every other kind of savage device are projected as the villains has been used by the Politburo with stunning effect in the United Nations. Almost unbelievably, this agency of 'peace', which is packed with Soviet client states, has affirmed in solemn session of the General Assembly that 'national liberation movements', even when patently Moscow-inspired revolutionaries, are fully justified in using terrorism and that elected governments which react by using counter-force to protect their citizens and their property are violating 'human rights'.[23]

When the active-measures apparatus is needed for use in frank military operations – what the Soviet theorists call 'the armed road' – the International Department is intimately involved because of the political implications and no initiatives may be taken by the KGB, the GRU or any military forces without detailed approval by the Politburo. Very large sums of money may be required, when, for example, it is proposed to give active support over an indefinite period to guerilla forces of a 'national liberation movement' or to surrogate forces like the Cuban troops fighting in Angola.

Large amounts of money and weapons were given to the left-wing revolutionaries who seized power in the Caribbean island of Grenada in 1979. Documents seized there by US forces in October 1983 showed that this had been the result of secret agreements between Russia and Grenada signed in 1980, but the money and aid had been funnelled through Cuba. The Politburo's purpose was to convert Grenada to a base from which pressure could be exerted on other Caribbean states, with a large airport and possibly a sea-port available to Cuba and the Soviet Union for military adventures in South and Central America. This attempt to militarize a previously peaceful island hardly accorded with the peaceful image which the Politburo tries to project.[24]

The brevity of the Soviet Bloc's response to the American operation in Grenada is evidence of its inability to disclaim involvement and of its respect for resolute action.

Another highly sensitive activity controlled by the International Department on the Politburo's behalf is the regular recruitment of foreign subversive agents – 'fifth columnists' – committed to assisting the Soviet forces in the event of an invasion. Such traitors, who are recruited mainly through ideology and money, were in position in advance of the invasions of Hungary and Czechoslovakia and, more recently, of Afghanistan, and assisted in the quick capture of key targets. What is not properly appreciated is that large numbers of similar traitors are in position as sleepers in Western Europe and in Britain. Specific targets have been allotted to them and their main function would be to strike in support of the Soviet commando forces, known as Spetsnaz units, which are trained for landing by air or sea in advance of a major assault on NATO.

Ranging in size from large airborne units to small groups, their purpose is to seize or destroy key targets such as nuclear storage depots, radio and radar stations, command and control posts and communication links. Their task could be enormously facilitated by small subversive units based in the country under attack as unsuspected 'sleepers', and springing into action, when instructed from Moscow, to act as guides, carry out diversions and actually attack some targets. The existence of such 'subversion units', regarded by the KGB as important 'clandestine assets' has been fully confirmed by KGB defectors, some details of those in Britain having been provided by Oleg Lyalin, the KGB officer stationed in the Soviet 'trade mission' in London who defected in 1971.

Subversion units are controlled by Spetsnaz officers working under diplomatic immunity as defence attachés, or in other guises such as officials of Aeroflot and the various timber, agricultural and industrial concerns established in Britain and Western Europe by the Soviet Government. All members of the Spetsnaz forces are required to be fluent in the language of their target countries and they are therefore rotated in the overseas posts available for linguistic advantages, as well as for the reconnaissance and surveillance of the key targets assigned to them. The security authorities suspect that there are also 'illegal' Spetsnaz officers and senior NCOs intruded as merchant seamen and living under deep cover until relieved by others. These Spetsnaz personnel are believed to maintain some contact with the most trusted British and European 'sleepers' who make up the bulk of the resident subversion units. Some of those GRU officers and officials of Aeroflot and other subversion front agencies who have recently been expelled from Britain, France and elsewhere were detected while engaging in Spetsnaz planning activities.

During the six months while Lyalin remained in his KGB post

after agreeing to work for British intelligence he provided documentary proof of Spetsnaz plans to blow up V-bombers on airfields, flood the London Underground railway system, sabotage military cable links and destroy the ballistic missile warning system at Fylingdales in Yorkshire. Lyalin described how he himself was to meet Spetsnaz troops landing from the sea near Fylingdales with the necessary explosives and probably wearing British uniforms or civilian clothes, and was to conduct them to the specially important site. Lyalin was a member of the KGB's Department Five, formerly known as SMERSH, and, like his colleagues, had been trained in assassination methods. He confirmed that the assassination of political and military leaders in the target countries was part of the Spetsnaz assignment and that subversion units would assist them.[25] The extent to which this assassination danger is appreciated was demonstrated by the immediate American reaction to the attempted murder of President Reagan in 1981. The US Forces were put on alert in case the assassination attempt had been a Spetsnaz move prior to a Soviet surprise attack on the US or on Europe.

Lyalin's evidence has been broadly confirmed by General Sejna who has revealed that 'the Warsaw Pact's contingency plans should not only provide for sabotage operations to cripple British industrial, defence and communications installations, as a prelude to war, but should also include measures whereby Soviet forces – or a progressive government established by them – could settle accounts with the bourgeois leaders'. A list of Britons considered hostile was seen by Sejna and ran to several hundred names, beside which were the actions contemplated, ranging from temporary detention to execution without trial. Sejna has also described how members of the British Communist Party were trained in sabotage techniques in Czechoslovakia at the KGB's request.[26] Another KGB defector, Major Aleksei Myagkov, who was in the directorate responsible for security within the Soviet armed forces, has confirmed the importance which the Soviet staff chiefs have assigned to Spetsnaz sabotage operations.[27]

Since then more detailed information about Spetsnaz forces, earmarked for use against the United Kingdom, has been made available to me by intelligence sources. Their military training concentrates on large-scale models of targets in Britain which they would be detailed to destroy. They practise landings on simulated British beaches and assaults on other simulated targets known to include 10 Downing Street and other Government headquarters in Whitehall, as well as radar stations, nuclear bases and military installations scattered throughout Britain. Those forces targeted on nuclear bases even have mock-ups of nuclear weapons, such as cruise missiles, on which to practise the placing of demolition charges designed to destroy the weapons without causing a nuclear blast. The Spetsnaz training also includes the mock assassination of political leaders, staff chiefs and senior civil servants.

The reality of this threat, which to some might seem far-fetched, has been recognized in the shape of the biggest military exercise to be staged in Britain since the war and named Brave Defender. It is specifically designed to test the home defences against clandestine assault by Spetsnaz forces and their British-based auxiliaries prior to a Soviet invasion of Europe. Scheduled for the week beginning 6 September 1985, and involving 65,000 troops of all services, including 1000 American personnel from US bases in Britain, Brave Defender's purpose is to expose vulnerabilities in the defence of key points known to be on the Soviet 'hit list' as well as to provide evidence of how they might be attacked. Troops from BAOR and other NATO forces will play the part of the invaders and their helpers and, since some of these will be posing as civilians, police from many areas will also be active. As with hunts for criminals, helicopters will be widely used.

The size and scope of Brave Defender indicates the vulnerability of Britain's open society and the authorities' appreciation of the ease with which Spetsnaz personnel and other subversives can enter the country. About 50,000 Soviet seamen come ashore each year with no limits on their movements since they enjoy the privileges afforded to all foreign merchant sailors. They can hire cars to familiarize themselves with the routes to their targets, if they are Spetsnaz men, and many are believed to have carried out reconnaissance operations in this manner. While a check is kept on the numbers of Russian seamen returning to their ships none is kept on identities. So Spetsnaz personnel remaining in Britain illegally can regularly be relieved and replaced. Igor goes ashore but it may be Ivan who returns. No comparable facilities are available to British seamen visiting the Soviet Union.[28]

Soviet-Bloc spies feed the Spetsnaz forces with continual updates

251

about their targets. This is, partly, what two Hungarian intelligence officers were about in April 1976 when they were seen taking photographs at the Royal Ordnance Factory at Burghfield, near Reading, which is involved in the production and maintenance of nuclear weapons. The information would also have been of use to terrorist organizations supported by the Soviets, for the seizure of nuclear explosive by terrorists is greatly feared by all Western governments as being likely to present a blackmail threat which would be almost impossible to counter.[29] 'Peace' protestors and others posing as such are well placed to keep Spetsnaz forces informed of local changes in guard arrangements and other security defences.

In addition to Lyalin, many of the 105 Soviet agents who were expelled from Britain after his defection had been engaged in active-measures operations and among these a high-priority requirement had been the recruitment of British fifth columnists, known to the Soviets as 'partisans'. The evidence of Major Levchenko given to a US Congress Select Committee is especially significant in that respect. He described how, in 1966, he was required to undergo specialized training as an illegal intelligence agent for infiltration into Britain in the event of a military emergency. His mission would have been 'to report on the state of readiness of British nuclear strike forces located in the area of one of their major seaports'. Describing the Illegal Service run by the KGB's Department Five he said, 'Its main activity is recruiting foreigners as agents for sabotage, assassinations and all kinds of things like that, primarily in case of a very serious aggravation of the international situation. This department also sends its own illegals abroad to sit and wait and recruit individuals who would be ready to blow up a certain bridge or telecommunications system and things like that.'[30]

Lyalin attested that subversion squads are ready to move into action when signalled to do so from Moscow and that each is equipped with a Russian radio receiver-transmitter which is used only infrequently to ensure that the set is in working order. The sets are normally concealed and one of them was accidentally dug up by a farmer near Llangollen, North Wales, in 1980. Inquiries showed that a party of six Russians had booked in at a nearby hotel describing themselves as part of a trade delegation and had gone out only when it was dark. Four of them were among those eventually expelled and there can be little doubt that they planted the set – a 'squirt' transmitter which sends messages on a punched tape at such speed that its location is difficult to pinpoint. The security authorities believe that the set, which was in excellent order and thoroughly protected against corrosion, was for the use of a subversion unit possibly based in Liverpool which is a high priority Spetsnaz target.[31] It was a fluke that the chance discovery of this set became public knowledge and others may have been found though the chances of doing so are obviously slight.

The British members of subversion units – so-called 'partisans' – are most likely to be recruited from among the many crypto-Communists, open Communists being too obvious for that purpose. There is considerable concern in MI5 about the extent to which trade unionists known to be of the extreme left are moving in and out of the Soviet Union and other Iron Curtain countries. One businessman has described to me how he was visited by an MI5 officer to be told that one of his 'shop-floor' union officials who was supposed to be away sick was actually in Moscow on a quick visit being paid for by the Soviets. It was the potential influence of left-wing extremists on the unions at GCHQ which finally drove the Government to ban union membership there. It was not thought – as the unions claimed – that membership entailed an increased danger of individual disloyalty. The fear lay in the risk that control of the GCHQ unions might fall into pro-Soviet extremist hands which would be prepared to interfere with its vital functions at times when intercepted intelligence might be crucial to survival. As already indicated, almost all the major defectors have underlined the importance the Politburo attaches to the penetration of the British trade unions not only because of their influence on political action through the Labour Party but for their disruptive capabilities in both peace and war.

According to Lyalin the 'partisans' are required to create chaos and terror at a time of mounting tension and to promote mass evacuation through fear of nuclear attack in order to interfere with the movement of British and American reinforcements to Europe, as well as to carry out sabotage operations. He could not name any because, as part of the security routine, they were handled by other officers. Nor could he give any information about the GRU espionage and subversion network in Britain which was even more closely involved with military operations. The security authorities have identified some of the would-be traitors and would be able to pick them up in an emergency but they cannot be touched under normal British law until they commit an offence. The security and intelligence services try to penetrate the Soviet subversion 'infrastructure' with their own agents and where this has been successful the units are best left undisturbed.

Similar legal restrictions apply to the subversion units that have been set up in West Germany and which, according to information given to me by a former chief of the Rhine Army, number at least four hundred. The total number of subversives in the West German 'sleeper' network may amount to 20,000 or more and there can be little doubt that many of them are East German professionals who have been 'permitted' to emigrate to the West or have arrived as refugees or students and then been recruited through the blackmail of threats to close relatives left behind. My questions to intelligence authorities concerning the size of the Soviet 'infrastructure' in Britain elicited only the cryptic comment that the importance attached by Moscow to Britain as a target would suggest that it is large. The number of NATO personnel serving as mock Spetsnaz invaders and their assistants in Exercise Brave Defender – understood to be about 5000 for operations involving only a few key points – offers some indication of the size of the problem. The size of individual subversion units depends on the nature and difficulty of their targets. Many may be no larger than a typical IRA 'active service unit' – perhaps a dozen people with two or three 'safe houses' for accommodation, planning and for weapons caches – but intelligence suggests that others are much bigger.

Spetsnaz forces demonstrated their value in a clever deception operation, planned by the International Department and the KGB, as the opening phase of the invasion of Czechoslovakia to remove the Dubchek régime and occupy the country permanently with Soviet forces. On 20 August 1968, shortly before midnight, a Soviet Antonov transport plane claimed to be in distress and secured permission to land at Prague main airport. It was filled with Spetsnaz troops which seized and occupied the control tower to facilitiate a major airborne landing of Soviet forces about an hour later. At the same time the first units of about half a million Warsaw Pact troops, who had collected on the false grounds of taking part in an exercise, crossed the Czech border at many points. To justify this massive invasion, which was to be explained away internationally as an invitation from the Czech government, active-measures operations had been in progress for many weeks. They included forgeries to indicate that Dubchek, a dedicated Communist who wanted some liberalizing of the régime, was a tool of the Americans who were planning to give 'counter-revolutionaries' military assistance. The KGB planted a cache of NATO weapons on Czech soil and when these were 'discovered' the controlled press was required to report that similar caches had been found in many other parts of the country.[31]

Spetsnaz forces were also involved, more recently, along with KGB personnel, in the storming of the presidential palace in Kabul in December 1979 and the assassination of President Hafizullah Amin and many of his staff.

In Western Europe Spetsnaz operations are essentially in the planning and training stages, but they have been conducted against neutral countries and with a considerable degree of contempt for the attitude of the free world and of the neutral countries themselves. Following the ruthless domination of Finland through threat of military action, the Politburo's main neutral target has been Sweden. Over the last twenty years the Soviet authorities have become increasingly blatant in their attempt to intimidate their small neighbour, which is so genuinely peaceful that it has not been involved in any war for well over a century. According to the intelligence reports on which the highly authoritative annual volume, *Jane's Fighting Ships*, depends, there have been more than 150 landings by Soviet reconnaissance parties along areas of the Swedish coast from Haparanda in the north to Malmö in the south since 1962. Raiding groups from the Soviet naval base of Kronstadt, near Leningrad, have been using Swedish territory to practise sabotage and the conquest of landing areas. The Swedes have been fully aware of the raids but have been reluctant to make much public complaint at this outrageous behaviour by its 'peace-loving' neighbour and any suggestions of Soviet impropriety have been angrily and threateningly denied from Moscow.

On 27 October 1981, however, an event occurred which laid bare the Politburo's behaviour beyond hope of effective denial. A 'Whiskey' class Soviet submarine ran aground in a highly restricted area of the Karlskrona Archipelago in southern Sweden near a major naval base. Such was the embarrassment and obvious fear of the stranded captain that the headline 'Whiskey on the Rocks' wrote itself into countless newspapers and has become a lasting symbol of Soviet malevolence and mendacity when exposed.[33]

For many months previously the Swedish authorities had been aware that the Soviets had increased their impudent invasions of their territorial waters by sending submarines into fjords and other sensitive defence areas. Using limited counter-measures, because of fear of the consequences, the Swedish forces had tried to make the submarines surface, but without success. When Soviet submarine No. 137 ran aground and was unable to extricate itself there could be no doubt that it had been on an espionage mission to probe the defences of the Karlskrona naval base and, perhaps, to take part in some mock invasion exercise as there is evidence that the boat was armed with nuclear torpedoes.

The Soviet Navy quickly had rescue ships and destroyers on the scene, but the Swedes courageously held the vessel for ten days during which it was boarded so that the log-book could be inspected, the captain questioned and the hull examined with the use of sensor devices. Meanwhile the International Department was required to take some emergency active measures to limit the damage. In answer to the strong formal protest which had been lodged by the Swedish Government, TASS made a totally false accusation that Sweden had been carrying out radio-signalling operations on behalf of NATO. About a dozen forged telegrams referring to an alleged secret agreement between the US and Sweden permitting the US to use Karlskrona were floated in Washington and Sweden itself.[34] Perhaps some gullible people believed them.

Any 'peace-loving' nation caught so blatantly and subjected to such worldwide publicity as the Soviet Union was with 'Whiskey on the Rocks' could have been expected to curb its activities towards the offended country, at least for a while. Instead, the Politburo authorized their intensification and in the following October an official investigation exposed a large-scale secret Soviet offensive involving new methods for the underwater infringement of sovereign territory. A number of submarines entered a restricted area of the Stockholm Archipelago and part of it penetrated into Harsfjarden, the chief base of the Swedish Navy. They were detected and hunted but escaped. The intrusion was so definite and so brazen that the Swedish Government set up a Commission of Inquiry under Sven Andersson, a former Defence Minister, while the Prime Minister, Olaf Palme, issued a warning that any submarines violating Swedish waters in future would be sunk.

The Commission's report, issued in April 1983, stated that the evidence indicated that probably six submarines had been involved. Three of these were conventional-sized vessels serving as mother-ships for the other three, which were midget manned submarines with a capability to remain suspended in the water or to crawl on the seabed on caterpillar tracks. This capability enabled them to operate in shallow water and they had left clear imprints on the sea-bottom. The recent Soviet Army defector now using the pseudonym Viktor Suvorov claims that the mini-submarines belong to naval Spetsnaz units. While the Swedish forces had done their best to hunt down and expose the intruders they had failed, largely because they had paid little attention to anti-submarine warfare in the past and did not have the requisite equipment.[35]

The Commission also reported on various violations of Swedish territorial waters which dated back to the 1970s, when there had been between two and nine per annum. These had risen gradually until there were more than forty in 1982. The Commission regarded this pattern as one of 'increasingly provocative behaviour' and was in no doubt that all the violations had been by Soviet vessels. It interpreted the Soviet intrusions as having two main purposes: the on-going collection of intelligence information and, more important, rehearsal for the deployment of commando forces against key Swedish targets in the event of a European war – in total breach of Swedish neutrality. A further purpose may have been to gauge the extent of the reaction from NATO which, regrettably, was slight.

On publication of the report the Swedish Government delivered a sharp protest to Moscow which responded, predictably, by repudiating the charges in a contemptuous way. Using the upside-down ploy it called on the Swedish Government to expose the officials who had been responsible for presenting the falsified information in the report! This response must have had the blessing of the Politburo.[36]

The violations have since continued in what is now quite obviously a Soviet campaign of intimidation and a clear warning to Sweden that in the event of war, or possibly through some other excuse,

Soviet forces would invade and occupy those parts of the country useful to them. Short of being defeated, they would be unlikely ever to depart without having first 'Finlandized' their peaceful neighbour and taken those facilities envied by the Soviet Navy. Meanwhile the shameless intimidation serves as an active measure aimed at making the Swedish Government and people realize that it has no alternative but to 'adjust' to Soviet interests and give in to whatsoever the Politburo may require of it.

The Politburo's cavalier treatment of Sweden demonstrates the total lack of respect it has for neutrals with no major military backing. The same attitude would be displayed towards Britain if ever it left NATO or caused NATO's collapse through Labour's unilateral nuclear defence policy. Currently, while Soviet intelligence forces fly and sail as close to the British shores as legally permitted, they do not infringe British air-space or territorial waters. The Politburo remains conditioned by Stalin's cynical remark, 'How many divisions has the Pope?'

Chapter 19

Counter-Offensive?

'To the question of what should the non-Communist countries do
. . . I will give the fairest and truest answer: "Don't do what you are
doing now."'

Jean-François Revel

Because the inherent vulnerabilities of the genuinely free and open society can so easily be exploited by those of evil intent, it is true democracy, rather than capitalism, which contains the seeds of its own destruction. The main vulnerabilities cannot be removed without destroying the cherished values which constitute real liberty – freedom of speech, writing, movement, assembly and ownership of property, freedom from arbitrary arrest and, above all, the right to expel an unpopular government and the means for doing that. But it is senseless that, having endured a terrible war to preserve these freedoms from the ravages of a Fascist dictatorship, Western civilization should allow itself to be progressively debilitated by an equally ruthless Communist dictatorship with even more menacing long-term tyrannical and territorial ambitions. Any objective observer looking through an all-seeing telescope from space at the nonchalant impotence of those who enjoy freedoms, secured by centuries of strife, while their institutions, their parliaments, media, trade unions, educational systems and churches are assiduously corrupted by left-wing extremists, could only conclude that the West is collectively suicidal. That very message has been conveyed, repeatedly, by down-to-earth observers with bitter experience of the Communist system, defectors and dissidents like Levchenko, Solzhenitsyn and Bukovsky. They are convinced that counter-measures which would not seriously erode civil liberties are not only possible but essential if the free world is to survive the alien onslaught. The West's predicament, as described in this book, confirms their fears and cries out for action to prevent true democracy and liberty being swept from the earth by an avalanche of Soviet-inspired active measures, helped on its way by apathy and resignation. The time available for such action may be shorter than most people appreciate.

Because the Soviet system and the Communist conspiracy as a whole are founded on fraud and held together by deceit, the instrument most feared by their directors and dependents is the searchlight of truth, wielded through publicity. Yet Western governments have been negligently reluctant to make use of their numerous publicity outlets for this purpose. No opportunity should ever be missed to expose the Politburo for what it is – an élite clique which seized power illegally and whose unelected successors have held on to it ever since by methods which, in any democratic country, would be regarded as criminal. It is an evil régime, which makes what amounts to war on its own people, yet when President Reagan called it that, some politicians, especially in Britain, complained that he had gone too far and that such truthful language was counter-productive.[1] In fact there has been far too much taking it on the chin and offering the other cheek, which the Soviets will always smite if it suits them. This is the policy of quiet diplomacy consistently advocated by Western foreign ministries and it has consistently failed to have any moderating impact on the Politburo's behaviour. Instead the Politburo has exploited the open-handedness of Western diplomats and their unfounded faith that friendship must eventually triumph over suspicion and guile. The Andrei Gromyko who directed Soviet foreign policy, with the assistance of the International Department and the KGB, until promoted to President in July 1985, is the same Gromyko who personally lied to President Kennedy during the Cuban missile crisis more than thirty years ago, and the motivating force behind that policy has not changed. This force, which remains the Marxist-Leninist requirement to foist Soviet-style Communism on the rest of the world, is like a monstrous fly-wheel into which so much energy has been pumped over the last sixty years that it cannot be stopped or slowed down without causing the collapse of the entire Soviet edifice. If freedom is to survive, there must be continuous appreciation of this threat with widespread realization of the scale and purpose of the enormous effort behind it. Only publicity can convince the all-too-silent majority, and particularly the young, that the target is all of us and that the Soviet marksmen continue to score hits on it. While some newspapers are courageously active in countering the 'it couldn't happen here' mentality, their efforts would be much more effective if backed more resolutely by Ministerial statements and disclosures for which there is almost daily scope if the Foreign Office gag were removed.

The British and European Governments would do their peoples a valuable service if they followed the US lead and publicized Soviet duplicities whenever these are exposed. Official reports on Soviet forgeries, for instance, are published in Washington and made available to the media while in Britain this appalling practice by a super-power is officially ignored.[2] The same applies to violations of various treaties and agreements by the Soviets. In the US the facts are published and the President comments on them. In Britain silence reigns, again, I suspect, at the instigation of the Foreign Office, which is overly concerned about offending the Politburo. Soviet leaders are permitted to falsify history at Western expense with little response from Ministers. At the fortieth anniversary celebration of VE Day in Moscow, Gorbachov had the gall to denounce the West for collusion with Hitler 'to destroy Soviet Socialism', when in fact it was the Politburo's collusion with Hitler which made Germany's war on the West and, eventually, on the Soviet Union possible.[3] The Politburo supplied the Nazi régime with petrol for the German tanks and bombers, grain to feed the German troops, leather for their jackboots and rubber for their armoured cars and copper and manganese for their shells and bullets. It helped Hitler to defeat Poland by occupying half the country and then handed over Jews there to the SS for concentration-camp treatment. It enabled German sea-raiders to avoid the British naval blockade and sink Allied merchant ships.[4]

Gorbachov could hardly have expected such an easily disprovable lie to be accepted in the West except by the purblind ideologues for whom the words of the Politburo constitute the truth, however

261

much at variance with the facts. It was, therefore, intended mainly for Soviet domestic consumption and was clear evidence that, under the new leadership, the mass deception of the Soviet people is to continue along with lying vilification of the true democracies.

The opportunity to nail that blatant falsehood and to demonstrate to the world that truth is of no concern to the top men in the Kremlin, be they old revolutionaries or young thrusters, was ignored by British Ministers, presumably to avoid upsetting Mr Gorbachov. The Government should not be surprised, therefore, if young British voters, born after the war, believe such disinformation and any more that Gorbachov has to offer. The same applies to the current Soviet claim, repeated many times by the Western media, that the Russians suffered 20 million killed in the war when the figure given by Stalin was less than 8 million. The difference is presumably made up by those killed by the Soviet régime itself, though some authorities put that figure, since the 1917 revolution, at 60 million. Equally misleading is the suggestion that these casualties were somehow suffered on behalf of freedom from Fascism in general when, in fact, Stalin would have sat back and seen Britain and Europe demolished had Hitler not made the mistake of attacking the Soviet Union.[5]

It is, of course, possible that some Ministers and the officials who advise them fail to appreciate how the Communist-trained mind works and cannot accept that after nearly seventy years the Soviet purpose is still to destroy the Western way of life and to clamp Moscow-style totalitarianism upon it. My inquiries suggest that few of them appreciate the extent of the active-measures offensive and its cumulative effects, which helps to explain why so little is being done to counter it. To quote Hans Huyn, in the West German context, 'Political decision-makers in the West must realize that Moscow has already been fighting the Third World War for a long time beneath the level of military conflict. Those who are not even prepared to acknowledge this fact will be unable to put up any resistance to the Soviet offensive.'[6]

Parliamentarians, who operate in the closed society of the Palace of Westminster, and are beset with constituency duties when outside it, are generally ignorant of the active-measures offensive. Not only do they fail to discuss it in the Commons, which would generate much-needed publicity, but they are actively discouraged from doing so because the issue impinges on security which is a taboo subject. In the US, Select Committees of Congress and the Senate have consistently served the cause of freedom by publishing reports on many aspects of Soviet subversion, but the comparable committees in Britain have lacked the courage to insist on their rights to investigate active measures, or any other threat, because of opposition which originates in the security services and is supported by senior civil servants determined to maintain secrecy about any activities involving the KGB.[7] The attempt by the All-Party Committee on Defence to investigate the efficiency of positive vetting was badly received by the authorities and was never completed. It is the Committee's duty to inform itself about the Spetsnaz threat but it has failed to do so. In April 1985 the House of Lords staged a revealing debate on certain aspects of the Soviet's secret offensive but this was largely ignored by the Commons where the 'table office' declines to accept most questions on such issues thereby preventing their discussion.[8]

The most perturbing finding of my inquiries into the Spetsnaz threat is the extent to which senior politicians and even some service chiefs prefer almost to ignore it on the grounds that they have so much to deal with already that they cannot spare the time or the resources for such a shadowy and perplexing problem.

Among some who do appreciate the seriousness of the Soviet active-measures effort, there is often a trusting belief that the danger is being cunningly countered by the secret services. In fact the published record shows that over the last forty years the secret services have been markedly ineffective in countering clandestine Soviet activities against the United Kingdom. I doubt that they have the strength or the resources to cope with the subversion threat, in addition to the burdens of IRA terrorism and counter-espionage. Further, the services have been repeatedly penetrated by Soviet agents, who have been able to nullify much of the counter-Soviet effort, and have been poorly manned and managed. When Shelepin, the KGB chief, was required to intensify the disinformation campaign he stressed the importance of penetration agents to feed back the results and he certainly succeeded in Britain as well as in France and West Germany.[9]

MI5 has had some successes but the Government has consistently avoided making use of them to alert the public to the Soviet Union's underhand activities and intentions. When KGB spies and active-measures agents have been expelled, the people, whose freedom they were threatening, should have been given some indication of what they had been doing, but there has been far too much concern with diplomatic niceties and avoidance of allowing the KGB to know the extent of MI5's discoveries. Intelligence sources must be protected, but in many instances some disclosure would have been a worthwhile trade-off, both by informing the nation about Soviet subversion and by embarrassing the Politburo internationally through the exposure they detest. Instead the secret services are allowed to play a private 'snubs to you' game with the KGB with little, if any, impact on the KGB's ensuing activities, except, perhaps, to spur them on. On the occasions when the secret-service chiefs favour publicity, political leaders lack the resolution to take advantage of the circumstances. In 1974, for example, thirteen Czech diplomats caught in espionage and active-measures activities were expelled, but the Prime Minister, Edward Heath, forbade publicity, even when this was recommended to him by the Minister at the Foreign Office, Julian Amery, with MI6 approval.[10]

Governments are prepared to make limited use of expulsions when it happens to suit some ministerial purpose. I am in little doubt, for instance, that the expulsion of five Soviet officials in April 1985 was timed to precede the Security Commission's report on the case of the MI5 officer, Michael Bettaney, who offered his services to the KGB.[11] The Prime Minister had received the report several weeks previously and knew that it was highly critical of MI5. The expulsions indicated that MI5 had been sufficiently alert to trap five KGB agents but the public were denied any information about what they had done and the penalty to the KGB and the Politburo was minimized. Such lack of political will was deplored by the late MI6 chief, Sir Maurice Oldfield, as the West's main weakness.[12] British and other Western governments would do well to follow the lead given by the Danish Government in the case of Arne Petersen which was given maximum publicity even though he was not prosecuted.[13] In Britain the case would have been covered up as it was with the comparable Soviet-Bloc agent Arthur Bax.[14]

The extent to which active measures are being steadily intensified is indicated by the increase in the number of Soviet agents being caught and expelled worldwide. In 1983 the publicized total was 147, with many more perhaps having been removed quietly. France alone expelled forty-seven and this bold action was followed by the US, Britain, Australia, Japan, Belgium, Holland and Denmark. More have since been expelled worldwide, including several in India.[15] To quote the US Deputy Under Secretary for Defense, Richard Stilwell, 'The Soviet Union and its surrogates have become far more active. . . . We have ten people awaiting trial on espionage charges, the highest figure in recent memory.'[16] This intensification is causing concern because it suggests that the Soviet leadership is in a hurry to achieve some purpose. Whatever it might be, there is urgent need for counter-measures. The secret services should be provided with additional resources, with more attention being paid to the International Department as well as to the KGB and GRU in the active-measures field. There needs to be additional surveillance of Soviet intelligence officers in all Western countries, with the same restrictions applied to the movements of those using UN organizations as cover that would be applied to Western officials if the organizations were based behind the Iron Curtain. By the same token restrictions should be applied to the movements of Soviet seamen in Western ports. In view of the blatant manner in which TASS and Novosti are used as cover for spies and active-measures operators, curbs should be placed on Soviet journalists, as they are on Western journalists in the Soviet Union.

Communists and other Britons serving as agents for Soviet intelligence and those suspected of it should continue to be subjected to surveillance, irrespective of the outcries from those involved with the civil liberties 'industry'. This may need political courage. When the Defence Secretary, Michael Heseltine, set up a small department in the Defence Ministry to examine the effects of only one aspect of the active-measures offensive – the manipulation of the CND – Labour and the far left attacked the move viciously, but democracy may not survive unless the Soviet offensive is taken seriously and countered. At the time of writing, CND is threatening to disrupt Exercise Brave Defender, which has no other purpose than the protection of the country and its people against a Soviet military takeover. There need to be more severe legal penalties for such deliberate interference with the nation's defences, and these should apply to the attempts to disrupt cruise missile convoys. Any nation which permits such outrages in the name of peaceful protest and civil liberties deserves all it is likely to get.

In this connection there is urgent need for the public to be disabused of the growing belief that the Communist Party is no longer a threat, being so reduced in size and rent with internal argument. The reason that the Communist Party has lost so many members is because they have joined the Labour Party to further their policies there. The Communist Party, as such, also remains active. In a meeting between British members of it and Soviet leaders in Moscow in September 1984, a joint press statement recorded that, 'The British comrades outlined the activity of the Communist Party of Great Britain, which is working consistently against Britain's nuclear rearmament, for halting the installation of US cruise missiles and removing those already installed, for the removal of all nuclear bases from Britain's soil and waters and for Britain's withdrawal from NATO.' Nothing was said about Soviet nuclear weapons which was, perhaps, understandable as the delegation was met by the active-measures chief, Boris Ponomarev, and Mikhail Gorbachov.[17]

There is equal need for the public to be made aware of the nature of the other revolutionary groups posing a serious threat to parliamentary democracy – the Workers' Revolutionary Party, the Socialist Workers' Party, the Militant Tendency ·and similar 'Trotskyist' organizations claiming to be different from the Communist Party and, in some respects, opposed to it. Bernard Levin has put the truth succinctly: 'To distinguish between a Communist and a Trotskyist is to declare that twice six is different from thrice four.'[18] All are playing the Politburo's game, whether wittingly or not.

The Thatcher Government has taken some constructive steps to reduce the manipulation of the trade unions by pro-Soviet Communists and other left extremists, with legal requirements for secret ballots and proposals for improved police powers to restrict the exploitation of picket lines and demonstrations.[19] More needs to be done, however, especially regarding secret ballots, which remain susceptible to rigging by left extremists as was shown in the recent election for the General Secretary of the Transport and General Workers' Union, when appalling malpractices necessitated a re-run.[20]

Understandably, all truly democratic governments are disinclined to consider any action to deal with the dangerous problem of extreme left-wing infiltration of the media. The Press Council in Britain has proved to be a near-useless organization and is now in such general disrepute that it carries no authority or clout. When Sir James Goldsmith urged it to draw up a code of behaviour for journalists, as the Royal Commission on the Press suggested that it should in 1977, he was told that the Council preferred to deal with specific cases after complaints had been lodged.[21] In the US, however, an excellent lead has been given by an independent, non-profit-making organization called Accuracy in Media (AIM) which monitors the American press, radio and television, from a base in Washington, and exposes misinformation and falsifications while applauding responsible journalism. It has repeatedly drawn attention to occasions when newspapers and press agencies have used items antagonistic to the US, some being of Soviet origin, without verification. In particular, it has been effective in focusing public attention on the many instances where television commentators and producers deliberately bias their questions and their shows to harass and damage the Government. There is need for such an organization in Britain and no modification of the Press Council will suffice. Meanwhile journalists and other media operatives need reminding, forcibly, that they would be among the first major casualties if the system which some of them seem so keen to promote ever gained power.

Regarding the excesses of radio and television, the British Government is in a position to exert some influence over the British Broadcasting Corporation but is disinclined to interfere, though individual MPs, and occasionally Ministers, object publicly to major distortions. The worst and most persistent offenders in the production of programmes biased in the extreme left-wing interest, and often viciously anti-American, are the independent television channels over which the Government has considerable potential control through the Independent Broadcasting Authority Act. The Authority is required to preserve 'due impartiality on the part of the persons providing the programmes as regards matters of political or industrial controversy or relating to current public policy'.[22] Nobody who watches Channel Four or ITV programmes like 'World in Action' is likely to believe that the Authority is making much effort to carry out this function, and the Government remains silent about it. As Channel Four is currently making huge losses it is pouring out a flood of extreme left-wing propaganda at the public expense. This has been pointed out privately to successive Home Secretaries by disenchanted viewers, but they have refused to interfere.[23] So the political warping of millions of minds, especially those of the young, continues.

The mind-warping being assiduously pursued in schools and colleges also demands some government action, if only through its repeated exposure in Parliament and elsewhere. This might, at least, induce parents to demand the right to have their children excluded from lessons and exhortations by visiting activists to which they take exception. Parents, as well as the Government, should take all the action they can to counter the erosion of discipline in the school and home which is showing itself in so many places as violent hooliganism and vandalism that are welcome to the revolutionaries but savagely suppressed in the Soviet Union.

In universities and colleges the elimination of compulsory membership of student unions would diminish or even eliminate many of the abuses practised by extremists who have captured control of those unions.

In a radio address to the American nation in June 1985, President Reagan announced high-priority 'reforms and improvements in counter-intelligence and security' to combat Soviet active measures, and later he urged all other true democracies to follow suit. A major constructive move in this context would be the setting-up of specialist agencies for this purpose in the countries under attack. A month later he called for similar support to counter the terrorist offensive and censured the Soviet Union for its close relationship with most of the countries and organizations promoting terrorism. The West should not descend to the dishonest level of the Politburo with its use of forgeries, lies and character assassinations and does not need to do so, as its most potent weapon is the truth. Britain formerly had a counter-propaganda agency which operated in a semiclandestine way under the cover-name of the Information Research Department (IRD), and was set up by the Attlee Government, mainly to counter the activities of Communists. It was modestly effective but was disbanded in 1977 by James Callaghan and David Owen, then the Foreign Secretary who controlled it. Their reasons have never been made plain but the Labour Government was in a phase when it desperately needed to pacify its far left to remain in office. It can be safely assumed that the Politburo was pleased. What is needed now is a more formidable and openly acknowledged organization properly funded and charged with specific responsibilities. It should be required to counter Soviet deceptions and disinformation with quick publicity so that their worldwide impact is nullified or at least reduced; it should monitor the media for deliberate disinformation and extremist slant and when instances are clearly established it should expose them; it could serve as an outlet for the secret services on occasions when it is in the national interest for the activities of Soviet agents to be exposed.

In an address to a forum of defence strategists in the US Sir James Goldsmith suggested that such organizations should be equipped with computers programmed to analyse the content of Communist-controlled media to identify trends in Soviet foreign propaganda and active-measures operations. Comparison with the products of the media could indicate which of the latter seem to be under Soviet influence or control.[24]

While such an organization in Britain would need to liaise on a continuous basis with the Cabinet Office, the Home Office and the Foreign Office it should be so constituted that it could resist the deadening hands which would be regularly raised in departmental interests. The mere existence of such organizations in the target countries of the International Department and the KGB would exert a moderating effect. Given a reasonably free hand, their repeated exposures of Soviet duplicities would draw attention to the dangerous realities of the Politburo's secret offensive and diminish the ignorance and gullibility on which the active-measures operators batten.

If the organizations were also given the responsibility for controlling radio broadcasts to the Soviet Union and Eastern Europe, perhaps making eventual use of the potential of satellite television, they could do much more than is currently being accomplished to make the Soviet-Bloc peoples aware of their true predicament and the benefits being denied to them. The Politburo's greatest fear is that the Soviet peoples should become really aware of the massive failures of the Communist system and the extent to which it has been bailed out by capitalist grain, goods and technology, and of the obscene curtailment of their liberties and rights compared with the true circumstances in the West.

Baroness Caroline Cox has suggested that NATO should devote some fraction of its budget to defence against Soviet 'psychological warfare' and to help to educate the Western allies about the Politburo's secret offensive. To quote Dr Maurice Tugwell in her support, 'To spend NATO's very substantial budget on physical defence and then to allow our wills to be destroyed so that we submit without fighting would be, as Lenin put it, "Behaving in an unwise or even criminal manner."'[25] This would be eminently sensible but should be additional to the organizations set up by the individual member countries. However the counter-offensive is eventually mounted, as it will have to be, such a life-and-death encounter cannot sensibly be left to private organizations currently making some attempt at it, like Aims of Industry and the Coalition for Peace through Security, nor to the philanthropy of a very few deeply concerned individuals like Sir James Goldsmith.

While anti-active-measures departments may be slow in materializing, given the inborn sloth of true democracies, the ubiquitous Department of Self-Delusion, which is most ably manipulated by Moscow, continues to manifest itself. Hope springs eternal in the humane West and the appearance of a young, urbane and personable Soviet leader, in the form of Mikhail Gorbachov, immediately generated prospects of major changes in Soviet attitudes inaugurating the long-awaited era of genuine East–West friendship and peaceful co-existence. Over the years the International Department has regarded the image of the Politburo chief as a deception objective in itself. Through disinformation successfully peddled to the Western media, Khrushchev projected himself as a reformer, officially confessing the horrors of the Stalin regime; Brezhnev, who built the Soviet offensive strength to new levels and took an iron-fisted attitude to the satellite states, was presented as a moderate; Andropov, the former KGB chief, was described in the American press as a secret liberal, and even the pitifully ill Chernenko raised hope of change. Now Gorbachov has even been compared to John Kennedy because of his comparative youth, though at fifty-three he is eight years older than Stalin was when he assumed power. What is certain is that Gorbachov, the product of fifty-three years of the Soviet system, with its unremitting deception, has been nurtured in a hard-line school and has been put where he is by hardline men, being a protégé of the strict ideologist, Mikhail Suslov, and, later, of Andropov, who regarded him as one of his 'young eagles'. It is, sadly, most unlikely that he will be allowed to make major foreign-policy changes, even if he would like to, because Marxism-Leninism and its requirement to spread the Soviet system and influence worldwide is fundamental to the whole structure and momentum of the Soviet system. As Levchenko, who was born and raised in that system, has pointed out, Marxism-Leninism is a perverted type of religion which has been imposed on hundreds of millions of people, and such beliefs are difficult to change. When 270 million Soviet people alone, apart from the satellite nations, have been conditioned to believe that the Sovietization of the world and the destruction of capitalism is like a *jihad* – a holy war – how can they suddenly be told that this is no longer necessary? At the same time, any serious internal reforms which might be expected to command Gorbachov's energies are unlikely because they would threaten the ruling clique and the *nomenklatura*. The only way he can effectively improve the lot of the Soviet people is by reducing the power of the Politburo and especially his own – a most unlikely eventuality. Substantial improvements in material living standards would also require much less spending on arms and Gorbachov knows that disarmament could quickly lead to the collapse of the Soviet empire, which is held in subjection only by force of arms.

The West has become so used to stone-faced Soviet leaders that a new man with a smile has induced the normally perceptive Margaret Thatcher to announce, on very short acquaintance, that she can 'do business with Mr Gorbachov' when his public utterances and actions to date give no support to such optimism. Before acquiring the top post he expressed his firm loyalty to the strict ideology impressed on him by Suslov in references to world revolution, the overthrow of capitalist-imperialism and support of the national liberation struggle. He has consistently pursued the deliberately deceptive line that the establishment of martial law in Poland was saving the country from counter-revolution and anarchy and that the Soviet invasion of Afghanistan was assistance against subversion from the West. He has expressed himself in favour of strengthening the Soviet Union's military might to increase its global influence. Since taking office he has increased the military pressure against the

271

Afghan tribesmen fighting to maintain their liberty and threatened President Zia of Pakistan for allegedly aiding them.[26] He has continued the basic policy of trying to drive wedges between the US and its NATO allies, using the so-called 'Star Wars' initiative as the means immediately to hand and threatening dire consequences if the West goes ahead with the research into this entirely defensive weapon.[27] There has been no let-up in the active-measures offensive and no sign of any. Gorbachov's upside-down ploy on the Red Square podium, when he accused the West of having colluded with Hitler, is proof that he is prepared to be used as a deception agent, as Gromyko and others have been in the past and that the falsification of history to suit the Soviet ideology is to continue.

It would seem, then, that Gromyko gave a more perceptive description of Gorbachov when he assured the Central Committee on 12 March 1985 that its new leader 'has a nice smile but he has iron teeth'. Western leaders would, therefore, be unwise to put any trust in any suggested deal or treaty with the Soviet Union, unless there can be genuine verification that its undertakings are being honoured. As a British Defence Ministry briefing stated bluntly in February 1983, negotiations on arms control between 1977 and 1980 failed because the parties 'could not agree on measures to prevent cheating'. The continuing danger of putting any faith in the Politburo's word was vividly publicized by Lord Home when he asked, in the Lords' debate on subversion 'When the ideology of the fellow on the other side of the table insists that he encompasses the destruction of your way of life, is it possible to think and talk in terms of trust?'[28] Only the Communists, the Labour Party and their supporters believe that it is.

The West will be equally unwise to put much faith in the influence of 'world opinion' on the Politburo concerning any military issue. Indeed, one can almost hear Gorbachov asking his colleagues, rhetorically, 'How many divisions has world opinion?' There is certainly no evidence to suggest that there will be any change in the myth that Soviet forces must be maintained and strengthened to cope with the 'external threat of the imperialist aggressors' – the everlasting excuse foisted on the Soviet people for the failure to provide material benefits. Gorbachov, like the millions of his compatriots who have heard the lie so often, may even believe it.

In any dealings with the Soviets, heed should be paid to those defectors from high inside the Soviet system, like Shevchenko, who stress that what the Politburo understands best is toughness, strength of will and political conviction backed by military and economic might.[29] A move that the Soviet leaders would respect, even though it would infuriate them, would be for them to be told that unless they carry out their obligations under the Helsinki Accord that agreement will be repealed by the West and with it will go the official acceptance that the current Western borders of the Soviet Empire are inviolable. This should apply particularly to the Baltic States – Latvia, Estonia and Lithuania – which were illegally seized by Soviet troops as a result of the Nazi-Soviet Pact of 1939 and have been savagely occupied and repressed ever since.

Lord Home has made a start in this respect by pointing out in the Lords' debate on subversion that the UN Commission for Human Rights in Geneva has condemned Soviet breaches of human rights as 'flagrant and massive'. The same Commission has also openly accused the Soviet Union – for the first time – of monstrous inhumanities in Afghanistan with 'systematic bombing of rural areas, the massacre of villagers and the pursuit of a scorched earth policy'. This report, issued in February 1985, was given all too little publicity.

At the Tenth Anniversary Conference of the Accord held in Helsinki in July 1985, the Soviet leaders were reminded of their gross failure to implement human rights, including the fact that of eighty Soviet citizens who joined groups to monitor the Politburo's progress on the issue, sixty were imprisoned for long terms, four dying after their treatment there, while fifteen were forced into exile. Their reaction was to dismiss the charge brusquely as 'entirely their business'.

The Western success, to date, in standing firm on the introduction of new NATO missiles to balance the Soviet SS20s should be a heartening beginning of all-round resistance to being manipulated, undermined and subverted for the purpose of sapping our determination to defend ourselves and our treasured liberties. In any summit meeting with Gorbachov or in any discussions with Gromyko it should be made clear that the West will judge the Soviets by their actions and, if active measures continue, the Politburo can expect a continuous response of a kind it will not like. This should include regular exposure of Soviet failures to keep promises. As Max Kam-

273

pelman, the chief negotiator at the resumed arms talks, has stated, 'It is essential in our negotiations in Geneva that we highlight the issue of Soviet violations of existing arms control agreements, even though they may yell like stuck pigs.'[30] The new Politburo should be made to understand that it can no longer bank on being forgiven for its appalling crimes as it has been, disgracefully, in the past.

Western political leaders must continue to go through the motions of talking with the Politburo and its representatives in an attempt to manage the differences between them, but any major change in the Soviet attitude, which would make meaningful disarmament safe, is unlikely in the foreseeable future. The essential aspects of the Soviet system are set in ideological concrete impervious to external impact – the immutable unholy writ of Marxism-Leninism, the pathological Iron Curtain mentality, which will always prevent on-site inspection of arms agreements, the compulsive acquisition of territory 'to protect borders', the implacable hostility towards all other systems, which have to be 'smashed', the unbreakable addiction to suspicion and duplicity which expresses itself in active measures applied, almost instinctively, as an instrument of first resort. Henry Kissinger had it right when he said, 'To expect the Soviet leaders to restrain themselves from exploiting circumstances they conceive to be favourable is to misread history.' It is also to misread the mentality of any man who can hoist himself to the position of General Secretary of the Communist Party of the Soviet Union.

Biographical Notes

Augstein, Rudolf

German journalist and publisher of *Der Spiegel*, which is based in Hamburg. Born in Hanover in 1923 he served in the artillery on the Eastern Front in the Second World War. Virtually founded *Der Spiegel* which he has run since 1947, specializing in political controversy which led to feuds with Adenauer and Strauss. He was arrested for alleged political offences in October 1962 and held until February 1963. He was elected to the Bundestag in November 1972 but resigned after only two months. Described as 'soft-spoken, mild-mannered' and small in build.

August, Frantisek

Formerly a senior officer of the Czechoslovak State Security Organization (STB) which is also responsible for espionage abroad. Defected to the US in 1968 following the Soviet invasion of his country. He was born in July 1928, of a working-class family and began working in the security service of the Communist régime in 1949. He was transferred to the British section at Prague headquarters in 1958 and was assigned to London for espionage and intelligence activities in 1961, working under cover at the Czech Embassy until his return to Prague in 1963 with the rank of major. In London he helped to penetrate the trade unions and the Labour Party.

Barron, John

A former American Naval Intelligence officer and a senior editor of *Reader's Digest* based in Washington. In 1974 he produced the most detailed and authoritative book on the KGB which clearly indicated profound access to official Western sources. He followed this with a sequel in 1983. During the research for the two books Barron interviewed almost every KGB officer who has fled to the West since 1954. He has testified in the US courts as an expert witness on the KGB and would have done so in the *Der Spiegel*/Goldsmith case.

Bittman, Ladislav

A major in the Czech intelligence service when he defected to the US in 1968. He spent eight of his fourteen years' service abroad recruiting and directing agents and from 1964 to 1966 was Deputy Chief of the Disinformation Department. He then operated in Vienna, under the cover of Press Attaché, still working on active measures by directing agents of influence and manipulating the Austrian media. He sought political asylum after the Soviet invasion of Czechoslovakia and became a college teacher in New England.

Cox, Baroness Caroline

After a career in nursing-education and sociology – when she was Head of the Department of Sociology at the Polytechnic of North London – she was created a life-peer in 1982 and has since concentrated on studying and exposing the Marxist infiltration of the educational system and peace movements. She is the author of several books and pamphlets.

Crozier, Brian

A writer and consultant on international affairs, Crozier, who was born in 1918, is a leading international authority on Communism and the author of many standard works. He was a co-founder of the prestigious Institute for the Study of Conflict and directed it for nine years.

Dzhirkvelov, Ilya

A Soviet defector of major importance because of the nature of his service with the KGB and International Department and his intellectual standing. Joined the KGB in 1944 when he was seventeen and graduated from the KGB 'Top School' and was then involved in disinformation work from 1947 to 1980. He operated first in the KGB itself in the Foreign Journalists' Development Department and then, in 1957, was made Deputy Secretary General of the newly created Union of Journalists of the USSR. From 1965

276

he worked mainly abroad – under the cover of being a TASS correspondent in Tanzania and the Sudan and then in the Public Information Department of the WHO in Geneva with the 'diplomatic' rank of counsellor. In 1980 he defected to Britain where he lives under an assumed name.

Epstein, Edward Jay

Renowned American investigative writer who has made a special study of Soviet deception. Born in New York in 1935 and still lives there.

Frolik, Josef

A former major of the Czech intelligence service who defected to the West in July 1969, claiming to be disenchanted with the Communist régime. He joined Czech counter-intelligence in 1955, being posted to the British Department at Prague headquarters in 1960. In 1964 he was transferred to London with the prime objective of penetrating NATO secrets. He was involved in the recruitment of trade unionists and MPs and after his defection named several who had been targets, some of whom had been recruited. Now lives under an assumed name in the United States.

Goldsmith, Sir James

A highly successful businessman who has made fortunes in Britain, France and, currently, in the US. Born in 1933, he has dual British and French nationality and began his business career in France in the drugs industry, later founding the Cavenham food empire in Britain and France. In 1977 he founded the unsuccessful British magazine *NOW!* and also bought the French journal, *L'Express*, which has been impressively successful. When he was knighted in the Wilson resignation honours list in 1976 it was falsely stated in the *Daily Express* that he had been proposed for a peerage. This was entirely due to disinformation deliberately planted on Sir Max Aitken, then the *Daily Express* proprietor, by someone determined to prevent Sir James from receiving any honour.

Sir James has since devoted considerable energy and resources to exposing the Soviet and Marxist threat to Western freedoms and democratic institutions.

Golitsin, Anatoli

Probably the most informative of all KGB defectors to the West. Golitsin's disclosures led to the identification of Soviet agents, mainly in Britain and

France, and he contributed enormously to the general knowledge of the KGB and its operations against most of the Western countries. Born in 1926 in the Ukraine, he joined the KGB in 1946 and served in departments responsible for operations against the US and Britain. He served later as a senior analyst in the NATO section of the Information Department of Soviet intelligence which gave him access to many highly sensitive documents which he committed to memory. He was posted to Finland from which he defected to the CIA in December 1961. He visited Britain, France and Canada to assist counter-espionage agencies there.

Gorbachov, Mikhail

Currently head man of the Soviet Politburo and of the Communist Party, Gorbachov was born in 1931 and, after becoming the chief Komsomol representative at Moscow State University, has risen steadily in the Soviet hierarchy. He developed close links with Suslov, the uncompromising Stalinist and chief ideologist. Andropov, the future KGB chief, became another mentor. After being moved to Moscow in the mid-1970s to cope with agriculture he became a member of the Politburo at the age of forty-eight in spite of a series of crop disasters requiring the purchase of Western grain. He succeeded Suslov in the ideological role and became General Secretary of the Party in 1985.

Hahn, Walter F.

Editor-in-Chief of the *Strategic Review*, the quarterly journal of the US Strategic Institute in Washington. He is a recognized authority on East–West relations.

Huyn, Count Hans

A member of the West German Bundestag and of the Christian Social Union party for which he often acts as a spokesman on foreign policy. Born in Warsaw in 1930, he studied law, political theory and languages at Munich University and served abroad with the West German Foreign Office. Since leaving the foreign service he has lectured and written widely on foreign affairs and such issues as the Soviet 'peace' offensive and disinformation.

Levchenko, Stanislav

Born in Moscow in 1941, the son of a major-general, Levchenko

278

specialized in the Japanese language and then worked for the International Department and, in 1972, entered the KGB, being assigned to Japan for active-measures operations in 1975. He defected to the US in October 1979 and has since provided the most detailed insider knowledge to date of the International Department's operations.

Ponomarev, Boris

An old-guard politician who was born in 1905 and claims to have been in the Red Army in 1919. He was 'elected' to the Supreme Soviet in 1958 and remains head of the International Department at the age of eighty.

Schuman, Tomas D.

Born under the name of Yuri Bezmenov in 1939, this defector contacted the CIA while serving in India in 1970. A considerable linguist, he was employed by the KGB in 1960 as an interpreter and two years later was assigned as a KGB officer to work in Novosti. Under Novosti cover he worked in India in close co-operation with the Soviet Information Department. He then worked for the Information Department in Moscow and was then formally recruited to the KGB for active-measures operations. He was assigned back to India in 1969 and defected the following year, living first in Canada and then in Los Angeles where he is now a lecturer and free-lance columnist for a Russian-American weekly newspaper.

Sejna, Jan

Born in Czechoslovakia in 1927, Sejna, whose parents were peasants, lived there until he defected in 1968. In his signed affidavit, Sejna claims that he became a dedicated Communist after his experiences with the Nazis during the war. He became a political commissar in the Sovietized Czech Army and was rapidly promoted as older army officers were purged by the KGB. On reaching the rank of lieutenant-colonel, he was appointed a member of the Czech Parliament and to membership of the Central Committee of the Czech Communist Party. His positions as Executive Secretary of the Defence Council of the Communist Party and then First Secretary of the Communist Party at the Defence Ministry gave him access to many KGB and other Soviet secrets. Further, he visited Moscow many times for discussions on Soviet global strategy attending meetings with such luminaries as Khrushchev and Brezhnev, while he encountered others such as Grechko and Ponomarev when they visited Prague. He was a particularly valuable source on active-measures operations when he defected to the CIA and is currently employed by the US Government.

Shevchenko, Arkady

Born in 1930 in the Ukraine, Shevchenko is the highest ranking Soviet official to defect to the West. He joined the Foreign Ministry in 1956 and from 1963 to 1970 served in the Soviet Mission to the UN as chief of the Security Council and Political Affairs Division. In 1973 he was promoted to Under Secretary General of the UN for Political and Security Council Affairs. He defected early in 1978 and lives openly, under his own name, in the United States. Critics have cast doubt on statements in his book, *Breaking with Moscow*, concerning his alleged espionage operations for the CIA before defecting. There is no doubt, however, about his service with Gromyko and his high-level knowledge of other Soviet leaders and their aims, as described in this book.

Strauss, Franz Josef

Prime Minister of Bavaria since 1978, Strauss remains a major political figure on the West German scene with a big following among the Catholic population. Born in 1915, he served in the Wehrmacht throughout the Second World War and joined the Christian Social Union (CSU) immediately afterwards. He was elected to the Bundestag in 1949 and remained there until becoming Prime Minister of his native Bavaria. He held office as Minister of Nuclear Energy (1955-6), of Defence (1956-62) and of Finance (1966-9). He remains a firm exponent of the alliance with the US and the deployment of medium-range ballistic missiles in Europe as a counter-force to Soviet military and political pressure.

Notes and Sources

Introduction (pages 1-6)

1 Arkady Shevchenko, *Breaking with Moscow*, Jonathan Cape, 1985. While serious doubt has been cast on Shevchenko's account of his espionage work for the CIA (Edward J. Epstein, *The New Republic*, 15 and 22 July 1985), his high-level career in the Soviet Foreign Service and access to information there is well documented

2 McGahey is an overt member of the CPGB. Scargill stated in *New Left Review*, July 1975, that he was in the Young Communist League for six years and 'played an important role'. His father was a member of the CPGB

3 Since the Bolsheviks seized power in 1917 there have been only seven established Soviet leaders – Lenin, Stalin, Khrushchev, Brezhnev, Andropov, Chernenko and Gorbachov, the last three with very short reigns to date. Malenkov and Bulganin held or shared power only briefly

4 As recorded by John Barron in his long interviews with Levchenko. See *The KGB Today*, Coronet, 1985

Chapter 1: Tailor-made for Moscow (pages 7-23)

1 *Defence and Security for Britain*, Statement to Annual Conference 1984 by the National Executive Committee, Labour Party B/038/84

2 See many references in *Soviet Military Strategy in Europe* by Joseph D. Douglass, Pergamon Press, 1980

3 See Duncan Campbell, *The Unsinkable Aircraft Carrier*, Michael Joseph, 1984

4 Denis Healey, for example, supported the independent British deterrent when in office and opposed unilateral disarmament until it was

adopted as Party policy. See also Dr Christopher Coker, *Naked Emperors: The British Labour Party and Defense*, US Strategic Review, Fall 1984

5   See *Daily Telegraph* and *The Times*, 5 March 1984 and preceding issues

6   See James Bamford, *The Puzzle Palace*, Sidgwick and Jackson, 1982

7   Coker, *op cit*

8   Clive Rose, *Campaigns Against Western Defence*, RUSI/Macmillan, 1985

9   Reinhard Gehlen, *The Gehlen Memoirs*, Collins, 1972

10   J. W. Pickersgill and D. F. Foster, *The Mackenzie King Record*, Vol. 3, University of Toronto Press, 1970

11   *Ibid* and Chapman Pincher, *Too Secret Too Long*, Sidgwick and Jackson, 1984

12   Pickersgill and Foster, *op cit*. Mackenzie King and Dean Acheson actually discussed the possibility of war with the Russians on the American continent. Also see H. Montgomery Hyde, *The Atom Bomb Spies*, Hamish Hamilton, 1980

13   See Brian Crozier *et alia*, *This War Called Peace*, Sherwood Press, 1984

14   Margaret Gowing, *Independence and Deterrence, Britain and Atomic Energy, 1945-1952*, Vol. 1, Macmillan, 1974

15   Information from confidential source. Lord Gladwyn and Sir Maurice Dean were other members. The secretary was Sir Michael Hadow

16   See Chapman Pincher *op cit*

17   Wilson called the projected Polaris fleet 'the so-called independent, so-called nuclear, so-called deterrent' when in opposition but he cancelled only the fifth boat, which the Tories intended to do anyhow. Most of the £1,000 million extra was spent on the 'Chevalline' warhead with improved penetration capability

18   See Chapman Pincher, *Inside Story*, Sidgwick and Jackson, 1978

19   CND resulted from a meeting at the house of Canon John Collins on 16 January 1958. In addition to Foot those present included J.B. Priestley, Sir Julian Huxley, Rose Macaulay. Collins was nominated chairman with Bertrand Russell as president

20   The extent to which some Communists are required to keep their Party membership and true beliefs secret was revealed in an extraordinary letter signed D. James in the *Morning Star* on 21 January 1985, which confirmed the existence of the secret membership lists and the importance attached to the undercover work of crypto-communists

21   As Bert Ramelson put it when acting as the Communist Party's 'industrial organizer', 'We have only to float an idea one month to see it adopted as policy by the Labour Party the next'

22   The statement headed 'Reagan is not welcome here' listed Kinnock as a sponsor along with seventy-eight others, almost all far left-wingers
23   Campbell, *op cit*
24   Information from confidential briefings. See also Douglass, *op cit.* According to Professor R. V. Jones there is decrypt evidence that Hitler refrained from using nerve gases because he believed, wrongly, that the Allies had them too. The Soviets are aware that NATO has none

Chapter 2: The Lie Machinery (pages 24-31)

1   *Soviet Active Measures*, US Government Printing Office, 1982. Richard Shultz and Roy Godson, *Dezinformatsia*, Pergamon-Brasseys, 1984. Reports by John Barron, Ilya Dzhirkvelov *et alia* supplied by Sir James Goldsmith. David Rees, *Soviet Active Measures: The Propaganda War*, Institute for the Study of Conflict, No. 169. Also declassified CIA documents
2   Ponomarev, born 1905, served with the Red Army in 1919 and has been actively involved with Communist politics ever since. Became a member of the Central Committee in 1956 and a non-voting member of the Politburo in 1972
3   See Shevchenko, *op cit*. Personal information from Ilya Dzhirkvelov
4   John Barron, *op cit*. William R. Corson and Robert T. Crowley, *The New KGB*, Morrow, New York, 1985
5   For detailed interviews with Levchenko see Barron, *op cit*, Shultz and Godson, *op cit*, *Soviet Active Measures*, US Government Printing Office, 1982, *L'Express*, 5 April 1985
6   Interview with Dzhirkvelov and his private report to Sir James Goldsmith
7   Anatoli Golitsin, *New Lies for Old*, Bodley Head, 1984. Chapman Pincher, *Too Secret Too Long*
8   Shultz and Godson *op cit*. *Soviet Active Measures*, US Government Printing Office, 1982
9   Also see Ladislav Bittman, *The Deception Game*, Ballantine, New York, 1972. Testimony of 'Lawrence Britt', Subcommittee on Internal Security of the Senate Judiciary Committee, 5 May 1971
10   Evidence of Levchenko. Also see E.J. Epstein, *Commentary*, July 1982
11   Information from MI5 officers. Golitsin, *op cit*

Chapter 3: The Der Spiegel Affair (pages 32-45)

1   See *The Times*, *Financial Times*, *Daily Telegraph*, *Die Welt*,

TSO – 10

Frankfurter Allgemeine Zeitung of 9 October 1984. Also biographical note on Sir James Goldsmith

2 Statement published in *NOW!* on 7 February 1981. Later issued separately for private circulation. See biographical note on Sejna

3 See biographical note on Strauss

4 Among those prepared to give evidence or who provided affidavits were Major-General Jan Sejna, Ilya Dzhirkvelov, Stanislav Levchenko, Dr Walter F. Hahn, Dr Joseph Douglass, Josef Frolik, Tomas Schuman, Dr Kepplinger, John Barron, Lord Chalfont and Iain Elliot

5 On 7 June 1957, for example, *Neues Deutschland*, the organ of the East German Communist Party, described Strauss as 'the murderer of his soldiers' following an accident in which fifteen soldiers were drowned in the River Iller

6 This material included a forgery involving Strauss with the German Communist Party in 1946

7 In December 1958 the 'Study Group', which issued its views in a magazine, carried an article called 'Strategist Strauss in Hitler's Footsteps'

8 *Neues Deutschland*, for example, ran a series of articles on 'War Agitator Strauss'. See issue of 25 April 1959. The East German Communist Party's propaganda chief, Albert Norden, named Strauss as the main target on 18 June 1957

9 Hans Graf Huyn, *Webs of Soviet Disinformation, US Strategic Review*, Fall 1984

10 Affidavit provided by Sejna

11 Gerd Schmuckle, Strauss's former press officer at the Defence Ministry, writing in *Der Spiegel*, 30 August 1982

12 Affidavit from Sejna

13 See biographical note on Augstein

14 Affidavit from Sejna

15 The many anti-Strauss articles by 'Jens Daniel' have been analysed by Helmut Baerwald, a German scholar, in a series of reports made available by Sir James Goldsmith. Reference to the 'Daniel' article using 're-vanchism' made in the West German weekly '*Christ und Welt*', 18 December 1958. For references to 'Minister for War' also see Gerd Schmuckle, *op cit*

16 *Der Spiegel*, 2 March 1960. The article was written by Augstein under the pseudonym Moritz Pfeil

17 Information from former BND officer

18 Issue of 18 March 1961, p. 18

19 Entitled 'The Finals: Strauss', in *Der Spiegel*, 5 April 1961

20 BND officer's reports

21 Bittman, *op cit*

22　Information from former BND officer

23　Issue of 5 July 1961

24　Gehlen, *op cit*. Information from Hermann Renner, a former writer for *Der Spiegel*, supplied by Sir James Goldsmith

25　BND officer's reports. On 22 October 1962 a West German Parliamentary Committee exonerated Strauss of any misconduct in the Fibag Affair

26　Kepplinger's reports also made available by Sir James Goldsmith

27　See Chapman Pincher reports from Athens conference, *Daily Express*, 3, 4 and 7 May 1962. On 11 April 1963 Strauss told the Institute of Strategic Studies in London that Germany would prefer to avoid making nuclear weapons but, if left to defend herself, would have to

28　Schmuckle, *op cit*

29　*Das Neue Schwarzbuch*, Kiepenheuer and Witsch, Cologne, 1980. It even suggested that Strauss was drunk at key moments during the Cuban missile crisis. Augstein's use of the pseudonyms Jens Daniel and Moritz Pfeil is recorded in *Meyers Enzyklopaedisches Lexicon*, Vol. 3, 1971

30　Schmuckle, *op cit*

31　Gehlen, *op cit*. Gehlen dates the recruitment as 'about a decade ago'. The memoirs were published in 1972. While much has been done to discredit Gehlen he was the single most knowledgeable man in the West about KGB activities because the Allies had virtually ended counter-intelligence operations against the Soviet Union after June 1941, while Germany had intensified them

32　Shevchenko, *op cit*, Chapman Pincher, *Too Secret Too Long*. John Barron, *KGB*, Corgi, 1975

33　Hermann Renner, *Augstein v Strauss*, report supplied by Sir James Goldsmith

34　See Chapman Pincher, *Their Trade is Treachery* and *Too Secret Too Long*

Chapter 4: Mission Accomplished (pages 46-55)

1　Affidavit supplied by Sejna

2　Written statement by Dzhirkvelov and interview. Also see biographical note on Dzhirkvelov

3　*Ibid*

4　*Ibid*

5　Affidavit supplied by Sejna. For Pâques see Chapter 8. For Hambleton see Chapter 11, Chapman Pincher, *Too Secret Too Long* and Leo Heaps, *Hugh Hambleton, Spy*, Methuen, 1983

6　Affidavit supplied by Sejna

7   Statement by Dzhirkvelov and interview
8   *Keesing's Contemporary Archives*, 14-21 September 1963
9   *Ibid*
10   *Ibid*. Schmuckle, *op cit*
11   *Keesing's Contemporary Archives*, 14-21 September 1963. Schmuckle, *op cit*
12   Issue of 29 September 1962
13   *Keesing's Contemporary Archives*, 24-31 December 1966. Statement by the Federal Prosecutor, Dr Walter Roemer, Karlsruhe, 25 January 1966
14   Debate on 7-9 November 1962. *Keesing's Contemporary Archives*, 14-21 September 1963
15   *Keesing's Contemporary Archives*, 14-21 September 1963. Statement by Dr Erich Mende in *Student*, Vol. 12, No. 86, December 1979. Stammberger's television broadcast was on 5 November 1962
16   Schmuckle, *op cit*
17   Mende, *op cit*. Schmuckle, *op cit*
18   Gehlen, *op cit*. Heinz Hohne and Hermann Zolling, *Network*, Secker and Warburg, 1972
19   *Keesing's Contemporary Archives* 5-12 June 1965. *Der Spiegel*, 17 May 1964. Gehlen, *op cit*. Usually reclusive, Gehlen claimed that he published the memoirs largely because of the damage caused to him and his organization (BND) by the *Der Spiegel* Affair

Chapter 5: Kremlin Conspiracy Exposed (pages 56-67)

1   *Keesing's Contemporary Archives*, 14-21 September 1963, 5-12 June 1965, 24-31 December 1966
2   Renner, *op cit*, confirms that a summary of all the information gathered by Ahlers from Martin was locked in Augstein's safe and remains unpublished
3   Information from confidential source
4   *Keesing's Contemporary Archives*, 24-31 December 1966
5   Schmuckle, *op cit*
6   Landgericht Munchen reports. Schmuckle, *op cit*, records that while Strauss won in the courts he lost politically
7   On 26 June 1963 *Der Spiegel* stated that Strauss had taken money which did not belong to him during his term as Minister. Hermann Renner, *Augstein v Strauss* (report supplied by Sir James Goldsmith). These allegations were dealt with in detail and disposed of by Brian Crozier in *NOW!*, 15 February 1980
8   The case of Dr Otto Praun, a gynaecologist who was murdered

along with his housekeeper. Praun's former mistress and her lover were sentenced for the crime, but the East German radio put out a story suggesting that Strauss had organized Praun's murder because he knew too much about some arms deals from which Strauss was alleged to have made profits

9   Before the Nuremberg and Munich Regional and Higher Regional courts on 28 July 1966, 29 October 1968, 18 February 1969, 16 May 1969 and 28 January 1970

10   William F. Buckley, *National Review (US)*, 8 February 1980

11   Gehlen, *op cit*

12   Bittman, *op cit*. The *Washington Post* printed the letter on 27 August 1969 followed by *Der Spiegel* on 8 September

13   Bittman, *op cit*. For details of Johnson case, see David C. Martin, *Wilderness of Mirrors*, Harper and Row, New York, 1980

14   Hahn has provided full details of his involvement with Sejna in a signed document made available by Sir James Goldsmith, who has also supplied an analysis, 'General Sejna and the Spiegel Affair', written by Hahn

15   *Ibid*

16   Jan Sejna, *We Will Bury You*, Sidgwick and Jackson, 1982

17   Statements by Dzhirkvelov and Bittman supplied by Sir James Goldsmith

18   Statement in the High Court of Justice Queen's Bench Division, 8 October 1984

19   A letter from Sir James Goldsmith's solicitors, Allen and Overy, states that 'the Hamburg Regional Court ordered that *Der Spiegel* publish a counter-statement by Sir James stating that the *Spiegel* article had erroneously suggested that Sir James had instigated the settlement discussions and correctly stating that it was *Der Spiegel*'s Counsel that first approached Lord Rawlinson'

20   Personal statement from Sir James Goldsmith

Chapter 6: *The Great Missile Deception (pages 68-86)*

1   *Daily Express*, 17 April 1970

2   Sejna, *Sunday Telegraph*, 24 January 1971

3   Marshal Malinovsky, '*Historical Exploits of the Soviet People and Their Armed Forces*', Voyennaya mysl, No. 5 1965, cited by Douglass, *op cit*

4   Douglass, *op cit*

5   *Ibid*

6   In September 1961 Khrushchev announced a series of Russian nuc-

lear tests following his suspension of tests in 1958. The move wrecked negotiations which had been proceeding since 1958 on a test-ban agreement. The atmospheric tests continued until October 31. Khrushchev spoke of a 50-megaton blast but analysis of fission products suggested a yield of 30 megatons. *Daily Express*, 1 September 1961, 5 October 1961, 18 October 1961

7   Chapman Pincher, *Their Trade is Treachery*, Oleg Penkovsky, *The Penkovsky Papers*, Collins, 1965

8   Chapman Pincher, *op cit*

9   The pilot was Francis Gary Powers who wrote an account of his experiences after his release, entitled *Operation Overflight*, Hodder and Stoughton, 1970

10   Georgi Bolchakov, then working out of the Soviet Embassy in Washington as a 'journalist' on a Novosti magazine

11   See David S. Sullivan, a former CIA strategic analyst, *Intelligence Requirements for the 1980s: Analysis and Estimates*, Roy Godson, National Strategy Information Center, Washington, 1980

12   Douglass, *op cit*. *Soviet Military Power*, US Government Printing Office, Washington, 1984

13   See Chapman Pincher, *Too Secret Too Long*. Henry Hurt, *Shadrin: The Spy Who Never Came Back*, Reader's Digest Press, New York, 1981

14   Chapman Pincher, *op cit*. Epstein, *op cit*

15   Epstein, *op cit*

16   *Ibid*

17   Chapman Pincher, *op cit*

18   Chapman Pincher, *op cit*

19   Chapman Pincher, *Their Trade is Treachery*

20   Information from confidential sources

21   *Ibid*

22   Epstein, *op cit*

23   *Ibid*. Information from confidential sources

24   Epstein, *op cit*. Felfe, a former West German police officer who joined the BND in 1951 had previously been recruited by the KGB for money. Until his exposure and arrest in November 1961 he handed over a mass of secret documents to the KGB, some of which were used in disinformation exercises. For further details of the Felfe case see Gehlen, *op cit*. David C. Martin, *op cit*

25   Epstein, *op cit*. Davis S. Sullivan, *op cit*. According to Max Kampelman (American Bar Association Intelligence Report Vol. 7, No. 2, February 1985) McNamara said that the Soviets should be allowed to catch up

26   Epstein, *op cit*

27   *The Soviet War Machine*, Hamlyn, 1976

28 Rose, *op cit.* David S. Sullivan, *op cit. The Soviet War Machine*, Hamlyn, 1976

29 *The Soviet War Machine*, Hamlyn, 1976

30 Epstein, *op cit*

31 Information from confidential GCHQ source

32 Epstein, *op cit.* The expert was William Harris of RAND

33 Bamford, *op cit.* Confidential GCHQ sources

34 *Ibid*

35 *Ibid.* See also Chapman Pincher, *Too Secret Too Long*

36 Report of the Security Commission, May 1983, Cmnd 8876

37 Rose, *op cit. Soviet Military Power* US Government Printing Office, Washington DC, 1984

38 *Ibid*

39 Epstein, *Intelligence Requirements for the 1980s: Analysis and Estimates*, Godson, National Strategy Information Center, Washington, 1980

40 Hurt, *op cit*

41 David S. Sullivan, *op cit*

42 Information from a US Senator

43 Report by the General Advisory Committee on Arms Control and Disarmament, released to Congress 10 October 1984. See also David S. Sullivan, *op cit*

Chapter 7: The Long March through the Media (pages 87-116)

1 *Daily Telegraph*, 8 April 1985

2 Sir Martin Furnival Jones, Departmental Committee on Section 2 of the Official Secrets Act 1911, Oral Evidence Vol. 3, HMSO Cmnd 5104, September 1972

3 The KGB man was Yuri Krotkov who, after his defection, and using the name George Karlin, gave evidence to a US Senate Subcommittee on Internal Security, 3-5 November 1969

4 The D Notice Secretary was Rear-Admiral Sir George Thomson

5 See Chapter 13. Stephen J. Morris, 'A Scandalous Journalistic Career', *Commentary*, November 1981

6 The prisoner was the Briton, Derek Kinne

7 Burchett brought the action in Sydney against Jack Kane, a politician who had published information based on Krotkov's ('Karlin's) testimony in the US. Kinne testified. Burchett lost the case in November 1974 and was ordered to pay heavy court costs

8 Letter to the author from William Stevenson

9 Burchett boasted of his friendships with leading Western journalists in his autobiography, *At the Barricades*, Times Books, New York 1981.

According to Reed Irvine (report, *Penetration of the American Mass Media*, supplied by Sir James Goldsmith), Burchett 'was able to get his articles placed in influential publications such as the *New York Times*'

10 See Chapman Pincher, *Too Secret Too Long*

11 Chapman Pincher, *Inside Story*

12 Information from an MI5 source

13 Allen Weinstein, *Perjury*, Knopf, New York, 1978

14 *The Times*, 28 March 1984. The medal was awarded on 26 March

15 Hearings on the Institute of Pacific Relations, Subcommittee on Internal Security of the Senate Judiciary Committee, Part 2 1951

16 Report by Reed Irvine. The *Daily World*, the official newspaper of the US Communist Party, claimed that writing for its columns, 'for which he would not take a penny', was Parker's 'great love'. AIM Report, 17 June 1978, Part 1

17 Burdett made his admission to the Subcommittee on Internal Security headed by Senator James O. Eastland, which examined Communist infiltration of the media. Whitman was subpoenaed. See *Strategy and Tactics of World Communism*, Subcommittee on Internal Security of the Senate Judiciary Committee, Part 17, 1956

18 *Soviet Active Measures*, US Government Printing Office, July 1982. Shultz and Godson, *op cit*

19 *Ibid*

20 *Information Digest*, 22 August 1980. The Minister was Christian Bonnet

21 *Soviet Active Measures*, US Government Printing Office 1982. Arne Herlov Petersen, *True Blues*, Joe Hill Press, 1980

22 *Ibid*

23 *Ibid*

24 *Ibid*. Evidence of Martin C. Portman of the CIA's Operations Directorate

25 *Ibid*. Statement of John McMahon, Deputy Director of Central Intelligence. Shultz and Godson, *op cit*. Barron, *op cit*. *L'Express*, Paris, 5 April 1985

26 *Ibid*

27 *Ibid*. Alexandr Kaznacheev, a KGB officer who defected to the US in 1959, while involved in active measures in Burma, stated 'The primary objective of Political Intelligence (Line PR) operations was penetration and subversion of local régimes and direct and active participation in the struggle between different political parties'. See Kaznacheev, *Inside a Soviet Embassy*, Lippincott, Philadelphia, 1962

28 Barron, *op cit*

29 *Ibid*

30   *Soviet Active Measures*, US Government Printing Office, 1982. Levchenko listed his reasons for defecting: 'I witnessed first-hand that the Soviet system was not working for the good of its citizens. It is a totally corrupt dictatorship with rotten moral standards. The Soviets rely on deception because the Communist ideology and the political system structured on it cannot stand on its merits. The Soviet intelligence community is just another tool in the hands of the Politburo and has even more disgusting features than any other part of the Soviet machine. I could not fight the Kremlin inside the country as an officer of the KGB – I would have ended up in one of the Siberian concentration camps, or in a mental asylum for the rest of my life.'

31   Dzhirkvelov, statement and interview

32   Permanent Select Committee on Intelligence, *Soviet Covert Action*, 96th Congress, 2nd Session, US Government Printing Office, 1980. See also Shultz and Godson, *op cit*

33   Duff Hart-Davis, *Sunday Telegraph*, 16 and 23 September 1984. Chapman Pincher, *Daily Express*, 19 September 1984, *Daily Telegraph*, 11, 15 and 19 September 1984, 7 March 1985

34   *Ibid*

35   Chapman Pincher, *Their Trade is Treachery*

36   Shevchenko, *op cit*. Barron, *op cit*. Corson and Crowley, *op cit*. The Institute was founded in 1967 and was the subject of a CIA special study declassified in 1982. Some Institute members were shown to be officers of the GRU and KGB. See *New Statesman*, 28 October 1983

37   *Soviet Active Measures*, US Government Printing Office, 1982. Barron, *op cit*. Corson and Crowley, *op cit*

38   A 'good' story may be held on file even when there has been proof of its falseness. The myth of the non-existent Dutch watchmaker at Scapa Flow, alleged to have been the spy responsible for the sinking of the Ark Royal is an example. See Chapman Pincher, *Inside Story*

39   Anthony Courtney, *Sailor in a Russian Frame*, Johnson, 1968. Chapman Pincher, *op cit*

40   Chapman Pincher, *Too Secret Too Long*, and *Their Trade is Treachery*, paperback edition, Sidgwick and Jackson, 1978

41   Statement to the Press on the action issued by Sir James Goldsmith, 11 July 1983

42   *Ibid*

43   Innumerable columns by 'Slicker'. See Sir James Goldsmith's submission to the Press Council, 16 February 1983

44   *Terrorist Activity*, Subcommittee on Internal Security of the Senate Judiciary Committee, July 5 1975

45   Statement by Tomas Schuman provided by Sir James Goldsmith

46   *Soviet Active Measures*, US Government Printing Office, 1982
47   Confidential information
48   Statement by Sir James Goldsmith to the Media Committee published in *NOW!* and later issued privately
49   According to Barron, *op cit*, Agee was forced to resign from the CIA for 'irresponsible drinking, continuous and vulgar propositioning of Embassy wives and inability to manage his finances'
50   Philip Agee, *Inside the Company: CIA Diary*, Penguin, 1975
51   The debates were held in February and May 1977. Stephen Hastings MP drew attention to the 'World in Action' programme shown 7 February 1977
52   *The Times*, 16 and 17 September 1978. While in prison Proll was visited by convicted terrorists

Chapter 8: The Agencies as Agents (pages 117-30)

1   The *Sunday Times* began serialization of the fake diaries on 17 April 1983
2   Tomas D. Schuman Novosti Press Agency (APN), 'KGB Front for Active Measures against the Free Media'. Supplied by Sir James Goldsmith. See also biographical note on Schuman
3   *Ibid*
4   Dzhirkvelov, statement and interview
5   Schuman, *op cit*. Sidney Hook, Lev Navrozov, Eric Waldman, *The Soviet Britannica*, Midstream, Vol. XXVI, February 1980
6   John Rees, *Infiltration of the Media by the KGB and its Friends*, Accuracy in Media Inc, 1978
7   *Soviet Active Measures*, US Government Printing Office, 1982
8   Schuman, *op cit*. According to the *Daily Telegraph*, Novosti's chief Swiss correspondent, Alexei Dumov was ordered to leave the country by 8 May
9   John Rees, *op cit*
10   Barron, *op cit*
11   *Daily Telegraph*, 2 April 1983
12   *Soviet Active Measures*, US Government Printing Office, 1982. Evidence of Edward O'Malley, Assistant Director FBI Intelligence Division
13   *The Times*, 26, 27, 28 February 1985, 21 June 1985. *Observer* 5 May 1985
14   Information from an MI5 officer involved with the Pâques case. Barron, *op cit*
15   Information from MI5 officer. Heaps, *op cit*

292

16   See Chapter 11. Also Chapman Pincher, *Too Secret Too Long*. Heaps, *op cit*

17   Chapman Pincher, *Inside Story* and *Too Secret Too Long*. Details of the case were first given to me by Lord George-Brown who dealt with it for the Labour Party

18   *Daily Telegraph*, 3 March 1984

19   In January 1966 Isakov, who had functioned as a disinformation officer in the US for four years, under the cover of UNICEF, was accused of trying to buy six accelerometers from a dealer in surplus equipment but managed to get out of the country. For Cairncross, see Chapman Pincher, *Too Secret Too Long*

20   See *Soviet Spies in the Shadow of the UN*, Ligue de la Liberté, Belgium 1969. Barron, *op cit*

21   Shevchenko, *op cit* and interview to *Daily Mail*, 29 August 1980. Written statement read out by Shevchenko's lawyers. Shevchenko claimed that of thirteen Russians in his department at least seven were KGB officers who did no UN work at all, receiving their orders direct from the KGB area 'resident'

22   The KGB colonel was Viktor Lessiovski, special assistant to Kurt Waldheim from 1961 to 1973 and from 1976 onwards

Chapter 9: Seeing Red (pages 131-45)

1   *The Times* and *Daily Telegraph*, 23 April 1985

2   Alan Whicker, *Within Whicker's World*, Elm Tree Books, 1982

3   'Money Programme', 7 November 1977. Goldsmith was interviewed by Hugh Stephenson and James Bellini

4   Letters Between Brigadier Ramsbotham and various MPs with Hughie Green. *Evening Standard*, 4 February 1982

5   The *Defence Attaché* article appeared under the name P.Q. Mann – probably a pseudonym

6   *The Times*, 20 November 1984. The case was heard in the High Court in London. It was claimed that the article implied that Korean Airlines 'intentionally took part in an adventure likely to result in disaster'

7   *Observer*, 31 March 1985. Nicholson was shot dead on 24 March

8   *The Times*, 23 April 1985

9   Called 'MI5's Official Secrets' and produced by 20/20 Vision, it was screened on 8 March 1985

10   *New Society*, 14 June 1984

11   Those taking part included Gerald Kaufman, Labour MP, and John Cartwright of the SDP. The second programme was screened on 14 March

1985. The Attorney General and the Director of Public Prosecutions decided against prosecuting Cathy Massiter for breach of the Official Secrets Act because the case would involve making damaging admissions in court

12   Copy of a statement by Nicholas Winterton. Called 'Where it Matters', the programme was broadcast nationwide on 9 June 1981

13   Whicker, *op cit*

14   Also see letter in *The Times*, dated 14 April 1980, from Sir Philip de Zulueta. The programme had been screened on 9 April

15   *Ibid*

16   *Sunday Express*, 21 April 1985. Also see *Sunday Telegraph* and *Observer*, 21 April 1985

17   Hans Graf Huyn, *op cit*

18   Michael Bentine, *The Door Marked Summer*, Granada 1981 and conversations

19   Statements from Hughie Green. Copy of letter from Admiral Troup. Statement from Philip Costello, former Command PRO to Flag Officer Submarines

20   IBA Act 1973, HMSO (No Cmnd no.). The £1,000 million was mainly on warhead improvements

21   Statements by Hughie Green and letter from Admiral Troup

22   Statement by Hughie Green. His manager was George Brightwell

23   Memo dated 3 January 1977 sent on behalf of Jack Smith of the IBA

24   Whicker, *op cit*

25   KGB recruits in Britain were urged to insinuate themselves into MI5, MI6, GCHQ, *The Times*, the BBC, Foreign Office or Home office – in that order – information from MI5 source

26   In the 20/20 Vision programmes (see notes 9 and 11) Cathy Massiter stated that a special desk was set up in MI5 to deal with 'subversion in the media' and that MI5 vetted BBC journalists who were candidates for politically sensitive posts

Chapter 10: The Disinformation Game (pages 148-61)

1   *Soviet Active Measures*, US Government Printing Office, 1982

2   Goldsmith, *op cit*

3   For details of the Katyn massacre see Nikolai Tolstoy, *Stalin's Secret War*, Jonathan Cape, 1981

4   Dzhirkvelov, *op cit*. The KGB man supplying the articles was Arkady Boiko

5   Hans Graf Huyn, *op cit*

6   Bittman, *op cit*

7   *Ibid*

8   Evidence that the Politburo makes the decisions on important assassinations has been provided by Sejna. Also intelligence information from MI5 sources

9   *Soviet Covert Action* (The Forgery Offensive), Hearings, Select Committee on Intelligence, House of Representatives, 6 and 19 February 1980, *Soviet Active Measures*, US Government Printing Office, 1982

10   Barron, *op cit*

11   *Sunday Times*, 8 January 1984

12   Foreign Affairs Note, US Department of State, April 1983

13   *Sunday Times*, 8 January 1984

14   *Morning Star*, 21 September 1983

15   *Soviet Active Measures*, US Government Printing Office, 1982

16   Foreign Affairs Note, US Department of State, April 1983

17   *Soviet Active Measures*, US Government Printing Office, 1982. See also Shultz and Godson, *op cit*

18   *Ibid*

19   *Ibid*

20   Statement by the US Attorney General, William French Smith, before the US American Bar Association, 6 August 1984

21   *Soviet Active Measures*, US Government Printing Office, 1982

22   *Ibid*

23   *Soviet Active Measures*, US Government Printing Office, 1982. Bittman, *op cit*

24   *Ibid*. The allegation may also have been intended to deflect attention from reports of the Soviet use of chemical warfare in Afghanistan. *Ethiopian Herald*, 12 March 1982. *Diario de Lisboa*, 13 April 1982

25   *Ibid*

26   Barron, *op cit*

27   *Soviet Active Measures*, US Government Printing Office, 1982

28   *Ibid*

29   *Ibid*

30   *Ibid*. Barron, *op cit*

31   *Ibid*

32   *Ibid*. Shultz and Godson, *op cit*

Chapter 11: Agents of Influence (pages 162-80)

1   Chapman Pincher, *Too Secret Too Long*

2   *The Times*, 19 March 1985. *Sunday Times*, 31 March 1985, Nicholas Bethell, *The Great Betrayal*, Hodder and Stoughton, 1984

3   Chapman Pincher, *Their Trade is Treachery*

4 Weinstein, *op cit*. James Barros, *Alger Hiss and Harry Dexter White*, Orbis, Vol. 21, No. 3, Fall 1977

5 Information from MI5 and FBI sources

6 Chapman Pincher, *Too Secret Too Long*

7 K.W. Fricke, *Die Staatsicherheit*, Verlag Wissenschaft und Politik, Berend von Nottbeck, 1982. Corson and Crowley, *op cit*. Information from MI5 source

8 Willy Brandt, *People and Politics*, Collins, 1978

9 Von Nottbeck, *op cit*

10 Brandt, *op cit*

11 *The Times*, 1 October 1981. *Daily Telegraph*, 2 October. The Soviets have developed the habit of seizing Westerners on slight pretexts to have them ready for possible exchanges for important agents

12 *The Times*, 28 February 1985

13 Trial transcript, November and December 1982. Heaps, *op cit*

14 Information from MI5 officer concerned with Operation Bride (later Venona) – the decipherment of wartime KGB traffic

15 Jan Sejna, *We Will Bury You*

16 John Rees, *Infiltration of the Media by the KGB and its Friends*, Accuracy in Media, 1978

17 Chapman Pincher, *Their Trade is Treachery* and *Too Secret Too Long*

18 *Ibid*

19 Barron, *op cit*

20 Chapman Pincher, *Their Trade is Treachery* (paperback edition), Sidgwick and Jackson, 1982

21 Information from MI5 sources

22 *Ibid*

23 Information about 'Party Piece' was given publicly by Peter Wright on the 'World in Action' television programme on 16 July 1984. Further details supplied by MI5 source

24 Bittman, Hearings of the Permanent Select Committee on Intelligence, House of Representatives, 6 and 19 February 1980. MI5 records show that the KGB has also tried to recruit women secretaries working for MPs serving on Select Committees

25 Josef Frolik, *The Frolik Defection*, Cooper 1975. Frantisek August and David Rees, *Red Star over Prague*, Sherwood Press, 1984. Evidence to Committee on the Judiciary, US Senate, 12 April 1976

26 *Ibid* and confidential information provided by Frolik

27 Departmental Committee on Section 2 of the Official Secrets Act 1911, Vol. 3, HMSO, 1972

28 Information from MI5 source

29 See *Freedom and the Security Services*, Labour Party, March 1983

30 P.M.S. Blackett, *Military and Political Consequences of Atomic Energy*, Turnstile Press, 1948. Information from Sir Frederick Brundrett, Chief Scientist M.O.D.

31 See Chapters 6, 13-18

32 *Soviet Active Measures*, US Government Printing Office, 1982

33 *Ibid.* Golitsin, *op cit*. Hans Huyn, 'The Soviet Peace Offensive', Heritage lecture, Heritage Foundation, 1982

34 E.g. *The Socialist Sixth of the World, Soviet Strength, Soviet Success* – all best-sellers

35 E.g. the Bishop of Durham

36 *Daily Telegraph*, 18 March 1985. *Daily Mail*, 19 March 1985

37 *Daily Mail*, 9 December 1981

38 Keith Jacka, Caroline Cox, John Marks, *Rape of Reason*, Churchill Press, 1975. Background briefing to issues at the Polytechnic of North London, supplied by Baroness Cox. See also Julius Gould, *The Attack on Higher Education*, Institute for the Study of Conflict, September 1977

39 'Financial abuse resulting from compulsory membership of Student Unions', confidential document by Caroline Cox and John Marks. Interview with Baroness Cox

40 See many newspaper reports from January to July 1976

41 *Daily Mail*, 19 and 30 April 1985. It was discovered later (*Daily Mail*, 14 May 1985) that the strike had been organized by a Trotskyist group operating from inside Labour Party headquarters

42 *Daily Telegraph*, 18 May 1981. Report by John Izbicki

43 See Caroline Cox and Roger Scruton, *Peace Studies, A Critical Survey*, Institute for European Defence and Strategic Studies, 1984

44 *Communist Bloc Intelligence Activities in the U.S.*, 12 April 1976, US Government Printing Office 1976

45 House of Lords *Hansard*, 23 April 1985

46 The review by General Sir Hugh Beach was printed in Chronicle Vol. 4, November 1984. In the *Daily Telegraph* of 19 November 1984, Baroness Cox claimed that there was a direct connection between 'the Kremlin's World Peace Council and the self-styled Generals for Peace Group'

Chapter 12: Active Measures and the Trade Unions (pages 181-95)

1 August, *op cit*

2 Frolik, *op cit*

3 House of Commons *Hansard*, 14 December 1977. *Daily Express*, 15 December 1977. The statement was made by Stephen Hastings MP and

Labour Ministers did all they could to smother the disclosures

4   Sejna, *op cit*

5   At a private dinner, which I attended, Len Murray, the Secretary of the TUC, described how he and the Government were 'dismantling' the legislation brought in by the Heath Government to curb the powers of the unions

6   August, *op cit*

7   Chapman Pincher, *Inside Story*

8   Chapman Pincher, *Too Secret Too Long*

9   Information from the Defence Ministry

10   The section is known as 'F Branch'. The issue of telephone tapping by MI5 was publicly ventilated on the TV programme 'MI5's Official Secrets', screened on 8 March 1985. It was then debated in Parliament following an investigation by Lord Bridge into allegations about the improper authorization of phone-tapping, which he rejected

11   Transcript of 'MI5's Official Secrets'

12   Confidential information

13   Transcript of Wright's broadcast and further information from MI5 source

14   Information from MI5 sources

15   *Ibid*

16   Lord Wigg, *George Wigg* Michael Joseph, 1972. Conversations with Wigg

17   Information from Maurice Macmillan

18   The journalist was Lord Chalfont. See his article, *The Times*, 2 October 1978

19   Statement made several times in Parliament by the Home Secretary, Leon Brittan

20   *Terms of Reference of the Three Advisers*, issued by 10 Downing Street

21   Information from former executive, Colin Valdar

22   Information from former executive, Robin Esser, and personal involvement

23   Statement by Frank Chapple to a meeting organized by Common Cause. Frank Chapple, *Sparks Fly*, Michael Joseph, 1984

24   See *Daily Mail*, 1 and 3 April 1985, *Observer*, 31 March and 14 April 1985, *Sunday Times*, 21 April 1985. In the re-run of the election Ron Todd won with an increased majority

25   *Daily Mail*, 4 January 1985. After inculcating the required tactics into Scargill, Watters was moved to Birmingham to simulate militancy among car-workers and now works for the Communist newspaper, *Morning Star*

26   In an interview published in the *Daily Express* on 17 October 1977
27   *The Times*, 29 March 1985
28   *The Times*, 29 November 1984
29   *Daily Mail*, 2 May 1985. *The Times*, 18 June 1985

Chapter 13: The Offensive called 'Peace' (pages 196-202)

1   Information from MI5 source concerned with the interrogation of Blunt

2   Barron, *op cit*

3   *Soviet Active Measures*, US Government Printing Office 1982. The current chairman of the Soviet Peace Fund is Anatoly Karpov, the chessmaster

4   *Ibid.* Rose, *op cit*

5   House of Lords *Hansard*, 23 April 1985, *The Times*, 24 April 1985 and letter from Lord Orr-Ewing, 26 April 1985

6   *De Telegraf*, 22 July 1981. *Moscow and the Peace Offensive*, Heritage *Foundation*, 1982

7   *Soviet Active Measures*, US Government Printing Office, 1982. Senior Defence Ministry sources have assured me that no evidence of any allotment of Soviet money to the British CND movement has been discovered in spite of efforts by MI5, including penetration of the movement

8   Information from CIA source. *Soviet Active Measures* US Government Printing Office, 1982

9   *Exhibition of Bacterial War Crimes Committed by the Government of the U.S.A.*, The Chinese People's Committee for World Peace, Peking, 1952. *Red's Photographs on Germ Warfare Exposed as Fakes*, *New York Times*, 3 April 1952

10   *Daily Express*, 9 July 1952

11   Gehlen, *op cit*

12   Sejna, affidavit. Eight months after the launching of 'peaceful coexistence' the Soviets smashed the Hungarian bid for freedom by military force

Chapter 14: The Détente Deception (pages 203-9)

1   Shevchenko, *op cit*

2   Brezhnev, Prague, 1973

3   David Hart, *The Times*, 3 June 1985

4   Brandt, *op cit*. *Daily Express*, 27 November 1975. Chapman Pincher, *Inside Story*. In *Red Star over Prague* (Sherwood Press, 1984) the Czech defector, August states, 'so-called détente facilitates the use of illeg-

als in the West as it lowers awareness of Soviet espionage at the very time when this process is being stepped up'

5   Rose, *op cit*. Shevchenko, *op cit*
6   Shevchenko, *Daily Mail*, 29 August 1980
7   *Ibid*
8   *Journal of Defence and Diplomacy*, April 1985
9   Max M. Kampelman, *Madrid Conference: How to Negotiate with the Soviets*, Intelligence Report, American Bar Association, Vol. 7, No. 2, February 1985. The Cuban capability to operate highly trained troops overseas was in itself the result of a Soviet breach of the Kennedy–Khrushchev deal which resolved the Cuban missile crisis in 1962

Chapter 15: The Neutron Bomb Offensive (pages 210-17)

1   S.T. Cohen, *The Neutron Bomb*, Institute for Foreign Policy Analysis, Washington, 1978
2   Joseph D. Douglass, *op cit*
3   Cohen, *op cit*
4   Khrushchev restarted nuclear tests in August 1961
5   Rose, *op cit*. *Soviet Active Measures*, US Government Printing Office, 1982.
6   *Ibid*. evidence of the FBI
7   *Washington Post*, 17 October 1977, 5 December 1977
8   Barron, *op cit*
9   *Ibid*
10   *Ibid*. Rose, *op cit*
11   *Soviet Active Measures*, US Government Printing Office 1982
12   *Ibid*
13   Janos Berecz

Chapter 16: 'Cruise' and the CND (pages 218-30)

1   MOD figures. *Soviet Military Power*, US Government Printing Office, 1984
2   *Ibid*. David J. Trachtenberg, *The Military Balance in 1985*, Journal of Defense and Diplomacy 1985
3   *Soviet Active Measures*, US Government Printing Office, 1982. Rose, *op cit*
4   *Ibid*; the country is not named
5   'MI5's Official Secrets', 20/20 Vision, 8 March 1985. Information from MI5 source
6   *Keep Death off the Roads*; *Telephone Trees*; *How we stop the Cruise Launcher* – documents issued through CND's *Campaign* following

the 1983 annual conference. Blake Baker, *Daily Telegraph*, 12 December 1984

7   Jon Bloomfield, *Marxism Today*, June 1983

8   Information from Newbury firms concerned as a result of action by Greenham 'peace women'

9   Information from senior MOD source

10   *Daily Telegraph*. Letter from Dr Julian Lewis (Coalition for Peace through Security), *Daily Telegraph*, 17 December 1984. Alun Chalfont, *Encounter*, April 1983. Patrick Cosgrave, *Daily Express*, 4 May 1983 Peter Jenkins, *Guardian*, 1 December 1982

11   Rose, *op cit*. Also see Paul Johnson, *Daily Mail*, 28 April and 16 May 1983

12   The official was Ian Davidson

13   *Morning Star*, 8 December 1984

14   *Newsweek*, The New Terror Network, 11 February 1985. *Sunday Times*, 3 February 1985

15   *Soviet Active Measures*, US Government Printing Office, 1982. Shevchenko, *op cit*

16   Rose, *op cit*

17   Dexter Jerome Smith, *Defence*, March 1983

18   *The Times*, 8 April 1985. *Daily Telegraph*, 9 April 1985

Chapter 17: 'Star Wars' (pages 231-6)

1   Douglass, *op cit*. *Soviet Military Power*, US Government Printing Office, 1984

2   Statement to Supreme Soviet quoted in the *Observer*, 3 March 1985

3   Stewart Menaul, *Space-based Strategic Defence*, Foreign Affairs Research Institute November 1981. Robert S. Dudney, *U.S. News and World Report*, 18 February 1985. Nigel Hawkes, *Observer*, 3 March 1985 American work on ABMs was frozen by Robert McNamara in 1962

4   Menaul, *op cit*. Menaul, *The Technology of Ballistic Missile Defence*, Aims of Industry, undated

5   *The President's Strategic Defence Initiative*, US Information Service, 3 January 1985. Robert C. Richardson, *Outline of Remarks to World Media Conference*, 23 October 1983. *Space Weapons, the Key to Assured Survival*, Heritage Foundation, 2 February 1984

6   Menaul, *op cit*. Menaul, *Military Uses of Space-Ballistic Missile Defence*. Space Policy, May 1985. Nicholas Ashford, *The Times*, 29 March 1985

7   Menaul, *op cit* and Europe's Stake in Ballistic Missile Defence, *Defence*, June 1984

301

8 Douglass, *op cit. Soviet Military Power*, US Government Printing Office, 1984. Soviet military literature continues to stress the importance of defence against nuclear attack

9 *The Times*, 17 December 1984. Margaret Thatcher's address to Congress, 20 February 1985, reported in *The Times* on the following day. Kinnock statement recorded in *The Times*, 7 March 1985

Chapter 18: The Sharp Edge of Active Measures (pages 237-58)

1 Widespread coverage of riots in newspapers of first fortnight of July 1981, e.g. *Daily Mail* 10 and 11 July; *Daily Telegraph* 11 July

2 The situation has been described by numerous exiles and dissidents, especially Aleksandr Solzhenitsyn. See also Nikolai Tolstoy, *Stalin's Secret War*, Jonathan Cape, 1981. Various authorities have estimated the number of Soviet citizens who have died, often violently, as a result of the Soviet revolution and régime at about 60 million

3 Information from Sejna's publishers

4 *Communist Bloc Intelligence Activities in the U.S.*, statement of Josef Frolik, US Government Printing Office, 1976. Also tapes of Frolik interviews

5 Information from Royal Canadian Mounted Police source. Also conversations with Gouzenko. Sabotka was interviewed on Canadian television (CBC) on 8 June 1982

6 Barron, *op cit. Soviet Active Measures*, US Government Printing Office, 1982

7 Ladislav Bittman, *The Deception Game*, Ballantine, 1972

8 Fenton Bressler, *Sunday Express*, 31 March 1985. Brian Freemantle, *KGB*, Michael Joseph, 1982

9 *Daily Mail*, 5 October 1981

10 Paul Hehnze, *The Plot to Kill the Pope*, Scribner, New York, 1983. Claire Sterling, *The Time of the Assassins: Anatomy of an Investigation*, Holt, Rinehart and Winston, New York, 1983

11 Statement by John Garrard, a 'Sovietologist' of the Wilson Centre (US) and statement by John Barron, made available by Sir James Goldsmith. Also writings of Duff Hart-Davis

12 Chapman Pincher, *Too Secret Too Long*, Sejna *op cit.*

13 Edward J. Epstein, *Legend*, Hutchinson, 1978. Warren Commission Report on the Kennedy assassination. Michael Eddowes, *The Oswald File*, Clarkson Potter, New York, 1977. Rowland Evans and Robert Novak, Lyndon B. Johnson, *The Exercise of Power*, Allen and Unwin, 1967

14 John J. Dziak, *Soviet Intelligence and the Security Services in the*

1980s: The Paramilitary Dimension, National Strategy Information Center, 1980

15   Sejna, *op cit*

16   Schuman, *op cit*

17   Carlos is the pseudonym for Ilich Ramirez Sanchez, son a Venezuelan lawyer, trained in terrorism in Cuba, then in Moscow. He has murdered French security officers and led the kidnap of oil ministers at the OPEC conference in Vienna in 1975

18   *Soviet Active Measures*, US Government Printing Office, 1982. Evidence of John McMahon, Deputy Director of Central Intelligence.

19   Schuman, *op cit*. According to John Rees (*op cit*) Novosti officials are also involved in the distribution of forged passports to terrorists

20   *Soviet Active Measures*, US Government Printing Office, 1982. An Italian Government report submitted to the Commission investigating the murder of Aldo Moro in 1978 and leaked to the newspapers accused the KGB of 'trying to pilot' the actions of the Red Brigades and of supplying terrorists with weapons and money

21   MI5 Source. The agents were Czechs – Ramon Narozny and Emil Merth

22   *Soviet Active Measures*, U.S. Government Printing Office, 1982. Barron, *op cit*

23   See Ambassador Jeane Kirkpatrick, *The Unauthorised Violence of Terrorism*, Journal of Defense and Diplomacy, November 1984

24   *Soviet Military Power*, US Government Printing Office, 1984

25   Spetsnaz is short for *spetsaznacheniya* (special designation). See *Soviet Military Power*, US Government Printing Office, 1984, Godson, *Intelligence Requirements for the 1980s: Counterintelligence*, National Strategy Information Centre, 1980. For Lyalin, see Chapman Pincher, *Too Secret Too Long* and House of Commons *Hansard*, statement by Attorney General, Sir Peter Rawlinson, 8 November 1971, col. 641

26   Sejna, *op cit*

27   Aleksei Myagkov, *Inside the KGB*, Foreign Affairs Publishing Co., 1976

28   Information from MI5 and MOD sources

29   *Daily Express*, 23 April 1976. *The Times*, 26 April

30   Levchenko, *op cit*

31   The Home Office confirmed the discovery of the set and that it was of Russian origin. A similar event in Austria is described by William Hood in *Mole*, Weidenfeld and Nicolson, 1982

32   Bittman, *op cit*. August and Rees, *op cit*

33   *The Times*, 28 and 29 October 1981 *et seq*. General Stig Lofgren, *Soviet Submarines against Sweden*, Strategic Review, Winter 1984

34   Lofgren, *op cit. Soviet Active Measures*, US Government Printing Office, 1982. Captain Guzjin, the submarine's commander, claimed 'problems with his rudder and radar in bad weather'

35   Lofgren, *op cit.* V. Suvorov, *Spetsnaz*, Int. Defense Review, Vol. 16, 1983

36   Lofgren, *op cit*

Chapter 19: Counter-Offensive? (pages 259-74)

1   Just as Anthony Eden thought that Churchill had gone too far in his Fulton speech exposing the fact of the Iron Curtain

2   See *Soviet Active Measures*, 1982, *Soviet Covert Action*, 1980, US Government Printing Office. *Soviet Active Measures: Focus on Forgeries*, US State Department, April 1983

3   *The Times*, 9 May 1985

4   Tolstoy, *op cit.* Writings of Margarete Buber-Neumann. Malcolm Muggeridge *Chronicles of Wasted Time*, Vol. 2; Collins 1973. The German raider, Komet, given safe passage by the Soviet Navy destroyed many ships

5   Tolstoy, *op cit*

6   Hans Graf Huyn, *op cit*

7   Chapman Pincher, *Too Secret Too Long.* The Commons Table Office usually refuses to accept questions on the security or intelligence services. The Select Committee on Defence undertook an inquiry into Positive Vetting but this had to be limited to the Defence Ministry and no witnesses from the security or intelligence services could be called. The inquiry was never completed

8   House of Lords *Hansard*, 23 April 1985. A previous Lords debate on subversion was held on 26 February 1975 with nothing comparable in the Commons in that period

9   Information from MI5 sources. See also Anatoly Golitsin, *New Lies for Old*, Bodley Head, 1984

10   Information from Julian Amery

11   The Commission's report was published on 9 May 1985

12   Conversations with Oldfield

13   See Chapter 7

14   See Chapter 8

15   *Daily Telegraph*, 11 February 1985. The spies who included Soviet 'journalists' had secured industrial secrets

16   Quoted in *Time*, 28 January 1985. Since then five more people have been arrested in the case of the US naval spy-ring centred on the Walker family

17   *Morning Star*, 29 September 1984

18   *The Times*, Levin Column, 5 December 1984

19   For the latest steps see *Review of Public Order Law*, HMSO May 1985. Summarized in *Daily Telegraph*, 17 May 1985

20   See Chapter 12, note 24

21   Information from Sir James Goldsmith

22   Independent Broadcasting Authority Act 1973, HMSO

23   See *Daily Express*, 10 May 1985, 'The Government is effectively picking up the bill of up to £175 million a year for ITV's Channel 4'. Based on statement by the Comptroller and Auditor General

24   The IRD has been studiously ignored in the memoirs of politicians involved with it. This may be because it was largely financed by the CIA. Various journalists worked for it. An MI5 informant told me that it was wound up because of the CIA involvement following the Watergate Affair. Labour's left-wingers would have been particularly incensed had they learned the facts. Sir James Goldsmith addressed the Defense Strategy Forum of the National Strategy Information Center in Washington on 22 May 1984

25   Quoted by Baroness Cox in *The Free Nation*, December/January 1985. Maurice Tugwell, NATO Fellowship Report (undated)

26   *Daily Telegraph* and *The Times*, 21 March 1985. *Daily Telegraph*, 25 March 1985. Zia Met Gorbachov in Moscow at Chernenko's funeral and was convinced that Gorbachov intended to intensify the war in Afghanistan, which has since happened. Gorbachov warned Zia against supporting the Afghan resistance

27   On 26 April 1985 Gorbachov threatened a fresh strengthening of the Soviet nuclear arsenal if Reagan continued with 'space wars' research (*Daily Telegraph*, 27 April 1985). Gorbachov was speaking in Warsaw when the Warsaw Pact was renewed for twenty years. On 27 May he met Willy Brandt in Moscow and attacked the 'Star Wars' programme claiming (falsely) that outer space was in danger of becoming a source of death and destruction

28   House of Lords *Hansard*, 23 April 1985

29   Shevchenko, *op cit*

30   Kampelman, *op cit*

Selected Bibliography

August, Frantisek and Rees, David, *Red Star over Prague*, Sherwood Press, 1984

Barron, John, *KGB Today, The Hidden Hand*, Coronet Books, 1984

Bittman, Ladislav, *The Deception Game*, Ballantine Books, New York, 1972

Bonds, Roy (Editor), *The Soviet War Machine*, Salamander Books/Hamlyn, 1976

Chapple, Frank, *Sparks Fly*, Michael Joseph, 1984

Corson, William R and Crowley, Robert T., *The New KGB*, Morrow, New York, 1985

Crozier, Brian; Middleton, Drew; Murray-Brown, Jeremy, *This War Called Peace*, Sherwood Press, 1984

Golitsin, Anatoli, *New Lies for Old*, Bodley Head, 1984

Nixon, Richard, *The Real War*, Sidgwick and Jackson, 1980

Pincher, Chapman, *Inside Story*, Sidgwick and Jackson, 1978

Pincher, Chapman, *Their Trade is Treachery*, Sidgwick and Jackson, 1981 and extended version (paperback edition), Sidgwick and Jackson, 1982

Pincher, Chapman, *Too Secret Too Long*, Sidgwick and Jackson, 1984

Rose, Clive, *Campaigns against Western Defence*, RUSI, Macmillan, 1985

Sejna, Jan, *We Will Bury You*, Sidgwick and Jackson, 1982

Shevchenko, Arkady N., *Breaking with Moscow*, Cape, 1985

Shultz, Richard H. and Godson, Roy, *Desinformatsia*, Pergamon-Brasseys, 1984

Soviet Active Measures, US Government Printing Office, 1982

Soviet Military Power, US Government Printing Office, 1984

Index

Accelerometers 80, 82
Accra 154
Accuracy in Media 167, 267
Action Gallows Cross 38
Active measures 2, 24, 30, 54, 65, 66, 104, 129,
    136, 186, 204, 212, 217, 235, 237, 260
Adenauer, Konrad 36, 39, 50, 52, 54, 61
Adjubei, Alexei 32, 47, 49
Aeroflot, 249
Afghanistan 2, 134, 149, 157, 159, 160, 198,
    207, 239, 244, 249, 271, 273
Afrique-Asie 100
Afro-Asian People's Solidarity Association 179
Agayants, Ivan 27, 37, 38, 48
Agca, Mehmet Ali 106, 241
Agee, Philip 113, 157
Agencies 117
Agents of Influence 52, 97
Ahlers, Conrad 51, 56
Aims of Industry 270
Aldermaston 8
Alderson, Ray 189
Algeria 127
Allen, Victor 225
Alsace-Lorraine 240
Amalgamated Union of Engineering Workers
    182, 189
Amin, Hafizullah 159, 244, 255
Amsterdam 215, 227
Andersson, Sven 257
Andronov, Ione 242
Andropov, Yuri 26, 166, 205, 208, 227, 270
Angola 207, 245, 248
Anti-ballistic missile treaty 232, 234
Antonov, Sergei 241
Apartheid 159
Arbatov, Georgy 107
Argentine 135, 152
Arts Council 177
Assassinations 27, 99, 243, 244, 250, 251
Associated Society of Locomotive Engineers
    and Firemen (ASLEF) 189
Association of Cinematographic, Television

and Allied Technicians 189
Astronautic conferences 74
Athens 43
Atlas 74, 79
Atomic bomb 15, 17
Atomic warheads 51, 56, 69, 72, 79
Attlee, Clement 14, 17, 268
ATV 138
Augstein, Rudolf 39, 40, 44, 49, 50, 51, 52, 57,
    61, 275
August, Frantisek 169, 181, 183, 275
Austria 149, 157, 160, 195
Ayvzov, Todor 241

Bl bomber 84, 207, 226
Baader-Meinhof 111, 115
Babaints, Yuri 199
Backfire 84, 85, 226
Bacterial warfare 152, 157, 201
Baker, Blake 224
Baltic States 273
BAOR 251
Baptists 214
Barak, Rudolf 60
Barents Sea 165
Barnes, Joseph F. 98
Barron, John 28, 56, 103, 104, 123, 151, 158,
    197, 275
Bavaria 53, 57, 58
Bax, Arthur 128
BBC 125, 131, 132, 140, 143, 144, 267
Beaverbrook, Lord 39, 42, 112
Becker, Hans-Detlev 50, 54
Beirut 154
Belenko, Viktor 123
Belgium 154, 213, 220, 221, 229
Belgrano 153
Belvedere Palace 68
Benes, Eduard 166
Benn, Anthony Wedgwood 136, 244
Bentine, Michael 140, 143
Berlin 139, 164, 212
Berlin crisis 128

Berliner Zeitung 40
Bernal J.D. 171
Berne 122
Bevin, Ernest 17
Biological weapons 59
Birmingham 238
Bitov, Oleg 65, 106, 242
Bittman, Ladislav 28, 41, 63, 105, 149, 156, 169, 240, 276
Blackett, Patrick 171
Blackjack 84, 226
Blackmail 150, 168, 169, 224, 252
Bloomfield, Jon 223
'Blue Peter' 173
Blunt, Anthony 29, 162, 163, 196
BND 37, 40, 54, 59
Bogdanov, Radomir 108, 172, 215
Bogopolev, Igor 117
Boiko, Arkady 49
Boilermakers' Union 182
Bonn 50, 53, 164, 205, 214
Boyce, Christopher 83
Brandt, Willy 164, 203
Brave Defender 251, 254, 265
Brezhnev, Leonid 83, 202, 203, 214, 221, 227, 229, 242, 270
Brezhnev Doctrine 203
Bridgwater 176
Brighton 244
Briginshaw, Lord 182
British Embassy (Moscow) 77
British Leyland 186, 190
British Peace Assembly 198
Brown, George 128
Bruck, Mikhail 119
Brussels 221, 236
Brzezinski, Zbigniew 154
Buckley, William F. 46, 61
Buckton, Ray 189
Buenos Aires 154
Buffalo 99
Bukovsky, Vladimir 207, 260
Bulgaria 154, 241
Burchett, Wilfred 45, 94
Burdett, Winston 98
Burgess, Guy 144, 162
Burghfield 253

Cabinet Office 269
Cairncross, John 129
Cairo 112
Calder, Ritchie 171
Callaghan, James 19, 170, 182, 215, 268
Cambridge 114
Cameron, Ken 189
Campaign for Nuclear Disarmament *see* CND
Campbell, Duncan 21, 170
Canada 119, 166, 167, 239
Capitol Times 98
'Carlos' 245
Carrington, Lord 126, 236
Carter, President Jimmy 83, 154, 159, 204, 207, 212, 226
Castro, Fidel 157
Caulfield, Justice 63
Central Intelligence Agency *see* CIA
Challet, Marcel 127

Chalmers, Malcolm 21
Chamberlain, Neville 204
Chambers, Whittaker 98
Chandra, Romesh 198, 215, 216
Channel Four 135, 136, 267
Chapple, Frank 190
Cheltenham 82
Chemical Research Establishment 243
Chemical weapons 22, 59, 157
Chernenko, Konstantin 208, 270
Chicago 246
'Chicken-feed' 75
Chile 149, 167, 207
China 95, 104, 155, 200, 218
Chou En-lai 155
Christian Democrats (CDU) 32, 52, 62
Christian Peace Conference 172, 179
Christian Social Union (CSU) 32, 36, 52, 58
Christie, Campbell 189
CIA 29, 33, 54, 60, 75, 79, 84, 101, 102, 104, 106, 108, 112, 114, 123, 133, 147, 153, 156, 159, 200, 242, 243
Civil liberties 222, 265
Civil and Public Services Association 183, 189
CND 17, 19, 21, 136, 138, 171, 173, 174, 218, 220, 222, 227, 265
Coalition for Peace through Security 270
Cohen, Samuel 210
Cohn-Bendit, Daniel 238
Cold launch 81
Cold War 14, 24, 112
Collins, Canon John 222
Comintern 25
Communist Party (Great Britain) 17, 18, 125, 169, 184, 189, 193, 223, 266
Copenhagen 101
Counter-spy 114
Courtney, Anthony 109
Crozier, Brian 276
Cox, Baroness Caroline 269, 276
Crucible Theatre Company 117
Cruise missiles 8, 85, 165, 217, 218, 220, 225, 227, 228, 266
Cruise missile convoys 136
Cruisewatch 222
Cuba 73, 85, 114, 157, 158, 167, 195, 207, 245, 246, 248, 260
Cultural attachés 178
Cyanide 22
Cypher machines 77
Czechoslovakia 7, 13, 28, 60, 69, 77, 128, 134, 149, 150, 166, 169, 193, 194, 198, 203, 249, 250, 254

D Notice Secretary 95
Daily Express 39, 42, 44, 47, 94, 112, 135, 196
Daily Mirror 189
Daily Worker 125
Dallas 243
Daniel, Jens *see* Rudolf Augstein
Dash, Jack 190
'Death of a Princess' 138
De Nieuwe 154
Defence Attaché 134
Defence Ministry 223, 224, 265, 272
Defence Strategy Forum 34

De Gaulle, President Charles 127, 168, 237
Dejean, Maurice 168
Delmer, Sefton 94
Denmark 12
Deptford 238
Der Spiegel 5, 33, 39, 44, 46, 49, 52, 57, 59, 64, 66, 105, 107, 152, 194, 212, 242
Der Spiegel Affair 31, 32, 54, 60, 93, 182
Desai, Moraji 111
Détente 9, 202, 203, 207
Deutsche Zeitung und Wirtschaftszeitung 51
Deutschland-magazin 56, 61
Diario de Lisboa 157
Die Deutsche Woche 111
Die Zeit 65
Dimbleby, Jonathan 133
Direct Action 226
Disinformation 22, 59, 63, 74, 76, 84, 118, 124, 146, 224, 242, 270
Dobrynin, Anatoly 76, 154
Dorchester Hotel 163
Douglass, Joseph D. 68, 70, 211
Dozier, General 158
Drama documentaries 137
Dubchek, Alexander 254
Dublin 247
Durham 183
Dusseldorf 214
Dutschke, Rudi 115
Dzhirkvelov, Ilya 47, 63, 104, 107, 119, 123, 148, 155, 245, 276

Eagleberger, Lawrence 216
East Berlin 111, 221
East Germany 13, 121, 150, 194
Egypt 152, 247
Egyptian Fundamentalists 245
Einstein, Albert 171
Eisenhower, President Dwight 73
El Triunfo 158
Encyclopaedia Britannica 121
Englemann, Berndt 44
Entryism 19, 20
Epstein, Edward J. 277
Estonia 273
Ethiopian Herald 157
Evening News 107

F 111 9, 16
Falin, Valentin 221
Falklands War 135, 153
Fallex '62 50, 54, 57, 66
Farnborough Air Show 124
Faslane 141
FBI 75, 84, 125, 150, 151, 159, 227, 244, 246
Federal Bureau of Investigation *see* FBI
'Fedora' 75, 76, 80, 84, 150
Felfe, Hans 78
Ferguson, Robert 173
Fibag 41
Fields, Tony 176
Fighting Communist Cells 226
Finland 12, 13, 160, 166, 255
Fire Brigades' Union 189
Food and Agriculture Organization 129
Foot, Michael 17, 182, 200
Foot, Paul 111

Ford, President Gerald 83, 178
Ford Motor Company 186
Foreign Office 186, 261, 269
Forgeries 118, 150, 261
Foxbat 123
France 13, 59, 97, 98, 100, 115, 125, 126, 149, 168, 171, 194, 205, 237, 263
Frankfurt 214, 238
Free Democratic Party 52
Frenzel, Alfred 169
Frolik, Josef 169, 178, 181, 239, 277
Furnival Jones, Sir Martin 170
Fylingdales 250

Gaitskell, Hugh 17, 242
Gale, George 135
Gandhi, Indira 111
GCHQ 11, 77, 81, 82, 150, 163, 170, 183, 253
Geneva 206, 236, 273
Geneva Convention 22
Genscher, Hans Dietrich 216
Gestapo 149
Ghana 122, 154, 214
Gibralter 155
Gill, Ken 185, 189
Gladwyn, Lord 163
Glasgow 148
Godson, Roy 28
Goebbels, Josef 111
Goldsmith, Sir James 5, 33, 62, 63, 93, 110, 113, 114, 119, 132, 133, 147, 191, 247, 267, 269, 270, 277
Goldwater, Barry 100
Golitsin, Anatoli 127, 172, 277
Gorbachov, Mikhail 25, 69, 134, 200, 208, 229, 235, 261, 266, 270, 278
Gouzenko, Igor 144, 112, 239
Granada Television 131, 132
Grand Mosque 146
Gratwohl, Larry 246
Great Soviet Encyclopaedia 88
Greater London Council 170, 177
Grechko, Marshal 166, 232
Green, Hughie 140, 143
Greenham Common 139, 222
Grenada 248
Gribanov, Oleg 167
Griffin, George 160
Gromyko, Andrei 2, 76, 204, 236, 260, 272
GRU 72, 73, 76, 98, 122, 128, 179, 249, 253, 265
Grunwick 175
Guillaume, Christl 164
Guillaume, Gunther 164
Gulags 239
Guardian 96

Hahn, Walter F. 60, 62, 278
Haig, Alexander 154, 215
Haldane, J.B.S. 171
Hambleton, Hugh 48, 128, 165
Hamburg 50, 54, 212
Hanoi 96
Hansard 182
Haparanda 255
Harrison, Sir Geoffrey 168
Harsfjaden 256

Hassel, Kai-Uwe von 58
Hastings, Max 132
Havana 246
Hayward, Ron 217
Heath, Edward 186
Heffer, Eric 21
Helsingin Sanomat 160
Helsinki 197, 206
Helsinki Accord 148, 166, 177, 205, 208, 272
Heseltine, Michael 265
High Frontier 233
High Time 98
Highgate cemetery 26
Hill, Ted 182
Hiroshima 177
Hiss, Alger 98, 163
Hitler, Adolf 4, 13, 14, 15, 40, 41, 51, 98, 204, 240, 261, 272
Hitler diaries 65, 118
Ho Chi Minh 96
Holland 115, 199, 213, 220, 221, 229
Hollis, Sir Roger 77, 163
Holocaust documents 160
Holy Loch 8
Home, Lord 207, 272, 273
Home Office 184, 269
Home Secretary 185, 268
Hoover, J. Edgar 77, 244
Housewives for Peace 199
Howe, Sir Geoffrey 195
Hull 238
Human rights 148, 206, 248, 273
L'Humanité 95
Hungary 13, 69, 95, 134, 194, 198, 208, 239, 249, 252
Huyn, Hans 38, 139, 149, 262, 278

IBA 135, 136, 141, 142
Independent Broadcasting Authority *see* IBA
Independent Broadcasting Authority Act 135, 267
India 160, 245
Information Research Department 268
Inge, Dean 7
Ingrams, Richard 110
Inner London Education Authority 175, 177
'Innocents Clubs' 180
Institute for Policy Studies 179
Institute of the US and Canada 108, 179
Institution of Professional Civil Servants 183
International Association of Democratic Lawyers 179
International Department 25, 29, 46, 76, 78, 82, 93, 102, 111, 118, 123, 125, 128, 133, 134, 140, 150, 173, 179, 215, 220, 225, 242, 244, 248, 256, 265, 270
International Federation of Resistance Fighters 179
International Information Department 25, 26, 113
International Institute for Peace 179, 198
International Organization of Journalists 179
International Radio and TV Organization 179
International Union of Students 179
Intourist Office 94
IRA 135, 224, 244, 245, 247, 254, 263
Iran 152

Irvine, Reed 1, 96, 98
Isakov, Vadim 80, 129
Islamabad 147, 159
Israel 245
Italy 59, 106, 115, 125, 149, 158, 220, 221, 236
Izvestia 51, 112

Jackson, Henry 100
Jacobi, Klaus 50
Jane's Fighting Ships 255
Japan 27, 95, 102, 104, 124, 158, 163, 177, 243
Jaruzelski, General 241
John Paul II, Pope 106, 154, 241, 258
Johnson, Hewlett 172, 200
Johnson, President Lyndon 78, 244
Johnson, Robert Lee 59
Joint Intelligence Committee 185
Joliot-Curie, Frédéric 171
Jones, Jack 182
Juan Carlos, King 155

Kabul 160, 225
Kaldor, Mary 21
Kampelman, Max 208, 218, 273
Kapfinger, Hans 41
Kapralov, Yuri 199
Karlskrona 255
Karlsruhe 57
Karmal, Babrak 159
Karpov, Vladimir 59
Katyn 148
Kekkonen, Urho 166
Kennedy, President John F. 50, 99, 148, 212, 242, 243, 260, 270
Kenny, General 95
Kent, Monsignor Bruce 173, 224, 225
Kent, Princess Michael of 138
Kenya 122
Kepplinger, Hans 42
Keys, Bill 195
KGB 25, 26, 28, 59, 61, 65, 72, 74, 80, 94, 96, 99, 101, 109, 111, 126, 128, 156, 158, 163, 167, 172, 179, 204, 242, 252, 264, 265
KGB Intelligence School 103, 121
Khrenov, Vladimir 127
Khrushchev, Nikita 17, 40, 47, 69, 72, 85, 96, 201, 212, 243, 245, 270
Kiev 172
King, MacKenzie 14
Kinnock, Neil 20, 236
Kissinger, Henry 126, 206, 274
Kitson, Alex 21, 195
Konkret 111
Knapp, Jimmy 189
Koch, Ed 154
Korczak, Boris 241
Korean airliner 1, 133, 148
Korean War 95, 162, 200
Kostov, Vladimir 241
Koucky, Vladimir 60
Krasnoyarsk 233
Kronstadt 255
Krotkov, Yuri 96
Ku Klux Klan 156
Kuriles 105
Kuznetsov, Igor 100
Kyodo 104

310

Labour Party 2, 7, 16, 69, 128, 141, 153, 170, 179, 185, 189, 200, 229, 238, 266
Labour Party Conferences 18
Labour Research Department 179
Lamond, James 198
Lasers 233
Latvia 273
Lenin, Vladimir Ilyich 1, 13, 15, 16, 24, 28, 32, 76, 87, 146, 181, 196, 199, 206, 269
Leningrad 255
Leonov, Vadim 199, 227
Letelier, Orlando 167
Levchenko, Stanislav 5, 27, 87, 93, 101, 122, 123, 124, 155, 165, 252, 260, 270, 278
The Leveller 114
Levin, Bernard 266
Libya 245
Line PR 103
Lisbon 227
Literary Gazette 106, 242
Lithuania 273
Live Aid concerts 161
Liverpool 190, 238, 253
Llangollen 252
Lockheed bribes scandal 58
London 72, 128, 160
London Underground 250
Long Kesh 135
Lonsdale, Gordon 150
Los Angeles 128, 156
Louis, Viktor 44, 107
Lui, Vitali *see* Viktor Louis
Lumumba University 159, 245
Luns, Joseph 100, 154
Luxemburg 155
Lwow 40
Lyalin, Oleg 249, 252

McCarthy, Joseph 98
McGahey, Mick 4, 173, 189, 191
Maclean, Donald 29, 120, 162
McLuhan Marshall 131
McMahon, John 162
Macmillan, Maurice 186
McNamara, Robert 78
Mader, Julius 156, 157
Madrid 115, 154, 155, 206, 208
Maiski, Ivan 94
Malaysia 165
Malley, Simon 100
Malmö 255
Manchester 238
Manley, Michael 114
Mao, Chairman 193
Markov, Georgi 240
Marnham, Patrick 110
Marshall Aid 16, 36, 194, 197
Marsland, Terry 189
'Martel' 127
Martin, Alfred 51, 56, 57, 61, 66
Martinique 127
Marx, Karl 26
Marxism Today 125
Maskirovka 73
Massing, Hede 98
Massiter, Cathy 136, 184, 222
Massu, General 237

May Day Parade 78
Mayne, Stanley 183
Meany, George 194
Mecca 146
Media Committee 33, 62, 113, 114, 148, 191, 247
Meinhof, Ulricke 111
Mende, Erich 52, 53
Merkulov, Vladimir 101
Mexico 246
Mexico City 244, 247
MI5 29, 45, 76, 93, 97, 106, 136, 145, 163, 169, 170, 183, 184, 186, 205, 222, 242, 243, 253, 263
MI6 72, 76, 97, 106, 129, 150, 157, 162, 170, 185
Microbiological Research Establishment 243
Mig 25 123
Militant Tendancy 144, 193, 238, 266
Milne, James 189
Mindszenty, Cardinal 95
Miner, The 188
Minuteman 78, 207
Mirving 79, 84
Missile gap 71, 74, 85
Mitterand, President François 100
'Moles' 29, 61, 66, 78, 126, 150
'Money Programme' 132
Montagu, Ivor 198
Montevideo 113
Morand, Charles *see* Pierre-Charles Pathé
Morning Star 125, 132, 154, 188, 217, 225
Moro, Aldo 158, 247
Morozov, Mikhail 199
Moynihan, Daniel 85
Mozambique 149, 245
MPs 169
Mugabe, Robert 172
Munich 60
Muslim Brotherhood 247
MX missile 207
Myagkov, Alexei 250

National Anthem 135
National Coal Board 143, 195
National Front 173
National Hotel 110
National Security Agency *see* NSA
National Union of Journalists 188
National Union of Mineworkers 188, 189, 195
National Union of Railwaymen 189
National Union of Seamen 189
National Union of Teachers 177
Nationality Bill 137
NATO 7, 9, 10, 16, 21, 22, 36, 40, 43, 47, 48, 50, 59, 66, 78, 126, 127, 154, 164, 179, 205, 211, 215, 219, 221, 226, 229, 236, 240, 256, 257, 269
Nazi Party 138, 164
Nazi-Soviet Pact 98, 261, 273
'Neptune' 149
Neues Deutschland 37, 41
Neutron bombs 8, 84, 148, 157, 208, 220
New Delhi 108, 160
New Orleans 159
New Society 136
New Times 48, 103, 104, 107, 124

311

New York 75, 129, 215
New York Herald Tribune 98
New York Times 98, 167
New Zealand 11, 21, 128
Newbury 222
Nicaragua 45
Nicholson, Arthur 134
Niven, Bill 21
Nixon, President Richard 204
Nkomo, Joshua 172
Nkrumah, Kwame 122
Nomenklatura 6, 102, 194, 271
Norman, Herbert 168
North Korea 246
North Sea 126
North Vietnam 203
Norway 12, 41, 126, 160, 165, 199, 227
Nosenko, Yuri 76
Novosti 106, 111, 118, 122, 197, 165
Novotny, Antonin 149
NOW! 33
NSA 77, 81
Nuclear free zones 20, 227
Nuclear freeze 21, 227, 229
Nuclear tests 72, 212
Nuclear warheads 214, 218

Oldfield, Sir Maurice 157, 181
Olympic Games 104, 129, 156, 246
'Opportunity Knocks' 140
Orientering 160
Orr-Ewing, Lord 179, 198
Oslo 126
Ostend 221
Ostpolitik 164
Oswald, Lee Harvey 243
Ottawa 167
Owen, David 268
Owen, Will 169
Oxford University Press 88

Pace e Guerra 154
Pakistan 160, 271
Pakistani Army 147
Palestine Liberation Organization 245, 247
Palme, Olaf 257
Panorama 132
Pâques, Georges 48, 127, 128
Paris 59, 72, 99, 126, 129, 166, 197, 237, 242
Parker, Cedric 98
Parliamentarians for Peace 199
Pathé, Pierre-Charles 99
Patriot 157
Patriotic Front of Zimbabwe 172
Peace camps 22
Peace movements 69, 86, 235
Peace studies 173
Peace women 139, 220, 222
Peaceful co-existence 201, 202, 204, 270
Pearl Harbor 163
Pechora 233
Peenemunde 94
Peking 201
Penkovsky, Oleg 72, 74
Penny, John 173
Pentagon 60, 74, 76, 78, 85, 153, 156

Pershing 2 missile 8, 165, 217, 219, 225, 227, 229
Peru 214
Petersen, Arne Herlov 100, 199
Philby, Kim 29, 97, 120, 123, 150, 162
Philips 143
Picket lines 174, 238
Pilger, John 96, 132
Pimen, Patriarch 172
Pinochet, General 167
Players Theatre Club 94
Plutonium 8
Poland 13, 15, 154, 155, 171, 193, 261
Polaris 2, 8, 17, 78, 141, 228
Polytechnic of North London 174
Ponomarev, Boris 25, 30, 46, 49, 66, 176, 205, 237, 266, 279
Positive vetting 263
Posner, Vladimir 161
Potsdam 13
Prague 60, 111, 172, 182, 194, 198, 199, 225, 254
Pravda 11, 38, 51, 112, 122, 124, 216, 227, 228
Press Council 266
Preston 238
Prime, Geoffrey 82, 85, 150
Private Eye 110
Profumo Affair 17, 107
Programme to Combat Racism 172
Proll, Astrid 115
Pushkino 233

Quakers 222
Quebec 246
Questions of Philosophy 70
Quisling, Vidkun 136

Rabb, Maxwell 154
Race relations 137
Radio Clyde 143
Radio-telemetry 81
Ramelson, 'Bert' 225
Ramsbotham, David 132
Rawlinson, Lord 34, 63
Reagan, President Ronald 20, 85, 98, 152, 155, 179, 216, 222, 229, 233, 234, 250, 260, 268
Red Army 13, 20, 22, 76, 166, 201, 203
Red Army Faction 226, 247
Red Brigade 158, 247
Red Square 176, 227, 271
Redgrave, Corin 177
Redgrave, Vanessa 177
Rees, John 121
Rees, Merlyn 114
Reibnitz, Baron von 139
René, Albert
Renner, Hermann 45
Reuters 124
Revel, Jean-François 254
Rhine Army 259
'Rhyolite' 82
Richardson, Jo 21
Ricin 240
Roberts, Ernie 182
Robinson, Derek 190
Rohl, Klaus Rainer 111

312

Romania 13
Rome 59, 154, 241
Roosevelt, Franklin D. 13, 163, 204
Royal Commission on the Press 267
Ruddock, Joan 225
Russell, Bertrand 171
Russia Committee 162
Russian Orthodox Church 133, 172

Sabotka, Anton 239
Sadat, Anwar 247
St Peter's Square 106, 241
Sakharov, Andrei 34
Saline, Guennadi 129
Salisbury Plain 243
Sankei 104
Sankei Shimbun 155
SALT 68, 80, 83, 84, 85, 205
Sapper, Alan 189
'Sapphire' 127
Saudi Arabia 138, 154
Scanlon, Hugh 182
Scargill, Arthur 4, 19, 140, 143, 189, 191, 195
Scarp 78
Schlesinger, James 81
Schmelz, Hans 50
Schmidt, Helmut 126
Schmuckle, Gerd 43, 44, 57
Schuman, Tomas 105, 111, 119, 245, 279
Seamen's strike 185
Security Commission 83
Sego 78
Sejna, Major-General Jan 29, 33, 38, 39, 46, 48, 60, 69, 166, 182, 202, 239, 243, 245, 250, 279
Senate Intelligence Committee 82
Service A (KGB) 26, 29, 150, 153, 156
Seychelles 159
Sheffield 177, 225
Shelepin, Aleksandr 27, 29, 30, 71, 194, 239, 263
Shevchenko, Arkady 2, 44, 107, 129, 204, 206, 227, 272, 280
Shorter Oxford Dictionary 88
Shultz, Richard 28
Siberia 218
Sikhs 160
Simon & Schuster 98
Slater, Jim 189, 195
'Sleepers' 249
SMERSH 250
Smolensk 148
Smolka, Peter 45
Social Democratic Party (West Germany) 23, 32, 164, 203
Socialist Workers' Party 20, 111, 138, 144, 173, 193, 266
Sofia 96
Solzhenitsyn, Alexander 260
Sorge, Richard 97
South Africa 149, 159
South Vietnam 203
Southampton 190
Soviet Kolony 168
Soviet Peace Committee 224
Soviet Peace Fund 197
Spain 51, 97, 158, 236
Spetsnaz 223, 249, 250, 257, 263

Sputnik 74
SS 138, 149, 227
SS9 78
SS11 78
SS16 84
SS17 80
SS18 80
SS19 80, 85
SS20 84, 207, 218, 229, 233, 273
Stalin, Joseph 7, 12, 13, 14, 15, 98, 163, 166, 204, 227, 239, 258, 262, 270
Stalin Peace Prize 172
Stammberger, Wolfgang 52
'Star Wars' 9, 148, 229, 231, 234, 271
Stashinsky, Bogdan 239
Stern 44, 65, 118, 123, 152
Stevenson, William 96
Stockholm Archipelago 256
Stockholm Conference 203
Stockholm Peace Pledge 200
Stonehouse, John 169
Straight Left 125
Strategic Arms Limitation Talks see SALT
Strategic Defence Initiative *see* 'Star Wars'
Strategic Missile Force 71
Strategic Review 60
Strauss, Franz Josef 2, 30, 32, 35, 36, 43, 46, 49, 52, 54, 56, 57, 60, 63, 69, 100, 105, 147, 178, 217, 280
Strelnikov, Anatoli 97, 112, 196
Strougal, Lubomir 48, 149
Students Union 174, 268
Stuttgart 214
Subversion units 250, 252
Sudan 148
Suez 127
Sullivan, David S. 84
Sunday Times 65, 118
Suslov, Mikhail 47, 48, 205, 242, 270
'Suvorov, Viktor' 257
Sweden 12, 115, 128, 255
Switzerland 115, 122
System Planning Corporation 70
Systemic lupus erythematosus 243
Synthesis 99
Syria 152

Tanzania 214
TASS 26, 121, 122, 124, 156, 157, 159, 199, 208, 216, 227, 234, 256, 265
Teachers for Peace 177, 199
Telephone-tapping 136
Templer, Sir Gerald 185
Terrorism 226, 245, 246, 252
Thailand 158
Thames Television 131, 135, 141
Thatcher, Margaret 19, 100, 152, 179, 216, 229, 235, 244, 271
Theatre 177
Theatre Centre 177
Thomas, Anthony 138
Thor 71, 73, 74, 78
Throw-weight 84
Tiempo 154
Time 39, 98
Times, The 64, 138, 161, 186, 192, 235
Tinian 95

Titov, Gennadiy 127
Titov, Igor 124
Tobacco Workers' Union 189
Todd, Ron 195
Tokyo 103, 104, 124, 155
'Tomahawk' 219
'Tophat' 76, 80
Trade Union Congress 183, 194
Trade unions 16, 181, 266
Transcaucasia 13
Transport and General Workers' Union
    (TGWU) 182, 190, 195, 226
Treholt, Arne 126, 165
Tremeaud, André-Marie 240
Trident 8, 228
Trotsky 193
Trotskyites 20, 266
Troup, Tony 141
Trudeau, Pierre 126
Truman, Harry 15
Tugwell, Maurice 269
Turkey 15, 127, 158
'TV Eye 131, 134
'Typhoon' 84, 228

U2 spy-plane 73, 243
UKUSA agreement 82
UNESCO 99, 127, 129
UNICEF 129
Union of Journalists (USSR) 47, 105
United Nations 75, 129, 204, 215, 227, 248
UN Commission for Human Rights 273
Upside-down ploy 2, 54, 148, 212, 236, 248
Urals 219, 228
USDAW 17
US Air Force 156
US Defense Intelligence Agency 60
US National Security Council 73, 154
US Peace Corps 148
US Peace Council 198
US Senate Judiciary Committee 180
US Strategic Air Command 156
US Strategic Institute 60

V1 219
V2 95
V-bombers 250
Vasilev, Zelio 242
Vassall, John 76
VE Day 261
Venice 106
Vienna 68, 197, 198
Virginia 241
Volkskrant 159

Waldheim, Kurt 215
Wallop, Malcolm 231
Warsaw 200

Warsaw Pact 9, 10, 166, 210, 213, 220, 250, 254
Washington 60, 61, 71, 74, 139, 154, 199, 215,
    227, 244, 256, 267
Washington Post 59, 167
Watergate 207
Watkins, John 167
Watters, Frank 191
Weathermen 246
Weber, C.A. 111
Weinberger, Caspar 85, 153
Welt am Sonntag 62
Wenland, Horst 59
West Berlin 82
West Germany 12, 58, 115, 154, 157, 205, 213,
    220, 221, 239, 263
Westmoreland, William 158
Whicker, Alan 131, 138, 143
White, Harry Dexter 163
White House 75
Whitelaw, William 135
'Whiskey on the Rocks' 255-6
Whitman, Alden 98
Wichts, Adolf 51, 54
Wiesbaden 57
Wigg, George 107, 186
William Tyndale school 175
'Willies' 3, 100, 110, 117, 126, 179, 234
Wilmers, John 35, 64
Winterton, Nicholas 137
Wilson, Sir Harold 17, 142, 171, 182, 185,
    204, 205
Wittfogel, Karl 98
Women's International Democratic Federation
    199
World Congress of Intellectuals for Peace 171
World Congress of Women 199
World Council of Churches 171
World Federation of Democratic Youth 179
World Federation of Scientific Workers 179
World Federation of Trade Unions 179, 194,
    199
'World in Action' 131, 267
World Peace Council 22, 167, 171, 179, 197,
    200, 214, 221, 227
Wolverhampton 238
Wright, Peter 169

Yalta 13, 208
Yamana, Takuji 104
Yermishkin, Oleg 128
Yorkshire Television 137

Zagladin, Vadim 221
Zamyatin, Leonid 26
ZAPU 245
Zeitung 155
Zhikov, Todor 241
Zia, President 271